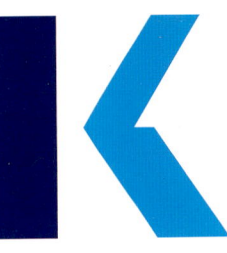

Kaplan Publishing are constantly f
ways to make a difference to your
exciting online resources really d
different to students looking for e...

This book comes with free EN-gage online resources so that you can study anytime, anywhere.

Having purchased this book, you have access to the following online study materials:

CONTENT	ACCA (including FFA,FAB,FMA)		AAT		FIA (excluding FFA,FAB,FMA)	
	Text	Kit	Text	Kit	Text	Kit
iPaper version of the book	✓	✓	✓	✓	✓	✓
Interactive electronic version of the book	✓					
Fixed tests / progress tests with instant answers	✓		✓			
Mock assessments online			✓	✓		
Material updates	✓	✓	✓	✓	✓	✓
Latest official ACCA exam questions		✓				
Extra question assistance using the signpost icon*		✓				
Timed questions with an online tutor debrief using the clock icon*		✓				
Interim assessment including questions and answers		✓			✓	
Technical articles	✓	✓			✓	✓

* Excludes F1, F2, F3, FFA, FAB, FMA

How to access your online resources

Kaplan Financial students will already have a Kaplan EN-gage account and these extra resources will be available to you online. You do not need to register again, as this process was completed when you enrolled. If you are having problems accessing online materials, please ask your course administrator.

If you are already a registered Kaplan EN-gage user go to www.EN-gage.co.uk and log in. Select the 'add a book' feature and enter the ISBN number of this book and the unique pass key at the bottom of this card. Then click 'finished' or 'add another book'. You may add as many books as you have purchased from this screen.

If you purchased through Kaplan Flexible Learning or via the Kaplan Publishing website you will automatically receive an e-mail invitation to Kaplan EN·gage online. Please register your details using this email to gain access to your content. If you do not receive the e-mail or book content, please contact Kaplan Flexible Learning.

If you are a new Kaplan EN-gage user register at www.EN-gage.co.uk and click on the link contained in the email we sent you to activate your account. Then select the 'add a book' feature, enter the ISBN number of this book and the unique pass key at the bottom of this card. Then click 'finished' or 'add another book'.

Your Code and Information

This code can only be used once for the registration of one book online. This registration and your online content will expire when the final sittings for the examinations covered by this book have taken place. Please allow one hour from the time you submit your book details for us to process your request.

Please scratch the film to access your EN-gage code.

Please be aware that this code is case-sensitive and you will need to include the dashes within the passcode, but not when entering the ISBN. For further technical support, please visit www.EN-gage.co.uk

ACCA

Paper P7 (INT/UK)

Advanced Audit and Assurance

Complete Text

British library cataloguing-in-publication data

A catalogue record for this book is available from the British Library.

Published by:
Kaplan Publishing UK
Unit 2 The Business Centre
Molly Millars Lane
Wokingham
Berkshire
RG41 2QZ

ISBN 978-0-85732-671-3

© Kaplan Financial Limited, 2013

The text in this material and any others made available by any Kaplan Group company does not amount to advice on a particular matter and should not be taken as such. No reliance should be placed on the content as the basis for any investment or other decision or in connection with any advice given to third parties. Please consult your appropriate professional adviser as necessary. Kaplan Publishing Limited and all other Kaplan group companies expressly disclaim all liability to any person in respect of any losses or other claims, whether direct, indirect, incidental, consequential or otherwise arising in relation to the use of such materials.

Printed and bound in Great Britain.

Acknowledgements

We are grateful to the Association of Chartered Certified Accountants and the Chartered Institute of Management Accountants for permission to reproduce past examination questions. The answers have been prepared by Kaplan Publishing.

All rights reserved. No part of this publication may be reproduced, stored in a retrieval system, or transmitted, in any form or by any means, electronic, mechanical, photocopying, recording or otherwise, without the prior written permission of Kaplan Publishing.

Contents

		Page
Chapter 1	Regulation in a global economy	1
Chapter 2	Code of ethics and conduct	27
Chapter 3	Professional appointments	67
Chapter 4	Quality control	77
Chapter 5	Advertising, publicity, obtaining professional work and fees	103
Chapter 6	Tendering	117
Chapter 7	Money laundering	127
Chapter 8	Professional responsibilities and liabilities	139
Chapter 9	Planning, materiality and assessing the risk of misstatement	183
Chapter 10	Group and transnational audits	227
Chapter 11	Evidence	263
Chapter 12	Completion	297
Chapter 13	Auditors' reports	341
Chapter 14	Reports to management	373
Chapter 15	Other assignments	385
Chapter 16	Prospective financial information	427
Chapter 17	Forensic audits	443
Chapter 18	Outsourcing	455
Chapter 19	UK syllabus only: Auditing aspects of insolvency	473
Chapter 20	Financial reporting revision	487
Chapter 21	Additional practice questions	539

Paper Introduction

How to Use the Materials

These Kaplan Publishing learning materials have been carefully designed to make your learning experience as easy as possible and to give you the best chances of success in your examinations.

The product range contains a number of features to help you in the study process. They include:

(1) Detailed study guide and syllabus objectives
(2) Description of the examination
(3) Study skills and revision guidance
(4) Complete text or essential text
(5) Question practice

The sections on the study guide, the syllabus objectives, the examination and study skills should all be read before you commence your studies. They are designed to familiarise you with the nature and content of the examination and give you tips on how to best to approach your learning.

The **complete text or essential text** comprises the main learning materials and gives guidance as to the importance of topics and where other related resources can be found. Each chapter includes:

- The **learning objectives** contained in each chapter, which have been carefully mapped to the examining body's own syllabus learning objectives or outcomes. You should use these to check you have a clear understanding of all the topics on which you might be assessed in the examination.

- The **chapter diagram** provides a visual reference for the content in the chapter, giving an overview of the topics and how they link together.

- The **content** for each topic area commences with a brief explanation or definition to put the topic into context before covering the topic in detail. You should follow your studying of the content with a review of the illustration/s. These are worked examples which will help you to understand better how to apply the content for the topic.

- **Test your understanding** sections provide an opportunity to assess your understanding of the key topics by applying what you have learned to short questions. Answers can be found at the back of each chapter.

- **Summary diagrams** complete each chapter to show the important links between topics and the overall content of the paper. These diagrams should be used to check that you have covered and understood the core topics before moving on.

- **Question practice** is provided at the back of each text.

Icon Explanations

Definition - Key definitions that you will need to learn from the core content.

Key Point - Identifies topics that are key to success and are often examined.

New - Identifies topics that are brand new in papers that build on, and therefore also contain, learning covered in earlier papers.

Expandable Text - Expandable text provides you with additional information about a topic area and may help you gain a better understanding of the core content. Essential text users can access this additional content online (read it where you need further guidance or skip over when you are happy with the topic)

Test Your Understanding - Exercises for you to complete to ensure that you have understood the topics just learned.

Illustration - Worked examples help you understand the core content better.

Tricky topic - When reviewing these areas care should be taken and all illustrations and test your understanding exercises should be completed to ensure that the topic is understood.

Tutorial note - Included to explain some of the technical points in more detail.

Footsteps - Helpful tutor tips.

Online subscribers

Our online resources are designed to increase the flexibility of your learning materials and provide you with immediate feedback on how your studies are progressing. Ask your local customer services staff if you are not already a subscriber and wish to join.

If you are subscribed to our online resources you will find:

(1) Online reference ware: reproduces your Complete or Essential Text online, giving you anytime, anywhere access.

(2) Online testing: provides you with additional online objective testing so you can practice what you have learned further.

(3) Online performance management: immediate access to your online testing results. Review your performance by key topics and chart your achievement through the course relative to your peer group.

Paper introduction

Paper background

The aim of ACCA Paper P7 (INT & UK), Advanced audit and assurance, is to analyse, evaluate and conclude on the assurance engagement and other audit and assurance issues in the context of best practice and current developments.

Objectives of the syllabus

- Recognise the legal and regulatory environment and its impact on audit and assurance practice;

- Demonstrate the ability to work effectively on an assurance or other service engagement within a professional and ethical framework;

- Assess and recommend appropriate quality control policies and procedures in practice management and recognise the auditor's position in relation to the acceptance and retention of professional appointments;

- Identify and formulate the work required to meet the objectives of audit and non-audit assignments and apply the International Standards on Auditing;

- Identify and formulate the work required to meet the objectives of non-audit assignments;

- Evaluate findings and the results of work performed and draft suitable reports on assignments;

- Understand the current issues and developments relating to the provision of audit related and assurance services.

Core areas of the syllabus

- Regulatory environment.
- Professional and ethical considerations.
- Practice management.
- Audit of historical financial information
- Other assignments.
- Reporting.
- Current issues and developments.

Approach to INT and UK syllabus elements

Due to the alignment of the INT and UK syllabus elements one text has been produced to address both variants. Both streams apply the principles of International Standards on Auditing (ISA's) and International Financial Reporting Standards (IFRS).

The International variant has been used as the basis of the text. Any variances relevant only to the UK syllabus (such as compliance with the Companies Act 2006) have been included at the end of each chapter (or section) in expandable text boxes headed "UK Syllabus Focus." All test your understandings have also been appended to reflect any UK specific variations.

Syllabus objectives

We have reproduced the ACCA's syllabus below, showing where the objectives are explored within this book. Within the chapters, we have broken down the extensive information found in the syllabus into easily digestible and relevant sections, called Content Objectives. These correspond to the objectives at the beginning of each chapter.

Syllabus learning objective	Chapter reference
A REGULATORY ENVIRONMENT	
1 International regulatory frameworks for audit and assurance services	
(a) Explain the need for laws, regulations, standards and other guidance relating to audit, assurance and related services.[2]	1

- (b) Outline and explain the need for the legal and professional framework including:[2]   1
    - (i) public oversight to an audit and assurance practice
    - (ii) the role of audit committees and impact on audit and assurance practice.

2 Money laundering

- (a) Define 'money laundering'.[1]   7
- (b) Explain how international efforts seek to combat money laundering.[2]   7
- (c) Explain the scope of criminal offences of money laundering and how professional accountants may be protected from criminal and civil liability.[2]   7
- (d) Explain the need for ethical guidance in this area.[2]   7
- (e) Describe how accountants meet their obligations to help prevent and detect money laundering including record keeping and reporting of suspicion to the appropriate regulatory body.[2]   7
- (f) Explain the importance of customer due diligence (CDD) (*UK: 'know you customer' information (KYC)*).[2]   7
- (g) Recognise potentially suspicious transactions and assess their impact on reporting duties.[2]   7
- (h) Describe, with reasons, the basic elements of an anti-money laundering program.[2]   7

3 Laws and regulations

- (a) Compare and contrast the respective responsibilities of management and auditors concerning compliance with laws and regulations in an audit of financial statements.[2]   8
- (b) Describe the auditors' considerations of compliance with laws and regulations and plan audit procedures when possible non-compliance is discovered.[2]   8
- (c) Discuss how and to whom non-compliance should be reported.[2]   8
- (d) Recognise when withdrawal from an engagement is necessary.[2]   8

B PROFESSIONAL AND ETHICAL CONSIDERATIONS
1 Code of ethics for professional accountants

(a)	Explain the fundamental principles and the conceptual framework approach.[1]	2
(b)	Identify, evaluate and respond to threats to compliance with the fundamental principles.[3]	2
(c)	Discuss and evaluate the effectiveness of available safeguards.[3]	2
(d)	Recognise and advise on conflicts in the application of fundamental principles.[3]	2
(e)	Discuss the importance of professional scepticism in planning and performing an audit.	9
(f)	Assess whether an engagement has been planned and performed with an attitude of professional scepticism, and evaluate the implications.	9

2 Fraud and error

(a)	Define and clearly distinguish between the terms 'error', 'irregularity', 'fraud' and 'misstatement'.[2]	8
(b)	Compare and contrast the respective responsibilities of management and auditors for fraud and error.[2]	8
(c)	Describe the matters to be considered and procedures to be carried out to investigate actual and/or potential misstatements in a given situation.[2]	8
(d)	Explain how, why, when and to whom fraud and error should be reported and the circumstances in which an auditor should withdraw from an engagement.[2]	8
(e)	Discuss the current and possible future role of auditors in preventing, detecting and reporting error and fraud.[2]	8

3 Professional liability

(a)	Recognise circumstances in which professional accountants may have legal liability.[2]	8
(b)	Describe the factors to determine whether or not an auditor is negligent in given situations.[2]	8
(c)	Explain the other criteria for legal liability to be recognised (including 'due professional care' and 'proximity') and apply them to given situations.[2]	8
(d)	Compare and contrast liability to client with liability to third parties.[3]	8

(e)	Evaluate the practicability and effectiveness of ways in which liability may be restricted.[3]	8
(f)	Discuss liability limitation agreements.[2]	8
(g)	Discuss and appraise the principal causes of audit failure and other factors that contribute to the 'expectation gap' (e.g. responsibilities for fraud and error).[3]	8
(h)	Recommend ways in which the expectation gap might be bridged.[2]	8

C PRACTICE MANAGEMENT

1 Quality control

(a)	Explain the principles and purpose of quality control of audit and other assurance engagements.[1]	4
(b)	Describe the elements of a system of quality control relevant to a given firm.[2]	4
(c)	Select and justify quality control procedures that are applicable to a given audit engagement.[3]	4
(d)	Assess whether an engagement has been performed in accordance with professional standards and whether reports issued are appropriate in the circumstances.[3]	4

2 Advertising, publicity, obtaining professional work and fees

(a)	Recognise situations in which specified advertisements are acceptable.[2]	5
(b)	Discuss the restrictions on practice descriptions, the use of the ACCA logo and the names of practising firms.[2]	5
(c)	Discuss the extent to which reference to fees may be made in promotional material.[2]	5
(d)	Outline the determinants of fee-setting and justify the bases on which fees and commissions may and may not be charged for services.[3]	5
(e)	Discuss the ethical and other professional problems, for example, lowballing, involved in establishing and negotiating fees for a specified assignment.[3]	5

3 Tendering

(a) Discuss the reasons why entities change their auditors/professional accountants.[2] — 6

(b) Recognise and explain the matters to be considered when a firm is invited to submit a proposal or fee quote for an audit or other professional engagement.[2] — 6

(c) Identify the information to be included in a proposal.[2] — 6

4 Professional appointments

(a) Explain the matters to be considered and the procedures that an audit firm/professional accountant should carry out before accepting a specified new client/engagement including:[3] — 3

   (i) client acceptance

   (ii) engagement acceptance

   (iii) establish whether the preconditions for an audit are present

   (iv) agreeing the terms of engagement.

(b) Recognise the key issues that underlie the agreement of the scope and terms of an engagement with a client.[2]

D AUDIT OF HISTORICAL FINANCIAL INFORMATION

1 (i) Planning, materiality and assessing the risk of misstatement

(a) Define materiality and performance materiality and demonstrate how it should be applied in financial reporting and auditing.[2] — 9

(b) Identify and explain business risks for a given assignment.[3] — 9

(c) Identify and explain audit risks for a given assignment.[3] — 9

(d) Identify and explain risks of material misstatement for a given assignment.[3] — 9

(e) Discuss and demonstrate the use of analytical procedures in the planning of an assignment.[3] — 9

(f) Explain how the result of planning procedures determines the relevant audit strategy.[2]   9

(g) Explain the planning procedures specific to an initial audit engagement.[2]   9

(h) Identify additional information that may be required in order to effectively plan an assignment.[2]   9

(i) Recognise matters that are not relevant to the planning of an assignment.[2]   9

1 (ii) Evidence

(a) Identify and describe audit procedures to obtain sufficient audit evidence from identified sources.[2]   11

(b) Identify and evaluate the audit evidence expected to be available to:[3]   11

   (i) support financial statement assertions and accounting treatments (including fair values); and

   (ii) support disclosures made in the notes to the financial statements.

(c) Apply analytical procedures to financial and non-financial data.[2]   11

(d) Explain the specific audit problems and procedures concerning related parties and related party transactions.[2]   11

(e) Recognise circumstances that may indicate the existence of unidentified related parties and select appropriate audit procedures.[2]   11

(f) Evaluate the use of written management representations to support other audit evidence.[2]   11

(g) Recognise when it is justifiable to place reliance on the work of an expert (e.g. a surveyor employed by the audit client).[2]   11

(h) Assess the appropriateness and sufficiency of the work of internal auditors and the extent to which reliance can be placed on it.[2]   11

1 **(iii) Evaluation and review**

    (a) Evaluate the matters (e.g. materiality, risk, relevant accounting standards, audit evidence) relating to:[3]   12

        (i) inventory and construction contract

        (ii) standard costing systems

        (iii) statement of cash flows

        (iv) changes in accounting policy

        (v) taxation

        (vi) segmental reporting

        (vii) non-current assets

        (viii) fair value

        (ix) leases

        (x) revenue recognition

        (xi) employee benefits

        (xii) government grants

        (xiii) related parties

        (xiv) earnings per share

        (xv) impairment

        (xvi) provisions, contingent liabilities and contingent assets

        (xvii) intangible assets

        (xviii) financial instruments

        (xix) investment properties

        (xx) share-based payment transactions

        (xxi) business combinations

        (xxii) assets held for sale and discontinued operations

        (xxiii) events after the end of the reporting period

        (xxiv) the effects of foreign exchange rates

        (xxv) borrowing costs

    (b) Explain the use of analytical procedures and checklists in evaluation and review.[3]   12

    (c) Explain how the auditor's responsibilities for corresponding figures, comparative financial statements, and 'other information' are discharged. [3]   12

    (d) Apply the further considerations and audit procedures relevant to initial engagements.[2]   12

Introduction

(e) Discuss the courses of action available to an auditor if an inconsistency or misstatement of fact exists in relation to other information.[2] — 12

(f) Specify audit procedures designed to identify subsequent events that may require adjustment to, or disclosure in, the financial statements of a given entity.[2] — 12

(g) Identify and explain indicators that the going concern basis may be in doubt and recognise mitigating factors.[2] — 12

(h) Recommend audit procedures, or evaluate the evidence that might be expected to be available and assess the appropriateness of the going concern basis in given situations.[3] — 12

(i) Assess the adequacy of disclosures in financial statements relating to going concern and explain the implications for the auditor's report with regard to the going concern basis.[3] — 12

2 Group audits

(a) Recognise the specific matters to be considered before accepting appointment as principal auditor to a group in a given situation.[3] — 10

(b) Identify and explain the matters specific to planning an audit of group financial statements including assessment of group and component materiality, the impact of non-coterminous year ends within a group, and changes in group structure. — 10

(c) Justify the situations where a joint audit would be appropriate.[2] — 10

(d) Recognise the audit problems and describe audit procedures specific to a business combination, including goodwill, accounting policies, intercompany trading, the classification of investments, equity accounting for associates, changes in group structure, and accounting for a foreign subsidiary[3] — 10

(e) Identify and explain the audit risks, and necessary audit procedures relevant to the consolidation process.[3] — 10

(f) Identify and describe the matters to be considered and the procedures to be performed at the planning stage, when a principal auditor considers the use of the work of component auditors.[3] — 10

(g) Consider how the principal auditor should evaluate the audit work performed by a component auditor.[2] — 10

(h) Explain the implications for the auditor's report on the financial statements of an entity where the opinion on a component is qualified or otherwise modified in a given situation.[2] — 10

E. OTHER ASSIGNMENTS
1 Audit-related services

(a) Describe the nature of audit-related services, the circumstances in which they might be required and the comparative levels of assurance provided by professional accountants and distinguish between:[2] — 15

  (i) audit-related services and an audit of historical financial statements

  (ii) an attestation engagement and a direct reporting engagement.

(b) Plan review engagements, for example:[2] — 15

  (i) a review of interim financial information

  (ii) a 'due diligence' assignment (when acquiring a company, business or other assets).

(c) Explain the importance of enquiry and analytical procedures in review engagements and apply these procedures.[2] — 15

2 Assurance services

(a) Describe the main categories of assurance services that audit firms can provide and assess the benefits of providing these services to management and external users.[3] — 15

(b) Justify a level of assurance (reasonable, high, moderate, limited, negative) for an engagement depending on the subject matter evaluated, the criteria used, the procedures applied and the quality and quantity of evidence obtained.[3] — 15

(c) Recognise the ways in which different types of risk (e.g. strategic, operating, information) may be identified and analysed and assess how management should respond to risk.[3] — 15

3 Prospective financial information

(a) Define 'prospective financial information' (PFI) and distinguish between a 'forecast', a 'projection', a 'hypothetical illustration' and a 'target'.[1] — 16

(b) Explain the principles of useful PFI.[1] — 16

(c) Identify and describe the matters to be considered before accepting a specified engagement to report on PFI.[2] — 16

(d) Discuss the level of assurance that the auditor may provide and explain the other factors to be considered in determining the nature, timing and extent of examination procedures.[1] — 16

(e) Describe examination procedures to verify forecasts and projections.[2] — 16

(f) Compare the content of a report on an examination of PFI with reports made in providing audit-related services.[2] — 16

4 Forensic audits

(a) Define the terms 'forensic accounting', 'forensic investigation' and 'forensic audit'.[1] — 17

(b) Describe the major applications of forensic auditing (e.g. fraud, negligence, insurance claims) and analyse the role of the forensic auditor as an expert witness.[2] — 17

(c) Apply the fundamental ethical principles to professional accountants engaged in forensic audit assignments.[2] — 17

(d) Plan a forensic audit engagement.[2] — 17

(e) Select investigative procedures and evaluate evidence appropriate to determining the loss in a given situation.[3] — 17

5 Internal audit

(a) Evaluate the potential impact of an internal audit department on the planning and performance of the external audit.[2] — 9

(b) Explain the benefits and potential drawbacks of outsourcing internal audit.[2] — 18

(c) Consider the ethical implications of the external auditor providing an internal audit service to a client[2] — 18

6 Outsourcing

(a) Explain the different approaches to 'outsourcing' and compare with 'insourcing'.[2] — 18

(b) Discuss and conclude on the advantages and disadvantages of outsourcing finance and accounting functions.[3] — 18

(c) Recognise and evaluate the impact of outsourced functions on the conduct of an audit.[3] — 18

7 UK Syllabus Only: Auditing Aspects of Insolvency (and similar procedures)

(a) *Explain the meaning of and describe procedures the involved in placing a company into voluntary or compulsory liquidation.*[2] — 19

(b) *Explain the consequences of liquidation or administration for a company and its stakeholders.*[2] — 19

(c) *Advise on the differences between fraudulent and wrongful trading and the consequences for the company directors.*[2] — 19

(d) *Examine the financial position of a company and determine whether it is insolvent.*[2] — 19

(e) *Identify the circumstances where administration could be adopted as an alternative to liquidation and explain the benefits of administration compared to liquidation.*[2] — 19

(f) Explain and apply the priority for the allocation of company assets.[2]   19

F REPORTING
1 Auditor's reports

(a) Critically appraise the form and content of an auditor's report in a given situation.[3]   13

(b) Recognise and evaluate the factors to be taken into account when forming an audit opinion in a given situation and justify audit opinions that are consistent with the results of audit procedures.[3]   13

(c) Assess whether or not a proposed audit opinion is appropriate.[3]   13

(d) Advise on the actions which may be taken by the auditor in the event that a modified report is issued.[3]   13

(e) Recognise when the use of an emphasis of matter paragraph and other matter paragraph would be appropriate.[3]   13

2 Reports to those charged with governance and management

(a) Critically assess the quality of a report to those charged with governance and management.[3]   14

(b) Advise on the content of reports to those charged with governance and management in a given situation.[3]   14

3 Other reports

(a) Analyse the form and content of the professional accountant's report for an assurance engagement as compared with an auditor's report.[2]   16

(b) Draft the content of a report on examination of prospective financial information.[2]   16

(c) Discuss the effectiveness of the 'negative assurance' form of reporting and evaluate situations in which it may be appropriate to express a reservation or deny a conclusion.[3]   16

G CURRENT ISSUES AND DEVELOPMENTS
1 Professional, ethical and corporate governance

(a) Discuss the relative advantages of an ethical framework and a rulebook.[2]   2

(c) Identify and assess relevant to emerging ethical issues and evaluate the safeguards available.[3]   2

(c) Discuss IFAC developments.[2]   1

Introduction

2 Information technology

(a) Describe recent trends in IT and their current and potential impact on auditors (e.g. the audit implications of 'cyberincidents' and other risks).[2] — 9

(b) Explain how IT may be used to assist auditors and discuss the problems that may be encountered in automating the audit process.[2] — 11

3 Transnational audits

(a) Define 'transnational audits' and explain the role of the Transnational Audit Committee (TAC) of IFAC.[1] — 10

(b) Discuss how transnational audits may differ from other audits of historical financial information (e.g. in terms of applicable financial reporting and auditing standards, listing requirements and corporate governance requirements).[2] — 10

4 Social and environmental auditing

(a) Plan an engagement to provide assurance on performance measures and sustainability indicators.[2] — 15

(b) Describe the difficulties in measuring and reporting on economic, environmental and social performance and give examples of performance measures and sustainability indicators.[2] — 15

(c) Explain the auditor's main considerations in respect of social and environmental matters and how they impact on entities and their financial statements (e.g. impairment of assets, provisions and contingent liabilities).[2] — 11

(d) Describe substantive procedures to detect potential misstatements in respect of socio-environmental matters.[2] — 11

(e) Discuss the form and content of an independent verification statement (e.g. on an environmental management system (EMS) and a report to society).[2] — 15

5 Other current issues

(a) Explain current developments in auditing standards including the need for new and revised standards and evaluate their impact on the conduct of audits.[3] — 1

(b) Discuss other current legal, ethical, other professional and practical matters that affect accountants, auditors, their employers and the profession.[3] — 7,8

The superscript numbers in square brackets indicate the intellectual depth at which the subject area could be assessed within the examination. Level 1 (knowledge and comprehension) broadly equates with the Knowledge module, Level 2 (application and analysis) with the Skills module and Level 3 (synthesis and evaluation) to the Professional level. However, lower level skills can continue to be assessed as you progress through each module and level.

The examination

Examination format

The examination is a three hour paper constructed in two sections. Questions in both sections will be almost entirely discursive. However, candidates will be expected, for example, to be able to assess materiality and calculate relevant ratios where appropriate.

Section A questions will be based on 'case study' type questions. That is not to say that they will be particularly long, rather that they will provide a setting within which a range of topics, issues and requirements can be addressed. Different types of question will be encountered in Section B and will tend to be more focused on specific topics, for example 'auditor's reports', 'quality control' etc. (This does not preclude these topics from appearing in Section A.) Current issues will be examined across a number of questions.

	Number of marks
Section A	
Two compulsory questions:	
Question 1	35
Question 2	25
Section B	
Choice of two from three questions, 20 marks each	40
	100

Total time allowed: 3 hours

Paper-based examination tips

Spend the first few minutes of the examination reading the paper.

Where you have a choice of questions, decide which ones you will do.

Unless you know exactly how to answer the question, spend some time **planning** your answer. Stick to the question and **tailor your answer** to what you are asked. Pay particular attention to the verbs in the question.

Spend the last five minutes reading through your answers and making any additions or corrections.

If you **get completely stuck** with a question, leave space in your answer book and return to it later.

If you do not understand what a question is asking, state your assumptions. Even if you do not answer in precisely the way the examiner hoped, you should be given some credit, if your assumptions are reasonable.

You should do everything you can to make things easy for the marker. The marker will find it easier to identify the points you have made if your answers are legible.

Essay questions: Your essay should have a clear structure. It should contain a brief introduction, a main section and a conclusion. Be concise. It is better to write a little about a lot of different points than a great deal about one or two points.

Computations: It is essential to include all your workings in your answers. Many computational questions require the use of a standard format. Be sure you know these formats thoroughly before the exam and use the layouts that you see in the answers given in this book and in model answers.

Scenario-based questions: Most questions will contain a hypothetical scenario. To write a good case answer, first identify the area in which there is a problem, outline the main principles/theories you are going to use to answer the question, and then apply the principles/theories to the case. It is vital that you relate your answer to the specific circumstances given.

Reports, memos and other documents: some questions ask you to present your answer in the form of a report or a memo or other document. So use the correct format – there could be easy marks to gain here.

Study skills and revision guidance

This section aims to give guidance on how to study for your ACCA exams and to give ideas on how to improve your existing study techniques.

Preparing to study

Set your objectives

Before starting to study decide what you want to achieve – the type of pass you wish to obtain. This will decide the level of commitment and time you need to dedicate to your studies.

Devise a study plan

Determine which times of the week you will study.

Split these times into sessions of at least one hour for study of new material. Any shorter periods could be used for revision or practice.

Put the times you plan to study onto a study plan for the weeks from now until the exam and set yourself targets for each period of study – in your sessions make sure you cover the course, course assignments and revision.

If you are studying for more than one paper at a time, try to vary your subjects as this can help you to keep interested and see subjects as part of wider knowledge.

When working through your course, compare your progress with your plan and, if necessary, re-plan your work (perhaps including extra sessions) or, if you are ahead, do some extra revision/practice questions.

Effective studying

Active reading

You are not expected to learn the text by rote, rather, you must understand what you are reading and be able to use it to pass the exam and develop good practice. A good technique to use is SQ3Rs – Survey, Question, Read, Recall, Review:

(1) **Survey the chapter** – look at the headings and read the introduction, summary and objectives, so as to get an overview of what the chapter deals with.

(2) **Question** – whilst undertaking the survey, ask yourself the questions that you hope the chapter will answer for you.

(3) **Read** through the chapter thoroughly, answering the questions and making sure you can meet the objectives. Attempt the exercises and activities in the text, and work through all the examples.

(4) **Recall** – at the end of each section and at the end of the chapter, try to recall the main ideas of the section/chapter without referring to the text. This is best done after a short break of a couple of minutes after the reading stage.

(5) **Review** – check that your recall notes are correct.

You may also find it helpful to re-read the chapter to try to see the topic(s) it deals with as a whole.

Note-taking

Taking notes is a useful way of learning, but do not simply copy out the text. The notes must:

- be in your own words
- be concise
- cover the key points
- be well-organised
- be modified as you study further chapters in this text or in related ones.

Trying to summarise a chapter without referring to the text can be a useful way of determining which areas you know and which you don't.

Three ways of taking notes:

Summarise the key points of a chapter.

Make linear notes – a list of headings, divided up with subheadings listing the key points. If you use linear notes, you can use different colours to highlight key points and keep topic areas together. Use plenty of space to make your notes easy to use.

Try a diagrammatic form – the most common of which is a mind-map. To make a mind-map, put the main heading in the centre of the paper and put a circle around it. Then draw short lines radiating from this to the main sub-headings, which again have circles around them. Then continue the process from the sub-headings to sub-sub-headings, advantages, disadvantages, etc.

Highlighting and underlining

You may find it useful to underline or highlight key points in your study text – but do be selective. You may also wish to make notes in the margins.

Revision

The best approach to revision is to revise the course as you work through it. Also try to leave four to six weeks before the exam for final revision. Make sure you cover the whole syllabus and pay special attention to those areas where your knowledge is weak. Here are some recommendations:

Read through the text and your notes again and condense your notes into key phrases. It may help to put key revision points onto index cards to look at when you have a few minutes to spare.

Review any assignments you have completed and look at where you lost marks – put more work into those areas where you were weak.

Practise exam standard questions under timed conditions. If you are short of time, list the points that you would cover in your answer and then read the model answer, but do try to complete at least a few questions under exam conditions.

Also practise producing answer plans and comparing them to the model answer.

If you are stuck on a topic find somebody (a tutor) to explain it to you.

Read good newspapers and professional journals, especially ACCA's **Student Accountant** – this can give you an advantage in the exam.

Ensure you **know the structure of the exam** – how many questions and of what type you will be expected to answer. During your revision attempt all the different styles of questions you may be asked.

Further reading

You can find further reading and technical articles under the student section of ACCA's website.

chapter 1

Regulation in a global economy

Chapter learning objectives

When you have completed this chapter you will be able to:

- Explain the need for laws, regulations, standards and other guidance relating to audit, assurance and related services.
- Outline and explain the need for the legal and professional framework including:
    (i) public oversight and principles of corporate governance
    (ii) the role of audit committees.

This chapter considers the reasons behind the mechanisms for regulating assurance services and how standards of corporate governance are maintained, including much of the background to developments in the profession. You need to have an awareness of recent developments in the profession, which will require you to read around the topic to develop your understanding and develop an ability to form your own opinion and reach your own conclusions.

1 Introduction

Why do clients pay for assurance services?

They do it to reduce their exposure to **risk**.

It is imperative that decision makers within financial markets have the confidence to make **informed decisions**. In order to make these decisions they need information that they can trust. The main investment decisions that take place concern the buying and selling of shares.

The successful operation of world financial markets requires a complex web of decision making. Many of those decisions are focused on the allocation of huge (almost inconceivably so) allocations of capital. Without credible, reliable information at their disposal investors cannot make those decisions.

However, it is not just shareholders that rely on this information; there are a range of other stakeholders who also rely on assurance services. For example; it is common for banks to seek audited financial statements and forecasts before making lending decisions. Many companies request audited financial statements before buying from or supplying a particular company, in case that company is nearing insolvency.

As well as investments in businesses other stakeholders must make decisions about how to deploy resources: suppliers, customers, employees and prospective lenders all need information before making significant decisions that could have damaging financial repercussions.

Confidence in the reliability of financial information is essential to the functioning of these markets. Whilst it is not the only factor in helping to achieve that confidence, good quality, independent audit and assurance has a key role to play. A series of recent and high profile corporate failures has eroded trust in the assurance market and as a result mechanisms for increased regulation of the auditing profession have been introduced.

chapter 1

The nature of assurance services

Assurance professionals provide reports that give an independent opinion as to whether subject matter complies with pre-determined criteria. This enables the end user of that information to place more or less reliance on that information when making decisions.

2 The need for regulation

Introduction

Business failures, particularly large, high-profile businesses, disturb the virtuous circle of confidence within global financial markets.

The requirement for audited financial statements was seen as a way to reduce this risk and to protect:

- the owners of a business from unscrupulous management
- the world at large from abuse of limited liability status.

Self-regulation

Initially the system relied on self-regulation. In the 1970s the accountancy profession began to introduce standards to regulate financial reporting and shortly afterwards auditing standards were introduced.

Standards were set **by** the accounting profession **for** the accounting profession to follow.

Self-regulation seemed to make sense because:

- the accountancy organisations usually had a 'public interest' remit written into their constitutions
- they understood the business of financial reporting and auditing better than anyone.

However, two factors have led to the questioning of self-regulation as a satisfactory mechanism, which are:

- globalisation
- high profile corporate failures, such as Enron.

Regulation in a global economy

Globalisation

The globalisation of business, professions and investment markets has been rapid.

Once businesses started to cross national borders it soon became clear that the variation of laws and regulations in different countries made life rather difficult, both for the multinationals and the professions trying to provide services to them.

The need for Global Accounting Networks

Although companies have had their securities listed in both the European and US markets for a number of years, the ability to be based virtually anywhere in the world, and to manufacture, sell and manage businesses on a truly global basis is a more recent phenomenon. Global businesses need global professional firms to support, advise and audit them. The emergence of the 'big 4' global practices has been an accelerating process that has its origins in the 1970s. Similar globalisation has happened in the banking and assurance industries and the introduction of external shareholders into the securities markets has led to, e.g. Nasdaq from the US investing in the London Stock Exchange.

Global Regulation

This realisation led to the foundation of **IFAC** – the International Federation of Accountants in 1977.

IFAC is structured to operate through a network of boards and committees.

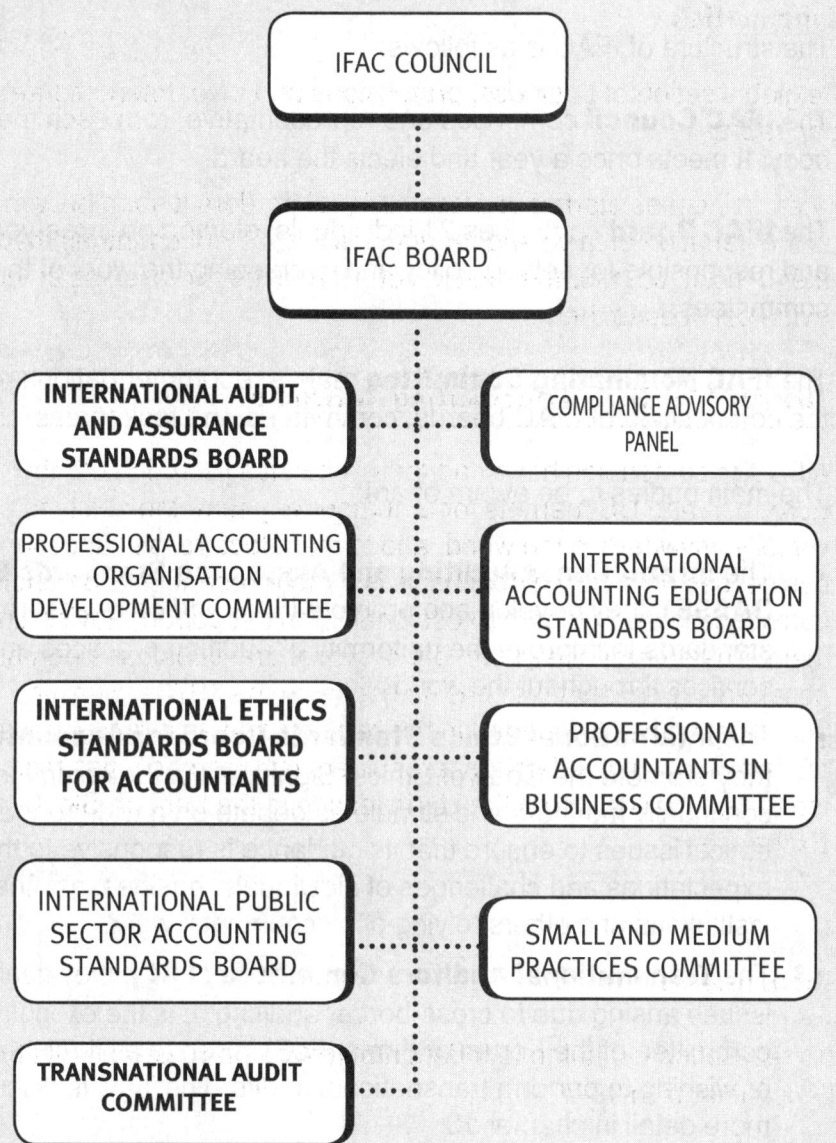

 Detailed explanation of IFAC structure

International Federation of Accountants

The International Federation of Accountants (IFAC) is the global organization for the accountancy profession. It was formed in 1977 and is based in New York. IFAC has more than 160 member bodies of accountants (including the ACCA), representing 2.5 million accountants from 125 separate countries.

IFAC's overall mission is to serve the public interest, strengthen the worldwide accountancy profession, and contribute to the development of strong international economies by establishing and promoting adherence to high-quality professional standards.

Regulation in a global economy

The structure of IFAC is as follows:

The **IFAC Council** comprises one representative from each member body. It meets once a year and elects the board.

The **IFAC Board** comprises 21 individuals, elected on three-year terms and responsible for setting policy and overseeing the work of the various committees.

The **IFAC Nominating Committee** makes recommendations regarding the composition of IFAC boards, committees and task forces.

The main bodies to be aware of are:

- The **International Auditing and Assurance Standards Board (IAASB)**: they develop and promote ISA's and other assurance standards to improve the uniformity of auditing practices and related services throughout the world.

- The **International Ethics Standards Board for Accountants**: they promote the Code of Ethics. Significantly, the committee continually monitors and stimulates debate on a wide range of ethical issues to ensure that its guidance is responsive to the expectations and challenges of individuals, businesses, financial institutions and others relying on accountants' work.

- The **Transnational Auditors Committee (TAC)**: they deal with issues arising due to cross-border auditing. It is the executive committee of the Forum of Firms (FoF), open to all firms performing or wishing to perform transnational audits. The TAC is discussed in more detail in chapter 10.

Other constituent bodies include:

- The **Compliance Advisory Panel (CAP)**
- The **Professional Accountancy Organisation Development Committee**
- The **International Accounting Education Standards Board**
- The **Professional Accountants in Business Committee (PAIB)**
- The **International Public Sector Accounting Standards Board**
- The **Small and Medium Practices Committee**

The trouble with IFAC

IFAC has encountered a number of difficulties in carrying out its role:

- It was set up by, and continues to be financed by, the accountancy profession worldwide. It therefore represents a self regulatory body. It is suggested that this is an inappropriate mechanism for regulating the audit profession.
- National interests still came into play leading to the implementation of international standards being bogged down in arguments between different national approaches.
- Its members are the professional accountancy bodies, whose authority, arguably, has been eclipsed to some extent by the power of the largest accountancy firms.

And then there was Enron!

The fraudulent financial reporting at the heart of the Enron collapse has had major repercussions for the accountancy profession worldwide. It was one of the largest and most complex bankruptcy cases the world has ever witnessed. Consequent investigations identified numerous creative accounting techniques designed to improve reported profits and hide significant debts from investors.

Ultimately the scandal that followed in the wake Enron's bankruptcy led to the collapse of one of the "Big 5" accountancy firms, Arthur Andersen, itself a massive multinational employer. The role of Arthur Andersen in the financial fraud came under close public scrutiny and much of the already fragile trust in the auditing profession, due to other high profile frauds, was lost.

What happened at Enron?

Before its bankruptcy, Enron employed approximately 22,000 people and was one of the world's leading electricity, natural gas, and communications companies. In 2001 its revenue peaked at nearly $101 billion. However, much of the reported profit and position was sustained by institutionalised and systematic accounting fraud.

The scandal also caused the dissolution of Arthur Andersen, at that point one of the "Big 5" global accounting firms. The firm was found guilty of obstruction of justice for destroying documents related to the Enron audit and was forced to stop auditing public companies (although the conviction was thrown out by the US Supreme Court in 2005).

The story can be briefly summarised as follows:

- a significant portion of Enron's profits were the result of deals with special purpose entities (SPE's), which it controlled;
- many of the entities were offshore, which – in summary – allowed Enron to avoid taxes, move currency and hide overall company losses;
- Enron used an accounting technique known as marking to market (MTM), which effectively meant that Enron could recognise sales and earnings on deals a long time before the actual revenue was realised;
- the huge profits Enron reported drove up its share price. This allowed executives (who knew about the offshore accounts and hidden losses!) to trade millions of dollars worth of Enron stock to their own benefit;
- share prices began to fall and Enron's massive liabilities started to exert pressure on its liquidity. This eventual lead to problems with its debt agreements and credit downgrades;
- the lower credit rating increased the cost of Enron's borrowing to unsustainable limits; and
- Wall Street analyst queries exposed a number of inconsistencies and problems with Enron's accounts until finally the veil was lifted and the extent of earnings management exposed.

Weak ethical leadership was partly to blame. However there was a deep flaw running right the way through Enron's corporate culture. Were these failures in ethical and business judgment caused by a few people at the top or was the flaw endemic within the whole business?

The fallout for the regulation of audits

As a result of the financial scandals, and the public concern that followed, many changes were implemented in the global auditing and accountancy profession. Examples of developments include:

- The IAASB's International Standards on Auditing have been adopted or are being used as a basis for national standards in over 100 countries worldwide;
- The World Federation of Exchanges endorsed the IAASB's standard setting process and ISA's;
- The Code of Ethics for Professional Accountants has been adopted by many member institutions;

- The largest accountancy firms have all committed to auditing in accordance with ISA's and to apply relevant sections of the Code of Ethics;

- Legislative changes have been established to introduce new corporate governance requirements. The most famous of these, The Sarbanes Oxley Act (SOX) in the US, lead to the creation of the Public Company Accounting Oversight Board, who create standards for listed entities and conduct inspections of audit firms' work; and

- The Public Interest Oversight Board (in conjunction with the International Organisation of Securities Commissions, the Basel Committee on Banking Supervision, the Financial Stability Forum and the World Bank) was set up in 2005 to oversee IFAC's auditing and assurance, ethics, and education standard setting activities and its membership compliance programme.

The trouble with regulation in a global market

Going global – Regulation

The main problem is that harmonisation requires national regimes to adopt International Standards on Auditing. IFAC cannot impose them on a global scale. Many countries have adopted ISAs but they have been adapted to suit local customs/laws and as a result many differences still exist in the quality of audits worldwide.

The most recent attempt to encourage worldwide harmonisation was the Clarity Project (discussed in greater detail later on). This simplified the structures of ISAs and made them more prescriptive so that they are easier to understand and apply in practice.

Providing some clarity

In 2004 the International Audit and Assurance Standards Board began a comprehensive overhaul of all the International Standards on Auditing (ISAs). The aim of the project was to issue a set of updated ISAs, which were easier to understand and encouraged more consistent standards of auditing across the world. The new "Clarified" ISAs became effective for audits of accounting periods beginning on, or after, 15 December 2009.

In order to achieve this aim the ISAs have been redrafted to make their objectives and the responsibilities of the auditor clearer. As a result all standards now adopt the following structure:

- Introduction;
- Objective;
- Definitions;

- Requirements; and
- Application and other explanatory information.

The language used in the standards is also less ambiguous. For example, the standards use the word "shall" instead of "should" to make it clearer that these are requirements that are applicable in virtually all engagements to which the ISA is relevant.

In addition to redrafting the existing standards, a number of them have also been revised with the aim of improving audit practice. This means that the guidance provided has been updated to reflect current issues and developments.

In August 2009 the P7 examiner published an article entitled "The IAASB Clarity Project," which summarises the key changes from the old regime. This article can be found on the ACCA website.

IFIAR: A current issue

IFIAR – a postscript

In September 2006, the national regulatory bodies from Australia, Austria, Brazil, Canada, Denmark, France, Germany, Ireland, Italy, Japan, Mexico, the Netherlands, Norway, Singapore, South Africa, Spain, Sweden, and the United Kingdom, announced the establishment of the International Forum of Independent Audit Regulators (IFIAR). PCAOB from the US was an observer, as were the bodies behind PIOB. The EU also sent observers. Its first meeting took place in Tokyo in March 2007.

It is possible, therefore, that a global regulatory authority may emerge. It is possible that it will set its own assurance standards, thereby supplanting IFAC and the ISA setting process. But then again …

Corporate governance

Introduction

The chapter has so far looked at mechanisms external to the audit firm and their clients (auditing standards, company law and the regulatory framework) that aid confidence and stability in the market place. The next section introduces an internal mechanism, namely corporate governance, and how its principles are enforced.

chapter 1

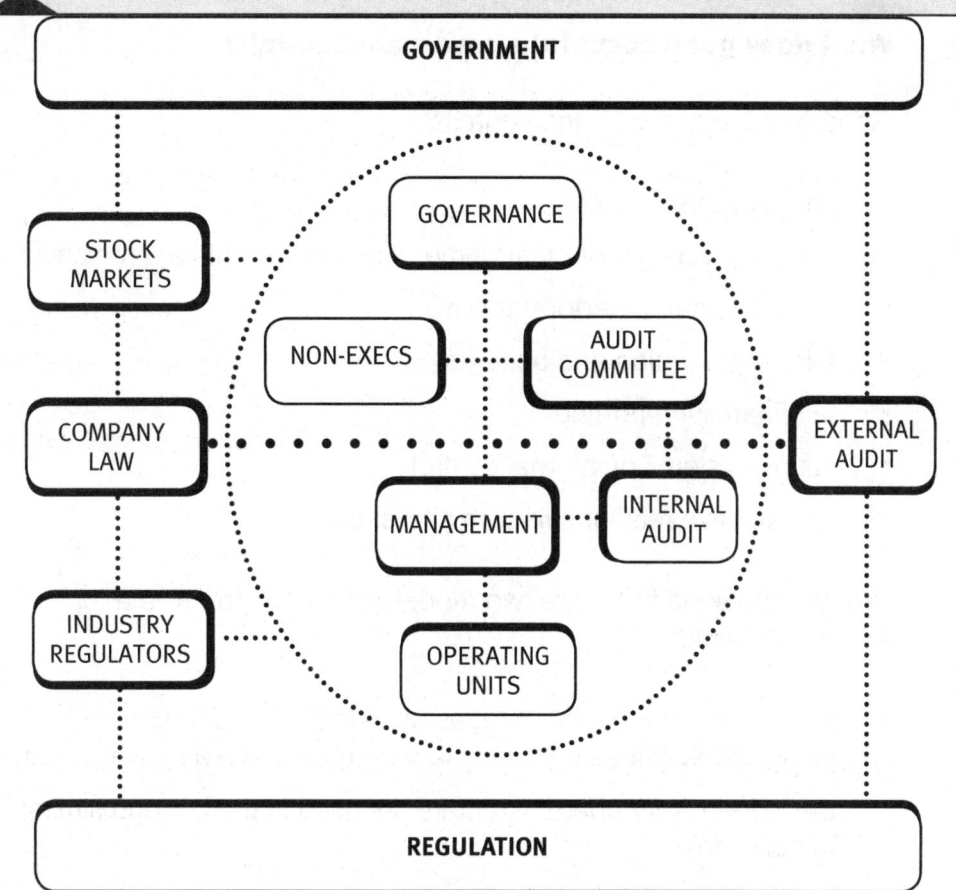

What is corporate governance?

Corporate governance is about ensuring that public companies are:

- managed effectively
- for the benefit of the company and its shareholders.

Why all the fuss?

Corporate governance pronouncements tend to happen in response to corporate scandals that arise because unscrupulous management has:

- manipulated the share price for personal gain
- disguised poor results /mismanagement
- extracted funds from the company
- raised finance fraudulently.

What does good corporate governance entail?

Good corporate governance entails:

- effective management
- support/oversight of management by non-executive directors
- fair appraisal of performance
- fair remuneration and benefits
- fair financial reporting
- sound systems of internal control
- constructive relationship with shareholders.

Broadly speaking there are two models of board structure adopted around the world:

- the 'unitary board' structure, as used in the UK and Ireland and jurisdictions whose company law systems have a similar basis; and
- the 'supervisory board' structure, as used in the US and similar jurisdictions.

Features of a unitary board include:

- collective board responsibility;
- no distinction in law between the responsibilities of executive and non-executive directors;
- the need to distinguish between the function of executive and non-executive directors; and
- the need to establish board committees to monitor and act on different functions – nominating committee, remuneration committee, audit committee, etc.

Features of a supervisory board include:

- executive management with operational responsibility for running the business – the CEO, CFO, Vice presidents, etc.
- the board, with its remuneration and audit committees, etc., which has purely an oversight role.

chapter 1

Sarbanes Oxley

Examples of how corporate governance has been enforced

In the **US** corporate governance is enshrined in law, namely the Sarbanes Oxley Act. As well as dealing with the oversight of auditors the act enforces certain governance responsibilities, such as:

- sound systems of controls.
- clear documentation of financial processes, procedures, risks, and controls.
- evidence that management has evaluated the adequacy of the design and the effectiveness of operation of procedures and controls.
- evidence that the auditor has adequately evaluated the design and operation of financial controls.
- evidence that the audit committee has taken a keen interest in the effectiveness of controls
- explicit 'sign off' procedures by the chief executive and chief financial officer (see 'Sarbanes Oxley').

Overview of the Act

'The primary benefit is to provide the company, its management, its board and audit committee, and its owners and other stakeholders with a reasonable basis to rely on the company's financial reporting.

The integrity of financial reporting represents the foundation upon which this country's public markets are built.'

The key characteristics of Section 302

CEO and CFO need to certify that:

- the SEC report being filed has been reviewed
- the report does not contain any untrue statements or omit any material facts
- the financial statements fairly present the financial position, results of operations and cash flows of the registrant
- they are responsible for, and have designed, established, and maintained disclosure controls and procedures as well as evaluated and reported on the effectiveness of those controls and procedures within 90 days of the report filing date

KAPLAN PUBLISHING   13

- deficiencies and material weaknesses in disclosure controls and procedures have been disclosed to the registrant's audit committee and external auditors
- significant changes in internal control affecting transactions in the period have been reported.

The key characteristics of Section 404

With the filing of their accounts, companies are required to include an annual internal control report of management over financial reporting including:

- responsibilities for establishing and maintaining adequate internal controls and procedures
- conclusions about the effectiveness of the company's internal controls and procedures
- an attestation by the company's registered public accounting firm on management's evaluation.

3 Audit committees

The broad objectives of an audit committee are threefold:

- To increase public confidence in the credibility and objectivity of published financial information;
- To assist directors in meeting their responsibilities in respect of financial reporting; and
- To strengthen the independent position of a company's external auditor.

Membership of audit committees

- A group of independent, non-executive directors
- At least one member should have recent and relevant financial experience.
- Committee members should be independent of operational management.

The functions of an audit committee

These could include the following.

- Review of a company's internal control procedures.
- Review of the internal audit function – the audit committee providing an independent reporting channel.
- Review of the company's current accounting policies and possible changes resulting from the introduction of new accounting standards.
- Review of regular management information (for example, monthly management accounts).
- Review of the annual financial statements presented to shareholders.
- Receiving and dealing with external auditors' criticisms of management, and ensuring that recommendations of internal and external auditors have been implemented.
- Recommending nomination and remuneration of the external auditors.
- Ensuring compliance with codes of practice on corporate governance set out by stock exchanges or other similar institutions.
- Providing a reporting channel for 'whistleblowing'.

Benefits:

- Improved credibility of the financial statements, through an impartial review of the financial statements, monitoring of the independence of the external auditors, and discussion of significant issues with the external auditors.
- Better quality of management accounting, as the audit commitee is better placed to criticise internal functions.
- Stronger control environment, as the internal audit function will report to the audit committee increasing their independence and adding weight to their recommendations.
- They should lead to better communication between the directors, external auditors and management.
- They help to avoid conflicts arising between management and auditors.
- The skills, knowledge and experience (and independence) of the audit committee members can be an invaluable resource for a business.
- It may be easier and cheaper to arrange finance, as the presence of an audit committee can give a perception of good corporate governance.
- It would be less burdensome to meet listing requirements if an audit committee (which is usually a listing requirement) is already established.

Drawbacks:

- Difficulties recruiting the right non-executive directors who have relevant skills, experience and sufficient time to become effective members of the committee.
- A fear that their purpose is to police executive management.
- Non-executive directors being over-burdened with detail.
- Additional cost. Non-executive directors are normally remunerated, and their fees can be quite expensive.

UK syllabus focus

Regulation of auditing

Regulation of auditing in the UK changed on 2 July 2012.

Audit and Assurance in the United Kingdom is regulated by the **Financial Reporting Council** (FRC). The FRC has two divisions, one of which is the **Codes and Standards** division. The Codes and Standards division is responsible for maintaining an effective framework of UK codes and standards for Corporate Governance, Stewardship, Accounting, Auditing and Assurance, and Actuary. The codes and standards division has three councils: the Auditing and Assurance Council, the Accounting Council, and the Actuarial Council. The Auditing and Assurance Council considers and advises the FRC Board and the Codes and Standards Committee on audit and assurance matters.

The FRC issues International Standards on Auditing for use within the United Kingdom and Republic of Ireland. The standards are supplemented and revised before issuing them, mainly in order to ensure that they remain compliant with national laws, such as the Companies Act 2006.

In addition the FRC:

- Develop and maintain ethical standards and guidance for auditors' and reporting accountants' integrity, objectivity and independence to facilitate the adoption of the Code of Ethics in the UK (see Ethics and Acceptance chapter for more detail).
- Has statutory responsibility for the oversight and regulations of the accountancy profession and of statutory auditors, which is managed by the Professional Oversight team, part of the Conduct division.
- Monitors the quality of the audits of listed and other major public interest entities; this is the responsibility of the Audit Quality Review team.

- Ensures that appropriate standards are maintained by members and member firms, by operating an independent professional disciplinary scheme for accountants, overseen by the Conduct division.

Audit exemption

In accordance with the Companies Act 2006 those companies falling below the small company threshold are not required, in law, to have an annual audit. Although they may still choose to have one voluntarily.

The main criteria for small company status are:

- Turnover not exceeding £6.5mn
- Gross assets not exceeding £3.26mn and
- The number of employees must not exceed 50.

In order to qualify the company must meet two out of the three criteria.

Reporting by exception

In the UK auditors take on additional reporting responsibilities from the Companies Act 2006. The matters are reported on by exception, meaning that the auditor would only make a separate report if the matters have not been concluded satisfactorily. These matters are that:

- adequate accounting records have been kept
- returns adequate for the audit have been received from branches not visited by the auditor
- the accounts agree with accounting records and returns
- director's remuneration has been adequately disclosed as required by law
- all information and explanations required for the audit have been received.

ISA 700 (UK & Ireland) also adds additional reporting responsibilities (by exception) for auditor's of listed companies in the UK, they are:

- A statement given by the directors that they consider the annual report and accounts taken as a whole is fair, balanced and understandable and provides the information necessary for shareholders to assess the entity's performance, business model and strategy, that is inconsistent with the knowledge acquired by the auditor in the course of performing the audit.

- A section describing the work of the audit committee that does not appropriately address matters communicated by the auditor to the audit committee.

- An explanation, as to why the annual report does not include such a statement or section, that is materially inconsistent with the knowledge acquired by the auditor in the course of performing the audit.

- Other information that, in the auditor's judgment, contains a material inconsistency or a material misstatement of fact.

FSA listing rules

The 'UK Corporate Governance Code' (formerly "the Combined Code" and last updated in October 2012) adopts what is commonly referred to as the "comply or explain" approach. It is not a rigid (or enforced) set of rules. Instead it consists of principles (main and supporting) and provisions.

In the UK all companies quoted on the stock exchange have to comply with the FSA listing rules. These include a requirement that all companies include in their annual report:

- An explanation from the directors of their responsibility for preparing the accounts and a statement that they consider that the annual report and accounts, taken as a whole, is fair, balanced and understandable and provides the information necessary for shareholders to assess and provide the company's performance, business model and strategy. There should also be a statement by the auditor about their reporting responsibilities.

- A report on progress with the company's policies on boardroom diversity.

- Information from the audit committee on how they have carried out their responsibilities including an explanation of how they have assessed the effectiveness of the external audit process and the approach taken to the appointment or reappointment of the external auditor, including the length of tenure of the current audit firm and when a tender was last conducted.

- If the external auditor provides non-audit services, an explanation of how auditor objectivity and independence is safeguarded, and

- A statement as to whether the company has complied with all relevant provisions set out in the Code, and explanations as to why they have chosen not to follow any particular provisions.

The FRC's *Guidance on Audit Committees* was also updated to reflect the changes to the UK Corporate Governance Code that relate to audit committees, explained above.

The main provisions of the Code are:

Leadership

- Every company should be headed by an effective board with collective responsibility;
- There should be a clear division of responsibilities between the Chairman and the Chief Executive;
- No one individual should have unfettered powers of decision; and
- Non-executive directors should constructively challenge and help develop proposals on strategy.

Effectiveness

- The board should have the appropriate balance of skills, experience, independence and knowledge;
- There should be a formal, rigorous and transparent procedure for the appointment of new directors;
- All directors should receive an induction and should regularly update and refresh their skills and knowledge;
- The board should be supplied with quality and timely information to enable it to discharge its duties;
- The board and individuals should be subject to a formal and rigorous annual evaluation of performance; and
- All directors should be submitted for re-election at regular intervals.

Accountability

- The board should present a balanced and understandable assessment of the company's position and prospects;
- The board is responsible for determining the nature and extent of the significant risks it is willing to take in achieving its strategic objectives;
- The board should maintain sound risk management and internal control systems; and
- The board should establish formal and transparent arrangements for corporate reporting and risk management and internal control principles and for maintaining an appropriate relationship with the company's auditor.

Regulation in a global economy

Remuneration

- This should be sufficient to attract, retain and motivate directors of the quality required to run the company successfully, but should not be excessive;
- A significant proportion of this should be structured so as to link reward to corporate and individual performance;
- There should be a formal and transparent procedure for developing policy on executive remuneration; and
- No director should be involved in deciding his or her own remuneration.

Relations with shareholders

- There should be a dialogue with shareholders based on the mutual understanding of objectives;
- The board as a whole has responsibility for ensuring that a satisfactory dialogue with shareholders takes place; and
- The board should use the AGM to communicate with investors and to encourage their participation.

Test your understanding 1

Becher is an independent construction company, dealing with large scale contracts throughout the UK and with some international interest in Europe, particularly in Spain. Becher has recently established an Audit Committee, the members of which are very concerned about meeting corporate governance 'best practice', particularly since they are currently looking at the possibility of obtaining a stock exchange listing.

You are an internal auditor with the company and have been asked to conduct a review of how well the company is meeting relevant corporate governance requirements.

You are required to prepare a report that addresses the following.

(a) What is meant by 'corporate governance' and why is it important that companies should comply with relevant corporate governance requirements?

(4 marks)

(b) What are the key issues for Becher to address to achieve effective corporate governance?

(5 marks)

(c) What is the role of the Audit Committee in relation to corporate governance?

(4 marks)

(d) List the types of regular reporting that would be useful for Becher in the context of establishing sound corporate governance.

(3 marks)

4 Chapter summary

This chapter has covered the following topics:

- the reasons for regulating the audit and assurance professions
- the difficulties facing national and international regulators in the global economy
- the difficulties facing national and international standard setting bodies
- the need for good standards of corporate governance
- how standards of corporate governance are maintained
- the function of the audit committee.

chapter 1

Test your understanding answers

Test your understanding 1

(a) **Corporate Governance**

Corporate Governance concerns the way that a company is directed and controlled. It encompasses the following key aspects:

- The role of the Board and Audit Committee.
- Overall control and risk management framework.

Corporate Governance has become increasingly important in the wake of high profile accounting frauds. These frauds have had a damaging impact on the effective operation of world stock markets due to reductions in investor (and public) confidence in the roles of directors and company auditors.

Management and control is often more difficult to achieve in larger, more complex organisations. In addition, shareholders (the owners) tend to be more remote from the directors who manage the company on their behalf. Having an agreed set of corporate governance standards therefore facilitates the adoption of good corporate governance practices and improves accountability to investor groups.

Failure to comply with these agreed standards of corporate governance could lead to significant penalties, namely:

- fines and penalties, where corporate governance is enforced through law, the US for example. This could, in the most extreme cases, lead to imprisonment of directors;
- penalties imposed by stock market regulators, such as removal from the listing; and
- replacement of board members.

(b) **Requirements of Corporate Governance**

The nature of issues to address depend upon the legal or listing requirements in place in the country of operation. However the following basic principles may be universally applied:

- The board should be responsible for the assessment of and response to risk;

KAPLAN PUBLISHING 23

- The board should be responsible for designing, implementing and monitoring the effectiveness of the system of internal control;
- An independent system (including the use of committees) should be established to enable the effective recruitment and retention of directors;
- Communication with, and independence of auditors, should be facilitated by the use of an audit committee; and
- There should be explicit and transparent reporting of compliance with corporate governance requirements/principles.7

UK Syllabus Focus

In the UK listed companies need to report upon how, and whether, they have complied with the UK Corporate Governance Code. This means adopting systems to address the following main principles of the Code:

- *Leadership;*
- *Effectiveness;*
- *Accountability;*
- *Remuneration; and*
- *Relations with shareholders.*

(c) **Role of the Audit Committee**

The role and importance of the Audit Committee has increased as corporate governance requirements have been strengthened. The Audit Committee should have at least three non-executive directors who should be independent of the company, i.e. have no direct involvement in the day to day running of its affairs.

The Audit Committee should:

- assess the framework for complying with corporate governance guidelines within the company, including the risk assessment procedures
- review the major risks identified including their chances of occurring and their likely impact
- require regular reporting from internal and external auditors and any other review bodies, showing how the risks are being managed
- receive and review internal audit assignment reports and follow up information

- discuss and consider any concerns of directors and internal audit staff
- review annual financial statements and the results of the external auditors' examination to ensure that the auditors have performed an effective, efficient and independent audit
- receive and deal with external auditors' comments on management and ensure that recommendations of internal and external auditors have been implemented.

(d) **Types of regular reporting**

Types of regular reporting that could be produced include:

- analysis of current operational risks, including assessment of likelihood and potential impact;
- report on strategy for current management of risks identified;
- details of any issues arising that had not previously been identified and, therefore, were not being managed;
- independent expert analysis of technical matters, for example: the structural condition of oil rigs, risk assessment for operating in politically unstable economies.

chapter 2

Code of ethics and conduct

Chapter learning objectives

When you have completed this chapter you will be able to:

- explain the fundamental principles and the conceptual framework approach
- identify, evaluate and respond to threats to compliance with the fundamental principles
- discuss and evaluate the effectiveness of available safeguards
- recognise and advise on conflicts in the application of fundamental principles.

Code of ethics and conduct

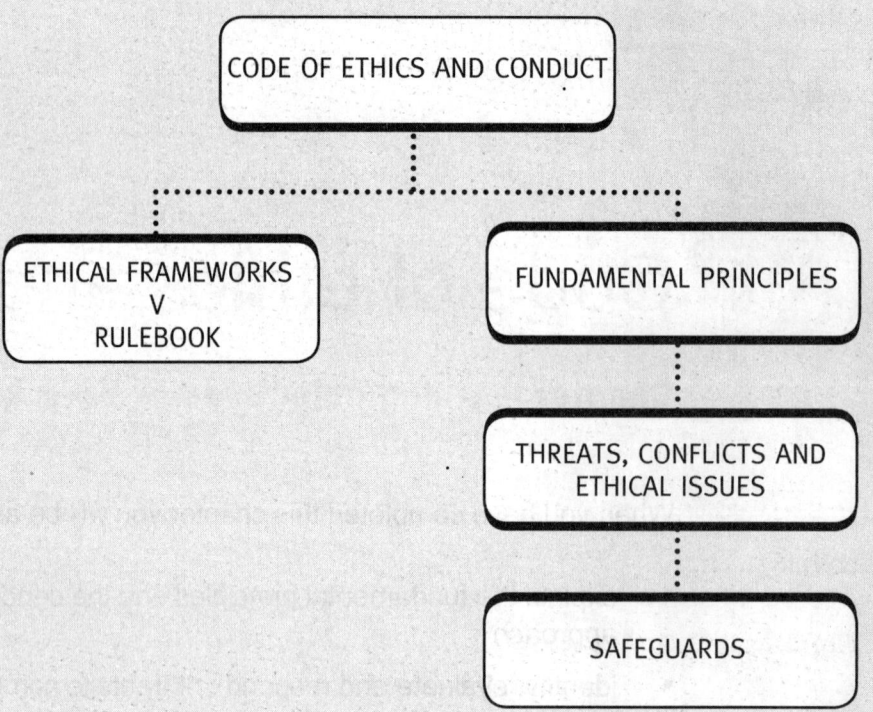

 Ethics always features in the P7 exam. A typical requirement will ask you to evaluate the ethical and professional issues in a scenario. Note that this incorporates all of the fundamental principles, not just objectivity, as well as professional issues discussed later in this text. Evaluation requires more than just identification and explanation of the threats. You will also need to consider the significance of the threat. As part of evaluating a threat a professional accountant would always consider what (if any) safeguards are available to reduce the threat to an acceptable level, and so in the exam you should always consider safeguards as part of this evaluation.

1 Framework versus rulebook approach to ethical guidance

Ethical guidance can either be principles-based (a conceptual framework approach) or rules-based.

Advantages of a 'rulebook' approach

- Certainty.
- Clarity regarding what is not permitted.

However, it is virtually impossible for rule-based systems to be able to deal with every situation that may arise, particularly across various national boundaries and in a dynamic industry.

They can also be interpreted narrowly in order to circumvent the underlying 'spirit' or intention of the rule.

chapter 2

Advantages of an 'ethical framework' approach

An ethical framework approach has advantages over rule-based systems.

- A framework is more appropriate to changing circumstances in a dynamic profession.
- Principles may be applied across national boundaries, where laws may not.
- The onus is placed on the auditor to demonstrate that **all matters** are considered within the principles of the framework.
- A framework approach may include some specific 'prohibitions' or deal with specific matters.

Both IFAC and the ACCA have decided on a principles-based approach.

The fundamental principles

IESBA develops and promotes the IFAC Code of Ethics for Professional Accountants, which applies to all professional accountants, whether in public practice or not. The IFAC Code serves as the foundation for codes of ethics developed and enforced by member bodies of IFAC. All ACCA members and students are obliged to follow the fundamental principles.

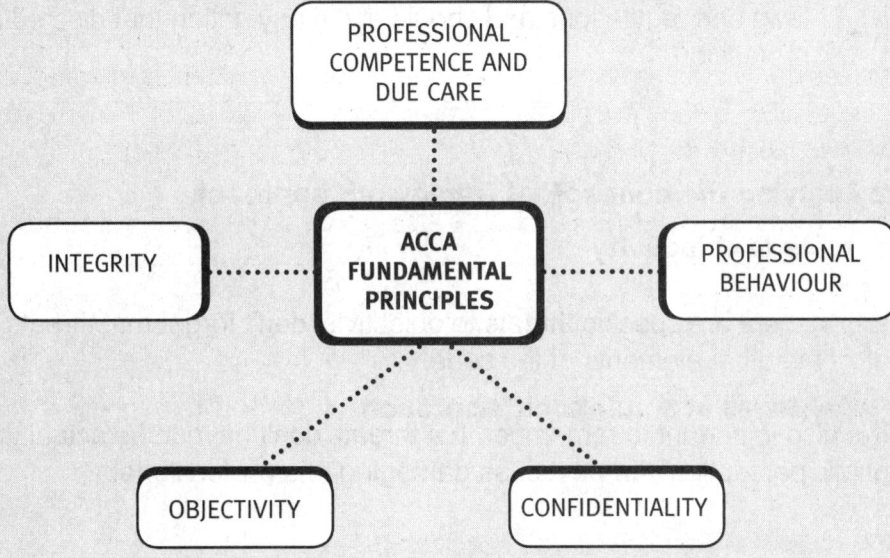

Code of ethics and conduct

Ethics definitions

- **Integrity:** Members should be straightforward and honest in all professional and business relationships.
- **Objectivity:** Members should not allow bias, conflicts of interest or undue influence of others to override professional or business judgments.
- **Professional competence and due care:** Members have a continuing duty to maintain professional knowledge and skill at a level required to ensure that a client or employer receives competent professional service based on current developments in practice, legislation and techniques. Members should act diligently and in accordance with applicable technical and professional standards when providing professional services.
- **Confidentiality:** Members should respect the confidentiality of information acquired as a result of professional and business relationships and should not disclose any such information to third parties without proper and specific authority or unless there is a legal or professional right or duty to disclose. Confidential information acquired as a result of professional and business relationships should not be used for the personal advantage of members or third parties.
- **Professional behaviour:** Members should comply with relevant laws and regulations and should avoid any action that discredits the profession.

2 Applying the conceptual framework approach

Threats to objectivity

Whilst there are specific threats to objectivity don't forget that threats exist to all of the other elements of the code.

It is also important to remember that threats don't have to be actual threats; public perception can be just as damaging to a professional.

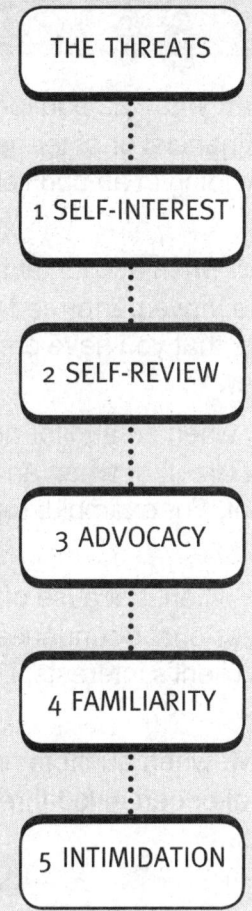

Assuming management responsibilities for an assurance client may also create threats to independence. In some jurisdictions this is referred to as the **management threat**. A firm must not assume management responsibilities as part of an assurance engagement or for an audit client.

- Activities that are routine and administrative, or involve matters that are insignificant, generally are deemed not to be a management responsibility.
- Providing advice and recommendations to assist management in discharging its responsibilities is not assuming management responsibilities.

The firm should take steps to ensure that client management make significant judgements and decisions.

Code of ethics and conduct

Threat definitions

(1) **Self-interest threat**: when an auditor (or a close family member of the auditor) has a financial or other beneficial interest in a client. For example: a shareholding in an audit client or a loan extended to a client.

(2) **Self-review threat**: when accountants review or re-evaluate work they, or a colleague, have performed. For example, auditing a set of financial statements that you have prepared yourself would constitute self-review.

(3) **Advocacy threat**: when an auditor acts on behalf of or as a representative of a client, or when an auditor promotes the position or opinion of a client. For example: representing a client in a legal case.

(4) **Familiarity threat**: when, because of a relationship with a client that goes beyond professional boundaries, the auditor becomes too sympathetic to the client's interests, i.e. the erosion of professional scepticism.

(5) **Intimidation threat**: when auditors are deterred from acting objectively by actual or perceived threats, e.g. the threat of litigation or withholding of fees.

Assessment and safeguards

The assessment of and response to ethical threats is a key element of the P7 exam. It is therefore critical that you can discuss the significance of a threat and recommend an appropriate safeguard.

chapter 2

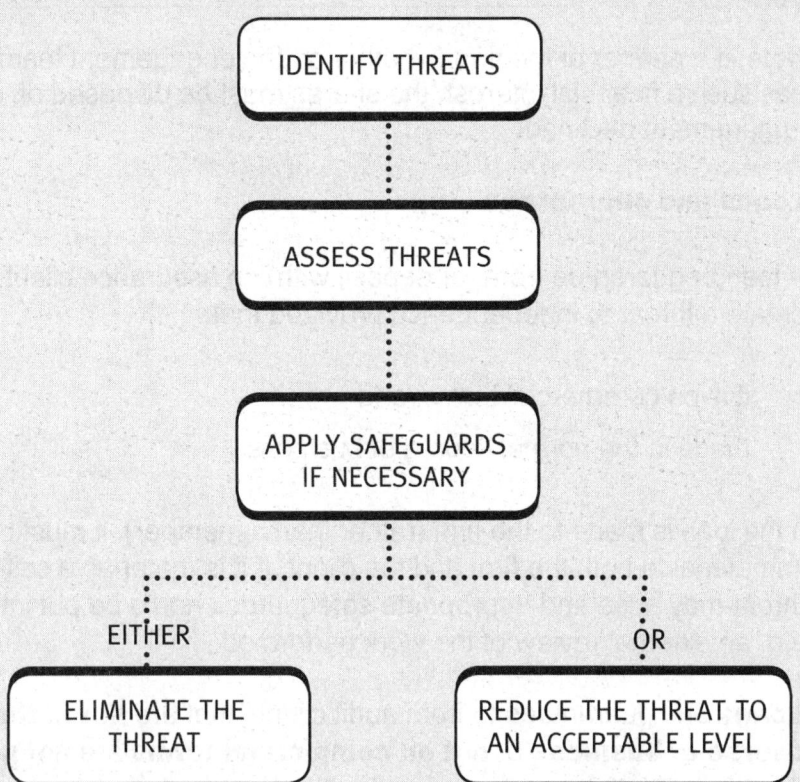

The ACCA Code of Ethics divides safeguards into two broad categories:

- **Safeguards created by the profession, legislation or regulation:** These include: requirements for entry into the profession, continuing professional development, corporate governance, professional standards, and monitoring and disciplinary procedures.
- **Safeguards created by the work environment:** These are discussed below, but include, rotation/removal of relevant staff from the engagement team, independent quality control reviews, using separate teams, etc.

 Further discussion of threats

Financial interests

A **self interest threat** may arise if a member (or their close family) holds any beneficial interest in the shares, or some other form of investment, in a client.

The significance of the threat depends on the role of the person holding the financial interest and the materiality of the investment.

Safeguards:

– Dispose of the shares; or

– Remove the individual from the engagement team.

KAPLAN PUBLISHING 33

Note, if a partner of the firm (whether on the engagement team or not) has such a financial interest, the shares must be disposed of, or the engagement declined.

Loans and guarantees

A loan or guarantee from (or deposit with) an assurance client will not create a threat to independence provided that:

- it is on commercial terms; and
- made in the normal course of business.

If the loan is made to the firm (rather than a member), it must be immaterial to both the firm and the client. If it is material, a self-interest threat may arise and appropriate safeguards should be put into place, e.g. an external review of the work performed.

Loans and guarantees to/from audit clients that are **not in the normal course of business** or **not on commercial terms** are **not permitted** (i.e. the self-interest threat is so significant, no safeguards could reduce the threat to an acceptable level).

Loans and guarantees to/from other assurance clients that are not in the normal course of business or not on commercial terms must be immaterial.

Relationships

(1) Family and other personal relationships

A familiarity threat, self-interest threat, or intimidation threat may occur when a member of the engagement team has a family or personal relationship with someone at the client who is able to exert significant influence over the financial statements (or subject matter of another assurance engagement).

Consideration should be given to the possibility that such a threat may also arise when a partner (or employee) of the firm has a family or personal relationship with someone at the client who is able to exert significant influence over the subject matter, even when the individual is not a member of the engagement team.

Safeguards

- Remove the individual from the engagement team.
- Structure the engagement team so that the individual does not deal with matters that are the responsibility of the close family member.
- Decline/resign from the engagement.

(2) **Business relationships**

If audit firms (or members) enter into business relationships (e.g. joint ventures, marketing arrangements) with clients this leads to self-interest because the auditor would have an interest in the successful operation of the client. In the case of audit firms, or partners of those firms, **no safeguard can reduce this threat to an acceptable level**.

The purchase of goods and services from an assurance client would not normally give rise to a threat to independence, provided the transaction is:

- in the normal course of business; and
- on commercial terms.

Employment

A self interest, familiarity or intimidation threat may arise where an employee of the firm becomes a director or employee of an assurance client (in a position to exert significant influence over the financial statements or subject matter of another assurance engagement).

Safeguards:

- Reviewing (and revising) the composition of the engagement team.
- Performing an independent partner/quality control review of the engagement.

If a member of the engagement team has reason to believe they may become an employee of the client, a self-interest threat arises.

Safeguards:

- The policies and procedures of the firm should require such individuals to notify the firm of the possibility of employment with the client.
- Removal of the individual from the assurance engagement.
- Performing an independent review of any significant judgements made by that individual.
- A key audit partner should not accept a key management position with an audit client until at least one set of financial statements covering a period of at least twelve months have been issued, since the partner was involved in the audit.

A self interest, self-review, or familiarity threat may arise where a director or employee of an assurance client (in a position to exert significant influence over the financial statements or subject matter of another assurance engagement) becomes an employee of the firm.

Safeguards:

- Such individuals should not be assigned to an engagement team until at least two years have elapsed (after the end of their employment with the client).

An employee or partner of a firm **cannot** also be an employee or director of an assurance client, as the self-interest and self-review threats created would be so significant that no safeguard could reduce the threats to an acceptable level.

Long-association of senior personnel

Using the same senior personnel in an engagement team over a long period may create a familiarity threat.

Safeguards:

- Rotation of senior personnel;
- Independent partner/quality control reviews;
- Note that it is a requirement to rotate key audit partners on listed clients after no more than seven years (with a minimum break of two years), unless in exceptional circumstances where necessary to maintain audit quality, in which case a maximum one year extension is permitted.

Fees and pricing

Objectivity may be threatened (or appear to be) by over-dependence on an audit client (a self-interest threat).

A firm's independence is threatened, and should be reviewed if a listed audit client's total fees exceed 15% of the firm's total fees for two consecutive years.

Safeguards:

- Disclosure to those charged with governance at the client;
- Performing an independent partner/quality control review of the engagement.

A self-interest threat may also be created if fees from an assurance client are overdue. A firm should consider whether the overdue fees may be regarded as a loan (loans are not permitted to an audit client).

Contingent fees for **assurance** work provided to **audit clients** are **not permitted.**

For non-assurance engagements provided to audit clients, a contingent fee may give rise to a self-interest or advocacy threat. It may not be possible to reduce the threat to an acceptable level with safeguards. Such safeguards would include disclosure to the client's audit committee, performing an independent partner review, and obtaining an external review (or determination) of the fee.

Provision of non-audit services to audit clients

There are occasions where objectivity may be threatened or appear to be threatened by the provision of additional services to audit clients. Such work can generate significant levels of income which may overly influence decisions made and conclusions reached during the statutory audit process (self-interest threat). This also increases the risk of self-review.

Where such services are permitted appropriate safeguards would include:

- Independent teams (i.e. different personnel with different reporting lines) providing each engagement;
- An independent partner review of the work performed.

Having custody of an audit or assurance client's assets may also give rise to such threats.

Some examples of these services include:

Accounting and bookeeping services

A firm **can** provide an audit client **that is not a listed** with accounting and bookkeeping services, including payroll services, of a 'routine or mechanical nature', as long as adequate safeguards are implemented.

> **Safeguards:**
>
> – Such services must not be performed by members of the audit team.
> – Managerial decisions must not be made by the firm, and the source data, underlying assumptions, and subsequent adjustments must be originated or approved by the client.

A firm **cannot provide** an **audit client** that is **listed** with **accounting and bookkeeping services**, except in an emergency (and only where the threat to independence can be managed).

Valuation services

Valuation of matters that are material to the financial statements and involve a significant degree of subjectivity should not be provided.

For listed audit clients, valuation services that are material to the financial statements (regardless of subjectivity) should not be provided.

Taxation services

Some taxation services create self-review and advocacy threats.

A firm **cannot prepare tax calculations** for an **audit client** that is **listed**, except in an emergency.

A firm **cannot represent an audit client** before a public tribunal or court in the resolution of a tax matter, where the amounts are material to the financial statements,.

Litigation services

Acting for an audit client in the resolution of a dispute or litigation in matters that are material to the financial statements is not permitted (self-review and advocacy threat).

Internal audit services

A firm cannot provide internal audit services for an audit client that is listed, where the service relates to internal controls over financial reporting, financial accounting systems, or in relation to amounts or disclosures that are material to the financial statements.

Hospitality

Objectivity may be threatened or appear to be threatened by acceptance of goods, services or hospitality from an audit client (self-interest and familiarity threats). Only 'clearly insignificant' gifts should ever be accepted and even these should be approved by a partner.

Actual or threatened litigation

A firm's objectivity may be threatened or appear to be threatened when it or a member of the engagement team is involved in, or threatened with, litigation in relation to a client (intimidation threat).

Litigation could represent a breakdown in the relationship of trust between auditor and client. This adversarial position may affect the impartiality of the auditor, and lead to a reluctance of management to disclose relevant information to the auditor. The firm must resign from or decline the audit.

It may be possible to continue other assurance engagements, depending on the significance of the threat by:

- Discussing the matter with the client's audit committee.
- If the litigation involves an individual, removing that individual from the engagement team.
- Obtaining an external review of the work done.

Confidentiality

The rule

Members acquiring information in the course of their professional work should not disclose such information to third parties without first obtaining permission from the client, unless there is a legal right or duty to disclose, or it is in the public interest to do so.

Circumstances in which disclosure is permitted or required

The general rule is that disclosure should only be made if:

- the client's permission has been given
- the client is suspected of treason, terrorism, drug trafficking, or money laundering
- such disclosure is required to protect the member's interests
- required by law
- it is in the public interest.

Public interest

There is no official definition of 'public interest'. The auditor must employ a combination of judgement and legal advice. However, a good rule of thumb is that if a member of the public could incur physical or financial damage that the auditor could knowingly have prevented it is likely that the auditor has failed in their public duty.

In determining the need to disclose matters in the public interest the auditor should consider:

- the potential monetary values involved;
- whether members of the public are likely to be or become involved;
- the gravity of the matter;
- the likelihood of repetition;
- the reasons for the client's unwillingness to make the disclosures;
- relevant legislation, accounting standards and auditing standards; and
- legal advice obtained.

chapter 2

> **Current Issue: IESBA: Responding to a Suspected Illegal Act**
>
> In August 2012, the IESBA issued *Responding to a Suspected Illegal Act* Exposure Draft.
>
> The Exposure Draft proposes:
>
> - For audit clients: to create a professional duty to disclose to an appropriate authority, suspected illegal acts (including fraud) that affect financial reporting (or are otherwise within the expertise of a professional accountant) that would be in the public interest (currently it is a right, not a duty).
>
> - For non-audit clients: to create a professional duty to disclose suspected illegal acts (including fraud) that would be in the public interest to the external auditor, where the accountant is unable to escalate the matter within the client or where the client has failed to take appropriate action. This would not affect the professional accountant's right to disclose these matters to an appropriate authority.
>
> The Exposure Draft states that in determining whether a disclosure would be in the public interest, the professional accountant must take into account the perspective of a reasonable and informed third party who knows all of the specific facts and circumstances. The determination requires professional judgement and consideration of the nature and magnitude of the matter, including the number of people who could be affected and the extent to which they could be affected.

Conflicts of interest

Professional accountants should always act in the best interests of the client. However, where **conflicts of interest** exist, such as **when a firm acts for competing clients** (which is common) the firm's work should be arranged to **avoid the interests of one being adversely affected** by those of another and to **prevent a breach of confidentiality.**

In order to ensure this, the firm must notify all affected clients of the conflict and **obtain their consent to act.** The following additional safeguards should be considered:

- advise the clients to seek independent advice

- separate engagement teams (with different engagement partners and team members)

- procedures to prevent access to information, e.g. physical separation of the team members and confidential/secure data filing

KAPLAN PUBLISHING

Code of ethics and conduct

- signed confidentiality agreements
- regular review of the application of safeguards by an independent person of appropriate seniority.

If adequate safeguards cannot be implemented (i.e. where the acceptance/continuance of an engagement would, despite safeguards, materially prejudice the interests of any clients) the firm must decline or resign from one or more conflicting engagements.

3 The auditor's integrity, objectivity and independence

Areas of risk to integrity, objectivity and independence

Common examples of threats to the auditor's integrity, objectivity and independence arise from:

- personal relationships between the auditor and the client
- financial and business relationships between the auditor and the client
- undue economic dependence on an audit client
- acceptance by the auditor of goods and services or hospitality from the client
- provision of non-audit services to an audit client (key ethical issue)
- overdue fees
- litigation between the auditor and the client.

Emerging ethical issues

Further possible measures to improve independence

The following possibilities might improve the independence of auditors still further:

- Compulsory rotation of audit firms (as already happens in some countries, e.g. Italy).
- A ban on the provision of non-audit services by auditors.
- A State Audit Board to audit all public interest companies.
- The government to appoint the auditors of all public interest companies.
- Tightening all the limits stated in the ACCA Code (e.g. no client to exceed 5% of a firm's total fee income, engagement partners to serve no more than two years, etc.).

Integrity in Ethics Discussion Paper

The Federation of European Accountants (FEE) Integrity in Ethics Discussion Paper

The FEE have an integrity working party aimed at:

- Promoting debate about the importance of integrity in the accountancy profession; and
- Engaging the public and stakeholders in the profession in considering what behaving with integrity in a professional and business context should mean.

The FEE have recommended the following characteristics expected of someone behaving with integrity in a professional context:

- Be straightforward, honest, and truthful.
- Deal fairly. This includes treating people on the same basis, without bias;
- Comply with the spirit as well as the letter of laws and regulations;
- Take into consideration the public interest;
- Show consistency;
- Be open-minded and open to consider new information and ideas;
- Take corrective action.

A professional accountant's advice and work should be uncorrupted by self-interest or other financial or behavioural motives and should not be influenced by the interests of other parties.

As well as individual traits the FEE have also identified a number of interlinked organisational traits required to promote integrity. These are:

- Leadership;
- Strategy;
- Policies;
- Information; and
- Culture.

To be effective, ethical values must be embedded within the way an organisation does business. In practice the success of this can be observed through a number of indicators:

- **Awareness:** an organisation that seeks to have integrity will recognise ethical dilemmas;

- **Predictability:** an organisation with integrity knows how to act when it faces an ethics dilemma, because it has, and applies, clear ethical values in a consistent and credible manner;

- **Transparency:** being open and honest about its behaviour;

- **Long term view:** in organisations with integrity short term actions support long term goals. This implies, for example, creating long term relationships with clients, suppliers and other stakeholders;

- **People:** there is a commitment to support employees to uphold the organisation's ethical values and to deal with any ethical dilemmas they may face.

UK syllabus focus

The FRC has issued a set of UK specific ethical standards designed to ensure practitioners comply with the IFAC Code of Ethics. These can be summarised as follows:

Ethical Standard 1 – integrity, objectivity and independence

- The audit firm shall establish policies and procedures to ensure that the firm, and all those involved in the audit, act with integrity, objectivity and independence;

- The leadership of the audit firm shall take responsibility for establishing a control environment that places adherence to ethical principles above commercial considerations;

- The audit firm shall designate an ethics partner;

- The audit firm shall establish policies and procedures to prevent employees from taking decisions that are the responsibility of management of the audited entity;

- The audit firm shall establish policies and procedures to assess the significance of threats to the auditor's objectivity:

    (i) when considering whether to accept or retain an audit or non-audit service;

    (ii) when planning the audit

    (iii) when forming an opinion on the financial statements; and

    (iv) when potential threats are reported.

- The audit engagement partner shall not accept or shall not continue an audit engagement if he or she concludes that any threats to the auditor's objectivity and independence cannot be reduced to an acceptable level.

- In the case of listed companies the engagement quality control reviewer shall:

    (i) consider the audit firm's compliance with the Ethical Standards; and

    (ii) form an independent opinion as to the appropriateness and adequacy of the safeguards applied.

Ethical Standard 2 – financial, business, employment and personal relationships

- The audit firm, or employees, shall not hold any financial interest in an audited entity;

- Audit firms and employees shall not make loans to, or guarantee the borrowings of, an audited entity (and vice versa);

- Audit firms and employees shall not enter into business relationships with an audited entity;

- An audit firm shall not second partners or employees to an audit client unless:
    - the agreement is for a short period of time; and
    - the audited entity agrees that the individual concerned will not hold a management position.

- Where a partner or employee returns to a firm on completion of a secondment to an audit client, that individual shall not be given any role on the audit involving any function or activity that they performed or supervised during that assignment.

- Where a partner joins an audited entity, the audit firm shall take action to ensure that no connections remain between the firm and the individual;

- Where a partner leaves a firm and is appointed as a director or to a key management position with an audited entity, having acted as audit engagement partner at any time in the two years prior to this appointment, the firm shall resign as auditor.

- A partner, or employee of the audit firm who undertakes audit work, shall not accept appointment:
    - to the board of directors of the audited entity; or
    - to any subcommittee of that board;

Code of ethics and conduct

ES 3 – Long association with the audit engagement

- The audit firm shall establish policies and procedures to monitor the length of time that senior staff serve as members of the engagement team for each audit;

- Where senior staff have a long association with the audit, the audit firm shall assess the threats to the auditor's objectivity and independence and shall apply safeguards to reduce the threats to an acceptable level. Where appropriate safeguards cannot be applied, the audit firm shall either resign as auditor or not stand for reappointment, as appropriate;

- Once an audit engagement partner has held this role for ten years, careful consideration must be given as to whether their objectivity would be perceived to be impaired;

- In the case of listed companies the audit firm shall establish policies and procedures to ensure that no one shall act as audit engagement partner for more than five years; and

- In the case of listed companies, the audit engagement partner shall review the safeguards put in place to address the threats arising where senior staff have been involved in the audit for a period longer than seven years.

ES 4 – Fees, remuneration and evaluation policies, litigation, gifts and hospitality

- The audit engagement partner shall ensure that audit fees are not influenced or determined by the provision of non-audit services;

- An audit shall not be undertaken on a contingent fee basis;

- Audit fee for the previous audit and the arrangements for its payment shall be agreed with the audited entity before the audit firm formally accepts appointment as auditor in respect of the following period;

- Where it is expected that the total fees receivable from a listed audited entity will regularly exceed 10% of the annual fee income (15% if non-listed) of the audit firm, the firm shall not act as the auditor of that entity;

- The audit firm shall establish policies and procedures to ensure that the objectives and appraisal of members of the audit team do not include selling non-audit services.

- Where litigation with a client is already in progress, or where it is probable, the audit firm shall either not continue with or not accept the audit engagement;

- The audit firm, including employees, shall not accept gifts from the audited entity, unless the value is clearly insignificant; and

- Audit firm employees shall not accept hospitality from the audited entity, unless it is reasonable in terms of its frequency, nature and cost.

ES 5 – Non-audit services provided to audited entities

- Before the audit firm accepts a proposed engagement to provide non-audit services to an audit client, the audit engagement partner shall:
    - consider whether a reasonable third party would regard the objectives of the proposed engagement as being inconsistent with the objectives of the audit;
    - identify and assess any threats to the auditor's objectivity, including any perceived loss of independence; and
    - identify and assess the effectiveness of the available safeguards to eliminate the threats or reduce them to an acceptable level.

- Where the audit partner considers it probable that a reasonable third party would regard the objectives of the proposed non-audit service engagement as being inconsistent with the objectives of the audit, the audit firm shall either:
    - not undertake the non-audit service engagement; or
    - not accept or withdraw from the audit engagement.

- Specifically, the audit firm shall not undertake an engagement to provide internal audit services to an audited entity where it is reasonably foreseeable that:
    - for the purposes of the audit of the financial statements, the auditor would place significant reliance on the internal audit work performed by the audit firm; or
    - for the purposes of the internal audit services, the audit firm would undertake part of the role of management.

- The audit firm shall not undertake an engagement to design, provide or implement information technology systems for an audited entity where:
    - the systems concerned would be important to any significant part of the accounting system and the auditor would place significant reliance upon them as part of the audit of the financial statements; or
    - for the purposes of the information technology services, the audit firm would undertake part of the role of management.

Code of ethics and conduct

ES – Provisions Available for Small Entities (PASE)

When auditing the financial statements of a small entity the audit firm is not required to:

- Comply with the requirement that an external independent quality control review is performed;
- Apply safeguards to address self-review threat provided:
  - the audited entity has 'informed management' (i.e. the threat and consequences have been explained to and understood by those charged with governance); and
  - the audit firm extends the cyclical inspection of completed engagements that is performed for quality control purposes.
- Adhere to the prohibitions in Ethical Standard 5, relating to providing non-audit services that involve the audit firm undertaking part of the role of management, provided that it discusses objectivity and independence issues related to the provision of non-audit services with those charged with governance, confirming that management accept responsibility for any decisions taken;
- Comply with Ethical Standard 5, paragraph 82 (acting as an advocate by providing tax services to an audit client during an appeal/tribunal); and
- Comply with Ethical Standard 2, paragraph 48 (partner leaving firm and being appointed as director of audit client) provided that it takes appropriate steps to determine that there has been no significant threat to the audit team's integrity, objectivity and independence.

Exam focus

- Professional and ethical considerations are a key element of the P7 paper. The examiner commented in her article on the approach to paper P7 (30 Jan 2007) "Ethics and professional issues are also important areas within the syllabus, likely to feature in every sitting, either in Section A or Section B."
- A question on ethics will not require you to 'dump knowledge' but to apply the rules and principles to a case study/scenario question, and apply your common sense!
- All the framework requires is that you apply the fundamental principles to unique situations, as observed in practice.

chapter 2

Exam-style question: Ethical and professional issues

You are an audit manager in Fox & Steeple, a firm of Chartered Certified Accountants, responsible for allocating staff to the following three audits of financial statements for the year ending 31 December 2012:

(a) Blythe Co is a new audit client. This private company is a local manufacturer and distributor of sportswear. The company's finance director, Peter, sees little value in the audit and put it out to tender last year as a cost-cutting exercise. In accordance with the requirements of the invitation to tender your firm indicated that there would not be an interim audit.

(b) Huggins Co, a long-standing client, operates a national supermarket chain. Your firm provided Huggins Co with corporate financial advice on obtaining a listing on a recognized stock exchange in 2011. Senior management expects a thorough examination of the company's computerized systems, and are also seeking assurance that the annual report will not attract adverse criticism.

(c) Gray Co has been an audit client since 2005 after your firm advised management on a successful buyout. Gray provides communication services and software solutions. Your firm provides Gray with technical advice on financial reporting and tax services. Most recently you have been asked to conduct due diligence reviews on potential acquisitions.

Required:

For these assignments, compare and contrast:

(i) **the threats to independence;**

(ii) **the other professional and practical matters that arise; and**

(iii) **the implications for allocating staff.**

(Total: 15 marks)

Code of ethics and conduct

Test Your Understanding 1

Aventura International, a listed company, manufactures and wholesales a wide variety of products including fashion clothes and audio-video equipment. The company is audited by Voest, a firm of Chartered Certified Accountants, and the audit manager is Darius Harken. The following matters have arisen during the audit of the group's financial statements for the year to 31 March 2009 which is nearing completion:

(i) During the annual physical count of fashion clothes at the company's principal warehouse, the audit staff attending the count were invited to purchase any items of clothing or equipment at 30% of their recommended retail prices.

(ii) The chief executive of Aventura International, Armando Thyolo, owns a private jet. Armando invoices the company, on a monthly basis, for that proportion of the operating costs which reflects business use. One of these invoices shows that Darius Harken was flown to Florida in September 2008 and flown back two weeks later. Neither Aventura nor Voest have any offices or associates in Florida.

(iii) Last week Armando announced his engagement to be married to his personal assistant, Kirsten Fennimore. Before joining Aventura in January 2009, Kirsten had been Voest's accountant in charge of the audit of Aventura.

Required:

Identify and discuss the ethical issues raised in each of the scenarios and the responses required by the auditor in relation to these matters.

(15 marks)

Test your understanding 2 'Audit Partner Rotation'

In order to comply with the ethical code of conduct it is widely recognised that senior audit personnel should be removed from engagements after a certain period (between five and ten years, depending upon the status of the client and national customs). To strengthen the ethical code of conduct further, professional accountancy bodies are currently debating whether to impose mandatory "rotation" periods for senior personnel as low as every two years.

Required:

(a) Discuss why audit partner rotation is important in an ethical code of conduct.

(4 marks)

(b) Identify and explain **TWO** problems a small or medium sized firm of chartered certified accountants might face if the threshold is lowered and identify a possible solution to each problem.

(4 marks)

Test your understanding 3 Blake Seven

(a) Explain the importance of the role of confidentiality to the auditor-client relationship.

(5 marks)

(b) Your firm acts as auditor and adviser to Blake Seven and to its four directors. The company is owned 50% by Brad Capella, 25% by his wife Minerva and 10% by Janus Trebbiano. Brad is the chief executive and Janus the finance director. Janus's sister, Rosella Trebbiano, has recently resigned from the executive board, following a disagreement with the Capellas. Rosella has now formed her own company, Blakes Heaven, in competition with Blake Seven.

Rosella is currently negotiating with her former co-executives the profit-related remuneration due to her and the sale of her 15% holding of shares in Blake Seven to one or all of them.

Rosella has contacted you to find out Brad's current remuneration package since he refuses to disclose this to her.

She has also requested that your firm should continue to act as her personal adviser and become auditor and adviser to Blakes Heaven.

Required:

Comment on the matters that you should consider in deciding whether or not your audit firm can comply with Rosella's requests.

(10 marks)

(Total: 15 marks)

4 Chapter summary

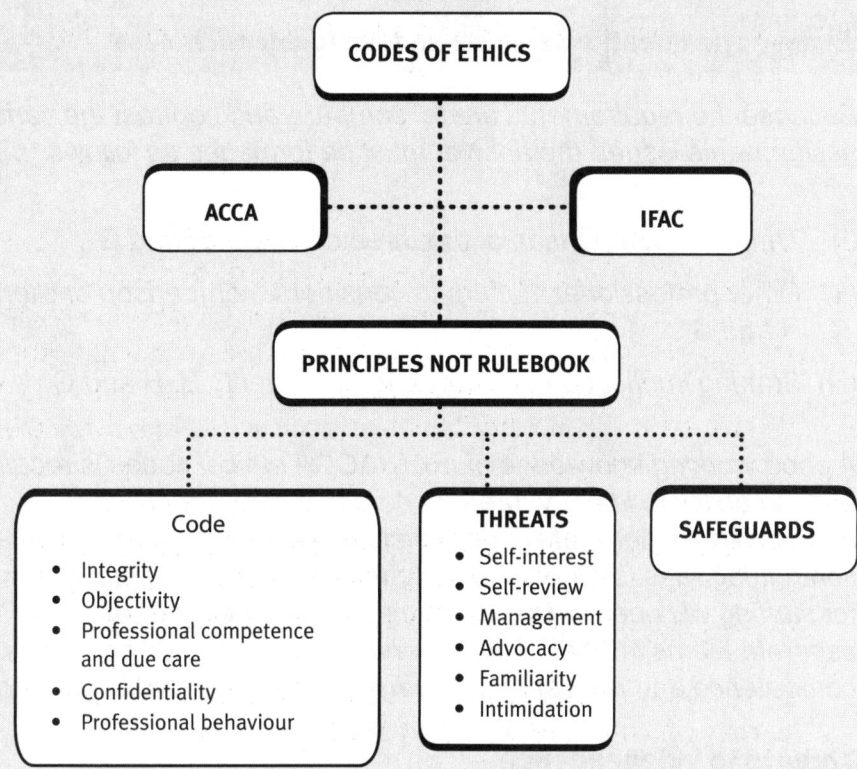

Code of ethics and conduct

Test your understanding answers

Exam-style question: Ethical and professional issues

Because the requirements are to 'compare and contrast the various assignments issues' the answer must be formatted as follows:

(i) *Threats – comparison of the three clients B, H and G*

(ii) *Other professional matters to consider – comparison of clients B, H and G*

(iii) *Staffing implications – comparison of clients B, H and G*

A good working knowledge of IFAC/ACCA ethical codes is required and the ability to identify threats and apply safeguards where appropriate. Other professional matters include for example, quality control, logistics, budgets/fees, staffing requirements, etc. Implications for staffing will need to take account of independence safeguards, e.g. separate teams for the different services provided, etc as well as competence and relevant knowledge/specialisms and experience.

Threats to independence

Self-interest

- A self-interest threat could potentially arise in respect of any (or all) of these assignments as, regardless of any fee restrictions (e.g. per IFAC's 'Code of Ethics for Professional Accountants'), the auditor is remunerated by clients for services provided.

- This threat is likely to be greater for Huggins Co (larger/listed) and Gray Co (requires other services) than for Blythe Co (audit a statutory necessity).

- The self-interest threat may be greatest for Huggins Co. As a company listed on a recognised stock exchange it may give prestige and credibility to Fox & Steeple (though this may be reciprocated). Fox & Steeple could be pressurized into taking evasive action to avoid the loss of a listed client (e.g. concurring with an inappropriate accounting treatment).

Self-review

- This threat is also likely to be greater for Huggins and Gray where Fox & Steeple is providing other (non-audit) services.

- A self-review threat may be created by Fox & Steeple providing Huggins with a 'thorough examination' of its computerized systems if it involves an extension of the procedures required to conduct an audit in accordance with International Standards on Auditing (ISAs).

- Appropriate safeguards must be put in place if Fox & Steeple assists Huggins in the performance of internal audit activities. In particular, Fox & Steeple's personnel must not act (or appear to act) in a capacity equivalent to a member of Huggins' management (e.g. reporting, in a management role, to those charged with governance).

- Fox & Steeple may provide Gray with accounting and bookkeeping services, as Gray is not a listed entity, provided that any self-review threat created is reduced to an acceptable level. In particular, in giving technical advice on financial reporting, Fox & Steeple must take care not to make managerial decisions such as determining or changing journal entries without obtaining Gray's approval.

- Taxation services comprise a broad range of services, including compliance, planning, provision of formal taxation opinions and assistance in the resolution of tax disputes.

- Such assignments are generally not seen to create threats to independence.

- The due diligence reviews for Gray may create a self-review threat (e.g. on the fair valuation of net assets acquired).

- However, safeguards may be available to reduce these threats to an acceptable level.

- If staff involved in providing other services are also assigned to the audit, their work should be reviewed by more senior staff not involved in the provision of the other services(to the extent that the other service is relevant to the audit).

- The reporting lines of any staff involved in the audit of Huggins and the provision of other services for Huggins should be different. (Similarly for Gray.)

Familiarity

- Long association of a senior member of an audit team with an audit client may create a familiarity threat. This threat is likely to be greatest for Huggins, a long-standing client. It may also be significant for Gray as Fox & Steeple have had dealings with this client for seven years now.

- As Blythe is a new audit client this particular threat does not appear to be relevant.

- Senior personnel should be rotated off the Huggins and Gray audit teams. If this is not possible (for either client), an additional professional accountant who was not a member of the audit team should be required to independently review the work done by the senior personnel.

- The familiarity threat of using the same lead engagement partner on an audit over a prolonged period is particularly relevant to Huggins, which is now a listed entity. IFAC's Code of Ethics for Professional Accountants requires that the lead engagement partner should be rotated after a pre-defined period, normally no more than seven years. Although it might be time for the lead engagement partner of Huggins to be changed, the current lead engagement partner may continue to serve for the 2012 audit.

Intimidation

- This threat is most likely to come from Blythe as auditors are threatened with a tendering process to keep fees down.

- Peter may have already applied pressure to reduce inappropriately the extent of audit work performed in order to reduce fees, by stipulating that there should not be an interim audit.

- The audit senior allocated to Blythe will need to be experienced in standing up to client management personnel such as Peter.

(ii) Other professional and practical matters

- The experience of staff allocated to each assignment should be commensurate with the assessment of associated risk. For example, there may be a risk that insufficient audit evidence is obtained within the budget for the audit of Blythe. Huggins, as a listed client, carries a high reputational risk.

- Sufficient appropriate staff should be allocated to each audit to ensure adequate quality control (in particular in the direction, supervision, review of each assignment). It may be appropriate for a second partner to be assigned to carry out a 'hot review' (before the auditor's report is signed) of:
    - Blythe, because it is the first audit of a new client; and
    - Huggins, as it is listed.
- Existing clients (Huggins and Gray) may already have some expectation regarding who should be assigned to their audits. There is no reason why there should not be some continuity of staff providing appropriate safeguards are put in place (e.g. to overcome any familiarity threat).
- Senior staff assigned to Blythe should be alerted to the need to exercise a high degree of professional skepticism (in the light of Peter's attitude towards the audit).
- New staff assigned to Huggins and Gray would perhaps be less likely to assume unquestioned honesty than staff previously involved with these audits.

Logistics (practical)

- All three assignments have the same financial year end, therefore there will be an element of 'competition' for the staff to be assigned to the year-end visits and final audit assignments. As a listed company, Huggins is likely to have the tightest reporting deadline and so have a 'priority' for staff.
- Blythe is a local and private company. Staff involved in the year-end visit (e.g. to attend the physical inventory count) should also be involved in the final audit. As this is a new client, staff assigned to this audit should get involved at every stage to increase their knowledge and understanding of the business.
- Huggins is a national operation and may require numerous staff to attend year-end procedures. It would not be expected that all staff assigned to year-end visits should all be involved in the final audit.

Time/fee/staff budgets

- Time budgets will need to be prepared for each assignment to determine manpower requirements (and to schedule audit work).

(iii) Implications for allocating staff

- Fox & Steeple should allocate staff so that those providing other services to Huggins and Gray (that may create a self review threat) do not participate in the audit engagement.

Code of ethics and conduct

Competence and due care (Qualifications/Specialisation)

- All audit assignments will require competent staff.
- Huggins will require staff with an in-depth knowledge of their computerized system.
- Gray will require senior audit staff to be experienced in financial reporting matters specific to communications and software solutions (e.g. in revenue recognition issues and accounting for internally-generated intangible assets).
- Specialists providing tax services and undertaking the due diligence reviews for Gray may not be required to have any involvement in the audit assignment.

Test Your Understanding 1

(i) **Goods**

Objectivity

The acceptance of gifts or hospitality, particularly during the inventory count, may be perceived to be a self-interest threat to objectivity. The audit team should be performing an inventory count, not going shopping for sale items. The count should be performed in an entirely neutral way but staff may ignore this in order to ensure they get their 'perk' of the engagement. Moreover, from an external perspective, this may be considered to be bribery for a more relaxed inventory count check.

Professional Due Care

Inventor counts should be performed with the least disruption possible. Movements in inventory during the count vastly increase the risk of incorrect procedures being performed. If staff are purchasing items during the day this constitutes inventory movement.

Response

If this was the first time that such an offer had been made to audit staff it should not have been accepted during the physical count. All offers of goods should be discussed with senior audit management.

The value of the goods in question should be considered. 30% of manufacturer's recommended price amounts to a 70% discount. This is unlikely to be material to the client but may be significant enough to the audit team to be considered more than a 'modest' gift.

The offer should be compared to any current staff discount schemes which Aventura offers to its employees. If Aventura does not offer staff discounts, the offer of discounted goods should have been declined.

In general it is prudent to avoid accepting gifts. If it later transpired that there was a problem with the count or the subsequent inventory valuation there would be increased risk of negligence claims (i.e. the audit team were not sufficiently diligent or that they accepted bribes).

(ii) **Services/Hospitality**

Objectivity

Once again a member of the audit team has self-interest in the audit. In this case Darius Harken has received a substantial benefit from his association with the audit client. The value of this gift is likely to be significant and it is unlikely that Darius can be considered to be neutral/objective any longer. In addition it could be argued that, as well as having a self-interest, Darius Harken is over-familiar with
the Chief Executive Armando Thyolo. This is quite an extravagant gift that could be perceived to be outside the boundaries of a normal, professional relationship. In this case Darius Harken should not have accepted the use of the jet without the express permission of the audit engagement partner. It is possible that Darius may have paid for the use of the jet. However, the question of over-familiarity would still be relevant, as he could have used a commercial airline.

Professional Behaviour

The fact that this arrangement only came to light during the audit of certain invoices suggests that Darius was intentionally withholding the beneficial transaction. Whilst there is no evidence that he tried to conceal it a manager should understand his ethical position and concerns should be raised about his conduct.

Response

Darius Harken should be removed from the audit and potentially disciplined. This could have serious consequences for the audit and the reputation of the firm. The requirement to have all gifts ratified by a senior member of the audit team should be communicated to all staff to ensure this does not happen again. All Darius' previous work on the client should now be re-reviewed before the audit report is signed to ensure that appropriate procedures have been carried out and that he has remained objective. Particular attention should be paid to all matters of the audit manager's judgement. Even if there is no evidence of the manager's work having been 'slack' in respect of the current year's audit, it would be appropriate to review how he dealt with any final review points on the prior year audit. Darius should be asked whether he has used the jet on other occasions and this should be confirmed with Armando.

(iii) Ex-audit staff employed by client

Objectivity As Kirsten was the accountant in change (AIC), not the audit manager or partner, it is unlikely that a significant lack of objectivity could have impaired the audit opinion for the year ended 31 March 2008 or for any interim work done in 2009. However, the objectivity of her work may have been impaired given that she has developed a personal relationship with Armando Thyolo. Upon beginning the relationship with Armando Kirsten should have been immediately removed from the audit engagement. Either the senior management team are responsible for a lack of professional due care when assigning team members or Kirsten has acted with a lack of professional behaviour. Kirsten is now a member of staff at Aventura. There is likely to be a strong familiarity threat between her and the current audit team. Again this could impair the objectivity of the 2009 and future audits.

Response

The audit files for 2008 and 2009, in particular the work of Kristen, should be re-reviewed. This should perhaps be done by an independent engagement partner. The members of the audit team assigned to Aventura may need to be rotated in order to reduce familiarity threat. Perhaps a team from a separate department/office could be used. At the very least the team will require a detailed briefing so that their roles, responsibilities and the ethical threats are clear.

Test your understanding 2 'Audit Partner Rotation'

Importance of rotation

Rotation of senior audit staff is important because it reduces the risk of **familiarity threat**. This arises when relationships between members of the audit team and the client develop beyond normal professional boundaries. This raises a number of concerns with regard to the professional completion of audit assignments.

Firstly, familiarity increases the risk of collusion between the director's of the client and senior audit personnel to bring about mutually beneficial ends, rather than performing the objective services required by shareholders. In the worst case scenario this could lead to fraud. Rotation of key staff reduces the likelihood of such undesirable relationships developing.

Secondly, familiarity could encourage the development of personal or business relationships between the auditor and their client. This would then create a self interest threat to objectivity, where the audit firm may benefit financially from the client. Once again rotating the partner reduces the likelihood of this occurring but also removes the partner in question away from engagements where relationships have already developed.

Finally, rotation reduces potential threats to professional competence/due care. This is due to the fact that an over-reliance on historical knowledge of a business and trust of directors can cause senior audit staff to overlook key issues. It is vital that auditors remain professionally sceptical at all times. Rotation freshens up perspectives and ideas, which should ensure consistently high quality services and professional due care.

Problems faced by small/medium sized firms

In some legislative authorities there are limits that restrict the requirement for small companies to have a statutory audit. For example: in the UK companies with turnover less than £6.5mn and a statement of financial position total of less than £3.25mn are exempt. Therefore many small firms have few, if any, remaining audit clients. The impact on these firms will be minimal.

In many firms partners specialise in certain industries, meaning there would only be a small pool of partners to rotate between. This could be overcome by allowing partners to return to a previous client after a "cooling off" period. It could also be overcome by firms pooling their audit teams to reduce specialist departments, replacing them with staff able to adapt to a broad range of industries.

Each time a new partner takes over a client there will be a necessary "transition of knowledge." It could potentially take a significant amount of time for a partner to get to grips with the key issues and risks relating to a client that the previous partner would have been aware of. To overcome this successor partners could be identified well in advance. They could then review the audit file each year prior to taking over the client to build an awareness of the key issues. Another solution might be the creation of a "knowledge bank" by the incumbent partner that they could give to their successor.

In small and medium sized firms many clients are won over by the local reputation of a certain partner. They may feel let down by the rotation policy and this could lead to problems accepting the new engagement partner. To manage this firms could work with their clients to ensure they are fully informed about the changes. They could include the client when deciding upon the replacement partner, perhaps even conducting interviews of the possible replacement.

Test your understanding 3 Blake Seven

(a) **The Importance of confidentiality to the auditor-client relationship**

That auditors should monitor and maintain the confidentiality and security of information is one of the mandatory competence requirements for membership of newly qualified Chartered Certified Accountants. It applies to all professional accountants.

In particular:

– confidential information is only disclosed to those entitled to receive it

– information obtained in the course of professional work is not used for purposes other than the client's benefit

– any decision to over-ride the duty of confidentiality (e.g. if required by a court order) is taken after due consideration and discussion with professional colleagues

– the duty of confidentiality continues even after an auditor-client engagement ceases

– an accountant who moves into new employment must distinguish previously gained experience from confidential information acquired from their former employment

– prospective accountants must treat any information given by existing accountants in the strictest confidence.

chapter 2

As well as being a fundamental principal of the Code of Ethics for Professional Accountants, confidentiality will also undoubtedly be an implied contractual term.

In order to fulfil their duties, auditors require full disclosure of all information they consider necessary. A duty of confidentiality is therefore essential to ensuring that the scope of the audit is not limited as a result of information being withheld.

(b) **Matters to consider**

Rosella has made three requests:

(1) disclosure of a former co-executive's level of remuneration
(2) continuing to act as personal adviser
(3) accepting an appointment as audit and adviser to Blakes Heaven.

(1) **Disclosure of remuneration package**

In an audit appointment, the auditor owes a duty of confidentiality to the client (i.e. the company not individual shareholders or executives). There is no legal or professional right or duty to disclose client information on an ad hoc basis merely because it is available to the auditor.

It would be a breach of the audit firm's duty of confidentiality to Blake Seven (in acting as auditor) and Brad (in acting as adviser) to disclose the information requested when clearly there is no process of law or 'public interest' involved.

The audit firm could only disclose the information to Rosella with Brad's consent. This is highly unlikely since Brad has refused to do so. Also, attempting to obtain permission from Brad is likely to result in a breach of the duty of confidence that the audit firm owes to Rosella (in their current role as adviser).

In general, the audit firm's working papers are its own property and any request for them (e.g. if Rosella requested a schedule of emoluments, etc) should be refused.

The latest audited financial statements (which are available to Rosella in her capacity as a shareholder) may disclose Brad's remuneration for the previous year (e.g. as chairman and/or highest paid executive). Rosella will need to wait for this information to be publicly available.

As a member of the company (i.e. shareholder), Rosella would also be entitled to inspect any relevant documents required to be held at Blake Seven's registered office (e.g. if Brad has a service contract with the company).

(2) **Continuing as personal adviser**

A conflict between the interests of Blake Seven (and its continuing directors) and Rosella Trebbiano (in a personal capacity) is likely to arise (e.g. over the valuation of Rosella's shareholding).

It would be inappropriate for one adviser to act for both parties in certain matters, such as negotiating a share price (in the event of subsequent disagreement) without appropriate safeguards.

Valuing Rosella's shareholding and negotiating her profit-related remuneration may appear to threaten the objectivity of the audit of Blake Seven. Rosella may try to exert influence to overstate profits (e.g. over Janus, as her brother and finance director, as well as the auditor).

However, the interests of these clients may not be materially prejudiced in all matters if:

- adequate disclosure is possible (i.e. of all relevant matters to all parties); and
- appropriate safeguards are implemented (e.g. advising one or all clients to seek additional independent advice).

In particular it may be possible to advise Rosella on personal tax matters.

(3) **Appointment as auditor**

A conflict between the interests of Rosella's new company, Blakes Heaven, and Blake Seven is likely to arise as the former has been set up in competition with the latter.

There is nothing improper in having both companies as audit clients if there are appropriate safeguards (e.g. different reporting partners and teams of staff for each audit engagement).

However, even with safeguards, the directors of Blake Seven (the Capellas in particular) may perceive that the involvement of the company's auditors with a competitor (in the capacity of auditor and adviser) could materially prejudice their interests. Also, that the new company has been set up with so similar a name suggests that Rosella may be quite aggressive in targeting Blake Seven's business.

In view of the adversarial relationship between Rosella and Blake Seven it would be prudent to include in their respective engagement letters a clause reserving the right to act for other clients subject to confidential information being kept secure.

The provision of other services (as adviser) could threaten the objectivity of the audit assignment. In particular, it would be inappropriate for the personal adviser to be the reporting partner or otherwise involved in the audit.

Conclusion

The request to disclose Brad's remuneration must be declined. However, Rosella may be directed to alternative sources of information, which may be of use (though not strictly current).

The firm may continue to act as Rosella's personal adviser subject to appropriate conditions and safeguards being put in place in respect of matters which may materially prejudice either client. For example:

- the agreement of Blake Seven (and the remaining directors)
- Rosella being advised to seek additional independent advice.

However, given the apparent acrimony between Rosella and her former associates, it seems unlikely that Blake Seven would agree to such an arrangement.

The audit appointment could only be accepted with appropriate safeguards (e.g. reporting partner and audit staff not involved in the audit of Blake Seven or the provision of other services). However, even with safeguards, if Rosella's appointments are accepted, Blake Seven may decide not to re-appoint the firm in future.

chapter 3

Professional appointments

Chapter learning objectives

Upon completion of this chapter you will be able to:

- explain the matters to be considered and the procedures that an audit firm/professional accountant should carry out before accepting a specified new client/engagement including:

    (i) client acceptance

    (ii) engagement acceptance

    (iii) establish whether the preconditions for an audit are present

    (iv) agreeing the terms of engagement.

- Recognise the key issues that underlie the agreement of the scope and terms of an engagement with a client.

Professional appointments

 A common requirement in the P7 exam is to explain the matters to consider and the procedures that should be performed after acceptance of an engagement, i.e. once the ethical and professional issues relating to acceptance of the engagement have been considered, and the engagement has been accepted in principle.

1 Accepting a new client or engagement

ISA 210 *Agreeing the Terms of Audit Engagements* and the Code of Ethics and Conduct provide guidance to the professional accountant when accepting new work.

According to ISA 210 before accepting (or continuing with) an engagement the auditor must establish whether the preconditions for an audit are present and that there is a common understanding between the auditor and management and, where appropriate, those charged with governance.

The preconditions for an audit are:

- That an acceptable financial reporting framework is to be applied to the preparation of the financial statements;
- That management understands and acknowledges its responsibilities for preparing the financial statements and providing the auditor with access to all relevant information and explanations.

If the client imposes a limitation on the scope of the auditor's work to the extent that the auditor believes it likely that a disclaimer of opinion will ultimately be issued then the auditor shall not accept the engagement, unless required to do so by law.

In addition, before accepting any engagement, the accountant should consider whether acceptance would create any threats to compliance with the fundamental ethical principles.

As in all circumstances, if the threats are other than clearly insignificant, then the accountant must apply appropriate safeguards to manage those threats. If the threat is considered so great that no safeguard would effectively reduce the risk then the engagement should be declined.

It is of particular importance to modern accountancy firms to consider whether they have the competence to perform engagements. Given the proliferation of services offered and the reduction in traditional audit services (due to the imposition of audit thresholds) many accountants may feel pressurised into offering unfamiliar services to keep up with competitors.

chapter 3

Acceptance procedures

The following procedures are necessary before accepting a new client. (It is assumed that the organization previously had an auditor. The same principles apply in respect of changes in appointments for all recurring professional work.)

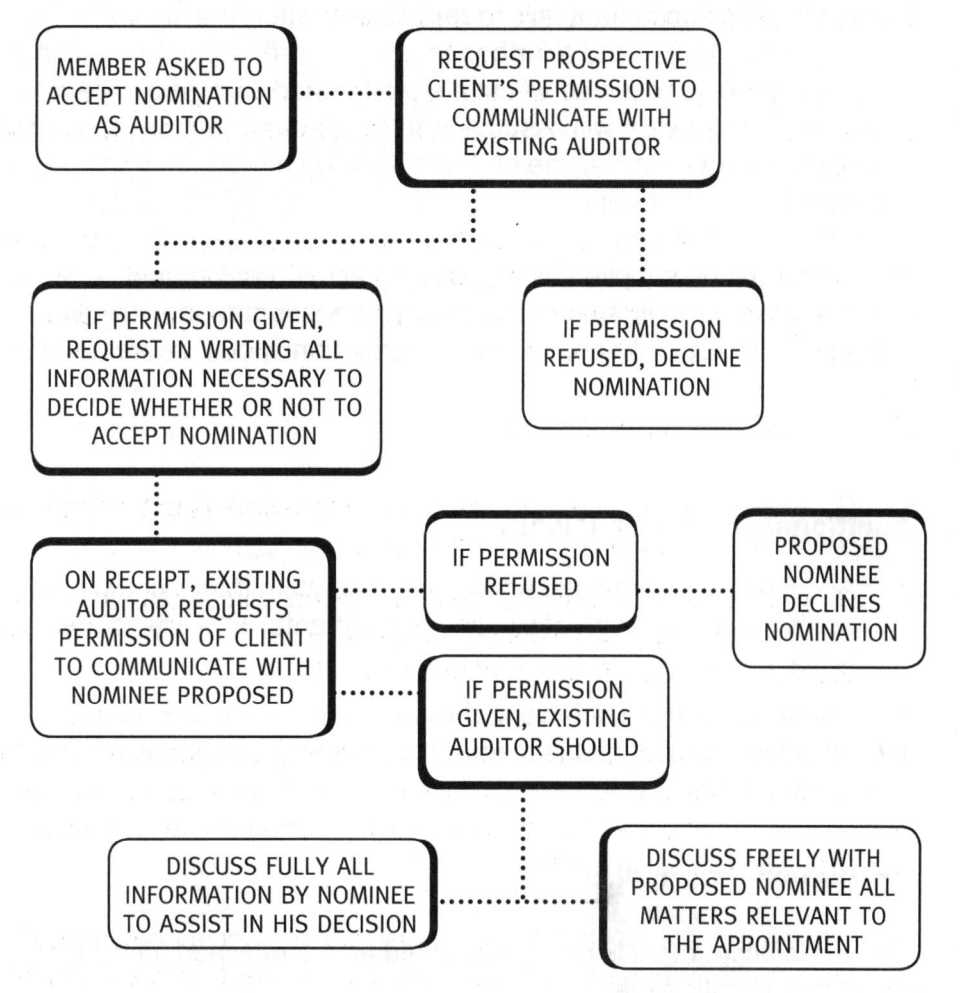

The etiquette letter

Accountants who are considering replacing an existing accountant should contact the existing accountant to determine whether there are any reasons that would preclude the accountant from taking on this engagement. The purpose of this professional etiquette letter is twofold:

- as a matter of professional courtesy to the existing accountant
- to enable the accountant to decide if there are any issues due to which, on ethical grounds, the accountant would not want to accept the appointment.

> Note that the client's permission must be obtained before sending this letter.
>
> Since the existing accountant is bound by the fundamental principle of confidentiality, he must obtain the client's permission before he can discuss any matters with the incoming accountant.
>
> If the existing accountant fails to reply to the letter, the incoming accountant should send a further letter by recorded delivery, stating that unless a reply is received within a stated period (e.g. seven days) the incoming accountant will assume that there are no matters of which they should be aware and, at the end of the stated period, they will proceed to accept the appointment.
>
> Any information supplied by the existing accountant should be considered carefully before the incoming accountant decides to accept or reject the appointment. All such information should be treated in confidence.

Additional professional work

- Accountants may be asked to undertake work that is complementary or additional to the work of existing accountants, who are not being replaced.
- Before accepting such work, the accountant should communicate with the existing accountants to inform them of the general nature of the work being done.

Appointment as auditor

Where an accountant is being appointed as the new auditor of a company they should confirm that:

- the outgoing auditor has vacated office in a correct manner
- they have been properly appointed as the incoming auditor in accordance with relevant local legislation. This is usually achieved through a majority vote at the AGM, which should be documented in a formal minute.

2 Agreeing the terms of engagement

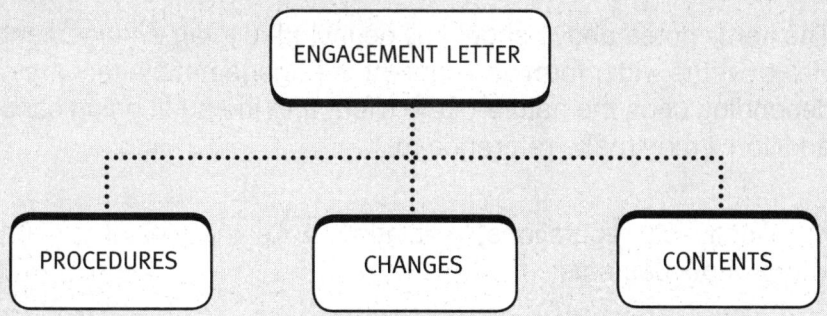

ISA 210 states that the auditor shall agree the terms of the audit engagement with management or those charged with governance, as appropriate. The terms are recorded in a written audit engagement letter and should include:

- The objective and scope of the audit of the financial statements;
- The responsibilities of the auditor;
- The responsibilities of management;
- Identification of the applicable financial reporting framework for the preparation of the financial statements; and
- Reference to the expected form and content of any reports to be issued by the auditor.

The content of the engagement letter should be agreed with the client before any engagement related work commences. The client's acknowledgement of the terms of the letter should be formally documented in the form of a director's signature.

Changes to the engagement letter

The engagement letter specifies the nature of the contract between the audit firm and the client. The auditor should issue a new engagement letter if the scope or context of the assignment changes after initial appointment.

Reasons for changes would include:

- changes to statutory duties due to new legislation
- changes to professional duties, for example: due to new or updated ISAs
- changes to 'other services' as requested by the client

Professional appointments

Engagement letter contents in detail

The items noted above should all be included in an engagement letter. However the wider form and content of engagement letters may vary depending upon the nature of the client and the audit being conducted. In addition it may make reference to:

- Applicable regulations, legislation, ISAs and ethical pronouncements;
- The form of any other communications as a result of the engagement;
- The inherent limitations of audit procedures;
- Arrangements regarding the planning and performance of the audit;
- The expectation that management will provide written representations;
- The agreement of management to make available to the auditor draft financial statements and any accompanying information in time to allow the auditor to complete the audit in accordance with the timetable;
- The agreement of management to make available to the auditor facts pertinent to the preparation of the financial statements, which management may become aware of during the period from the date of the auditor's report to the date the financial statements are issued;
- The basis upon which fees are computed and billed;
- A request for management to acknowledge receipt of the engagement letter and to agree to the terms of engagement outlined therein;
- Arrangements concerning the involvement of other auditors and experts (where relevant);
- Arrangements concerning the involvement of internal auditors (where relevant);
- Any restriction on the auditor's liability, when such possibility exists; and
- Any obligations to provide audit working papers to other parties.

chapter 3

Audit of components of a group

- Where the auditor of a parent company is also the auditor of a subsidiary, branch or division of the group, the audit firm must decide whether to issue a single engagement letter covering all the components, or a separate letter to each component.

- If the audit firm sends one letter relating to the group as a whole, it is recommended that the firm should identify in the letter the components of the group for which the firm is being appointed as auditor.

Test your understanding 1

AB Accountants has been invited to become the auditors of XY Ltd, a company with a poor reputation since several senior managers were convicted of corruption recently. The company is adamant that it has now changed its culture, and is hoping that AB Accountants will become its auditors as part of this new ethical outlook.

Identify possible safeguards AB Accountants might consider using.

Test your understanding 2

An accountant has been invited to carry out an engagement for a client, but she has only limited experience in this area. What safeguards could she apply to ensure that the threat to professional competence and due care is reduced to an acceptable level?

3 Chapter summary

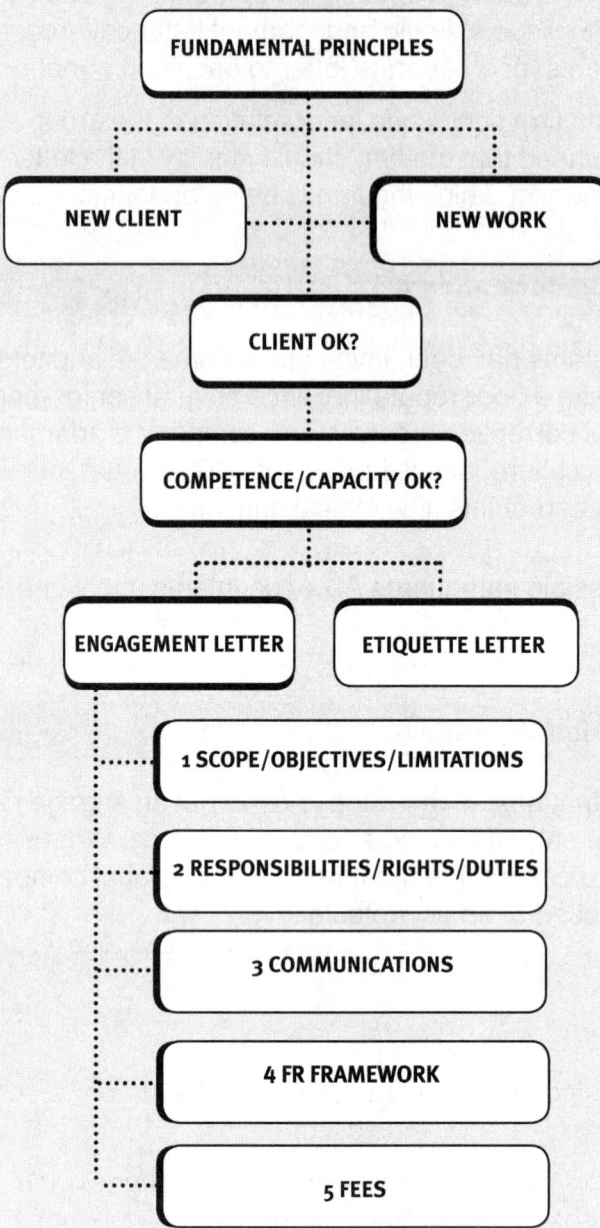

chapter 3

Test your understanding answers

Test your understanding 1

AB Accountants must weigh up the possible costs and benefits of accepting nomination. The firm may wish to apply safeguards such as:

- obtaining a detailed knowledge of the client before accepting nomination
- securing the client's commitment to implement strong internal controls and the highest standards of corporate governance
- allocating the senior partner of the firm to be the engagement partner rather than a more junior partner.

If the firm does not believe that any such safeguards could reduce the threats to compliance with the fundamental principles to an acceptable level, then the firm should decline nomination.

Test your understanding 2

Possible safeguards could include:

- acquiring technical knowledge of the relevant subject area
- assigning specific staff members who possess particular skills and experience
- using external experts per ISA 620
- increasing the expected duration of the engagement to allow for learning time and gaining experience
- ensuring that the documentation of the engagement is comprehensively reviewed once the fieldwork has been completed.

Professional appointments

chapter

4

Quality control

Chapter learning objectives

When you have completed this chapter you will be able to:

- explain the principles and purpose of quality control of audit and other assurance engagements.

- describe the elements of a system of quality control relevant to a given firm.

- select and justify quality control procedures that are applicable to a given audit engagement.

- assess whether an engagement has been performed in accordance with professional standards and whether reports issued are appropriate in the circumstances.

Quality control

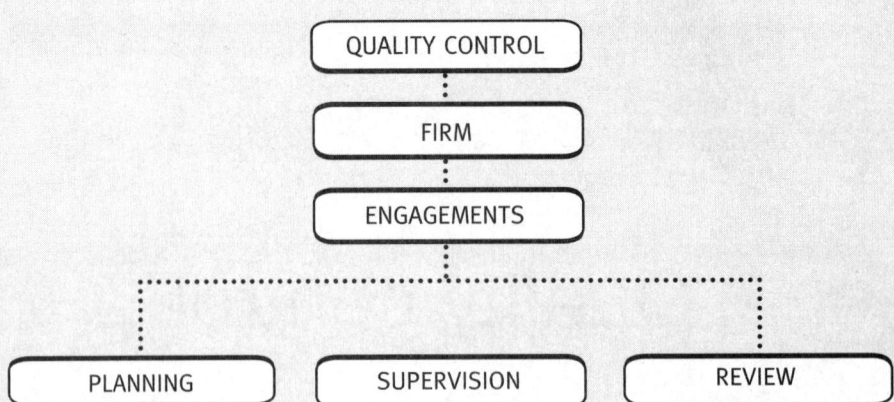

Quality control is one of the professional issues that must be considered before acceptance of a new client. In addition, a common requirement in the P7 exam is to critically evaluate the audit work already performed on an engagement. Quality control is a key part of this.

1 The principles and purpose of quality control

The purpose of assurance services is to boost confidence by reducing investors' risk.

In order to achieve this, assurance firms need to have policies and procedures that ensure the quality of their work is satisfactory, otherwise:

- in the short term there may be individual audit failures, leading to professional negligence claims,
- in the long term public confidence in the assurance process as a whole will be diminished.

Quality control ensures that assurance work is of a sufficiently high standard so that failures simply do not happen. Quality control ensures that reports issued by a firm are appropriate in the circumstances. If a professional negligence claim is made, and the firm has followed suitable quality control procedures, they should be able to defend the claim.

In other words, quality control ensures that an assurance engagement is completed to an appropriate standard, and that the risk to the firm is reduced to an acceptable level.

In order to achieve this, quality control procedures are based on a number of key principles, including:

- strong and ethical leadership, and ethical behaviour by all a firm's employees;
- only 'suitable' clients and engagements are accepted and retained;
- a firm and its employees have the necessary knowledge, technical competence, and experience;

- a firm and its employees follow proper working practices;
- effective communication, including briefing team members before, and supervising team members during each engagement;
- professional scepticism and professional judgement; and
- continuous improvement through adequate monitoring.

Quality control standards

There are two standards that set out the responsibilities of auditors regarding quality control:

- ISQC 1 *Quality Control for Firms that Perform Audits and Reviews of Financial Statements, and Other Assurance and Related Services Engagements.*
- ISA 220 *Quality Control for an Audit of Financial Statements.*

ISQC 1 sets out an accountancy firm's responsibilities with regard to their systems of quality control for audits, reviews and other assurance engagements. Those quality control systems should include policies designed to ensure that the firm and its personnel comply with applicable professional standards and regulatory requirements and that reports issued are appropriate. The system should also include procedures necessary to implement those policies and monitor compliance with them.

ISA 220, by contrast, establishes the responsibilities of the auditor (mainly the engagement partner and engagement quality reviewer) regarding their quality control procedures during audits. It states that within the context of the firm's system of quality control, the engagement team have a responsibility to implement quality control procedures applicable to the audit engagement.

2 Quality control and the firm

ISQC1 identifies six building blocks of a firm's system of quality control:

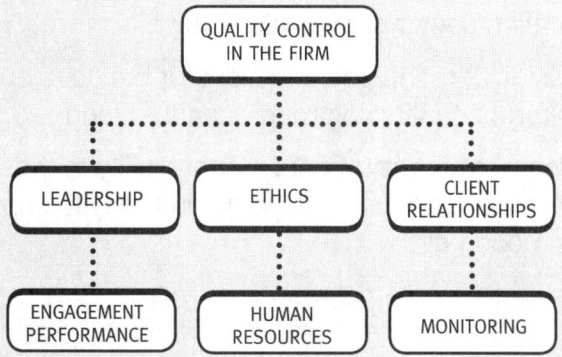

We saw in chapter 2 how important ethics are, and the arrangements for the acceptance and continuance of client relationships and specific engagements are dealt with in chapter 3.

A firm must have policies and procedures in place designed to ensure it meets the requirements of IFAC and ACCA's code of ethics and that only appropriate clients are accepted and retained.

In this chapter we will focus on the remaining four 'building blocks'.

Independence

The independence and objectivity of the firm is crucial to the credibility of any assurance engagement. If that independence is perceived to be flawed, however technically skilled the work may be, the quality of the work may still be called into question. It is vital that all independence issues are discussed and relevant safeguards adopted before any fieldwork is performed.

3 Leadership

The underlying message is simple – firms must:

- perform work that complies with professional standards and regulatory and legal requirements; and
- issue reports that are appropriate in the circumstances.

To achieve this firms must establish policies and procedures to **promote an internal culture that recognises the importance of quality** in performing engagements. This requires the firm's management team (i.e. managing partners) to assume ultimate responsibility for the system of quality control. In accordance with ISQC 1 this requires:

- the establishing of policies and procedures to address performance evaluation, compensation and promotion to demonstrate commitment to quality;
- the assignment of management responsibility so that commercial consideration does not override quality;
- the provision of resources sufficient for the development, documentation and support of quality control procedures; and
- the assignment of operational responsibility to those with sufficient and appropriate experience, ability and authority to implement those quality control procedures.

chapter 4

Communicating the message

The promotion of quality depends on clear, consistent and frequent actions and messages from all levels of the firm's management that emphasise the firm's quality control policies and procedures. This can be achieved via:

- training seminars.
- meetings.
- formal or informal dialogue.
- mission statements.
- newsletters.
- briefing memoranda.
- training materials.
- partner and staff appraisals.

Really meaning it

At the heart of this part of the standard are some clear and quite tough messages:

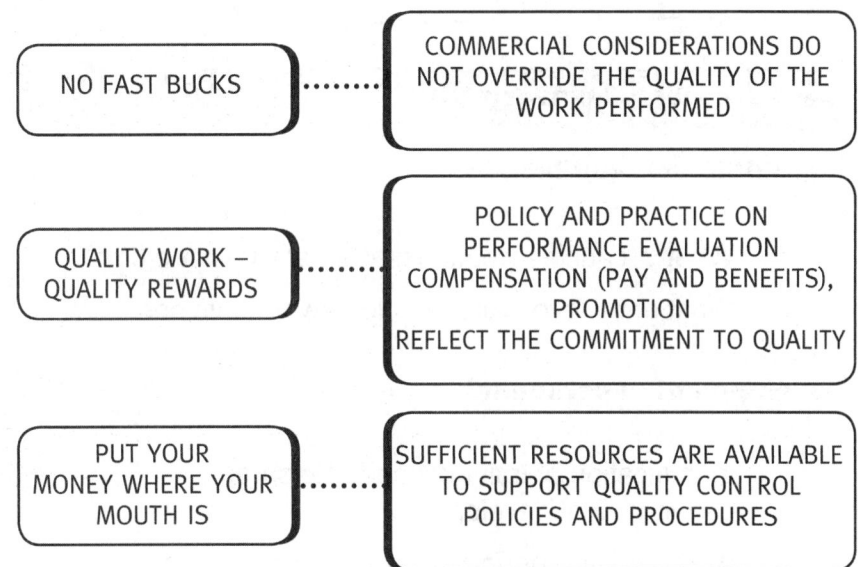

You should not use the expressions on the left in your exam answers, but hopefully they sum up what the standard setters had in mind.

4 Human resources

The standard sets out a comprehensive – albeit brief – guide to the HR function. It stresses that if a firm wants quality flowing through all levels of staff it must go through the steps outlined below.

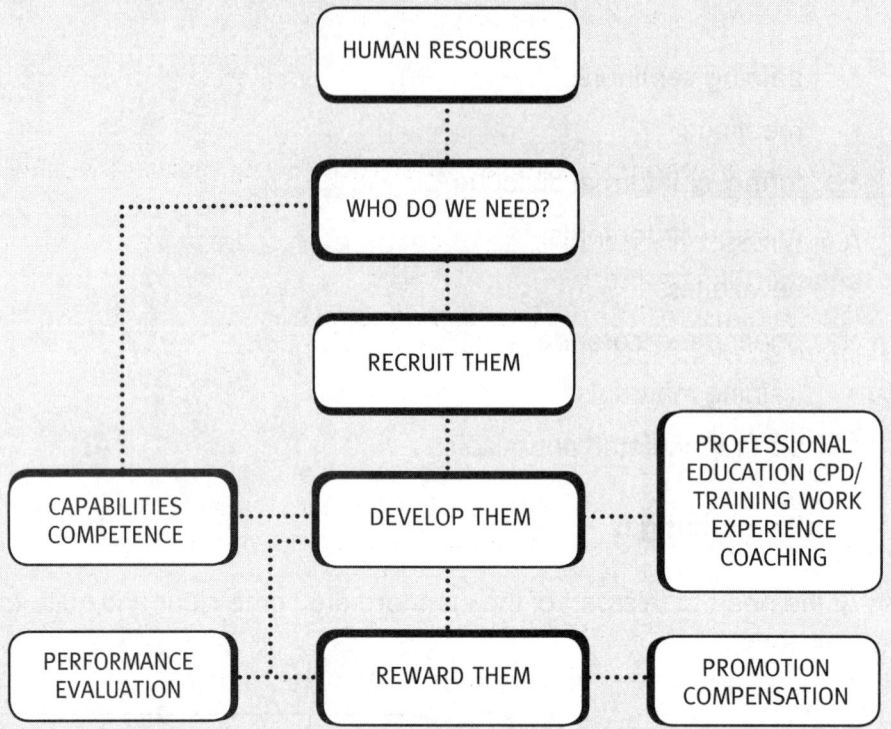

Human resource management

Recruiting the right people:

- What vacancies/weaknesses exist within the firm?
- What entry level skills should new recruits possess?

Development of personnel:

- Identification of training needs for career enhancement/development;
- Appraisal and performance evaluation;
- Development of capabilities and competences through education, training and professional development.

Reward systems:

- Appraisal and performance evaluation;
- Career development opportunities/promotion;
- Appropriate remuneration/compensation.

The role of planning: Allocation of staff to engagement teams

A firm must have policies and procedures in place to ensure the right engagement partner (i.e. one who has the competence, capability and time to perform the role) is assigned to an engagement and the client is informed of the identity and role of that partner.

People

The engagement partner should then ensure the right people are allocated to the engagement team, including considering:

- Do they have the necessary levels of training for this engagement?
- Do they have sufficient knowledge of the client?
- Do they have sufficient experience of this type of engagement?
- Do they have sufficient technical knowledge?
- Have they been briefed?

5 Engagement performance

ISQC1 requires firms to establish policies and procedures designed to provide it with reasonable assurance that engagements are performed in accordance with professional standards and applicable legal frameworks, and that the reports issued are appropriate in the circumstances.

ISQC 1 identifies three areas of policy and procedure relevant to the performance of an engagement:

- Matters relevant to promoting **consistency** in the quality of engagements;
- **Supervision** responsibilities; and
- **Review** responsibilities.

Consistency in the quality of engagement performance

Firms promote consistency through their policies and procedures. This is often accomplished through written manuals, software tools and standardised documentation. Particular matters that can be addressed include:

- How engagement teams are briefed to obtain an understanding of the engagement and their objectives;
- Processes for complying with engagement standards;
- Processes of engagement supervision, training and coaching;
- Methods of reviewing work, judgements and reports issued;
- Documentation of work performed and the timing and extent of reviews; and
- Processes to keep policies and procedures current.

Supervision responsibilities

Supervision responsibilities include:

- tracking the progress of the engagement;
- considering the competence and capabilities of the team members;
- addressing significant matters that arise during the engagement;
- and identifying matters for consultation.

Good quality supervision

Supervisors should consider:

- whether the right decisions were made at the planning stage - **ISA 330** stresses that audit procedures must be targeted at assessed risks. At the planning phase those risks must be identified so that appropriate, targeted procedures can be performed during fieldwork.
- whether the staff conducting the work have the knowledge and experience to be able to execute the plan whether. unforeseen circumstances have arisen in the course of the engagement.
- whether progress is satisfactory.
- whether unforeseen risks have arisen.
- whether there is a need for consultation over and above anything foreseen in the original plan.

The delegation problem

The hardest thing about supervision is knowing how tight or loose control should be.

- Supervise too closely and you risk demotivating staff or even causing disruption.
- Supervise too loosely and things could go badly wrong before you are aware of it.

Review responsibilities

Work of less experienced team members should be reviewed by more experienced team members, to identify whether the work has been:

- properly performed;
- concluded; and
- documented, and;
- that the evidence is sufficient and appropriate to achieve the objectives of the engagement.

All reviews should be timetabled in advance to enable timely completion. This includes identifying the need to perform second partner and 'hot' reviews - see the section on monitoring later in this chapter.

Review procedures are discussed in more detail later, in the chapter on Completion.

Good quality review

The role of review is to consider whether:

- Work has been performed in accordance with identified standards;
- Significant matters have been raised for further consideration;
- Appropriate consultations have taken place and been documented;
- There is a need to revise the nature, timing and extent of procedures;
- The work performed supports the conclusions reached and is appropriately documented;
- The evidence obtained is sufficient and appropriate to support the report; and
- The objectives of the engagement procedures have been achieved.

Quality control

The broader role

Because the review phase is the final link in the chain, it plays a wider part in the firm's quality control procedures than simply ensuring that an individual engagement has been completed satisfactorily.

- Lessons learned about failures at the planning stage can be communicated so that similar mistakes are not made elsewhere in the firm.
- Staff appraisals, conducted promptly after an engagement, are an immensely powerful tool in quality control for the firm as a whole. If good work is praised and rewarded and poor work constructively criticised and plans made for improvement, there can be a lasting effect on the quality of the firm's work.

Consultation

ISQC1 and ISA 220 both contain the requirement for appropriate consultation on difficult or contentious matters. Clearly, as far as possible, areas requiring consultation (both internally and externally) should be organized in advance to facilitate timely – and cost effective – completion of the engagement.

6 Monitoring

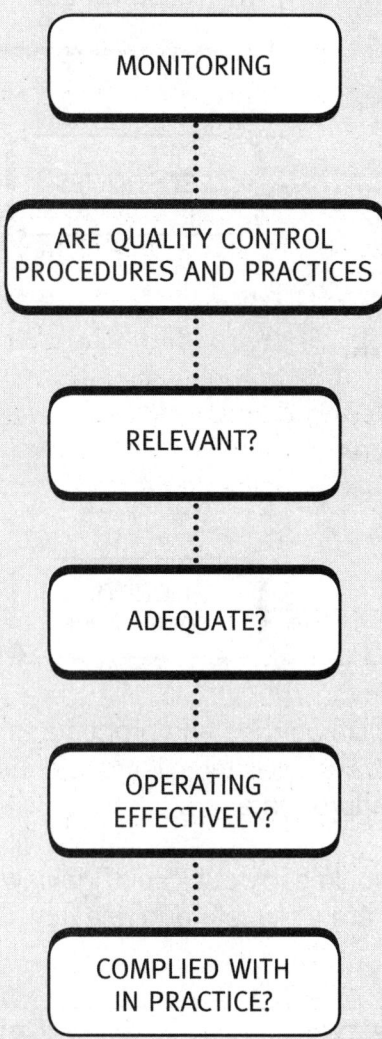

Quality control policies alone do not ensure good quality work. They must be implemented effectively. Therefore firms need systems to evaluate:

- adherence to professional standards and regulatory/legal requirements;
- whether quality controls have been implemented on a day-to-day basis; and
- whether the firm's quality control policies and procedures are effective so that reports issued by the firm are appropriate in the circumstances.

Quality control

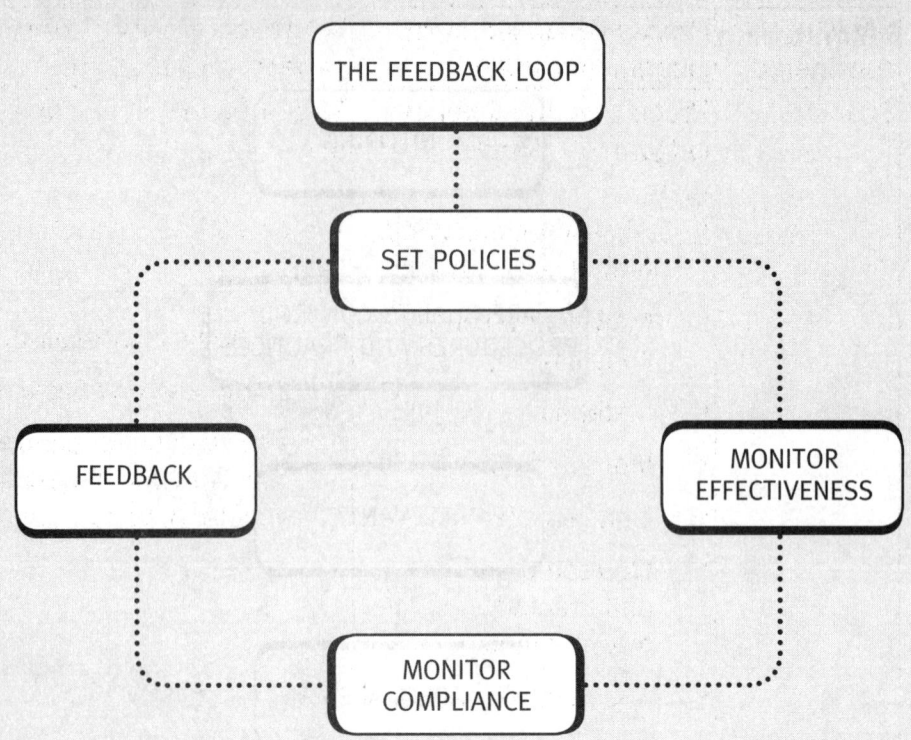

Firms should establish policies and procedures for performing engagement quality ("hot") reviews for all listed clients and for other risky, public interest engagements, as appropriate.

In addition, firms should carry out ("cold") reviews to ensure that quality control procedures are adequate and relevant, are operating effectively and are complied with.

	Hot review	**Cold review**
Purpose...	To enhance the quality of assurance work.	Monitoring, i.e. to assess whether policies and procedures were put into place during an engagement and to identify any deficiencies there in.
When...	Before the firm's report is issued/finalised.	After an engagement has been completed.
Which files...	Listed clients; public interest engagements; or engagements where there are particular risks. Each partner should have some of their engagements reviewed.	A selection of completed engagements.
Who by...	An independent partner (or senior manager).	A dedicated compliance or quality department/team; a qualified external consultant; or an independent partner.

What considered...	Processes underpinning judgements made.	Wholesale review of all working papers on an audit file.
Specifically...	Processes underpinning judgements about: • Significant risks and responses to them; • Matters requiring consultation; • Materiality; • Independence; • Conclusions; • Corrected and uncorrected mistatements; • The audit opinion; and • Matters to be communicated to management and those charged with governance.	To ensure that all working papers are: • On file; • Complete; • Signed as completed; • Evidenced as reviewed; and • The work undertaken is sufficient and has been documented appropriately.
Outcomes...	A reduction in audit risk, i.e. the risk that the auditor expresses an inappropriate audit opinion when the financial statements are materially misstated.	An annual report of the results will be provided to the partners in a firm flagging systemic deficiencies that require corrective action. Recommendations will be made including (as appropriate): • Additional quality control reviews; • Training; • Communication of findings; • Changes to the firm's policies and procedures; and/or • Disciplinary action.

> **Good quality monitoring**
>
> The clarified version of ISQC 1 requires that monitoring is performed on an ongoing, cyclical basis, including an inspection of at least one completed engagement for each engagement partner. The responsibility for this monitoring process should be assigned to a partner and those performing the inspections should not have had any involvement in the engagements under review.
>
> The monitoring process goes beyond the simple enforcement of policies and procedures. It has to consider:
>
> - how does the firm respond to new developments in professional standard and regulatory and legal requirements?
>
> - how does the firm ensure compliance with, e.g. independence rules, by all its partners and staff? (Usually achieved through the use of independence or 'fit and proper' forms, which will need checking for completeness)
>
> - how does the firm ensure that all partners and staff comply with continuing professional development requirements? (Often achieved by controlling course bookings centrally, or by the maintenance of training logs.)
>
> - how does the firm ensure that appropriate decisions are made about the acceptance of new appointments or the continuance of client relationships? (Should be covered as part of the independent review of assignments.)
>
> Arrangements then need to be made for follow up where breaches of policy or ineffective procedures are revealed.

7 Documentation

In addition to the main elements of quality control identified in the previous sections ISA 220 also requires auditors to document certain matters:

- Issues with respect to ethical requirements and how they were resolved;
- Conclusions on compliance with independence requirements;
- Conclusions reached regarding the acceptance and continuance of engagements; and
- The nature, scope and conclusions resulting from consultations undertaken during the course of the audit.

During completion of the audit the engagement quality reviewer has to document:

- The procedures required by the firm's engagement quality review procedures;
- That the engagement quality review has been completed (on or before the date of the auditor's report); and
- That the reviewer is not aware of any unresolved matters that would cause the reviewer to believe that the significant judgements of the team were not appropriate.

Test your understanding 1: 'Cello'

You are a senior manager with Flute and Co. and are a member of the team conducting cold reviews this year. In your review of Cello Ltd, a subsidiary of a listed overseas parent, which imports and distributes office furniture, usually manufactured by other group companies. The company is large enough to require a statutory audit, but is still not a particularly large company.

In the course of your review you notice the following.

- Minutes of the planning meeting are on file but were not signed by the partner.
- The company has a December 31 year end. Fieldwork was completed by February 15 and the financial statements together with the audit report were signed on April 15. The subsequent events checklist was completed on February 15.
- The company has very little headroom in its overdraft and apparently no other borrowing facilities.
- There is a letter of support on file from the holding company dated April 15.
- Materiality is calculated at $60,000, which is in line with the firm's recommended procedures.
- Non-current assets consist of office furniture, office equipment and racking and forklifts for the rented warehouse. Net book value is $250,000 and additions in the year were $40,000. Copy invoices for all the additions are on file but you find it difficult to see precisely what work was done and the working papers other than the pre-printed audit programme and lead schedule were neither initialled nor dated.
- The receivables circularization was successful except for one non-reply for $40,000.

Quality control

Required:

- What conclusions are you able to draw about the quality of the audit of Cello Ltd?
- What recommendations would you make to the firm's audit quality committee?

Test your understanding 2: 'Agnesal'

(a) 'The objective of the auditor is to implement quality control procedures at the engagement level that provide the auditor with reasonable assurance that:

– The audit complies with professional standards and applicable legal and regulatory requirements; and

– The auditor's report issued is appropriate in the circumstances.'

(**ISA 220** *Quality Control for an Audit of Financial Statements*)

Required:

Describe the nature and explain the purpose of quality control procedures appropriate to the individual audit.

(7 marks)

(b) You are the manager responsible for the quality of the audits of new clients of Signet, a firm of Chartered Certified Accountants. You are visiting the audit team at the head office of Agnesal, a limited liability company, the date is 5 June 2013. The audit team comprises Artur Bois (audit supervisor), Carla Davini (audit senior) and Errol Flyte and Gavin Holst (trainees). The company provides food hygiene services which include the evaluation of risks of contamination, carrying out bacteriological tests and providing advice on health regulations and waste disposal.

Agnesal's principal customers include food processing companies, wholesale fresh food markets (meat, fish and dairy products) and bottling plants. The draft accounts for the year ended 31 March 2013 show turnover $19.8 million (2012 $13.8 million) and total assets $6.1 million (2012 $4.2 million).

You have summarised the findings of your visit and review of the audit working papers relating to the audit of the financial statements for the year to 31 March 2013 as follows:

(i) Against the analytical procedures section of the audit planning checklist, Carla has written 'not applicable – new client'. The audit planning checklist has not been signed off as having been reviewed by Artur.

(ii) Artur is currently assigned to three other jobs and is working from Signet's office. He last visited Agnesal's office when the final audit commenced two weeks ago. In the meantime, Carla has completed the audit of non-current fixed assets (including property and service equipment) which amount to $1.1 million as at 31 March 2013 (2012 $1.1 million).

(iii) Errol has just finished sending out requests for confirmation of trade receivable balances as at 31 March 2013 when trade receivables amounted to $3.5 million (2012 $1.6 million).

(iv) Agnesal's purchase clerk, Jules Java, keeps $2,500 cash to meet sundry expenses. The audit program shows that counting it is 'outstanding'. Carla has explained that when Gavin was sent to count it he reported back, two hours later, that he had not done it because it had not been convenient for Jules. Gavin had, instead, been explaining to Errol how to extract samples using value-weighted selection. Although Jules had later announced that he was ready to have his cash counted, Carla decided to postpone it until later in the audit. This is not documented in the audit working papers.

(v) Errol has been assigned to the audit of inventory (comprising consumable supplies) which amounts to $150,000 (2012 $90,000). Signet was not appointed as auditor until after the year-end physical count. Errol has therefore carried out tests of controls over purchases and issues to confirm the 'roll-back' of a sample of current quantities to quantities as at the year-end count.

(vi) Agnesal has drafted its first 'Report to Society' which contains health, safety and environmental performance data for the year to 31 March 2013. Carla has filed it with the comment that it is 'to be dealt with when all other information for inclusion in the company's annual report is available'.

Required:

Identify and comment on the implications of these findings for Signet's quality control policies and procedures.

(18 marks)

(Total: 25 marks)

8 Chapter summary

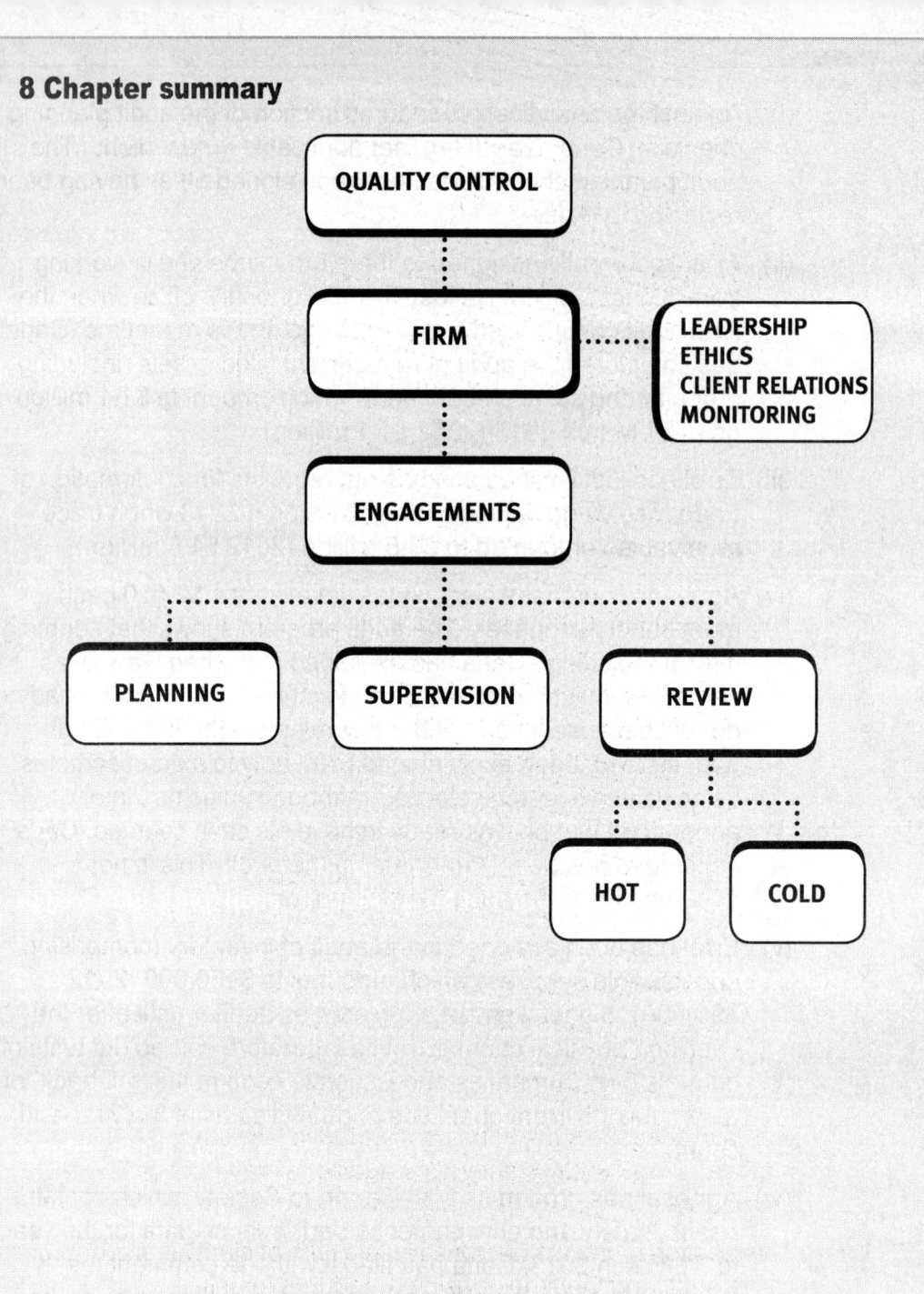

chapter 4

Test your understanding answers

Test your understanding 1: 'Cello'

Planning meeting

The planning should be documented fully and approved by the partner before the start of fieldwork. It is possible that evidence of this approval is to be found elsewhere on the file, but it would have been better if the partner had signed off the meeting minutes as soon as they were available.

Going concern and subsequent events

- The subsequent events review should be updated to the date of signing the audit report. The review should arguably be more rigorous and comprehensively documented because of the lack of financial facilities and the raised risk of going concern issues.

- It may be that the letter of comfort from the holding company is sufficient to eliminate this risk, but this should be made clear on the file, and the checklist still needs updating.

- The fact that the parent is listed overseas does not, of itself, mean that the comfort letter is valid evidence that Cello Ltd is a going concern and there may be an increased level of risk, because of the parent's listed status.

Non-current assets

- Non-current assets might be considered low risk, but the total is material even if the current year's additions may not be in themselves.

- This section of the file demonstrates a lack of clarity in the approach to the audit and the firm's basic procedures for initialling and dating working papers have not been observed, albeit in what may be a relatively low-risk area.

Receivables

- The uncleared item may not be material as such, but it may well be in excess of the tolerable error threshold.

- The item should have been followed up and other evidence obtained and, if this was impossible, the potential mis-statement should have been calculated in theoretical terms to see if the mis-statement in the financial statements as a whole might have been material.

Quality control

Conclusions/recommendations

- There is a risk that the audit report (on the assumption that an unmodified opinion was given) might have been wrong because of the going concern and debtor questions.
- Laid down audit procedures need to be followed for the planning meeting, subsequent events review, non-current assets working papers and receivables sample.
- Training implications need to be considered.

Test your understanding 2: 'Agnesal'

The first part of this question requires knowledge of standard quality control procedures and policies that should be incorporated in to each audit undertaken. Knowledge of the requirements under ISA 220 and ISQC 1 is required here.

(a) **QC procedures**

Quality controls are the policies and procedures adopted by a firm to provide reasonable assurance that all audits done by a firm are being carried out in accordance with the objective and general principles governing an audit.

Individual audit level

Work delegated to assistants should be directed, supervised and reviewed to ensure the audit is conducted in compliance with ISAs.

Assistants should be professionally competent to perform the work delegated to them with due care.

Direction (i.e. informing assistants about their responsibilities and the nature, timing and extent of audit procedures they are to perform) may be communicated through:

- briefing meetings and on-the-job oral instruction
- the overall audit plan and audit programs
- audit manuals and checklists
- time budgets.

Supervisory responsibilities include monitoring the progress of the audit to ensure that assistants are competent, understand their task and are carrying them out as directed. Supervisors must also address accounting and auditing issues arising during the audit (e.g. by modifying the overall audit plan and audit program).

The work of assistants must be reviewed to assess whether:

- it is in accordance with the audit program
- it is adequately documented
- significant matters have been resolved
- objectives have been achieved
- conclusions are appropriate (i.e. consistent with results).

Documentation which needs to be reviewed on a timely basis includes:

- the overall audit plan (including risk assessments)
- the audit program (and modification thereto)
- results from tests of control/substantive procedures and conclusions drawn
- financial statements, proposed audit adjustments and the proposed audit opinion.

An independent review (i.e. by personnel not otherwise involved in the audit), to assess the quality of the audit (before the issue of an audit report) should be undertaken for listed and other public interest or high risk audit clients.

Additional point

Quality control procedures reduce the risk of litigation claims (thereby reducing PII costs).

Quality control

(b) **Implications of findings for QC policies and procedures**

Key answer tips

'Planning an answer' means, as a minimum, deciding how marks are likely to be allocated and structuring the answer accordingly. In general, the more a question is broken down into parts, the less time needs to be spent on 'formal' writing out of an answer plan. In this question there are 18 marks for addressing six matters, i.e. just 3 marks of answer for each. However, there are also 'pervasive' issues which can be brought out as overall conclusions on QC policies and procedures at the level of the audit firm. It is a higher skill to recognise causes and effects or other links between the findings.

(i) **Analytical procedures**

Applying analytical procedures at the planning stage, to assist in understanding the business and in identifying areas of potential risk, is an auditing standard and therefore mandatory. Analytical procedures should have been performed (e.g. comparing the draft accounts to 31 March 2013 with prior year financial statements).

Audit staff may have insufficient knowledge of the highly specialised service industry in which this new client operates to assess risks. In particular, Agnesal may be exposed to risks resulting in unrecorded liabilities (both actual and contingent) if claims are made against the company in respect of outbreaks of contamination (e.g. CJD, BSE, foot and mouth, listeria, etc).

The audit has been inadequately planned and audit work has commenced before the audit plan has been reviewed by the audit supervisor. The audit may not be carried out effectively and efficiently.

(ii) Supervisor's assignments

The senior has performed work on non-current assets which is a less material (18% of total assets) audit area than trade receivables (57% of total assets) which has been assigned to an audit trainee. Non-current assets also appear to be a lower risk audit area than trade receivables because the carrying amount of non-current assets is comparable with the prior year ($1.1m at both year ends), whereas trade receivables have more than doubled (from $1.6m to $3.5m). This corroborates the implications of (i).

The audit is being inadequately supervised as work has been delegated inappropriately. It appears that the firm does not have sufficient audit staff with relevant competencies to meet its supervisory needs.

(iii) Direct confirmation

It is usual for direct confirmation of trade receivables to be obtained where trade receivables are material and it is reasonable to expect customers to respond. However, it is already more than two months after the statement of financial position date and, although trade receivables are clearly material (57% of total assets), an alternative approach may be more efficient (and cost effective). For example, monitoring of after-date cash will provide evidence about the collectability of trade receivables (as well as corroborate their existence).

This may be a further consequence of the audit having been inadequately planned.

Alternatively, monitoring of the audit may be inadequate. For example, if the audit trainee did not understand the alternative approach but mechanically followed circularisation procedures.

Depending on the reporting deadline, there may still be time to perform a circularisation. However, consideration should be given to circularising the most recent month end balances (i.e. May) rather than the year end balances (which customers may be unable or reluctant to confirm retrospectively).

Quality control

(iv) **Cash count**

Although $2,500 is very immaterial, the client's management may well expect the auditor to count it, albeit routinely, to confirm that it has not been misappropriated.

Monitoring of the trainee may have been inadequate. For example, Gavin may not have understood the need to count the cash immediately the request was made of the client. However, the behaviour of Gavin also needs to be investigated in that he failed to report back to the audit senior on a timely basis and allowed himself to be unsupervised.

The trainees do not appear to have been given appropriate direction. Gavin may not be sufficiently competent to be explaining sample selection methods to another trainee.

Although it is not practical to document every matter, details should have been recorded to support Carla's decision to change the timing of a planned procedure. (Carla's decision appears justified as it is inappropriate to perform a cash count when the client is 'ready' for it.) Also, if some irregularity is discovered by the client at a later date (e.g. if Jules is found to be 'borrowing' the cash), documentation must support why this was not detected sooner by the auditor.

(v) **Inventory**

Inventory is almost as immaterial as the cash in (4) from an auditing perspective, being less than 2.5% of total assets (2012 2.1%). Although it therefore seems appropriate that a trainee should be auditing it, the audit approach appears highly inefficient. Such in-depth testing (of controls and details) on a immaterial area provides further evidence that the audit has been inadequately planned.

Again, it may be due to a lack of monitoring of a mechanical approach being adopted by a trainee.

This also demonstrates a lack of knowledge and understanding about Agnesal's business – the company has no inventory-in-trade, only consumables used in the supply of service.

(vi) 'Report to society'

The audit senior appears to have assumed that this is 'other information' to be included in a document containing audited financial statements (the annual report). 'To be dealt with' presumably means 'to be read' with a view to identifying significant misstatements or inconsistencies. However, Agnesal may be intending to publish it as an entirely separate report and require an assurance service (other than audit) such as an independent verification statement on performance standards.

As the preceding analysis casts doubts on Signet's ability to deliver a quality audit to Agnesal, it seems highly unlikely that Signet has the resources and expertise necessary to provide such assurance services.

QC policies procedures at audit firm level/Conclusions

That the audit is not being conducted in accordance with ISAs (e.g. ISA 315 Identifying and Assessing the Risks of Material Misstatement Through Understanding the Entity and Its Environment and ISA 520 Analytical Procedures) means that Signet's quality control policies and procedures are not established and/or not being communicated to personnel.

That audit work is being assigned to personnel with insufficient technical training and proficiency indicates weaknesses in procedures for hiring and/or training of personnel.

That there is insufficient direction, supervision and review of work at all levels to provide reasonable assurance that audit work is of an acceptable standard suggests a lack of resources.

Procedures for acceptance of clients appear to be inadequate as the audit is being conducted so inefficiently (e.g. procedures are inappropriate and/or not cost-effective). In deciding whether or not to accept the audit of Agnesal, Signet should have considered whether it had the ability to serve the client properly. The partner responsible for accepting the engagement does not appear to have evaluated the firm's (lack of) knowledge of the industry.

chapter 5

Advertising, publicity, obtaining professional work and fees

Chapter learning objectives

Upon completion of this chapter you will be able to:

- recognise situations in which specified advertisements are acceptable.

- discuss the restrictions on practice descriptions, the use of the ACCA logo and the names of practising firms.

- discuss the extent to which reference to fees may be made in promotional material.

- explain the determinants of fee-setting and justify the bases on which fees and commissions may and may not be charged for services.

- discuss the ethical and other professional problems involved in establishing and negotiating fees for a specified assignment.

Advertising, publicity, obtaining professional work and fees

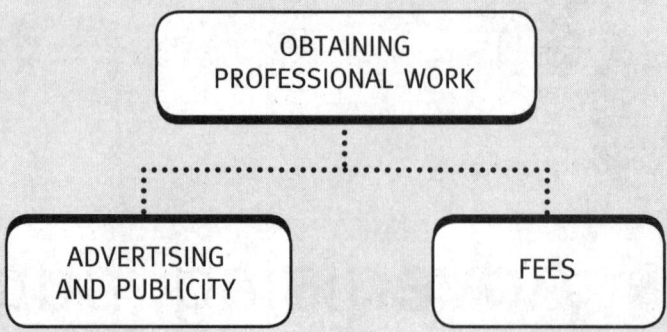

 Fees is a particular important part of this chapter as one of the ethical and professional issues that should be considered during the acceptance phase of an engagement, and as a common feature in the exam.

1 Advertising

The ACCA Rules of Professional Conduct state that it is perfectly acceptable in principle for ACCA members to advertise their services, but there is a general proviso that the advertising must not reflect adversely on:

- the member
- the ACCA or
- the accountancy profession as a whole.

The aim of adverts should be 'To inform, rather than impress'.

ACCA rules

The rules state that advertisements and promotional material should not:

- bring ACCA into disrepute or bring discredit to the member, firm or the accountancy profession
- discredit the services offered by others whether by claiming superiority for the member's own services or otherwise
- be misleading, either directly or by implication
- fall short of the requirements of any relevant national Advertising Standards Authority's Code of Advertising Practice, notably as to legality, decency, clarity, honesty, and truthfulness.

2 Restrictions on practice names and descriptions

There are restrictions on practice names and descriptions and the use of the ACCA logo, which all members should be aware of.

Members' descriptions

- Members of the ACCA are entitled to call themselves Chartered Certified Accountants or just Certified Accountants, and may use the letters ACCA (as members) or FCCA (if they are fellows).
- These descriptions may **not** be used in the registered names of companies. For example you may not set up a company called John Smith Certified Accountant Ltd.

Practice descriptions

- An accountancy firm may describe itself as a 'firm of Chartered Certified Accountants', or a 'firm of Certified Accountants', or an 'ACCA practice' provided that:
    - at least half of the partners (or directors) are ACCA members, and
    - these partners (or directors) control at least 51% of the voting rights under the firm's partnership agreement (or constitution).
- On its professional stationery, a firm in which all the partners are ACCA members may use the description 'Members of the Association of Chartered Certified Accountants'.
- In the case of a mixed firm (e.g. some partners are ACCA members and others are members of other Chartered Accountancy bodies), the firm should not use the description 'Certified Accountants and Chartered Accountants' or similar, since this could be misleading.
- Instead they may print the following statement on their stationery: 'The partners of this firm are members of either the Association of Chartered Certified Accountants or (e.g.) the Institute of Chartered Accountants in England and Wales'.

Use of the ACCA logo

- A firm that has at least one ACCA member as a partner (or director) may use the ACCA logo (also called the ACCA 'mark') on its professional stationery and on its website.
- The ACCA logo should be separate from the logo of the firm.
- The positioning, size and colour of the ACCA logo should be chosen so that it is clearly recognizable.
- The logo can be downloaded by members from the ACCA website in electronic format.

Names of practising firms

Generally, members may practice under whatever name they want, but:

- a practice name should be consistent with the dignity of the profession
- a practice name should not be misleading (e.g. a firm could not trade as 'PQ International Accountants' if all its offices were in one country)
- a practice name should not run the risk of being confused with the name of another firm
- a sole practitioner should not add 'and partners' to the name under which he practices.

3 Fees

The need for guidance

The setting of fees is a sensitive subject, so the ACCA Rules of Professional Conduct contain a number of important provisions, to:

- Minimize the possibility of a dispute between a member and his clients.
- Ensure that the member behaves at all times in accordance with the fundamental principles.

References to fees in promotional material

- Where reference is made in promotional material to fees, the basis on which those fees are calculated, hourly or other charging rates, etc. should be clearly stated.
- Members may make comparisons in such material between their fees and the fees of other accounting practices, whether members or not, provided that any such comparison does not give a misleading impression, and does comply with relevant codes of conduct.
- Promotional material that is based on the offer of percentage discounts on existing fees is permitted but must not detract from the professional image of the firm and the profession as a whole.
- Members may offer a free consultation to potential clients, at which levels of fees will be discussed.

Determinants for fee-setting

- The general principle is that members are entitled to charge a fair and reasonable fee for their services. This amount will be:
    - the fee considered appropriate for the work undertaken
    - the fee in accordance with the basis agreed with the client
    - the fee by reference to custom in certain specialized areas.

- Members will usually consider the following matters in setting a fee:
  - the seniority of the persons necessarily engaged on the work
  - the time spent by each person
  - the degree of risk and responsibility that the work entails
  - the urgency of the work to the client
  - the importance of the work to the client
  - the overhead expenses of the firm.
- The fee charged should include the recovery of any expenses properly incurred by the audit staff in the course of the engagement.
- The general basis on which fees are normally computed should be communicated to clients or potential clients in the letter of engagement, in order to reduce the risk of misunderstandings.

Bases on which fees and commissions may be charged

Hourly rates

The basis used by most accountancy practices is to set an hourly rate for each grade of staff and to invoice the client for the number of hours involved in the assignment.

Introductions

Members may, in return for the introduction of a client, pay a referral fee to a third party. The payment of such a fee may create a self-interest threat, therefore safeguards should be established to eliminate the threat or reduce it to an acceptable level (usually by disclosing any such arrangements to the client).

Contingency fees

A **contingency fee** is an arrangement made at the outset of an engagement under which a pre-determined amount or percentage is payable to the accountant upon the completion of a specified event, or the achievement of a particular outcome.

4 The ethical problems involved in setting fees

In establishing and negotiation fees for a specific assignment, members may come across ethical and other professional problems.

Advertising, publicity, obtaining professional work and fees

Contingency fees

Contingency fees could lead to practitioners forcing a specific outcome that would not normally have been obtained to try and achieve higher fees. For example, tax fees may be agreed based upon the tax savings the practitioners create or an auditor may be paid for unusually rapid completion of an audit. Of course this could lead to the engagement being conducted without necessary due care and objectivity.

The ACCA's position is that **fees should not be charged on a percentage, contingency or similar basis**, save where that course of action is generally accepted practice for certain specialized work or as specifically permitted by the Rules of Professional Conduct.

Fee quotations

When negotiating fees for a particular assignment members may quote a fixed total fee that is believed to be appropriate to the engagement. This can obviously lead to price cutting in order to secure work and can lead to aggressive price competition. However, if a fee quoted is so low that it becomes difficult to perform the engagement in accordance with applicable professional standards for that price, then an ethical threat to professional competence and due care may be created.

Safeguards may be applied to eliminate this threat or to reduce it to an acceptable level, for example:

- making it clear to the client which services are covered by the quoted fees and the basis upon which fees are to be charged;
- performing a rigorous budgeting process to ensure that costs can be recovered; and
- assigning sufficient time and appropriate staff to the assignment to ensure it is performed effectively.

If a member is investigated following allegations of unsatisfactory work, an inappropriate fee quote may be taken into account during the disciplinary process.

Lowballing

Lowballing is the setting of a low price at the start of an arrangement in order to secure the business, with the intent of later raising it or recovering the losses made on that engagement with other, more lucrative, services.

This could lead to self-interest threat as the auditor may try and keep their client happy simply in order to win other contracts with them. It could also lead to 'corner cutting' on the audit to try and minimise losses. This would obviously impair professional competence and due care.

However, it should be noted that there is no evidence that lowballing has actually lead to negligent auditing. The regulatory system and the keenness of audit firms to maintain their reputation should be sufficient to maintain audit quality regardless of the fee. The cost of litigation and the fear of high profile public scandals is a significant deterrent.

The pressure to cut fees

During the period 2002 to 2006 audit fees charged to large European companies were high, due to a combination of the transition to IFRSs and the regulatory burden of complying with the US Sarbanes-Oxley Act. Finance directors now hope that audit fees in future can be reduced year by year, due to:

- stability in accounting standards (the IASB intend to make no major amendments to IASs/IFRSs during the next two years, to give standards a chance to 'bed in')
- improved internal controls in companies should enable more systems-based and less substantive auditing
- an ongoing learning curve effect as audit firms build up cumulative audit knowledge about their clients.

Test your understanding 1

Possible advertisement

Comment on whether the following advertisement is acceptable?

Deidre Jones ACCA
www.djonesacca.co.uk
Advice for small businesses
Friendly and professional service
Business start-up specialist
'The best and friendliest service in this town'

Advertising, publicity, obtaining professional work and fees

Test your understanding 2

Ethical aspects of auditing

The provision of audit services to clients (as opposed to other assurance services or non-assurance services) brings with it specific ethical issues in relation to fees. What do you believe are the appropriate responses to the following ethical problems?

(1) The assignment of audit staff to a low audit fee engagement.

(2) The acceptability of contingency fees.

(3) Overdue fees from the previous audit.

Test your understanding 3 'Hawk'

You are a training manager in Hawk Associates, a firm of Chartered Certified Accountants. The firm has suffered a reduction in fee income due to increasing restrictions on the provision of non-audit services to audit clients. The following proposals for obtaining professional work are to be discussed at a forthcoming in-house seminar:

(a) 'Cold calling' (i.e. approaching directly to seek new business) the chief executive officers of local businesses and offering them free second opinions.

(5 marks)

(b) Placing an advertisement in a national accountancy magazine that includes the following:

'If you have an asset on which a large chargeable gain is expected to arise when you dispose of it, you should be interested in the best tax planning advice. However your gains might arise, there are techniques you can apply. Hawk Associates can ensure that you consider all the alternative fact presentations so that you minimise the amount of tax you might have to pay. No tax saving – no fee!'

(6 marks)

(c) Displaying business cards alongside those of local tradesmen and service providers in supermarkets and libraries. The cards would read:

> 'Hawk ACCA Associates
> For PROFESSIONAL Accountancy, Audit,
> Business Consultancy and Taxation Services
> Competitive rates. Money back guarantees.'

(4 marks)

Required:

Comment on the suitability of each of the above proposals in terms of the ethical and other professional issues that they raise.

(Total: 15 marks)

Advertising, publicity, obtaining professional work and fees

5 Chapter summary

OBTAINING PROFESSIONAL WORK
Professional guidance is needed on obtaining professional work in order to ensure that ACCA members apply the Fundamental Principles of the ACCA Code of Ethics in their daily conduct

ADVERTISING AND PUBLICITY
Material must not:
- Bring disrepute to the ACCA
- Discredit the services offered by others
- Be misleading
- Fall short of any advertising codes

FEES
Fees should be:
- Fair and reasonable
- Based on factors such as staff seniority, time spent, urgency of the work, etc.
- Contingency fees should be avoided except where customary (e.g. in merger and acquisition work)

TENDERING FOR ENGAGEMENTS
See next chapter

chapter 5

Test your understanding answers

Test your understanding 1

In short: no.

Deidre Jones is entitled to inform the public of her special skills (e.g. advice for small businesses, business start-ups, etc.) but claiming that she offers the best service in the area discredits the services offered by other accountants. The 'smiley' symbols are not consistent with an image of professionalism and should be replaced. Finally, she should state a business telephone number or physical address in the advertisement, not just a web address.

Nowhere in the advertisement does Deidre Jones state that she is an accountant (although obviously the ACCA designation states this for those who know what it means). If this advertisement is to be included in a directory of accountants, there is no need to include this point. However, if the advertisement is to go in a general publication, it is probably best to clearly state the fact that Deidre Jones is a certified accountant or chartered certified accountant (as well as including the ACCA designation after her name).

Deidre is also not permitted to use the term "ACCA" in her web address as this indicates that she works for them, when in fact she is simply a professional member of the ACCA.

Test your understanding 2

(1) Every audit must have assigned to it sufficient staff and sufficient time to carry out the audit properly, regardless of the audit fee to be charged. There are no circumstances in which a low audit fee can justify any lack of appropriate resource or time taken to perform a proper audit in compliance with auditing and ethical standards.

(2) No audit can be carried out on a contingency fee basis. The threat to objectivity from such an arrangement would be too great.

(3) Arrangements to pay such overdue fees must be agreed with the client before an auditor can accept appointment as auditor for the following period. If the amounts overdue are significant, the engagement partner should consider whether the firm can continue as auditors, or whether it is necessary to resign.

Advertising, publicity, obtaining professional work and fees

Test your understanding 3 'Hawk'

A good working knowledge of the professional codes is required here and an ability to apply them. However, it should be helpful to identify issues which common sense would indicate do not sit comfortably with a professional approach (that must be independent where assurance is given)

(a) **'Cold calling'**

Tutorial note: Recognising that there are three issues to address (i.e. 'cold calling', 'free' and 'second opinions') is likely to earn more marks than focusing on just one.

- Until relatively recently 'cold calling' has been largely prohibited throughout the profession (and still is in some countries e.g. Hong Kong). Therefore the 'direct' approach may not be suitable.

- Where 'cold-calling' restrictions have been relaxed it may still only be permitted for existing business clients (i.e. to offer them additional services), the direct approach to non-business clients being prohibited. This inhibits competition.

- Although the practice may be viewed as 'a bit grubby and commercial' it is now generally regarded as an accepted modern business practice. Along with other professional bodies, ACCA removed its prohibition on 'cold calling' in 2002.

- Whilst Hawk is permitted to 'cold call', the fundamental ethical principles must be adhered to. Whilst solicitation which is decent, honest and truthful may be acceptable, cold calling which amounts to harassment is not.

- Offering a service for 'free' is not prohibited provided that the client is not misled about future levels of fees.

- There are strict ethical codes regarding 'second opinions' (on accounting treatments). Practitioners are advised NOT to provide second opinions, when requested, without following a procedure of contacting the incumbent auditor/accountant. Therefore to be offering second opinions clearly goes against ethical guidelines – as the practice is to be discouraged.

(b) **Tax planning**
- Advertising is generally allowed subject to the observance of the fundamental principles of ethical codes (e.g. IFAC's Code of Ethics for Professional Accountants, ACCA's Code of Ethics and Conduct).
- Although direct advertising (i.e. on television, radio, cinema) is prohibited in many jurisdictions (e.g. Hong Kong), an advertisement in a national accountancy magazine is generally permitted.
- Where advertising is permitted, the minimum requirements are that it be decent, honest, truthful and in good taste. These criteria may not be met in this proposal as:
    - expectations of favourable results (lower tax liabilities) may be unjustifiable (or created deceptively);
    - 'techniques you can apply' may imply an ability to influence taxation authorities;
    - 'the best' is likely to be a self-laudatory statement and not based on verifiable facts;
    - 'the best' may also be making an unjustifiable comparison with other professional accountants in public practice;
    - 'the best tax planning advice' may be an unjustifiable claim of expertise or specialism in the field of tax.
- 'Can ensure …' and the assertion of 'all' may not be supportable claims, therefore the advertisement is not honest in these respects.
- There is a 'fine line' between tax avoidance and tax evasion and 'techniques you can apply' and 'alternative fact presentations' may lean toward the latter and so not be in keeping with the integrity of the profession.
- The assertion of being able to 'minimise the amount of tax' may expose Hawk Associates to litigation. The engagement risk associated with taking on this work would be high and so should carry commensurately high fees.
- The 'no tax saving – no fee' offer does not compensate for the risk associated with undertaking the work advertised.
- Contingency fees, whereby no fee will be charged unless a specific result is obtained, are prohibited by IFAC (unless otherwise permitted by statute of member body).

Advertising, publicity, obtaining professional work and fees

(c) **Business cards**

- Business cards may be considered a form of stationery and should be of an acceptable professional standard and comply with legal and member body requirements concerning names of partners, principals, professional descriptions, designatory letters, etc.

- Whilst placing such an advertisement where a target audience might reasonably be expected to exist (e.g. in an Institute of Directors or Business Men's Club), displaying it alongside 'local tradesmen' may appear to belittle the status of professional accountants.

- An advertisement the size of a business card would be sufficient to provide a name and contact details and in this respect is suitable. However, the danger of giving a misleading impression is pronounced when there is such limited space for information.

- However, the tone of the advertisement may discredit the ACCA name. It is also unsuitable that it seeks to take unfair advantage of the ACCA name. Although the ACCA mark can be used by Hawk Associates on letterheads and stationery (for example) it cannot be used in any way which confuses it with the firm.

- The emphasis on 'professional' may be unsuitable as it could suggest that there are other than professional accounting, audit (etc) services to be had.

- Offering a range of non-audit services in the same sentence as 'audit' may mislead interested persons picking up the card into thinking that Hawk can provide them together. This conflicts with the fact that Hawk is restricted in providing non-audit services to audit clients.

- There is no basis for asserting 'competitive rates'.

- It is unlikely that any professional would offer 'money back'. In the event of dispute (e.g. over fees), the matter would be taken to arbitration (with their member body) if a satisfactory arrangement could not be reached with the client.

- A tradesman may guarantee the quality of his work – and that it can be made good in the event that the customer is not satisfied. However, an auditor cannot guarantee a particular outcome for the work undertaken (e.g. reported profit or tax payable). Most certainly an auditor cannot guarantee the truth and fairness of the financial statements in giving an audit opinion.

chapter 6

Tendering

Chapter learning objectives

Upon completion of this chapter you will be able to:

- discuss the reasons why entities change their auditors/professional accountants
- recognise and explain the matters to be considered when a firm is invited to submit a proposal or fee quote for an audit or other professional engagement
- identify the information to be included in a fee proposal.

Tendering

 Tendering does not feature in every exam in P7, but it is a crucial part of the audit process; it is the main method by which audit/accounting firms obtain work. Remember that the purpose of tendering is to sell the firm's services to the client.

1 Changing auditors/professional accountants

Why change auditors?

Companies may change their auditors or other professional accountants for a number of reasons, with the impetus for change coming either from the company or from the audit firm.

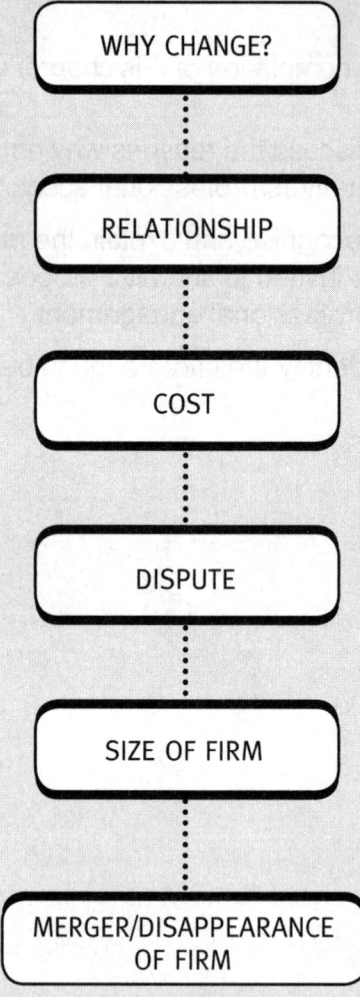

chapter 6

Why change auditor?

Reasons why a company may wish to change their auditors include:

- a change in the relationship between auditor and client;
- an attempt to reduce costs;
- a dispute between the company and the incumbent firm, maybe over financial reporting practices;
- the company might seek a larger audit firm who can offer a wider range of services;
- the audit firm may have ceased trading.

Why step down?

Audit firm may not seek re-appointment for many reasons. Examples include:

- independence issues
- doubts regarding the integrity of the company's management
- strategic decision making, such as: concentrating in other markets.

EU research into reasons for changing auditor

The EU has carried out research on the reasons why companies in practice have changed their auditors. The results were as follows.

Reason	Percentage of responses (%)
Company policy of regular rotation of audit firm	24
Appointment of a group auditor	16
Audit fees of incumbent auditor are too high	8
Dissatisfaction with quality of incumbent's work	4
Differences of opinion regarding financial statements	4
Insufficient advisory suggestions from incumbent	4
Other/not specified	40
	100

KAPLAN PUBLISHING

Tendering

> The prominence of rotation reflects the special case of Italy where there is a statutory requirement to rotate audit firms. The situation of a parent company imposing a group auditor is relevant across Europe and often arises when a company is sold to a new group.

2 Matters to be considered when a firm is invited to tender

Tendering is the process of quoting a fee for work before the work is carried out.

Tendering and changes in the market

As a consequence of being required to tender for audits, audit firms have found that fees have been substantially reduced. This has (in theory) resulted in certain changes in the accountancy market:

- mergers of audit practices to become more efficient. The 'Big 4' firms (PwC, Deloitte, Ernst & Young and KPMG) now dominate audit provision throughout the world
- adoption of risk-based auditing techniques so that fewer hours of auditing are needed to reach the same standard of audit conclusion
- acceptance that audit fees might fall in amount, but a hope that money can be made by carrying out lucrative non-audit work for the client (e.g. consultancy, tax planning, recruitment services, etc.).

When invited to tender, a firm must decide whether it wishes to take part in the tendering process. The following should be considered:

Ethical issues	Legal issues	Commercial issues
• Is the firm independent? • Will the quoted audit fee exceed accepted ethical fee limits? • Does the firm have the necessary resources to complete the engagement with competence and due care?	• Is the firm eligible under company law to be appointed, e.g. are any partners of the firm also employees of the company?	• Are the firm's resources available to complete the engagement on time? • Need for external experts? • Do the expected rewards outweigh the perceived costs/risks? • How much was the prior year audit fee? • Is the potential client profitable and growing? • What additional services could be sold?

In addition to the risk associated with any new client the specific risks of being involved with the tender include:

- wasted time – if the audit tender is not accepted.
- setting an uncommercially low fee in order to win the contract (see 'lowballing' in the previous chapter).
- making unrealistic claims or promises in order to win the contract.

3 The engagement proposal document

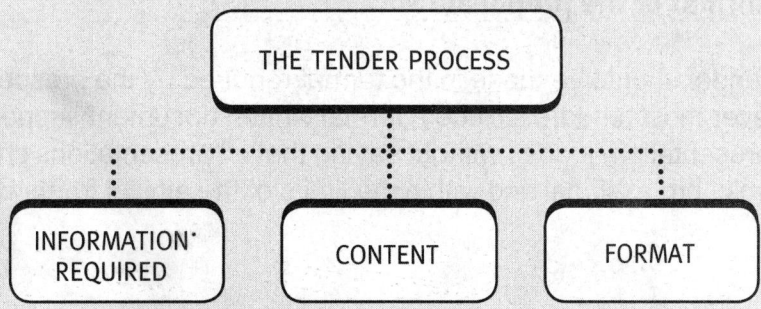

The preparation of an engagement proposal document is an important step in obtaining new work.

Information required for the proposal

Prior to drafting any proposals an audit firm should consider the following:

- precisely what does the potential client expect from its auditors?
- what timetable does the client expect: an interim audit followed by a final audit, or a longer final audit after the year end?
- by what date are the audited financial statements required?
- what are the company's future plans, e.g. public flotation, expansion, contraction, concentration on certain markets?
- are there any perceived problems with the potential client's current auditors?

The content of the proposal

The content of the proposal should include:

- the fee and how it has been calculated
- the nature, purpose and legal requirements of an audit (clients are often not clear about this)
- an assessment of the requirements of the client
- an outline of how the audit firm proposes to satisfy those requirements
- the assumptions made, e.g. on geographical coverage, deadlines, work done by client, availability of information, etc.
- the proposed approach to the audit or audit methodology
- an outline of the firm and its personnel
- the ability of the firm to offer other services.

The format of the proposal

The tender should be made in the format required by the prospective client. However most tenders include a formal written document supported by an oral presentation. It goes without saying that all presentations should be dynamic, professional and within the limits of the ethical framework.

UK syllabus focus

The UK Corporate Governance Code states:

- The audit committee should have primary responsibility for making a recommendation on the appointment, reappointment and removal of the external auditors.
- **FTSE 350 companies should put the external audit contract out to tender at least every ten years** (but can retain the current auditor if they provide the best quality and most effective audit) - or explain in the annual report why they have not.
- If the board does not accept the audit committee's recommendation, it should include in the annual report, and in any papers recommending appointment or re-appointment, a statement from the audit committee explaining the recommendation and should set out reasons why the board has taken a different position.

Benefits and drawbacks of tendering process

The benefits and drawbacks to the process of tendering and possible practice of constantly changing auditors include the following:

Benefits

- More efficient auditing.
- A tendency by companies to boost their internal audit departments so as to reduce external audit costs.
- Companies have also tended to simplify their group structures to reduce audit costs (among other reasons).

Drawbacks

- Greater market concentration, which has in fact reduced market choice.
- Loss of long-term relationships with auditors.
- A slight loss of perceived independence. The audit firms would deny this.

Tendering

You decide

- Greater emphasis by audit firms on other services they can sell the client (auditing could be a loss leader).
- Lowballing – the tendency for audit firms to tender below cost with the objective of getting the audit and hoping to raise the fee later, and to get lucrative non-audit work to compensate for the low audit fee. Surveys have found no correlation between lowballing (predatory pricing) and negligent auditing.

Exam hint

Almost everything on this list is double edged – greater concentration may be interpreted as an increase in expertise or as a reduction in choice.

In the exam you may be required to express the arguments clearly and to have a grasp of both sides of the argument. You may even be required to form a conclusion based upon your interpretation of the argument.

Test your understanding 1

How can small and mid-tier audit firms win the audits of large companies if those companies don't even invite them to tender for the audit?

4 Chapter summary

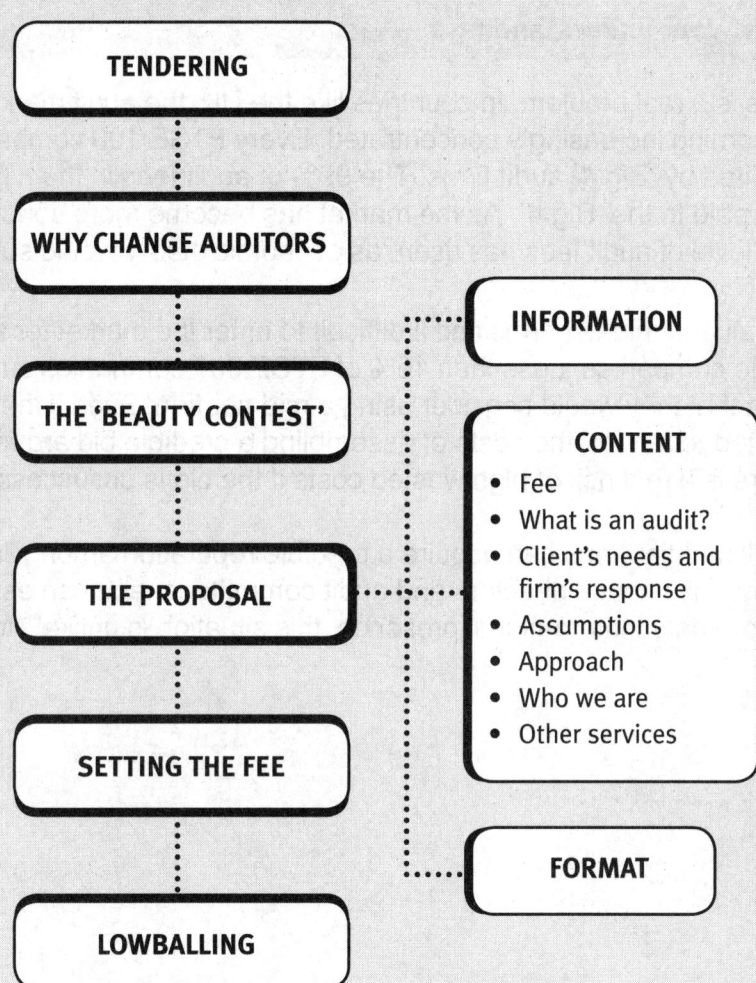

Test your understanding answers

Test your understanding 1

This is a real problem. In countries like the UK, the audit market is becoming increasingly concentrated. Every FTSE 100 company is audited by 'Big 4' audit firms. The 99% of audit fees in the FTSE 350 are paid to the 'Big 4'. As the market has become more concentrated, the level of audit fees has risen, as economic theory would suggest.

Small and mid-tier firms find it difficult to enter the market for auditing large companies. Less than 10% of FTSE 350 companies surveyed said that they would consider using a mid-tier firm. Even if they are invited to tender, the costs of assembling a credible bid are high, so there is a real risk of high wasted costs if the bid is unsuccessful.

Until mid-tier firms can acquire a credible reputation among large company finance directors and audit committees, and can establish a co-ordinated international presence, this situation is unlikely to change.

chapter 7

Money laundering

Chapter learning objectives

When you have completed this chapter you will be able to:

- define 'money laundering'
- explain the scope of criminal offences of money laundering
- explain the need for ethical guidance in this area
- describe how accountants meet their obligations to help prevent and detect money laundering
- explain the importance of customer due diligence (CDD)
- recognise potentially suspicious transactions and assess their impact on reporting duties.

Money laundering

Money laundering can be examined as part of professional issues to be considered when deciding whether or not to accept an engagement, or as a distinct requirement. Money laundering requirements may be knowledge based, in which you are required to explain the basic elements of an anti-money laundering program or define and give examples of money laundering offences. You may also need to identify a potentially suspicious transaction and explain the requirement to report knowledge or suspicion of money laundering.

1 Definition of money laundering

Money laundering is the process by which criminals attempt to conceal the true origin and ownership of the proceeds generated by illegal means, allowing them to maintain control over the proceeds and, ultimately, providing a legitimate cover for their sources of income.

Examples

Consider the following scenarios.

- Whilst preparing or auditing accounts you realize that a client has incorrectly reclaimed value added tax (or other national recoverable taxes) on the purchase of a motorcar. You point this out to the client and propose an adjustment to the financial statements to provide for the additional tax that is due. You also advise the client that they must rectify this with the tax authorities. However, the client tells you that they have just had an inspection by the tax authorities that did not reveal the error and they do not wish to do anything further.

- An auditor knowingly receives payment for one invoice twice (i.e. payment has been duplicated). The sole director has told the accounts department to ignore negative balances when they issue statements of account to customers hoping that they fail to notice.

    Errors and mistakes of the type illustrated above may not constitute criminal conduct, provided that they are corrected. However, in both cases there appears to be an intention to gain a permanent benefit from another's mistake or to avoid a legal liability. In the UK, for example, this is criminal conduct. As such, each of these cases would result in the accountant knowing or suspecting that a client is involved in money laundering.

2 International efforts to combat money laundering

The Financial Action Task Force (FATF) is an international body that promotes policies globally to combat money laundering and terrorist financing. In 1990 FATF issued recommendations to combat the misuse of financial systems to launder drug money.

The recommendations included:

- making money laundering a criminal offence
- measures to be taken by businesses and professions to prevent money laundering, including:
    - customer due diligence and record-keeping
    - reporting of suspicious transactions to an appropriate authority
- international co-operation including extradition of suspects.

These recommendations have become the benchmark against which a country's rules are assessed.

FATF recommendations

FATF focuses on three principal areas:

- setting standards aimed at combating money laundering and terrorist financing
- evaluating the degree to which countries have implemented measures that meet those standards, and
- identifying and studying money laundering and terrorist financing techniques.

In 1990, FATF drew up a document entitled "The Forty Recommendations" as an initiative to combat the misuse of financial systems to launder drug money. These recommendations (including the ones noted above) were endorsed by over 130 countries worldwide and now form the benchmark against which national anti-money laundering systems are assessed. Although different countries have moved forward in different ways.

The UK has adopted the recommendations of FATF.

The USA has a number of similar Acts:

- the Bank Secrecy Act 1970: this requires all cash deposits, withdrawals and transfers above $10,000 to be reported to the Inland Revenue Service
- the Money Laundering Control Act 1986
- the Uniting and Strengthening America by Providing Appropriate Tools Required to Intercept and Obstruct Terrorism (USA PATRIOT) Act 2001: this requires all financial institutions to establish an anti-money laundering program, including the development of internal policies and the designation of a compliance officer.

3 Examples of legislation

Introduction

Different countries have moved forward in different ways with the implementation of the FATF recommendations. The main legislation and requirements below relate to the money laundering regulatory regime as it stands in the UK. The principles, however, are appropriate on an international basis.

UK legislative background

Following the 1993 Criminal Justice Act, four further laws have tightened up the regulations in the UK:

- Terrorism Act 2000
- Proceeds of Crime Act 2002 (POCA)
- Money Laundering Regulations 2007 (the Regulations)
- Serious Organized Crime Police Act (SOCPA) 2005

In 2003 the ACCA issued Technical Fact Sheet 94 'Anti-money Laundering (Proceeds of Crime and Terrorism)' giving guidance to accountants in this area.

Money laundering offences

There are five basic money laundering offences:

- Acquiring, possession or use of criminal property.
- Concealing or disguising or transferring criminal property, or removing it from the UK.
- Failure to disclose knowledge or suspicion of money laundering.
- Tipping off.
- Failure by a financial services business to meet their obligations under money laundering regulations.

'Tipping off' means to carry out any action that may make suspected money launderers aware that they are under investigation, or prejudicing the outcome of an investigation.

Failure to disclose knowledge or suspicion of money laundering may include:

- failure by an individual in the regulated sector to inform the Serious Organised Crime Agency (SOCA), a Financial Intelligence Unit (FIU) or the business's Money Laundering Reporting Officer (MLRO), as soon as practicable, of knowledge or suspicion that another person is engaged in money laundering; or
- failure by MLROs in the regulated sector to make the required report to SOCA as soon as practicable if an internal report leads them to know or suspect that a person is engaged in money laundering.

Money Laundering Regulations impose certain obligations on financial services businesses, which are designed to assist in detecting money laundering and preventing the financial services organisations being used for money laundering purposes. These obligations are:

- To put in place internal controls and policies to ensure compliance with the legislation;
- To appoint a Money Laundering Reporting Officer (MLRO);
- To establish/enhance record keeping systems for:
  - all transactions;
  - the verification of clients' identities;
- To establish internal reporting procedures; and
- To educate and train all staff in the main requirements of the legislation.

> **Criminal property and criminal conduct**
>
> Criminal property is property that has arisen from criminal conduct. Examples include:
>
> - Property acquired by theft;
> - The proceeds of tax evasion
> - Bribery or corruption
> - Saved costs arising from a criminal failure to comply with a regulatory requirement

4 Anti-money laundering program: basic elements

Some of the recommendations of FATF cover measures to be incorporated into an anti-money laundering program by financial institutions, non-financial businesses and professions to prevent money laundering and the financing of terrorist activities.

At a minimum, an anti-money laundering program should incorporate:

- Customer identification procedures;
- Enhanced record keeping;
- Procedures for the reporting of suspicious transactions and compliance to the Financial Intelligence Unit (FIU), including appointment of a Money Laundering Reporting Officer ('MLRO');
- Communication and training; and
- Systems and controls that effectively manage the risk that the firm is exposed to in relation to money laundering activities.

In the UK, for example, some of these measures are covered by the Money Laundering Regulations 2007.

5 Customer identification procedures

Accountants are required to establish that new clients are who they claim to be by obtaining satisfactory evidence of identity from the client. This is often referred to as 'customer due diligence' or 'know your customer' procedures.

Customer due diligence is an essential part of the anti-money laundering requirements. It ensures that accountants:

- know who their clients are; and
- do not unknowingly accept clients which are too high risk.

chapter 7

Detailed procedures

Customer due diligence must performed as soon as is reasonably practicable after contact is first made between the two parties. Where satisfactory evidence of identity is not obtained by the accountant, the business relationship or one-off transaction must not proceed any further.

Basic identification procedures include:

- For individuals (including key management personnel where the client is an entity): inspection of evidence to establish the full name and permanent address of the client, e.g. a driving licence or a passport (which include a photograph) and a recent utility bill to confirm the address.

- For businesses: inspection of evidence including: the certificate of incorporation; lists of registered members and directors; certificate of registered address.

- For trusts: inspection of evidence to establish and confirm: the nature and purpose of the trust; its original source of funding; and the identities of the trustees, controllers and beneficiaries.

It may be helpful for the auditor to explain to the client the reason for requiring evidence of identity and this can be achieved by including this matter in the engagement letter.

It may also be helpful to inform clients of the auditor's responsibilities to report knowledge or suspicion that a money laundering offence has been committed and the restrictions created by the 'tipping off' rules on the auditor's ability to discuss such matters with their clients.

Example engagement letter money laundering clauses

'In accordance with the *Proceeds of Crime Act 2002* and *Money Laundering Regulations 2007* you agree to waive your right to confidentiality to the extent of any report made, document provided or information disclosed to the *Serious Organised Crime Agency (SOCA)*.

You also acknowledge that we are required to report directly to *SOCA* without prior reference to you or your representatives if during the course of undertaking any assignment the person undertaking the role of Money Laundering Reporting Officer becomes suspicious of money laundering.

> As a specific requirement of the Money Laundering Regulations we may require you to produce evidence of identity of the company and its owners and managers. This will include for the business proof of registration and address and for the individuals proof of identity and address. Copies of such records will be maintained by us for a period of at least five years after we cease to act for the business.'
>
> (ACCA Technical Guidance and Support, 2008)
>
> **Note:** The above clauses include references to the relevant legislation and regulatory bodies in the United Kingdom. The references would be amended for the specific jurisdiction(s).

6 Enhanced record keeping

It is very important that accountants keep comprehensive records to show that they have complied with money laundering regulations, and protect themselves if there is an investigation into one of their clients.

Records must be kept of:

- all customer due diligence completed, including copies of the evidence inspected;
- transactions with each client;
- internal and external money laundering/suspicious activity reports.

Records must be held for five years after a relationship with a client has ended or the date a transaction is completed.

7 Reporting procedures

The FATF recommend reporting procedures. In the UK these are codified in the MLR 2007 that are typical of procedures adopted internationally. This requires that:

- a person in the organisation is nominated to receive disclosures under this regulation (usually an MLRO)
- anyone in the organisation, to whom information comes in the course of the relevant business as a result of which he suspects that a person is engaged in money laundering, must disclose it to the MLRO
- where a disclosure is made to the MLRO, they must consider it in the light of any relevant information which is available to the organisation and determine whether it gives rise to suspicion, and
- where the MLRO does so determine, the information must be disclosed to a regulatory body authorised for the purposes of these regulations, such as the SOCA in the UK.

Potentially suspicious transactions

There is no formal definition of "suspicious". A suspicious transaction will often be inconsistent with the client's known or usual legitimate activities. Examples include:

- Unusually large cash deposits;
- Frequent exchanges of cash into other currencies; and
- Overseas business arrangements with no clear business purpose.

Remember it is a criminal offence not to report knowledge or suspicion of money laundering.

'De minimis' concessions

Note that in the UK the obligation to report does not depend on the amount involved or the seriousness of the offence. There are no de minimis concessions.

The MLRO

The MLRO should be an individual of suitable seniority and experience. Alternative arrangements must be made when the MLRO is unavailable (on holiday, sick, jury service, etc). The MLRO receives and assesses money laundering reports from colleagues, and passes on valid suspicions to a regulatory agency (SOCA) on a standard form that identifies:

- the suspect's name, address, date of birth and nationality
- any identification or references seen
- the nature of the activities giving rise to suspicion
- any other information that may be relevant.

Sole practitioners with no employees or associates are exempt from the requirement to appoint an MLRO, since clearly they would be reporting to themselves.

8 Communication and training

Financial services firms in the conduct of relevant business must take appropriate measures to ensure that employees are:

- made aware of the provisions of anti-money laundering regulations, and are
- given training in how to recognise and deal with transactions which may be related to money laundering.

This is because businesses and their employees must:

- comply with the requirements of regulations; and
- establish procedures of internal control and communication as may be appropriate for the purposes of forestalling and preventing money laundering.

9 Systems and controls

The systems and controls described above (client due diligence, record keeping, reporting and communication and training of employees) should be testing periodically to ensure that they comply with the relevant money laundering laws and regulations.

This would include checking that employees are completing available training, and testing their understanding of it.

10 The need for ethical guidance on money laundering

ACCA provides guidance in its Code of Ethics and Conduct in the area of money laundering.

- This is needed because there is a clear conflict between:
  (1) the accountant's professional duty of confidentiality in relation to his client's business, and
  (2) the duty to report suspicions of money laundering to the appropriate authorities as required by law.

- Professional accountants are not in breach of their professional duty of confidentiality if they report in good faith their knowledge or suspicions of money laundering to the appropriate authority.

- Disclosure in bad faith or without reasonable grounds would possibly lead to the accountant being sued for breach of confidence.

- Auditor's duty of confidentiality will not be breached if they report, in good faith, any money laundering knowledge or suspicions to the appropriate authority. Statutory protection also applies where reports are made in good faith.

11 Chapter summary

MONEY LAUNDERING

FINANCIAL ACTION TASK FORCE ON MONEY LAUNDERING (FATF)

Legislation
(UK example)
Proceeds of Crime Act 2002
Money Laundering Regulations 2007

Offences
- Money laundering
- Tipping off
- Not setting up procedures
- Not complying with procedures

Ethical guidance
- Conflict with confidentiality

Duties
Client identification
- Client due diligence

Appointing a MLRO
- With specified responsibilities

Staff training
- For all relevant personnel

Reporting
- Internal to MLRO
- External to FIU

Basics of a client system
To enable auditors to review client anti money laundering procedures.

chapter 8

Professional responsibilities and liabilities

Chapter learning objectives

When you have completed this chapter you will be able to:

- compare and contrast the respective responsibilities of management and auditors concerning:
    (i) compliance with laws and regulations; and
    (ii) fraud and error.
- describe the matters to be considered at planning and the procedures to be carried out to investigate possible non-compliance and fraud;
- discuss how and to whom instances of non-compliance and fraud should be reported;
- recognise circumstances in which professional accountants may have a legal liability;
- explain the criteria for legal liability to be recognised (including 'due care' and 'proximity'); and
- evaluate the practicability and effectiveness of ways in which liability may be restricted.

Professional responsibilities and liabilities

 Professional responsibilities and in particular liability, is one of the professional issues to be considered before accepting an engagement. The exam may also incorporate a specific requirement relating to liability. In addition, scenario based questions may incorporate a breach of laws or regulations or a fraud in which case the matters to be considered would incorporate the auditor's responsibilities in relation to each of these.

1 Laws and regulations

Guidance regarding responsibility to consider laws and regulations in an audit of financial statements is provided in ISA 250 Consideration of Laws and Regulations in an Audit of Financial Statements.

Responsibilities are considered from the perspective of both auditors and management.

Responsibilities of management

ISA 250 clearly states that it is the responsibility of management, with the oversight of those charged with governance, to ensure that the entity's operations are conducted in accordance with relevant laws and regulations, particularly those that determine the reported amounts and disclosures in the financial statements.

Preventing and detecting non-compliance

In order to help prevent and detect non-compliance, management can implement the following policies and procedures:

- Monitoring legal requirements applicable to the company and ensuring that operating procedures are designed to meet these requirements;
- Instituting and operating appropriate systems of internal control;
- Developing, publicising and following a code of conduct;
- Ensuring employees are properly trained and understand the code of conduct;
- Monitoring compliance with the code of conduct and acting appropriately to discipline employees who fail to comply with it;
- Engaging legal advisors to assist in monitoring legal requirements; and
- Maintaining a register of significant laws and regulations with which the entity has to comply.

In larger entities, these policies and procedures may be supplemented by assigning appropriate responsibilities to:

- An internal audit function;
- An audit committee; and/or
- A compliance function.

Responsibilities of the auditor

The auditor is responsible for obtaining reasonable assurance that the financial statements taken as a whole, are free from material misstatement, whether caused by fraud or error (ISA 200). Therefore, in conducting an audit of financial statements the auditor must take into account the applicable legal and regulatory framework.

More specifically the auditor must obtain sufficient, appropriate evidence regarding compliance with **those laws and regulations generally recognised to have a direct effect** on the determination of material amounts and disclosures in the financial statements.

The auditor must also perform specified audit procedures to help identify instances of non-compliance with those laws and regulations that may have a material impact on the financial statements. If non-compliance is identified (or suspected) the auditor must then respond appropriately.

Effect of laws and regulations

ISA 250 distinguishes between two types of laws and regulations: those which are generally recognised to have a **direct effect** on the determination of material amounts and disclosures in the financial statements; and **other laws and regulations**.

Examples of laws and regulations with a **direct effect** include:

- company law (e.g. the Companies Act in the UK).
- taxation legislation.

The auditor must obtain sufficient, appropriate evidence regarding compliance with laws and regulations that have a direct effect on the financial statements.

Professional responsibilities and liabilities

Examples of **other laws and regulations** include:

- environmental legislation.
- employment laws.

Compliance with other laws and regulations that do not have a direct effect on the determination of material amounts and disclosures in the financial statements, may nevertheless be fundamental to the ability of an entity to continue to operate as a business, or to avoid material penalties, and may therefore still have a material effect on the financial statements.

The auditor must perform specified audit procedures to help identify non-compliance with laws and regulations that may have a material impact on the financial statements.

Further discussion of auditor responsibility

IFAC recognises that the auditors have a role in relation to non-compliance with laws and regulations. Auditors plan, perform and evaluate their audit work with the aim of providing reasonable, though not absolute, assurance of detecting any material misstatement in the financial statements which arises from non-compliance with laws or regulations.

However, auditors cannot be expected to be experts in all the many different laws and regulations where non-compliance might have such an effect. There is also an unavoidable risk that some material misstatements may not be detected due to the inherent limitations in auditing.

2 The auditors' considerations and procedures

Non-compliance with laws and regulations may have a fundamental effect on:

- the operations of the entity (and its ability to continue as a going concern); and
- disclosures in the financial statements (most notably provisions and contingencies).

The auditors should perform procedures to help identify instances of non-compliance with those laws and regulations by:

- **obtaining a general understanding** of the legal and regulatory framework applicable to the entity and the industry, and of how the entity is complying with that framework
- **inspecting correspondence** with relevant licensing or regulatory authorities
- **enquiring of the management and those charged with governance** as to whether the entity is in compliance with such laws and regulations
- **remaining alert** to the possibility that other audit procedures applied may bring instances of non-compliance to the auditor's attention
- **obtaining written confirmation** from the directors that they have disclosed to the auditors all those events of which they are aware which involve possible non-compliance, together with the actual or contingent consequences which may arise from such non-compliance.

How to obtain a general understanding

ISA 250 provides some guidelines to assist auditors when obtaining an understanding of their clients' legal and regulatory environments. The standard provides the following examples:

- Using the auditor's existing understanding of the industry;
- Updating the auditor's understanding of laws and regulations that directly determine reported amounts and disclosures in the financial statements;
- Enquiry of management as to other laws and regulations that may be expected to have a fundamental effect on the operations of the entity;
- Enquiry of management concerning the entity's policies and procedures regarding compliance;
- Enquiry of management regarding the policies or procedures adopted for identifying, evaluating and accounting for litigation claims.

(ISA 250, A7)

Professional responsibilities and liabilities

Indications of non-compliance

The appendix to ISA 250 sets out examples of the types of information or situations that may come to the attention of the auditor and may indicate non-compliance with laws or regulations.

These include:

- investigation by government department
- payment of fines or penalties
- loans or payments for unspecified services to consultants, related parties, employees or government employees
- sales commissions or agents' fees that appear excessive in relation to those normally paid by the entity or in its industry
- unusual payments in cash
- unusual transactions with companies registered in tax havens
- an accounting system that fails to provide an adequate audit trail or sufficient evidence (either by design or by accident)
- transactions that are unauthorised
- improperly recorded transactions
- comment in the media.

When the auditors become aware of information concerning a possible instance of **non-compliance** with laws or regulations, they should:

- understand the **nature of the act**
- understand the **circumstances** in which it has occurred
- obtain sufficient other information to **evaluate** the possible effect on the financial statements
- **document** their findings
- **report** their findings to an appropriate level of management (subject to any requirement to report directly to a third party)

chapter 8

3 Reporting non-compliance

The auditor should report non-compliance to management. However, in certain circumstances they should consider reporting directly to shareholders or third parties (perhaps in cases of fraud or money laundering?)

Where the auditors conclude that suspected non-compliance with laws or regulation has a material effect on the financial statements and they disagree with the accounting treatment or with the extent, or the lack, of any disclosure in the financial statements they should consider a modified audit opinion.

Reporting non-compliance to third parties

Confidentiality is an implied term of the auditors' contract. The duty of confidentiality, however, is not absolute. In certain exceptional circumstances auditors are not bound by the duty of confidentiality and have the right to report matters to a proper authority in the public interest. Auditors need to weigh the public interest in maintaining confidential client relationships against the public interest in disclosure to a proper authority. Determination of where the balance of public interest lies requires careful consideration. Auditors whose suspicions have been aroused need to use their professional judgement to determine whether their misgivings justify them in carrying the matter further or are too insubstantial to deserve report.

The auditor may need to seek legal advice before deciding on a course of action.

4 Engagement withdrawal

The auditor may decide that the situation is so serious that they need to withdraw from the engagement (i.e. resign as auditor).

From the perspective of financial reporting, the auditor can issue a disclaimer of, an adverse or a qualified opinion on the accounts. However, there may have been a breakdown of trust between the auditor and management, or the auditor may have doubts about the competence of management that could lead to the auditor considering resignation. The auditor should take legal advice before embarking on this course of action.

5 Laws and regulations – summary

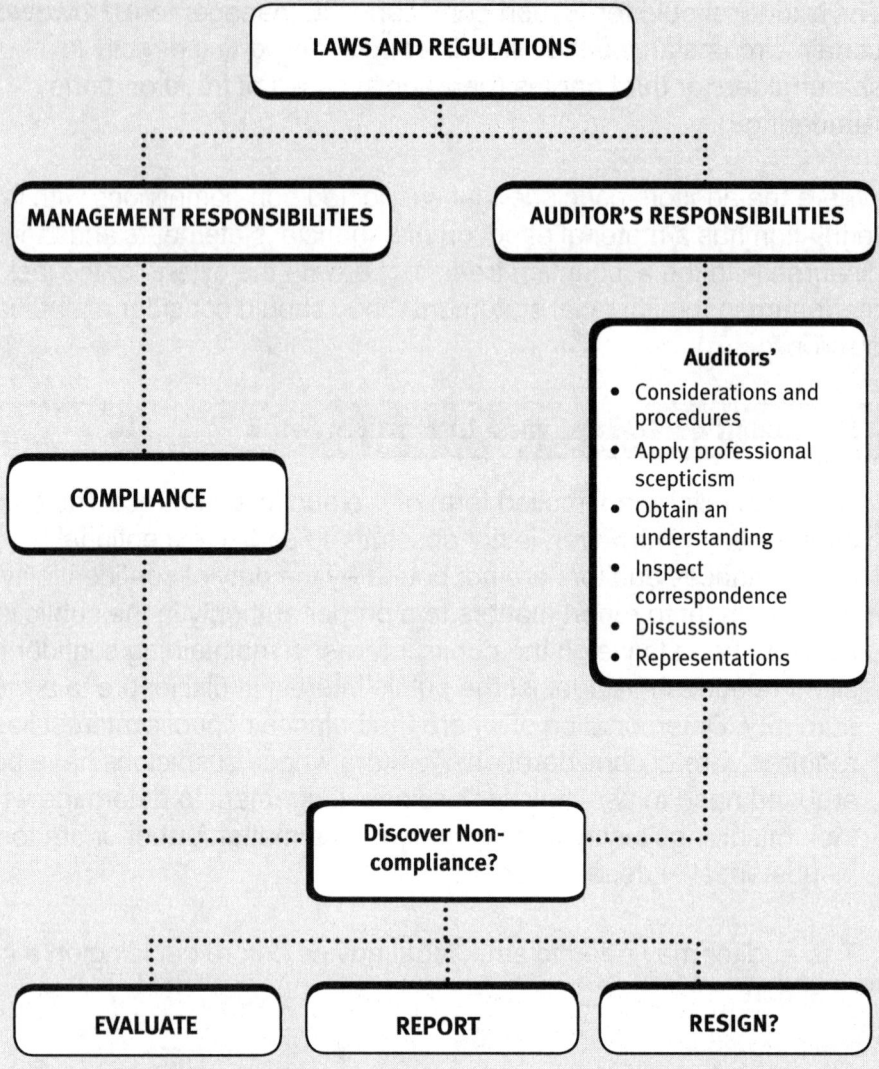

6 Fraud and error, mistatements and irregularities

Definitions

Irregularity

An 'Irregularity' is the collective term for fraud, error, breaches of laws and regulations, and deficiencies in the design or operating effectiveness of controls. An irregularity may or may not result in a misstatement in the financial statements.

Misstatement

A misstatement is defined by ISA 450 as "A difference between the amount, classification, presentation, or disclosure of a reported financial statement item and the amount, classification, presentation, or disclosure that is required for the item to be in accordance with the applicable financial reporting framework."

In ISA 240 the *Auditor's Responsibilities Relating to Fraud in an Audit of Financial Statements*, it states that "misstatements in the financial statements can arise from fraud or error. The distinguishing factor between fraud and error is whether the underlying action that results in the misstatement of the financial statements is intentional or unintentional."

Fraud

Fraud is an intentional act involving the use of deception to obtain an unjust or illegal advantage. It may be perpetrated by one or more individuals among management, employees or third parties.

ISA 240 identifies two categories of fraud that are of concern to auditors:

- Fraudulent financial reporting; and
- Misappropriation of assets.

Examples of financial statement fraud could include: the creation of dummy suppliers or ghost employees to divert company funds into a personal bank account; or the intentional concealment of company loans within complex networks of special purpose entities (Enron!) so that they do not appear on the statement of financial position.

Each case needs to be considered but, depending on the severity of the fraud, the police may become involved and court proceedings launched against the perpetrator. It is important to note that it is not up to an auditor to make legal determinations of whether fraud has occurred.

Error

An 'error' can be defined as an unintentional misstatement in financial statements, including the omission of amounts or disclosures, such as the following:

- A mistake in gathering and processing data from which financial statements are prepared;
- An incorrect accounting estimate arising from oversight or a misinterpretation of facts; or

- A mistake in the application of accounting principles relating to measurement, recognition, classification, presentation or disclosure.

Errors are normally corrected by clients when they are identified. If a material error has been identified but has not been corrected, it may affect the ultimate audit opinion (see audit reporting chapter for further explanations).

Article focus

The examiner classifies fraud into three distinct areas: corruption, misappropriation of assets, and financial statements fraud.

The article "Forensic Auditing" (Sep 2008) provides further detail and provides a link between fraud and forensic accounting, a topic covered later in these notes. It can be found on the ACCA website under P7 resources.

A subsequent article "Massaging the Figures" (April 2009) picks up on this topic and explores how creative accounting techniques, when intentionally misleading, can lead to fraudulently prepared financial statements.

7 Responsibilities for fraud and error

ISA 240 explains that the "primary responsibility" for the prevention and detection of fraud rests with both those charged with governance of an entity and with management.

However, auditors are required to provide reasonable assurance that the financial statements are free from material misstatement, whether caused by fraud or error. In order to meet this responsibility auditors must plan, perform and review audits in light of the risk of misstatement due to fraud.

Of fundamental importance to this is the concept of professional scepticism. This means that auditors should always remain aware of the possibility that fraud could take place. They must always consider the potential for management override of controls and recognise the fact that audit procedures that are effective for detecting error may not be effective for detecting fraud.

ISA 240 also recognises the inherent limitations of an audit and that there is an unavoidable risk that some material misstatements may not be detected, even though the audit is properly planned and performed in accordance with ISAs. This risk is greater in relation to misstatement due to fraud, rather than error, because of the potentially sophisticated nature of organised criminal schemes.

chapter 8

Management vs. auditor

Management should:

- place a strong emphasis on fraud prevention and error reduction
- reduce opportunities for fraud to take place
- ensure the likelihood of detection and punishment for fraud is sufficient to act as a deterrent
- ensure controls are in place to provide reasonable assurance that errors will be identified
- foster, communicate and demonstrate a culture of honesty & ethical behaviour
- consider potential for override of controls or manipulation of financial reporting
- implement and operate adequate accounting and internal control systems.

Auditors

- ISA 315 requires a discussion amongst the engagement team regarding the susceptibility of the client's financial statements to material misstatement due to fraud.
- The auditor shall than perform risk assessment procedures to obtain an understanding of the client and its environment. According to ISA 315 this should include the following procedures:
    - Enquiry of management regarding their assessment of fraud risk, the procedures they conduct and whether they are aware of any actual or suspected instances of fraud;
    - Enquiry of the internal audit function to establish if they are aware of any actual or suspected instances of fraud;
    - Enquiry of those charged with governance with regard to how they exercise oversight of management processes for identifying the risk of fraud and whether they are aware of any actual or suspected fraud; and
    - Consideration of relationships identified during analytical procedures.

KAPLAN PUBLISHING

- In response, in accordance with ISA 330, the auditor shall determine overall responses to address the risks of material misstatement due to fraud at the financial statements level. This includes: the design of further audit procedures; the allocation of – and supervision of – team members to particular procedures; evaluation of accounting policies; and incorporation of an element of unpredictability in the selection of the nature, timing and extent of audit procedures

(ISA 240, P.29)

The future of fraud and the audit

Fraud is a controversial area for auditors, and the extent of auditor responsibility for the prevention and detection of fraud continues to be debated by those in the profession, governments and other users of financial statements.

The Kingston Cotton Mill case (1896) emphasised that the reader of an audit report should have a realistic viewpoint of what the auditor's role should actually be.

The judge in the case set the benchmark for auditor responsibility when he said "An auditor is not bound to be a detective, or… to approach his work with suspicion, or with a foregone conclusion that there is something wrong. He is a watchdog, not a bloodhound."

As the remainder of this section will explore, auditing has evolved since 1896. Auditors do have a recognised responsibility for considering fraud when conducting an audit of financial statements, but the primary responsibility for fraud and error continues to rest with management, and those charged with governance. However, the auditor's responsibility with respect to fraud could change.

Auditors are currently responsible for detecting material misstatements whether caused by fraud or error. However, misstatements due to fraud are, by their very nature, extremely difficult to detect. Auditors are not trained as nor expected to be forensic investigators and even the most experienced auditor may have failed to detect a material misstatement caused by fraud. The auditor's responsibility for detecting material misstatements could be limited to exclude those caused by fraud.

Conversely, many users would like to see auditors' responsibility for fraud extended. In order to achieve this, auditors would have to be given the training necessary to identify fraud. In addition, the extent of auditor's responsibilities would have to be defined. It would not be possible to expect the auditor to detect all fraud. Some frauds (especially where collusion is involved) are almost impossible to identify. However, auditors could be given responsibility for performing audit procedures specifically to detect fraud, possibly in those areas that are more susceptible to fraud (e.g. payroll).

The audit profession is dynamic and subject to much debate at the current time. It is not possible to know what the future holds, but perhaps auditors will be required to move towards the role of a bloodhound in the not too distant future.

Absolute assurance – never!

An auditor **cannot obtain absolute assurance** over the accuracy of the financial statements because of such factors as:

- the use of judgement
- the use of testing
- the inherent limitations of internal control, and
- the fact that much of the audit evidence available to the auditor is persuasive rather than conclusive in nature.

8 Investigations of possible misstatements

When an actual or potential misstatement is identified by an auditor, a number of matters must be considered, and procedures carried out, to determine the impact (if any) on the audit.

- The nature of the event and the circumstances in which it has occurred should be understood.

- Sufficient information should be gathered to allow evaluation of the possible effect on the financial statements.

- If the auditors believe that the indicated fraud or error could have a material effect on the financial statements, they should perform appropriate modified or additional procedures.

- ISA 240 requires that where a fraud is identified or information indicating that one may exist the auditor should communicate the matter to the appropriate level of management.

Professional responsibilities and liabilities

Implications for the audit

Modified or additional procedures

Procedures will depend on the nature of the fraud indicated, the likelihood of its occurrence and the likely effect on the financial statements. Auditors cannot assume that frauds are isolated. Where such additional procedures do not dispel the suspicion of fraud or error, the auditor should discuss the matter with management and consider whether it has been properly reflected in the financial statements.

Implications for the audit

Auditors should consider the effect of the fraud or error on their preliminary risk assessment and on the reliability of management representations. This is particularly important where senior management is involved.

Discuss with management

Regardless of the materiality of the actual or suspected fraud or error, the auditor will need to communicate factual findings with management and those charged with governance in order to:

(i) keep them informed and to ensure that they understand the position correctly

(ii) discover what action they have taken or intend to take to rectify the position, e.g. management may consider amending the system of internal control in order to reduce or eliminate the risk of such irregularities in the future

(iii) evaluate the likelihood that the irregularity has recurred or will recur (iv) discover what, if any, legal advice has been taken.

Management override

Management is uniquely placed to commit fraud due to their access to and ability to manipulate accounting records and financial statements. This is due to the fact that many controls rely on the effective operation of management and management can abuse their power to override those controls.

All the famous, high profile (and most economically damaging) cases, such as Enron and Maxwell, include some form of managerial fraud.

Although the risk of management override varies it is always present and auditors must always consider this possibility when planning, performing and evaluating their audit.

In response auditors should design and perform procedures to:

- Test the appropriateness of journal entries in the general ledger and adjustments made in the preparation of the financial statements. These procedures include:
  - Enquiring of those involved in financial reporting about unusual activity relating to adjustments;
  - Selecting journal entries and adjustments made at the end of the reporting period; and
  - Considering the need to test journal entries throughout the period.
- The auditor should also consider the accounting estimates made by management and the possibility of bias or direct manipulation affecting their judgement. In performing this review auditors shall:
  - Evaluate the reasonableness of judgements and whether they indicate any bias on behalf of management; and
  - Perform a retrospective review of management judgements reflected in the prior year.
- If there are any significant transactions that are outside the normal course of business, or appear unusual, the auditor should consider whether this suggests an increased risk of fraudulent financial reporting.

9 Fraud, error and the role of auditors

The action taken by auditors to report an event varies in relation to its nature and the gravity of its consequences.

Reporting to management

If the auditor has identified a fraud, or obtained evidence that indicates one may have occurred, the auditor should communicate this on a timely basis to an appropriate level of management.

If the auditor suspects either management, employees with a significant role in internal control or others where the fraud results in a material misstatement, then the auditor should communicate the matter to those charged with governance.

The requirement to report such matters also stems from ISA 260, which requires the auditor to communicate matters of governance interest in a timely fashion. If the matter is significant it should be reported in writing.

If the auditor has doubts about the integrity of those charged with governance then the most appropriate course of action would be to obtain legal counsel before any reports are made.

Reporting to shareholders

If the matter leads to a material misstatement or an inability to obtain sufficient appropriate evidence then the auditor must consider the impact upon the nature and wording of their audit report. If matters are significant the auditor may choose to speak directly to the shareholders at the AGM, however, if the matter relates to fraud the auditor would obtain legal advice first.

Reporting to third parties

Where the auditor believes that a suspected fraud should be reported to an appropriate authority in the public interest, they should notify the directors in writing of their view and, if the entity does not voluntarily do so, should report it themselves.

Where the suspected fraud casts doubt on the integrity of the directors, the auditor should make a report direct to the proper authority in the public interest without delay and without informing the directors in advance.

10 Fraud and error – summary

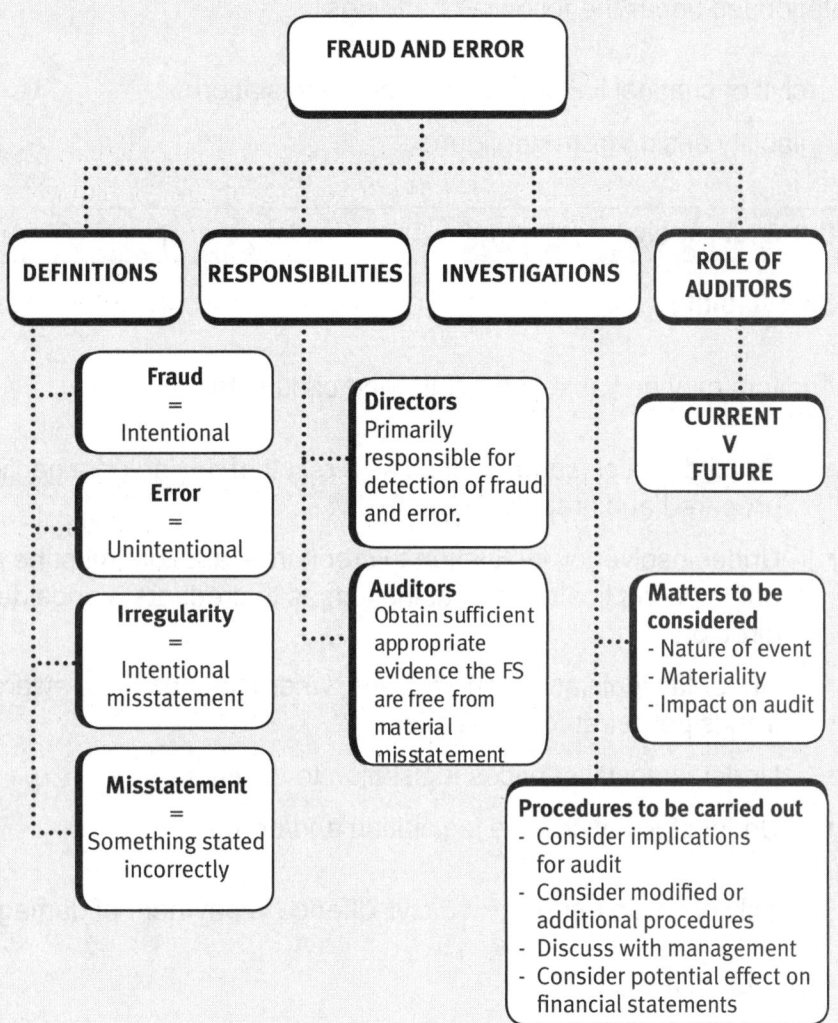

11 Legal liability

The circumstances in which auditors may have legal liability

Typically, the auditor has a statutory duty to report to the members on whether:

- the financial statements are free from material misstatement;
- the financial statements have been properly prepared in accordance with relevant national legal frameworks (e.g. in the UK - the Companies Act); and
- the Directors' Report is consistent with the financial statements

Professional responsibilities and liabilities

Such duties impose liabilities if things go wrong. Auditors' liability can be categorised under the following headings:

- civil or criminal liability arising under legislation
- liability arising from negligence

Criminal vs. civil

Civil liability

Auditors may be liable in the following circumstances.

- To third parties suffering loss as a result of relying on a negligently prepared audit report – see below.
- Under insolvency legislation to creditors – auditors must be careful not to be implicated in causing losses to creditors alongside directors.
- Under tax legislation – particularly where the auditor is aware of tax frauds perpetrated by his client.
- Under financial services legislation to investors.
- Under stock exchange legislation and/or rules.

The only possible penalty for a civil offence is payment of damages.

Criminal liability

Criminal liability can arise in the following circumstances:

- Acting as auditor when ineligible;
- Fraud, such as: theft; bribery and other forms of corruption; falsifying accounting records; and knowingly publishing misleading financial statements;
- Insider dealing; and
- Knowingly or recklessly making false statements in connection with the issue of securities.

Penalties for criminal liability include fines and/or imprisonment.

In addition to the various civil and criminal liabilities the professional bodies that regulate accountants and auditors have various sanctions, such as; warnings, fines, reprimands, severe reprimands and exclusion from membership for misconduct by members. Conviction of a criminal offence involving financial misconduct is normally sufficient to warrant exclusion from membership of a reputable professional body.

Liability to the client and liability to third parties

Liability in contract

- Liability to the client arises from contract law. The company has a contract with the auditor and hence can sue the auditor for breach of contract if the auditor simply fails to deliver, or delivers a negligently prepared, audit report.
- When carrying out their duties the auditor must exercise due care and skill. The degree of care and skill to be shown, in particular in relation to the depth of investigation and the types of check to be made, is shown by judicial precedent.
- In the ACCA's Rules of Professional Conduct the fundamental principles in respect of professional competence and due care state that:

  'Members have a continuing duty to maintain professional knowledge and skill at a level required to ensure that a client or employer receives competent professional service based on current developments in practice, legislation and techniques. Members should act diligently and in accordance with applicable technical and professional standards when providing professional services.'

- Generally if auditors can show that they have complied with generally accepted auditing standards, they will not have been negligent.

Liability in tort

A third party (i.e. a person who has no contractual relationship with the auditor) may sue the auditor for 'damages', i.e. a financial award.

In the tort of negligence, the plaintiff (i.e. the third party) must prove that:

- the defendant (i.e. the auditor) owes a duty of care; and
- the defendant has breached the appropriate standard of care as discussed above (i.e. has been negligent); and
- the plaintiff has suffered loss as a direct result of the defendant's breach.

On the whole litigation is not concerned whether the auditor has in fact been negligent but whether a duty of care is owed in the first place. If no duty is owed, it cannot be breached.

> **Case Study: Lloyd Cheyham v Littlejohn de Paula**
>
> **Lloyd Cheyham v Littlejohn de Paula (1985)**
>
> Littlejohn de Paula successfully defended themselves against a negligence claim in this case by showing:
>
> - that they had followed the standard expected of the normal auditor, i.e. the standard in Accounting Standards and Auditing Standards
> - that their working papers were good enough to show consideration of the problems raised by the plaintiff and reasonable decisions made after consideration
> - that the plaintiff had not made all the reasonable enquiries one could expect when, in this case, purchasing a company. For example a review of the business was not undertaken upon investigating the purchase but only after purchase
> - the judge, therefore, held that far too much reliance was placed on the accounts by the plaintiff and he awarded costs against the plaintiff to the defendant.

12 Negligence

The critical matter in most negligence scenarios is whether a duty of care is owed in the first place.

When is a duty of care owed?

A duty of care exists when there is a special relationship between the parties, i.e. where the auditors knew, or ought to have known, that the audited accounts would be made available to, and would be relied upon by, a particular person (or class of person).

The injured party must therefore prove:

- that the auditor knew, or should have known, that the injured party was likely to rely on the financial statements
- that the injured party has sufficient 'proximity', i.e. belongs to a class likely to rely on the financial statements
- that the injured party did in fact so rely, and
- that the injured party would have acted differently if the financial statements had shown a different picture.

chapter 8

> **Case Study: ADT Ltd v BDO Binder Hamlyn**
>
> **ADT Ltd v BDO Binder Hamlyn (1995)**
>
> BH were the joint auditors of the Britannia Security Systems Group. Before the 1989 audit was finished, ADT were considering bidding for Britannia, so an ADT representative met the BH audit partner and asked him to confirm that the audited accounts gave a true and fair view and that he had learnt nothing subsequently which cast doubt on the accounts. The partner said that BH stood by the accounts and there was nothing else that ADT should be told. ADT then bought Britannia for $105m, but it was found to be worth only $40m.
>
> It was held that BH owed ADT a duty of care when the partner made his statements, and the accounts had been negligently audited, so ADT were awarded $65m plus interest. The shortfall in BH's insurance cover was $34m; the partners were therefore individually liable for that amount.
>
> BH appealed, and ADT agreed an out-of-court settlement.

Has the auditor exercised due professional care?

The term due professional care cannot be explained in precise terms. There is no absolute standard. The following points are relevant in determining what is a reasonable standard of care:

- applying the most up-to-date accounting and auditing standards.
- adhering to all standards of ethical behaviour laid down by the relevant professional bodies.
- being aware of the terms and conditions of appointment as set out in the letter of engagement and as implied by law.
- employing competent staff who are adequately trained and supervised in carrying out instructions.

Has the injured party suffered a loss?

This is normally provable as a matter of fact. For example, if X relies on the audited financial statements of Company A and pays $5m to buy the company, but it soon becomes clear that the company is worth only $1m, then a loss of $4m has been incurred.

Case Study: Caparo

The Caparo case (Caparo Industries v Dickman and others (1984))

Caparo Industries took over Fidelity plc in 1984 and alleged that it increased its shareholding on the basis of Fidelity's accounts, audited by Touche Ross. Caparo sued Touche Ross for alleged negligence in the audit, claiming that the stated $1.3m profit for the year to 31 March 1984 should have been reported as a loss of $460,000.

It was held in this case that the auditors owed no duty of care in carrying out the audit to individual shareholders or to members of the public who relied on the accounts in deciding to buy shares in the company.

The House of Lords looked at the purpose of statutory accounts. They concluded that such accounts, on which the auditor must report, are published with the principal purpose of providing shareholders as a class with information relevant to exercising their proprietary interests in the company. They are not published to assist individuals (whether existing shareholders or not) to speculate with a view to profits.

Case Study: Bannerman

The Bannerman case (Royal Bank of Scotland (RBS) v Bannerman Johnstone Maclay (2002))

RBS provided overdraft facilities to APC Limited and Bannerman were APC's auditors. The relevant facility letters between RBS and APC contained a clause requiring APC to send RBS, each year, a copy of the annual audited financial statements.

In 1998 APC was put into receivership with approximately $13.25m owing to RBS. RBS claimed that, due to a fraud, APC's financial statements for the previous years had misstated the financial position of APC and Bannerman had been negligent in not detecting the fraud. RBS contended that it had continued to provide the overdraft facilities in reliance on Bannerman's unqualified opinions.

Bannerman applied to the court for an order striking out the claim on the grounds that, even if all the facts alleged by RBS were true, the claim could not succeed in law because Bannerman owed no duty of care to RBS.

> The judge held that the facts pleaded by RBS were sufficient in law to give rise to a duty of care and so the case could proceed to trial. The judge held that, although there was no direct contact between Bannerman and RBS, knowledge gained by Bannerman in the course of their ordinary audit work was sufficient, in the absence of any disclaimer, to create a duty of care owed by Bannerman to RBS. In order to consider APC's ability to continue as a going concern, Bannerman would have reviewed the facilities letters and so would have become aware that the audited financial statements would be provided to RBS for the purpose of RBS making lending decisions. Having acquired this knowledge, Bannerman could have disclaimed liability to RBS but did not do so. The absence of such a disclaimer was an important circumstance supporting the finding of a duty of care.

13 Restricting auditors' liability

Ways in which liability may be restricted

Audit firms may take the following steps to minimise their exposure to negligence claims:

- screening potential audit clients to accept only clients where the risk can be managed
- using a letter of engagement as per ISA 210 in order to establish the respective responsibilities and duties of directors and auditors
- carrying out high quality audit work
- using clauses to disclaim liability to third parties
- taking out professional indemnity insurance (PII)
- attempting to regulate the use of documents and restrict their use to their specific, intended purpose
- obtaining specialist legal advice where appropriate.

Current issue: Disclaimer statements

Reaction to the Bannerman decision – disclaimer statements

In the Bannerman case the judge commented that, if the auditors had inserted a disclaimer statement in their audit report, then they would have had no legal liability to RBS who was suing them.

Following this case, the ICAEW recommended additional wording to be routinely included in all audit reports by ICAEW members, on the lines of:

'This report is made solely to the company's members as a body. Our audit work has been carried out so that we might state to the company's members those matters we are required to state to them in an audit report and for no other purpose. We do not accept responsibility to anyone other than the company and the company's members as a body, for our audit work or for the opinions we have formed.'

The ACCA's view (in Technical Factsheet 84) is that standard disclaimer clauses should be discouraged since they could have the effect of devaluing the audit report. Disclaimers of responsibility should be made in appropriate, defined circumstances (e.g., where the auditor knows that a bank may rely on a company's financial statements) but the ACCA does not believe that, where an audit is properly carried out, such clauses are always necessary to protect auditors' interests.

In practice, the difference of opinion between the ICAEW and the ACCA may not be so great. If an ACCA auditor is not aware that a bank is going to place reliance on an audit report (so no disclaimer is given), then it seems likely under Caparo or Bannerman that no duty of care would be owed to the bank in any event.

The impact of limiting audit liability

Some commentators have argued that limiting audit liability is contrary to the public interest, since auditors will be less motivated to do a first class job if they know that they won't have to pay for their mistakes.

Other commentators say that this ignores the professional nature of the audit discipline. People choose to be audit partners because they want to do a high quality job for themselves and for society.

Possible methods of limiting audit liability

(a) **A financial cap on liability**

This could be a fixed amount (as in Germany) or a multiple of the audit fee. A possible adverse effect of the latter would be to either reduce the quality of work done, or to reduce the fee, as the lower the fee, the lower the liability.

(b) **Incorporating audit firms as limited liability partnerships (now permitted in the UK under the Limited Liability Partnerships Act 2000).**

chapter 8

(c) **Permitting auditors to agree the limits of their liability with their clients**

In the UK such agreements were illegal until the Companies Act 2006, which now permits 'liability limitation agreements' between auditors and companies, subject to shareholders' approval. The Act does not specify what sort of limit can be agreed, so a fixed cap, or a multiple of fees, or any other type will all now be possible once this section of the Act has been implemented.

(d) **Modification of the 'joint and several liability' principle**

Auditors are jointly and severally liable with directors where negligence claims are made, either under legislation, or under case law. This means that directors and auditors are held responsible together for the issue of negligently prepared and audited financial statements. If, say, the auditors and directors share the blame for falsifying records (i.e. the auditors did not detect it), the auditor may bear all of the costs if the directors have no resources to pay. The objective is to protect the plaintiff and maximise their chances of recovery of losses. The effect in practice is to load all of the costs onto auditors who have to be insured!

An associated problem is the fact that all partners and directors are responsible for the misconduct of other partners and directors in audit firms, regardless of whether they were directly involved in a particular audit. In the US - and now the UK - this problem is partly dealt with by limited liability partnerships.

(e) **Compulsory insurance for directors – for the reasons noted in above.**

Professional indemnity insurance

One of the obligations of practising as a professional accountant is to ensure that, if an accountant's negligence has caused loss to a client, the accountant has an insurance policy to ensure that he can pay any damages awarded.

- **Professional indemnity insurance (PII)** is insurance taken out by an accountant against claims made by clients and third parties arising from work that the accountant has carried out.

- **Fidelity guarantee insurance (FGI)** is insurance taken out by an accountant against any liability arising through acts of fraud or dishonesty by any partner or employee in respect of money or goods held in trust by the accountancy firm.

If an accountant did not have PII, it is possible that a successful claim could be made against him in excess of his personal resources, so that the claimant could not be paid.

Settlements out of court

On occasions legal cases may be settled out of court due to negotiation between the plaintiff and the dependent.

Benefits

- Cost saving (i.e. lower fees);
- Time saving;
- Less risk of damage to reputation.

Drawbacks

- Does not address the importance of the practitioner's legal responsibilities; and
- May be due to pressure from insurers, who are willing to risk a court settlement; and
- Insurance premiums may still rise.

14 The expectation gap

The **expectation gap** is the gap between what the public believe that auditors do (or ought to do) and what they actually do.

This expectation gap can be categorised into:

- a **standards gap** – where the public believe auditing standards to be different from what they actually are.
- a **performance gap** – where auditors operate below current standards.
- a **liability gap** – where the public do not understand to whom the auditor is legally responsible.

chapter 8

Expectations gap: Examples

Typical manifestations of the expectation gap are:

- the public believe that auditors are responsible for preventing and detecting fraud and error, while auditors maintain that they need only have a reasonable expectation of detecting material fraud and error.

- the public believe that they can sue the auditors if companies fail, while auditors maintain that it is the directors' responsibility to run their business as a going concern, and following Caparo it is not the auditor's function to protect individual shareholders if they make a poor investment decision.

Bridging the gap

Recent developments include:

- educating the public to reduce the standards gap e.g. the 'long-form' audit report now specifically states the auditor's responsibilities, detail that was not included in the shorter wording used previously

- improving the quality of audits to reduce the performance gap.

- possible changes in auditors' liability.

Exam style question: Ethical, professional and legal issues

Study note: this question is typical of the current P7 exam. It is one of the 'core' topics identified in the 'Examiner's Approach to Paper P7' article (January 2007). Therefore a question of this nature (or similar case style presentation) should be expected in each sitting of P7.

You are an audit manager in Ebony, a firm of Chartered Certified Accountants. Your specific responsibilities include planning the allocation of professional staff to audit assignments. The following matters have arisen in connection with the audits of three client companies:

(a) The Finance Director of Almond, a private limited company, has requested that only certain staff are to be included on the audit team to prevent unnecessary disruption to Almond's accounting department during the conduct of the audit. In particular, that Xavier be assigned as accountant in charge (AIC) of the audit and that no new trainees be included in the audit team. Xavier has been the AIC for this client for the last two years.

(5 marks)

KAPLAN PUBLISHING   165

Professional responsibilities and liabilities

(b) Alex was one of the audit trainees assigned to the audit of Phantom, a private limited company, for the year ended 31 March 2004. Alex resigned from Ebony with effect from 30 November 2004 to pursue a career in medicine. Kurt, another AIC, has just told you that on the day Alex left he told Kurt that he had ticked schedules of audit work as having been performed when he had not actually carried out the tests.

(5 marks)

(c) During the recent interim audit of Magenta, a private limited company, the AIC, Jamie, has discovered a material error in the prior year financial statements for the year ended 31 December 2003. These financial statements had disclosed an unquantifiable contingent liability for pending litigation. However, the matter was settled out of court for $4.5 million on 14 March 2004. The auditor's report on the financial statements for the year ended 31 December 2003 was signed on 19 March 2004. Jamie believes that Magenta's management is not aware of the error and has not drawn it to their attention.

(5 marks)

Required:

Comment on the ethical, quality control and other professional issues raised by each of the above matters and their implications, if any, for Ebony's staff planning.

Note: The mark allocation is shown against each of the three issues.

(Total: 15 marks)

Test your understanding 1

You are the auditor of Promise Co. The Finance Director has asked for a meeting with you. She recently discovered that the purchase ledger manager has diverted company funds into his own bank account. The Finance Director has identified funds of $50,000 to date as being diverted and wants and explanation as to why you did not highlight this issue during the course of your recently completed audit. The profit for the year was $17.5m. Prepare a set of briefing notes to assist you in your meeting with the Finance Director.

chapter 8

Test your understanding 2

You are the auditor of a chain of restaurants. You have noticed a newspaper report that guests at a wedding have fallen ill after eating at one of your client's restaurants.

What impact should this report have on your considerations of compliance with laws and regulations and what audit procedures would you perform?

Test your understanding 3

The directors of Jubilee Ltd have asked your firm to produce a much more detailed report at the end of the audit than usual, listing down all the deficiencies in the internal control system. They are unhappy that during the course of the year discounts had been given to customers who did not qualify for them, as a result of the non-application of an internal control process. They have expressed dissatisfaction with your audit firm as this control deficiency was not reported to them by your firm.

Draft points to include in your reply to Jubilee Ltd.

Test your understanding 4

A recent industry commentator has written: "In respect of the many recent corporate collapses, the auditor is often seen as the easy scapegoat. Not least because of their professional indemnity insurance. This damages the reputation of the profession and over time can only lead to reduction in the number and quality of skilled audit practioners, and a consequential increase in costs to their clients. Legislation has to be changed, in order to protect the auditor and the future of the profession, to allow auditors to agree a contractual cap on their liability for statutory audits."

Set out what you believe are the arguments for and against allowing auditors to agree on a contractual cap as described above.

Professional responsibilities and liabilities

Test your understanding 5: 'Lambley'

The partner in charge of your audit firm has asked your advice on frauds which have been detected in recent audits.

(a) The audited financial statements of Lambley Trading were approved by the shareholders at the AGM on 3 June 20X2. On 7 June 20X2 the managing director of Lambley Trading discovered a petty cash fraud by the cashier. Investigation of this fraud has revealed that it has been carried out over a period of a year. It involved the cashier making out, signing and claiming petty cash expenses which were charged to motor expenses. No receipts were attached to the petty cash vouchers. The managing director signs all cheques for reimbursing the petty cash float. Lambley Trading has sales of about $2 million and the profit before tax is about $150,000. The cashier has prepared the draft financial statements for audit.

The partner in charge of the audit decided that no audit work should be carried out on petty cash. He considered that petty cash expenditure was small, so the risk of a material error or fraud was small.

You are required to:

(i) briefly state the auditor's responsibilities for detecting fraud and error in financial statements

(ii) consider whether your firm is negligent if the fraud amounted to $5,000

(iii) consider whether your firm is negligent if the fraud amounted to $20,000.

(9 marks)

(b) The audit of directors' remuneration at Colwick Enterprises, a limited company, has confirmed that the managing director's salary is $450,000, and that he is the highest paid director. However, a junior member of the audit team asked you to look at some purchase invoices paid by the company. Your investigations have revealed that the managing director has had work amounting to $200,000 carried out on his home, which has been paid by Colwick Enterprises. The managing director has authorised payment of these invoices and there is no record of authorisation of this work in the board minutes. The managing director has refused to include the $200,000 in his remuneration for the year, and to change the financial statements. If you insist on qualifying your audit report on this matter, the managing director says he will get a new firm to audit the current year's financial statements. The company's profit before tax for the year is $91 million.

Assuming the managing director refuses to amend the financial statements, **you are required to:**

(i) consider whether the undisclosed remuneration is a material item in the financial statements

(ii) describe the matters you will consider and the action you will take:
– to avoid being replaced as auditor; and
– if you are replaced as auditor

assuming the managing director owns 60% of the issued shares of Colwick Enterprises.

(iii) describe the matters you will consider and the action you will take to avoid being replaced as auditor, assuming Colwick Enterprises is a listed company with an audit committee, and the managing director owns less than 1% of the issued shares.

(11 marks)

(Total: 20 marks)

15 Legal liability – summary

> **AN AUDITOR MAY HAVE A CIVIL OR CRIMINAL LIABILITY ARISING FROM LEGISLATION, OR A LIABILITY UNDER COMMON LAW ARISING FROM NEGLIGENCE.**

> **IN THE TORT OF NEGLIGENCE, THE PLAINTIFF MUST PROVE:**
> - the auditor owes them a duty of care
> - the auditor has breached this duty
> - the plaintiff has suffered loss as a direct result.

> **KEY LEGAL CASES INCLUDE CAPARO AND BANNERMAN. THE BANNERMAN CASE EMPHASISES THE ADVANTAGES OF INCLUDING DISCLAIMER STATEMENTS IN THE AUDIT REPORT IN RELEVANT CIRCUMSTANCES.**

> **THE BEST WAY TO AVOID PAYING OUT MONEY FOR NEGLIGENCE CLAIMS IS TO CARRY OUT HIGH QUALITY AUDITS IN THE FIRST PLACE.**

> **HISTORICALLY THERE HAS BEEN AN EXPECTATION GAP BETWEEN WHAT THE PUBLIC BELIEVE AUDITORS DO, AND WHAT THEY ACTUALLY DO. THE PROFESSION IS TRYING TO EDUCATE THE PUBLIC, IN ORDER TO CLOSE THE GAP.**

chapter 8

Test your understanding answers

Exam style question: Ethical, professional and legal issues

Study note: as indicated in the 'Examiner's Approach to Paper P7' article (January 2007) the majority of marks will be awarded for application of knowledge to the scenario. Regurgitation of rote-learned facts will not score well in P7. Therefore, in your answer keep referring to the situations, companies and individuals described in the question.

It is also important to answer the question set! Too many candidates focus solely on ethical issues and therefore restrict the pool of marks they can access. Therefore, breakdown each sub question into its basic components and structure your plan and answer around those components. The use of headings (as shown below) is an effective (and neat) way of doing this.

Although a good working knowledge of the professional codes is required here and an ability to apply them, students must be able to deal with these situations in a way which satisfies the professional requirements, maintains audit quality and is satisfactory in maintaining a mutually beneficial relationship with the clients concerned. A common sense approach is required. In situation (c) the accounting/reporting implications must be considered.

(a) **Audit team**

- There are many factors to be taken into account when allocating staff to an assignment, for example:
    - the number of staff and levels of technical expertise required;
    - logistics of time and place;
    - the needs of staff (e.g. for study leave); and
    - what is in the client's (i.e. the shareholders') best interest (e.g. an expeditious audit).

- As a matter of practice management, a client should not dictate who staffs their audit. If the Finance Director's requests are based solely on the premise that to have staff other than as requested would cause disruption then he should be assured that anyone assigned to the audit will be:
    - technically competent to perform the tasks delegated to them;
    - adequately briefed and supervised; and
    - mindful of the need not to cause unnecessary disruption.

KAPLAN PUBLISHING

171

- Ebony may have other (more complex) assignments on which Xavier (and other staff previously involved in the audit of Almond) could be better utilised.

- To re-assign Xavier to the job may be to deny him other on-the-job training necessary to his personal development. For example, he may be ready to assume a more demanding supervisory role with another client – or he may wish to expand the client base on which he works to obtain a practicing certificate (say).

- To keep Xavier with Almond for a third year may also increase the risk of familiarity with the client's staff – a threat to the independence of the audit.

- If it is usual to assign new trainees to Almond then the Finance Director should be advised that to assign a higher grade of staff is likely to increase the audit fee (as more experienced staff cannot necessarily do the work of more junior staff in any less time).

Conclusion

The Finance Director's requests should be granted only if:

(1) it is in the interests of Almond's shareholders (primarily);

(2) meets the needs of Ebony's staff; and

(3) Almond agrees to the commensurate audit fee.

(b) **'Phantom ticking'**

- Ebony's quality control procedures should be such that:
    - the work delegated to Alex was within his capability;
    - Alex was supervised in its execution; and
    - the work performed by Alex was reviewed by appropriate personnel (i.e. someone of at least equal competence).

- Alex's working papers for the audit of Phantom should be re-reviewed to confirm that there is evidence of his work having been properly directed, supervised and reviewed. If there is nothing which appears untoward – it should be discussed with Alex's supervisor on the assignment whether Alex's confession to Kurt could have been 'a joke'.

- As Alex has already left not only the firm, but the profession, it may not seem worth the effort taking any disciplinary action against him (e.g. reporting the [alleged] misconduct to ACCA). However, ACCA's disciplinary committee would investigate such a matter and take appropriate action.

- It is likely that Ebony will have given Alex's new employer a reference. This should be reviewed in the light of any evidence which may cast aspersions on Alex's work ethics.

- As there are now doubts about the integrity of Alex, his work should now be re-reviewed, to determine the risk (if any) that the conclusions drawn on his work may be unsubstantiated (in terms of the relevance, reliability and sufficiency of audit evidence).

- It should also be considered whether the reviewer of Alex's work should have seen the problem. (For example, in a purchase test, the reviewer should have been put upon enquiry if a test indicated that a goods received note had been inspected where a purchase was clearly for services provided and not goods received.) If the reviewer did not detect an evident problem they should be (re)trained as necessary.

- The work undertaken by Alex for audit clients other than Phantom should also be subject to scrutiny.

Conclusion

As Kurt is already aware of the potential problem, it may be appropriate that he be assigned as AIC to audits on which Alex undertook audit work, as he will be alert to any ramifications. It is possible that Ebony should not want to make the situation known to its staff generally.

(a) **Prior year audit failure**

- It appears that the subsequent events review was inadequate in that an adjusting event (the out-of-court settlement) was not taken account of.

- The financial statements for the year ended 31 December 2003 contained a material error in that they disclosed a contingent liability (of unspecified amount) when a provision should have been made (for a known liability).

- The reasons for the error/oversight should be ascertained. For example:
  - who was responsible for signing off on the post statement of financial position event review?
  - when was the review completed?
  - for what reason, if any, was it not extended to the date of signing the audit report?
  - on what date was the management representation letter signed?
  - did the management representation letter cover the outcome of pending litigation (for example)?

- The error has implications for the firm's quality control procedures. For example:
    - was the AIC adequately directed and supervised in the completion of the post statement of financial position event review?
    - was the work of the AIC adequately reviewed, to notice (for example) that it was not extended up until the date on which the auditor's report was signed?
- Ebony may need to review and improve on its procedures for the audit of provisions, contingent liabilities and post statement of financial position events.
- If the AIC (or other staff) involved in the prior year audit of Magenta were not as thorough as they should have been, with respect to the post statement of financial position event review, then other audit clients may be similarly affected.
- The auditor has a duty of care to draw the error/oversight to Magenta's attention. This would be an admission of fault for which Ebony should be liable if Magenta were to take action against the firm.
- If Ebony were to remain silent and hope the error is unnoticed there is the risk that Magenta will find out anyway.
- As the matter is material it warrants a prior period adjustment (IAS 8 Accounting Policies, Changes in Accounting Estimates and Errors). If this is not made the financial statements will be materially misstated with respect to the current year and comparatives – because the expense of the out-of-court settlement should be attributed to the prior period and not the current year's net profit or loss.
- The most obvious implication for the current year audit of Magenta is that a more thorough post statement of financial position event review will be required than the previous year. This may have a consequent effect on the time/fee/staff budgets of Magenta for the year ended 31 December 2004.
- As the matter is material, it needs to be brought to the attention of Magenta's management, so that a prior year adjustment is made. In the absence of which a qualified auditor's report 'except for' should be required.

Conclusion

The staffing of the final audit of Magenta should be reviewed and perhaps a more experienced person assigned to the post statement of financial position event review than in the prior year. The assignments allocated to the staff responsible for the oversight in Magenta's prior period should be reviewed and their competence/capability re-assessed.

Test your understanding 1

Notes for meeting with Finance Director

- Engagement letter:
  - Refer to any specific points regarding work in this area
  - Refer to section on auditors and directors responsibilities
  - Client signed engagement letter
- Responsibility for detection of fraud primarily responsibility of management
- Implementation of internal control system is responsibility of management
- Auditors role is to obtain *reasonable assurance* that financial statements are free from *material error*
- Amounts in question not material
- Ascertain how FD discovered fraud
- Ascertain how amounts of diverted funds were quantified
- Discuss whether there might be further unidentified sums

Professional responsibilities and liabilities

Test your understanding 2

The auditor should consider whether any laws or regulations have been broken (for example laws and regulations over health and safety, food hygiene, product use by dates etc.).

Procedures include:

- obtaining a general understanding of the relevant legal and regulatory framework
- talking to the directors and other appropriate management (perhaps at the local level) to assess compliance or not
- examining relevant documentation, for example correspondence with the local authority and hygiene inspectors
- evaluating the financial impact of the non-compliance (for example, possible penalties, the cost of compensation claims, the cost of remedial action, the impact on the value of the brand name)
- obtain management representations re full disclosure of non-compliance and its impact
- consult experts in the area if considered necessary.

Test your understanding 3

Auditors must determine the most effective approach to each area of the financial statements. This may involve testing of the internal controls or substantive procedures, or a combination of the two.

Where the auditors choose to test the internal control systems of the company, they must design their work so as to have a reasonable expectation of detecting any weaknesses which would be likely to result in a material misstatement in the financial statements.

The area of discounts may have been one which did not involve testing of the internal controls as analytical procedures are likely to be effective.

Even if the controls in this area were tested, if the discounts given to customers were recorded accurately in the financial statements then no material error is likely to result. This would again make detection less likely. Jubilee must be reminded that the control weaknesses report issued at the conclusion of the audit is simply a by-product of the audit function and is not intended to be a comprehensive list of all possible weaknesses.

Should Jubilee Ltd require a more comprehensive review, then this could be undertaken as a separate assurance assignment.

Test your understanding 4

For

- Avoid firms exiting from the statutory audit market and thus maintaining choice and competition
- Management of costs for both audit firms and their clients
- Clearly quantifies the extent of auditors liability – clear to the public
- Reduces risk of auditors being used as scapegoats and hence:
- Ensures that directors bear their extent of liability

Against

- Auditors may not feel as accountable or be seen to be as accountable
- Auditors who carry out their work with due professional skill and care should not fear unlimited liability
- May reduce the perceived value of an audit if risk to auditors is reduced
- Extent of cap may be a difficult and contentious issue to agree with the client
- Shareholders, or other parties to whom the auditors owe a duty of care may find themselves inadequately protected
- Level of cap would have to be agreed with directors who may be tempted to agree to a lower cap in order to save on fees – this may not afford shareholders sufficient protection

Professional responsibilities and liabilities

Test your understanding 5: 'Lambley'

There are three main aspects of auditing examined in this question – the role of and potential liability of the auditor in connection with the detection and prevention of fraud, the concept of materiality and the position of the auditor when threatened with dismissal and replacement.

Note that in questions involving materiality, the usual assumption is that, as regards the effect on profit and/or assets and liabilities, a difference of less than 5% is not material, a difference of more than 10% is material, and differences between these limits may be material depending on the circumstances.

(a) **Lambley Trading**

　(i) ISA 240 The Auditor's Responsibility to Consider Fraud in an Audit of Financial Statements says that auditors should design their audit procedures so as to have a reasonable expectation of detecting material fraud and error in the financial statements. So, an auditor is probably liable (in negligence) if he fails to detect material fraud and error. However, the auditor may not be liable if the fraud is difficult to detect (i.e. the fraud had been concealed and it is unreasonable to expect the auditor to have detected the fraud).

For immaterial fraud and error, a claim for negligence against the auditor for not detecting immaterial fraud or error would be unsuccessful (except in the circumstances described in the next section). An auditor may be negligent if he:

– finds an immaterial fraud while carrying out his normal procedures and does not report it to the company's management (but he may not be negligent if the evidence to support a suspected fraud is weak)

– carries out audit procedures on immaterial items, of which the company's management is aware, and these procedures are not carried out satisfactorily, so failing to detect an immaterial fraud. For instance, there may be a teeming and lading fraud, and the auditor may check receipts from sales are correctly recorded in the cash book and sales ledger, but fail to check that the cash from these sales is banked promptly.

– carries out audit procedures on immaterial items at the specific request of the company's management, and the auditor failed to detect an immaterial fraud due to negligent work. The management would have a good case to claim damages for negligence against the auditor.

(ii) The fraud of $5,000 is 3.3% of the company's profit before tax, so it is immaterial. As the auditor has carried out no work in this area, and is not responsible for detecting immaterial fraud, it is probable that he is not negligent. It could be argued that the other audit procedures should have detected an apparent irregularity, such as analytical review. This might have indicated an increase in motor expenses compared with the previous year and budget, or the auditor could have looked at petty cash expenditure, which would show an increase compared with the previous year.

It could also be argued that the auditor should have looked at the absolute level of petty cash expenditure in order to decide whether to carry out work on the petty cash system. However, these arguments against the auditor are relatively weak, and it is unlikely that a claim for negligence would be successful. However, not detecting the fraud is likely to lead to a deterioration of the client's confidence in the auditor.

(iii) The fraud of $20,000 is 13.3% of the company's profit before tax, so it is material. It appears that the auditor is negligent in not carrying out any audit work on petty cash, as he/she has contravened the advice given in ISA 240.

ISA 240 says the auditor should design audit procedures so as to have a reasonable expectation of detecting material fraud or error, so as he/she performed no work on petty cash there is no chance of him/her detecting the fraud. As a minimum, the auditor should have looked at the level of petty cash expenditure, comparing it with the previous year and the budget. This should have highlighted the increase in expenditure and led to the auditor carrying out further investigations. As this is a petty cash fraud, it could be difficult to detect, but the cashier writing out and signing the petty cash vouchers, with no receipt attached, should have led the auditor to suspect the fraud.

It could be argued that the company has some responsibility for allowing the fraud to take place, as there was a serious weakness in the system of internal control (i.e. the cashier recorded and made petty cash payments, and appeared to be able to authorise petty cash vouchers). So, some employee (e.g. the managing director) should have checked the cashier's work. Also, the managing director would have signed cheques which reimburse the petty cash, and he should have been aware that these had increased and investigated the reasons for the increase.

Professional responsibilities and liabilities

(b) **Colwick Enterprises**

(i) In terms of profit before tax, the sum of $200,000 is immaterial. Normally a material item, in terms of profit before tax is an error which exceeds either 5% of the profit before tax (i.e. $4.55m) or 10% of the profit before tax (i.e. $9.1m), so $200,000 is very small. However, in terms of the director's remuneration, the $200,000 is 44% of the managing director's annual salary of $450,000. Directors' remuneration is a very important item in financial statements, both as far as legal requirements are concerned, and to the readers of accounts. For example, recent press reports and public interest in the remuneration of directors of public companies in the UK (particularly the privatised utilities) has confirmed the importance of this figure in financial statements. The company is proposing that the financial statements should show only 69% of the managing director's remuneration, so the understatement is very material.

(ii) If the managing director refused to change the financial statements, I would have to qualify my audit report and state his total emoluments are $650,000. However, it seems probable that he will try to dismiss me as auditor before I am able to give an audit report on the financial statements. In order to change the auditor, he must:

- find another auditor who is prepared to replace me as auditor and
- call a general meeting to vote on the change of auditor and
- notify the shareholders, the new auditor, and myself, as retiring auditor.

I may have the right to make representations to the shareholders, which can either be sent to the shareholders before the meeting, and/or I can make the representations at the meeting when it is proposed that I am replaced.

Although these representations are likely to have little effect on the change of auditor (as the managing director owns 60% of the shares, and only a 50% vote is required to change the auditor), it would alert the other shareholders to the action of the managing director and concealment of information.

As a further point, provided the new auditors are a member of the ACCA or one of the recognised bodies, the ethical rules require the new auditor to write to me asking if there are any matters I ought to bring to their attention to enable them to decide whether or not they are prepared to accept the audit appointment. I will reply to their letter, saying that the managing director has had $200,000 of benefits-in-kind, which he refuses to allow to be disclosed in the financial statements. I have explained to the managing director that I would have to qualify my audit report if these emoluments are not disclosed, and this is the reason why he is proposing that I should be replaced as auditor. If the proposed new auditors have the expected amount of integrity, they should discuss this point with the managing director, and point out that they will have to qualify their audit report if the benefits of $200,000 are not included in his remuneration in the financial statements.

If the new auditors take over the appointment and give an unqualified report, I will take legal advice. The action I could take would include:

- disclosing information about the director's remuneration to the new auditor's professional body, and the fact that the audit report has not been qualified

- notifying the authorities of the alleged understatement of the managing director's remuneration

- disclosing the benefit to the tax authorities (as it may not have been subject to income tax)

- disclosing the benefit to the police.

(iii) If the managing director owned less than 1% of the issued shares, my position as auditor would be much stronger than in the situation in part (ii) above. If the managing director refused to increase his remuneration in the draft accounts, I would explain that I would have to contact the audit committee. If he still refused to change the remuneration, I would contact the chairman of the audit committee and arrange a meeting with its members. I would explain that I would have to qualify my audit report, unless the remuneration was increased to $650,000. Also, it is likely that either the company or the managing director is committing an offence by not disclosing this benefit to the tax authorities. It seems probable that this meeting will decide to incorporate the benefit in the financial statements.

However if the audit committee believes the financial statements should not be changed, I will have to insist on qualifying my audit report. If, at this stage, the directors decide to replace me as auditor, they will have to convene a general meeting for this purpose. I may be able to make representations in writing to the shareholders, and/or make those representations at the general meeting.

As Colwick Enterprises is a listed company, this information is likely to be picked up by the press and financial institutions, and result in adverse publicity for the company. In addition, it will make shareholders suspicious of the honesty of the managing director and the other directors.

It seems probable that the directors would realise the problems of adverse publicity if they try to replace me as auditor, and this will prevent them from proposing the change of auditor. So, it seems probable that the other directors will insist that the full remuneration of the managing director should be shown in the financial statements.

chapter 9

Planning, materiality and assessing the risk of misstatement

Chapter learning objectives

Upon completion of this chapter you will be able to:

- define materiality and performance materiality and demonstrate how it should be applied in financial reporting and auditing;
- identify and explain business risks, audit risks and risks of material misstatement for a given situation;
- discuss and demonstrate the use of analytical procedures in the planning of an assignment;
- explain how the result of planning procedures determines the relevant audit strategy; and
- explain the planning procedures specific to an initial audit engagement.

Planning, materiality and assessing the risk of misstatement

 This is a very important chapter. Planning, including risk assessment, normally makes up a significant number of marks in one of the compulsary questions within section A of the exam. It is also essential for all areas of the exam that you are able to assess the materiality of a matter. Materiality is explained in this chapter.

1 The audit strategy and plan

The auditor should establish an overall strategy for the audit. This addresses such matters as:

- Which resources to deploy for specific audit areas;
- The amount of resources to deploy;
- When resources are deployed; and
- How those resources are managed, directed and supervised.

In establishing the strategy ISA 300 *Planning an Audit of Financial Statements* states that the auditor shall:

- Identify the characteristics of the engagement that define its scope;
- Ascertain the reporting objectives of the engagement;
- Consider the factors that are significant in directing the engagement team's efforts;
- Consider the results of preliminary engagement activities; and
- Ascertain the nature, timing and extent of resources necessary to perform the engagement.

Once the strategy has been established the auditor should develop an audit plan. This is more detailed than the strategy and includes a description of:

- The nature, timing and extent of planned risk assessment procedures;
- The nature timing and extent of further audit procedures;
- The nature, timing and extent of direction and supervision of engagement team members and the review of their work; and
- Other planned audit procedures required to comply with ISA's.

Both the strategy and the plan must be formally documented in the audit working papers.

2 The impact of ISAs

The risk-based approach to auditing

The adoption of International Standards on Auditing was an important junction in the evolution of audit methodology. Certain standards included direct reference to the need for auditors to consider and reduce their exposure to audit risk.

This overwhelming principle is laid out in ISA 200 *Overall Objectives of the Independent Auditor and the Conduct of an Audit in Accordance with International Standards on Auditing*. It lists the objectives of an audit, including: the need for the auditor to express an opinion on the truth and fairness of the financial statements; the need to carry out the audit in accordance with ISAs; and the need for professional scepticism, etc.

It also introduces the concept of audit risk:

'Reasonable assurance is a high level of assurance. It is obtained when the auditor has obtained sufficient appropriate evidence to reduce audit risk to an acceptably low level.'

In other words, for an audit to be conducted in accordance with ISAs, the auditor **must** use a risk-based approach.

ISAs 315 and 330

These two ISAs are vitally important!

ISA 315 (Revised) *Identifying and Assessing the Risks of Material Misstatement through Understanding the Entity and Its Environment* (issued March 2012, effective for audits of financial statements for periods ending on or after December 15, 2013) clearly prescribes the responsibility of the auditor for adopting a risk based approach:

"The objective of the auditor is to identify and assess the risks of material misstatement, whether due to fraud or error, at the financial statement and assertion levels, through understanding the entity and its environment, including the entity's internal control, thereby providing a basis for designing and implementing responses to the assessed risks of material misstatement."

In a nutshell: an assessment of risk must take place at the planning phase of an audit to assist with the design of further audit procedures.

ISA 330 *The Auditor's Response to Assessed Risks* further develops the concept by stating that:

Planning, materiality and assessing the risk of misstatement

"The objective of the auditor is to obtain sufficient appropriate audit evidence regarding the assessed risks of material misstatement, through designing and implementing appropriate responses to those risks."

The ISA's are clear: auditors should assess the risk of misstatement at the planning phase and design audit tests to respond to that risk assessment. Failure to comply with these requirements (or failure to document that these processes have been followed) could constitute professional negligence.

> ### F8 recap: Audit risk
>
> **Audit Risk = Inherent Risk x Control Risk x Detection Risk.**
>
> **'Inherent risk'** is the susceptibility of an assertion about a class of transaction, account balance or disclosure to a misstatement that could be material, before consideration of any related controls (i.e. that it occurs in the first place).
>
> **'Control risk'** is the risk that a misstatement that could occur (as above) will not be prevented, or detected and corrected, on a timely basis by the entity's internal control.
>
> **'Detection risk'** is the risk that the procedures performed by the auditor to reduce audit risk to an acceptably low level will not detect a misstatement that exists that could be material.
>
> (ISA 200)

3 Risk assessment

According to ISA 315 auditors are required to identify and assess the risks of material misstatement through understanding the client entity and its environment and through understanding the internal control environment.

The revised ISA 315 states that when assessing the control environment the auditor may also consider how management has responded to the findings and recommendations of the internal audit function regarding identified deficiencies in internal control relevant to the audit, including whether and how such responses have been implemented, and whether they have been subsequently evaluated by the internal audit function.

ISA 315 requires auditors to perform the following (minimum) risk assessment procedures:

- **Enquiries** with management, of appropriate individuals within the internal audit function (if there is one), and others (with relevant information) within the client entity (e.g. about external and internal changes the company has experienced)
- **Analytical procedures**
- **Observation** (e.g. of control procedures) and **inspection** (e.g. of key strategic documents and procedural manuals).

Analytical procedures

The term 'analytical procedure' means the evaluation of financial information through the analysis of plausible relationships among both financial and non-financial data. This is defined in ISA 520 *Analytical Procedures*

The purpose is to identify trends and/or relationships that are inconsistent with other relevant information or the auditor's understanding of the business. The purpose of this is to identify risk areas and guide the design of further audit procedures that are aimed at detecting and quantifying material misstatement.

Analytical procedures are used at varying stages throughout the audit:

- As part of risk assessment, in accordance with ISA 315
- As part of substantive audit procedures, in accordance with ISA's 500 and 520; and
- As part of the review of audit procedures, towards the end of the audit, in accordance with ISA 520.

The entity and its environment

Auditors should obtain an understanding of:

- Relevant industry, regulatory and other external factors;
- The nature of the entity, including:
    - Its operations;
    - Its ownership and governance structures;
    - The types of investment the entity makes; and
    - The way the entity is structured and financed.
- The entity's selection and application of accounting policies;

- The entity's objectives and strategies, and those related business risks that may result in material misstatement; and
- The measurement and review of the entity's financial performance.

If the entity has an internal audit function, obtaining an understanding of that function also contributes to the auditor's understanding of the entity and its environment, including internal control, in particular the role that the function plays in the entity's monitoring of internal control over financial reporting. This understanding, together with the information obtained from the auditor's inquiries described above may also provide information that is directly relevant to the auditor's identification and assessment of the risks of material misstatement.

The entity's internal control

Most controls relevant to the audit are likely to relate to financial reporting, although others may also have an impact. It is a matter of judgement whether an auditor ultimately considers a control to be relevant to the audit or not.

The components of internal control include:

- The control environment;
- The entity's risk assessment process;
- The information system relevant to financial reporting;
- The control activities; and
- The monitoring system.

The auditor must evaluate the design of the controls to determine whether they have been implemented during the financial reporting period and whether they are effective at preventing and detecting potentially material fraud and error.

Example risk assessment procedures

It is impossible to prepare a comprehensive list of risk assessment procedures that need to be carried out; the procedures need to be prepared in light of the unique circumstances of the client. However, examples include:

Enquiries of management:

- Have any share issues occurred during the year?
- Has the company invested in any new capital assets during the year?
- Have any new competitors or products entered the market?
- How does the company manage exposure to exchange rate risk?
- Have there been any changes in senior management during the year?

Analytical procedures:

- Compare actual results to the forecast to identify any significant changes to plan;
- Compare the client's performance and position to any available industry data to identify significant variations;
- Compare the client's financial statements in comparison to the prior year to identify and unexpected changes in performance or position.

Observe:

- The application of controls over the counting of inventory during the year;
- The performance of year-end reconciliations (bank, supplier statement) to ensure they are performed thoroughly;
- Month end adjustments/reconciliations being performed during an interim visit to ensure controls are applied throughout the year as well as at the end of it.

Planning, materiality and assessing the risk of misstatement

> **Inspect:**
>
> - Organisation charts to identify changes in key staff;
> - Company targets/strategic objectives to identify how they are performing in comparison or if there are any changes in product/market;
> - Examples of controls operating throughout the year, e.g. evidence of review of month end reconciliations, evidence of review of aged receivables on a monthly basis;
> - HR records/payroll records to identify movements in staff;
> - News/media reports to identify any significant issues, such as potential legal action.

4 Risk and the exam

In the examination it is likely you will get a question asking you to perform a risk assessment for a given scenario. The three types of risk examinable are:

- Business risk;
- Risk of material misstatement (financial statement risk);
- Audit risk.

It is vital that you understand the difference between these types of risk to ensure you answer the question appropriately.

Risk of material misstatement (financial statement risk)

Risk of material misstatement is the risk of a material misstatement in the financial statements (either due to fraud or error), prior to audit. Risk of material misstatement is comprised of **inherent and control risk**.

When evaluating the risk of material misstatement it is crucial to discuss the specific impact of the risk on the financial statements, i.e.

- the specific account balance, transaction or disclosure affected
- whether the item might be overstated, understated, omitted, inappropriately recognised, etc.

e.g. a technically complex area of accounting or client incentive and ability to manipulate the financial statements. Estimates are good examples of account balances that are prone to misstatement due to director bias and the simple inaccuracy of this process.

The auditor is also required to determine whether any of the risks are a significant risk. A significant risk is a risk of material misstatment that requires special audit consideration.

P7 includes four professional marks in one of the Section A questions, for clarity of explanation or evaluation, the use of logical structure and an appropriate format. In the exam, you should prioritise risks identified as this adds to the professionalism of the risk assessment performed.

The importance of financial reporting standards

The unmodified audit opinion states:

"In our opinion, the financial statements present fairly, in all material respects (or *give a true and fair view of*) the financial position of ABC Company as at December 31, 20X1, and (*of*) its financial performance and its cash flows for the year then ended **in accordance with International Financial Reporting Standards**."

Therefore, in order to reach this opinion, the auditor must fully understand the relevant financial reporting standards, and must evaluate whether the financial statements comply with these standards. This knowledge and understanding needs to be applied throughout the audit. Chapter 20 summarises the key points from these standards.

At the **planning** stage the auditor needs to undertake a **risk assessment**, including assessing the risk of material misstatement in the financial statements. The auditor must understand financial reporting standards in order to identify potential omission or incorrect measurement, recognition, presentation or disclosure of an item.

The risk of material misstatement will increase with the complexity of the financial reporting issue, and where the matter requires the use of significant judgement.

Audit risk

Audit risk is the risk that the auditor offers an inappropriate opinion. Therefore you are firstly required to identify any area of the financial statements that is prone to misstatement (i.e. risk of material misstatement). In addition to this you can factor in detection risk and discuss issues that might affect the conduct of the audit, such as: this is the first year of audit or the client is putting the auditor under undue time pressure.

Business risk

A business risk is one resulting from "significant events, conditions, circumstances, actions or inactions that could adversely affect an entity's ability to achieve its objectives and execute its strategies" (ISA 315). Business risk is broader than the risk of material misstatement.

A business risk is a **threat to an ongoing business objective**.

Auditors must assess business risk in order to:

- develop business understanding
- increase the likelihood of identifying specific risks of material misstatement
- evaluate overall audit risk.

Most business risks will eventually have financial consequences, and therefore an effect on the financial statements.

The difference between business risk and the risk of material

Operating in a technologically fast paced market could lead to a company's products being superseded by superior products. This is a **business risk** because it may stop a company achieving desired profit margins.

The **risk of material misstatement** is that inventory may be overstated in the financial statements: the net realisable value of inventory may have fallen below cost, requiring a write-down of inventory balances.

Business risks are often linked to inherent risk, or sometimes control risk. However, it is vital that you identify and discuss the specific risk category being examined.

Article focus

The examiner's article, *Exam technique for Paper P7* (May 2012), explains the difference between the types of risk examinable and the need for a different focus when answering the relevant requirements.

Another article, *Syllabus and study guide update* (March 2012), explains more about this distinction and the approach to risk assessment questions in the exam.

chapter 9

Examples of business risks

These risks are often categorised as being 'external' or 'internal' risks.

Typical 'external risks'	Typical 'internal risks'
changing legislation	employees
changing interest rates (N.B. Highly geared companies)	failure to modernise products, processes, labour relations, marketing
changing exchange rates	excessive reliance on a dominant CEO
public opinion, attitudes, fashions	cash flow difficulties
price wars initiated by competitors	rapidly increasing gearing
import competition	inappropriate acquisitions
untried technologies and ideas, political factors	overtrading
natural hazards	fraud
	excessive reliance on one or few products, customers, suppliers
	computer systems failures

5 Factors influencing the assessment of risk

As part of the risk assessment process auditors have to consider the significance of the identified risks, including:

- Whether the risk is one of fraud;
- Whether it is related to recent economic, accounting or other developments that require specific attention;
- The complexity of the related transactions;
- Whether it involves related parties;
- The degree of subjectivity involved in measuring financial information; and
- Whether it involves transactions outside the normal course of business.

If the auditor determines that a significant risk exists they must then obtain the necessary understanding of how the entity controls that risk. Only then can the auditor determine an appropriate response in terms of further audit procedures.

6 Response to risk assessment

The main purpose of performing risk assessment is to guide the auditor in the design and performance of further audit procedures to obtain sufficient appropriate audit evidence. On the whole the only way the auditor can reduce audit risk is by manipulating their **detection risk**. They can manipulate detection risk by:

- allocating complex or risky areas of the engagement to suitably experienced and competent staff, such as the audit of related party transactions and complex inventory calculations.
- placing more or less reliance on the results of systems and controls testing.
- altering the volume of substantive procedures performed after the year-end.
- altering the volume of balances tested by changing sample sizes.
- performing more or less substantive analytical procedures as opposed to other, more detailed ones.
- consulting external experts on technically complex or contentious matters.
- changing the timing and frequency of review procedures, including using additional partners to review work.
- developing expectations that can be used when performing substantive analytical procedures.
- emphasising the need for professional scepticism.

Professional scepticism

Professional scepticism is defined in ISA 200 as: 'An attitude that includes a questioning mind, being alert to conditions which may indicate possible misstatement due to error or fraud, and a critical assessment of audit evidence'.

It is both an ethical and professional issue; professional scepticism includes maintaining independence of mind.

The auditor must maintain professional scepticism throughout the planning and performance of the audit; recognising that circumstances may exist that cause the financial statements to be materially misstated.

Professional scepticism requires the auditor to be alert to:

- Audit evidence that contradicts other audit evidence.
- Information that brings into question the reliability of documents and responses to enquiries to be used as audit evidence.

- Conditions that may indicate possible fraud.
- Circumstances that suggest the need for audit procedures in addition to those required by ISAs.

In February 2012, the IAASB released *Questions and Answers: Professional Scepticism in an Audit of Financial Statements*, which provides additional explanations relating to professional scepticism.

Specifically, professional scepticism:

- is fundamentally a **mindset** that drives auditor behaviour to adopt a questioning approach
- is inseparably **linked to objectivity** and auditor independence
- forms an integral part of the auditor's skill set and is closely interrelated with **professional judgement**, both of which are key inputs to audit quality
- enhances the **effectiveness** of an audit procedure and **reduces** the **risk** of giving an inappropriate opinion.

The Q&A reiterates the **importance** of the components of **quality control** in enhancing the awareness of the importance and application of professional scepticism.

In addition, the Q&A emphasises that although professional scepticism is not referred to within each ISA, it is **relevant and necessary throughout the audit** and is particularly important in when considering the risks of material misstatement due to fraud and when addressing areas of the audit that are more complex, significant or highly judgemental (e.g. accounting estimates, going concern, related party transactions, non-compliance with laws and regulations).

Audit **documentation is critical in evidencing professional scepticism**, particularly documentation demonstrating how significant judgements and key audit issues were addressed, which may provide evidence of the auditor's exercise of professional scepticism.

Effective oversight and inspection of audits by regulators and oversight bodies should incorporate challenging, influencing and stimulating auditors to be sceptical and focusing auditors on the importance of professional scepticism and how it can be appropriately applied through constructive dialogue.

Planning, materiality and assessing the risk of misstatement

UK syllabus focus

In March 2012, the FRC released a Briefing Paper *Professional Scepticism*.

The briefing paper takes a theoretical approach to discussing the importance of professional scepticism in the audit - specifically:

- Exploring:
  - the roots of scepticism and identifying lessons for its role in the conduct of the audit
  - scientific scepticism
  - the origins of modern audit
- Concluding about professional scepticism and the audit and
- Discussing the conditions necessary for auditors to demonstrate professional scepticism.

The paper highlights the **significance of scepticism to the quality of the audit**. It defines scepticism as 'examination, inquiry into, hesitation or doubt' specifically, **doubt that stimulates challenge and inquiry**.

It explains that scientific scepticism is a 'systematic form of continual informed questioning', or **critical appraisal**, looking for evidence that contradicts management's assertions and suspending judgement about the validity of those assertions. In the context of an audit, this means **actively looking for risks of material misstatement**.

Assessing whether professional scepticism has been applied

In the exam you may be required to critically evaluate the planning or performance of an audit engagement. This will include assessing whether an engagement has been planned and performed with an attitude of professional scepticism.

Examples of circumstances where professional scepticsim has not been applied include:

- Contradictory evidence has not been questioned.
- The reliability of documents and responses to enquiries from the client has not been evaluated.
- The sufficiency and appropriateness of evidence has not been considered.

- The authenticity of a document has not been considered, when there are indications of possible fraud.
- Past experience of the dishonesty or lack of integrity of the client has been disregarded.
- The auditor has accepted less persuasive evidence because of their past experience of the honesty and integrity of the client.

If professional scepticism is not maintained, the auditor may:

- overlook unusual circumstances
- use unsuitable audit procedures
- reach inappropriate conclusions.

Professional skepticism reduces audit risk.

Current issues: Going concern

During times of economic hardship, particularly during recession, there is always an increase in the number of failed businesses. This does not just include small businesses, even significant institutions fail, for example; Lehman Brothers, a large Wall Street investment bank, filing for chapter 11 bankruptcy protection in September 2008.

During such times auditors must be aware that there is a heightened risk that companies may not be going concerns and that the basis of preparing the financial statements and the nature of disclosures relating to uncertainty must be closely scrutinised.

In response to the economic crisis, the FRC produced a Bulletin (2008/10) - *Going Concern Issues During the Current Economic Conditions* in December 2008 and in January 2009 the IAASB produced a practice alert *Audit Considerations in Respect of Going Concern in the Current Economic Environment*. Both publications explain the particular challenges the current economic conditions create including the need for increased disclosure about going concern and liquidity risk, and aim to raise auditors' awareness about matters relevant to the consideration of the use of the going concern assumption.

In response the P7 examiner produced an article entitled "Going Concern" (Feb 2010). This must therefore be considered an important issue. The nature of the auditor's responsibilities are considered in more detail in chapter 11 "Completion." However, it should be noted that consideration of going concern risks should be incorporated into all aspects of planning, performing and reviewing audit procedures.

7 Materiality

As stated in ISA 200, the objective of an audit is to express an opinion as to whether the financial statements are prepared, in all material respects, in accordance with an applicable financial reporting framework. It is therefore of vital importance for auditors to apply the concept of materiality in the planning and performance of the audit.

Various frameworks discuss materiality in slightly different terms. However, a generally accepted definition of materiality in the context of an audit is as follows:

"Misstatements, including omissions, are considered to be material if they, individually or in aggregate, could reasonably be expected to influence the economic decisions of users taken on the basis of the financial statements."

Unfortunately many practitioners have, in the past, applied materiality in a purely mechanical, numerical fashion. Whilst numerical guidelines are an accepted method for identifying a starting point in the consideration of materiality, arbitrary pre-conceived thresholds do not meet the above definition.

Calculation

ISA 320 recognises, and permits, the use of benchmark calculations of materiality. However, it must be stressed, that these should be used in the initial assessment of materiality. The auditor must then use judgement to modify materiality so that it is relevant to the unique circumstances of the client.

A traditional calculation basis is as follows:

	Value	Comments
Pre-tax profit	5 – 10%	Users usually interested in profitability of the company.
Turnover	½ – 1%	Materiality relates to the size of the business, which can be measured in terms of revenue
Total assets	1 – 2%	Size can also be measured in terms of the asset base

When deciding on an appropriate benchmark the auditor must consider:

- The elements of the financial statements;
- Whether particular items tend to be the focus of the users;
- The nature of the entity, its life cycle and its environment;
- The ownership and financing structure; and
- The relative volatility of the benchmark.

chapter 9

Performance materiality

Once materiality has been derived this does not act as a threshold for the performance of the entire audit in such a way that any uncorrected misstatement below the threshold will always be evaluated as immaterial. The circumstances surrounding some misstatements may cause the auditor to evaluate them even if they are below the threshold.

For this reason auditors must also consider what is known as 'performance materiality.'

This is an amount, established by the auditor, set below the materiality to be used when designing the nature, timing and extent of further procedures. The aim is to reduce the risk that misstatements in aggregate exceed materiality for the financial statements as a whole.

Performance materiality also considers the significance of individual classes of transaction, account balances or disclosures to the users of accounts.

Case Study: Performance materiality

LeJoG Co is a company that organises accommodation, luggage transportation, and support for charitable sporting enthusiasts attempting to travel from one end of the country to the other. All customers pay in full when booking their trip. LeJoG has a complicated cancellation policy; the amount refundable decreases with the length of time before the start of the trip.

The audit engagement team has planned the audit of the financial statements for the year ended 30 June 2012. The team has determined a materiality level for the financial statements as a whole, of $100,000, which has been calculated using an average of 1% of turnover, 2% total assets and 10% profit before tax. Performance materiality needs to be applied to revenue and the associated liabilities recognised when taking payment from customers in advance, as revenue recognition is an area of audit risk.

Performance materiality could be determined as a percentage of financial statement materiality, say 75%, i.e. a performance materiality of ($100,000 x 75%) $75,000 could be set for the audit of revenue and the associated liabilities. The audit team could use a higher or lower percentage, or use a different calculation, depending on their professional judgement.

The aim of performance materiality is to reduce the risk that misstatements in aggregate exceed materiality for the financial statements as a whole. For example, if a misstatement was identified of, say $80,000, without performance materiality the auditor would conclude that revenue is not materially misstated. However, the audit may not have detected further misstatements which when added to the $80,000 identified would result in a material misstatement. By using performance materiality, the auditor would conclude that a misstatement of $80,000 is material, reducing the risk of giving an inappropriate opinion.

Planning an initial audit engagement

There are additional considerations and procedures that are relevant for an audit where it is the first year that a firm has undertaken the audit of that client (an initial audit engagement).

ISA 510 *Initial Audit Engagements - Opening Balances* defines an audit engagement as:

An engagement in which either:

(i) The financial statements for the prior period were not audited; or

(ii) The financial statements for the prior period were audited by a predecessor auditor.

The procedures for auditing opening balances are dealt with in the chapter "Completion".

However, there are additional matters that the auditor will need to consider when planning an audit for an initial engagement. These are detailed in ISA 300 *Planning an Audit of Financial Statements* and include:

- Client acceptance procedures (see "Ethics and acceptance" chapter).

- Professional clearance (communicating with the predecessor auditor, see "Ethics and acceptance" chapter).

- Making arrangements to review the predecessor auditor's working papers.

- Holding consultations with management to discuss any major issues (including the application of accounting principles or of auditing and reporting standards), and consideration of how these matters affect the overall audit strategy and plan.

- Other procedures required by the firm's own system of internal control, e.g. "the involvement of another partner to review the overall strategy prior to commencing" the audit, or to review the audit report for an initial engagement prior to signing.

- Further expansion of planning procedures, because the auditor does not have "the previous experience with the entity that is considered when planning recurring engagements", e.g. familiarisation with the nature of the business, industry, and internal control systems of the client.

Additional time and resource may be necessary in the first year of an audit for a new client, in order to obtain the required knowledge of the client, e.g. documenting the internal control systems of the client for the first time.

In addition, it may be difficult to place reliance on analytical procedures as a source of substantive audit evidence as these require knowledge and experience of the client in order to set appropriate expectations, and therefore increased tests of detail may be necessary.

Social and environmental issues

Auditors must appreciate that their clients' social and environmental obligations may lead to liabilities that must be recognized in the financial statements.

- Certain types of enterprises are 'high risk' bodies in terms of social and environmental reporting.
- Typical examples are companies engaged in oil and gas exploration, shipping, and nuclear waste reprocessing.

Possible areas that might lead to the risk of material mis-statements include the following:

- provisions, e.g. for site restoration costs
- contingent liabilities, e.g. arising from pending legal action
- impairment of asset values, e.g. non-current assets or inventories that may be subject to environmental concern or contamination
- accounting for capital or revenue expenditure on cleaning up the production process or to meet legal or other standards
- product redesign costs
- product viability/going concern considerations.

When an auditor realizes that his client may have environmental issues that could have an impact on the financial statements, additional procedures should be designed and carried out to detect any potential mis-statements.

The following substantive procedures might be appropriate to detect potential mis-statements in respect of social-environmental matters:

- Obtain an appropriate understanding of the company, its operations, and, in particular, its environmental issues.
- Enquire of management as to any systems or controls that are in place to identify risk, evaluate control, and account for environmental matters.
- Obtain written representations from, and seek corroborative evidence of any statements by, management on any environmental matters.
- Obtain evidence from environmental experts where necessary.
- Use professional judgment to consider whether the evidence in relation to environmental matters is sufficiently persuasive.
- Review available documentation (board minutes, expert's reports, correspondence with authorities or lawyers etc)
- Review all assets for impairment.
- Review liabilities and provisions to ensure all have been included and contingencies to ensure adequate disclosure.
- Include environmental issues in the review of the appropriateness of going concern.

Auditing small and medium sized entities

Applying ISA's Proportionately with the Size and Complexity of an Entity (IAASB - August 2009)

The IAASB issued a publication to highlight how the design of the ISAs issued by the IAASB under the Clarity Project enables them to be applied in a manner proportionate with the size and complexity of an entity. Specifically, it focuses on matters that are likely to be of particular relevance to an audit of a small- and medium-sized entity (SME).

The auditor's objectives are the same for audits of entities of different sizes and complexities. This, however, does not mean that every audit will be planned and performed in exactly the same way. In particular ISAs explain that the appropriate audit approach for designing and performing audit procedures depends on the auditor's risk assessment and the exercise of appropriate professional judgment.

Often, SMEs engage in relatively simple business transactions, which means that their audits under will generally be relatively straightforward. For example, consider the requirement in ISA 315 for the auditor to obtain an understanding of the entity and its environment; the typically simpler structure and processes in an SME often mean that the auditor may obtain understanding quite readily and document this in a straightforward manner. Similarly, internal control in the context of an SME may be simpler.

Of particular relevance is the fact that the ISAs include useful guidance that assists the auditor in applying specific requirements in the ISAs in the context of an SME audit. Where appropriate, guidance is included in ISAs under the subheading, Considerations Specific to Smaller Entities. For example:

- Standard audit programs drawn up on the assumption of few relevant control activities may be used for the audit of an SME audit provided that they are tailored to the circumstances of the engagement;

- In the absence of interim or monthly financial information the auditor may need to plan to perform analytical procedures when an early draft of the entity's financial statements becomes available; and

- Given the potential lack of documentary evidence concerning control activities, the attitudes, awareness, and actions of management are of particular importance to the auditor's understanding of an SME's control environment.

Other guidance indicates that specific aspects of the audit will vary with the size, complexity, and nature of the entity, for example:

- The nature and extent of the auditor's planning activities;
- The auditor's consideration of fraud risk factors;
- The communication process between the auditor and those charged with governance;
- The level of detail at which to communicate significant deficiencies in internal control; and
- The judgment as to whether a control is relevant to the audit.

Not all of the ISAs are necessarily relevant in every audit—that is, the circumstances in which an ISA applies may not exist in the engagement. For example, some of the ISAs that may not be relevant in an SME audit include:

- ISA 402, if the client does not use a service organization;
- ISA 510, if it is a continuing, and not an initial, engagement;

- ISA 600, if it is not a group audit; and
- ISA 610, if there is no internal audit function.

Even if an ISA is relevant, not all of its requirements may be relevant in the particular circumstances of an audit. A few examples include:

- Holding an engagement team if it is only a one-person team;
- Performing the specified substantive procedures if the auditor has not identified previously unidentified or undisclosed related parties or related party transactions; and
- Obtaining sufficient appropriate audit evidence to determine whether a material uncertainty exists if the auditor has not identified any event or condition that casts doubt on the entity's ability to continue as a going concern.

Finally, to further assist the auditor, the ISAs provide examples of how the documentation in an SME audit can be approached in an efficient and effective manner. For example:

- It may be helpful and efficient to record various aspects of the audit together in a single document, with cross-references to supporting working papers as appropriate;
- The documentation of the understanding of the entity may be incorporated in the auditor's documentation of the overall strategy and audit plan;
- The results of the risk assessment may be documented as part of the auditor's documentation of further procedures;
- It is not necessary to document the entirety of the auditor's understanding of the SME and matters related to it; and
- A brief memorandum may serve as the documented audit strategy. At the completion of the audit, a brief memorandum could be developed and then updated to serve as the documented audit strategy for the following year's audit engagement.

Auditing significant, unusual or highly complex transactions

In August 2010, the IAASB issued a Questions & Answers publication called "Auditor considerations regarding significant unusual or highly complex transactions" in response to specific requests for information on how the ISAs deal with this particular topic.

The publication highlights that "because of their nature, these transactions may give rise to risks of material misstatement of the financial statements and, accordingly, may merit heightened attention by auditors."

The publication does not provide any additional guidance beyond that which is contained within the ISAs themselves. Instead, it highlights the most salient points from the ISAs for auditors to consider when approaching the audit of significant, unusual or highly complex transactions, and in particular highlights:

- What considerations in the ISAs are relevant when forming an opinion on the financial statements.

- What general considerations in the ISAs are relevant in relation to audit documentation, quality control, and interim reviews of financial statements when dealing with such transactions.

- How the ISAs guide the auditor in the auditor's communication with those charged with governance when dealing with such transactions.

The publication highlights many specific requirements of the ISAs, including:

- The requirement to "exercise professional judgment and maintain professional scepticism throughout the planning and performance of an audit".

- The need to "identify and assess the risks of material misstatement by performing risk assessment procedures designed to obtain the required understanding of the entity and its environment, including the entity's internal control".

- The requirement to "design and implement overall responses to address the assessed risks of material misstatement" and to "design and perform further audit procedures whose nature, timing, and extent are based on and are responsive to the assessed risks of material misstatement at the assertion level."

When approaching the audit of significant, unusual or highly complex transactions, the auditor should consider the need to obtain more persuasive audit evidence in responding to the assessed risks, as the auditor's assessment of risk is likely to be higher, in particular there is the possibility of i ncreased risk of bias in management's judgments due to the complexity involved therein.

Planning, materiality and assessing the risk of misstatement

Article focus

The P7 examiner, Lisa Weaver, has produced a two part article that discusses how she believes well prepared candidates should approach the reading, planning and writing of planning style questions.

The articles, entitled "How to Tackle Audit and Assurance Case Study Questions" (part 1 and 2) (Aug and Sep 2007) can be found on the ACCA website.

Test your understanding 1: 'Ivor'

You are the audit senior in a firm of accountants. One of the partners has given you some financial information for a client, Ivor Ltd, whose final audit is due to take place in a month's time. The partner has asked you to conduct an analytical review of the management accounts in comparison to the prior year's financial statements.

	31.12.2007 (Management Accounts)		31.12.2006 (Audited Financial Statements)	
	$000	$000	$000	$000
Statement of profit or loss				
Turnover		13,095		10,160
Sales discounts		(525)		(200)
		12,570		9,960
Cost of sales				
Opening inventory	1,200		1,085	
Purchases	10,150		7,830	
Purchase discounts	(154)		(112)	
Closing inventory	(1,640)		(1,200)	
		(9,556)		(7,603)
Gross profit		3,014		2,357
Distribution costs		(762)		(498)

206   KAPLAN PUBLISHING

Admin expenses

Wages and salaries	1,275		960	
Directors' salaries	125		115	
Depreciation:				
Land & buildings	18		40	
Plant & machinery	42		49	
Amortisation	26		25	
Rent	35		12	
Rates	5		4	
Gas and electricity	5		2	
Profit on disposal	(510)		(75)	
Bad Debts	8		7	
Insurance	16		15	
Cleaning	2		1	
Miscellaneous	15		10	
	────	(1,062)	────	(1,165)

Net profit before tax 1,190 694

Statement of financial position

Non-current assets

Tangible assets (note 1)		1,073		2,130
Intangible assets (note 2)		54		75
		────		────

Current assets 1,127 2,205

Inventory	1,640		1,200	
Trade receivables (note 3)	2,204		1,353	
Other receivables	46		42	
Cash	104		–	
	────	3,994	────	2,595
		5,121		4,800

Equity and liabilities			
Ordinary share capital		1,700	1,000
Retained earnings		1,894	1,004
		3,594	2,004
Non-current liabilities			
Bank loan		500	1,000
Current liabilities			
Overdrafts		–	129
Trade payables		703	1,479
Other payables		32	20
Tax payable		292	168
		1,027	1,796
		5,121	4,800

Note 1	Land & buildings $000	Plant & machinery $000	Total $000
Cost			
B/fwd at 1 Jan 2007	2,000	750	2,750
Disposals	(1,100)	–	(1,100)
C/fwd at 31 Dec 2007	900	750	1,650
Depn			
B/fwd at 1 Jan 2007	200	420	620
Disposals	(110)	–	(110)
Charge	18	49	67
C/fwd at 31 Dec 2007	108	469	577
NBV			
At 31 Dec 2007	792	281	1,073
At 31 Dec 2006	1,800	330	2,130

Buildings are depreciated over 50 years on a straight line basis.

Plant and machinery are depreciated at 15% using the reducing balance method.

Note 2
Development costs

	Total $
Cost	
B/fwd at 1 Jan 2007	125
Additions	5
C/fwd at 31 Dec 2007	130
Amortisation	
B/fwd at 1 Jan 2007	50
Charge	26
C/fwd at 31 Dec 2007	76
NBV	
At 31 Dec 2007	54
At 31 Dec 2006	75

Development costs are being depreciated over five years using the straight line method.

Note 3

	31.12.2007 $000	31.12.2006 $000
Trade receivables	2,274	1,423
Provision for doubtful debt	(70)	(70)
	2,204	1,353

Required:

Prepare an internal report for the partner that identifies and explains the audit risks discovered during your analytical review of the financial information that should be taken into consideration when planning the final audit of Ivor Ltd.

Note: Calculations for materiality are not required.

One professional mark is available.

(12 marks)

Planning, materiality and assessing the risk of misstatement

Test your understanding 2

Engine Ltd

You are the audit senior in a firm of accountants. You are assisting with the planning for the year end audit of one of your main clients, Engine Limited. The senior manager has asked you to perform an analytical review of the financial statements that she can use to brief the engagement partner of the key audit risks.

	30.06.2009 (Draft)		30.06.2008 (Audited)	
	$m	$m	$m	$m
Statement of profit or loss				
Turnover		128		107
Cost of sales				
Opening inventory	9		6	
Purchases	87		74	
Closing inventory	(14)		(9)	
		(82)		71
Gross profit		46		36
Distribution costs		(11)		(9)
Admin expenses (note 1)		(20)		(18)
Net profit before tax		15		9
Statement of financial position				
Non-current assets				
Tangible assets (note 2)			77	67
Intangible assets (note 3)			17	13
			94	80

Current assets

Inventory (note 4)	14	9
Trade receivables	17	13
Cash	3	3
	34	25

Total assets	**128**	**105**

Equity and liabilities

Ordinary share capital	20	20
Revaluation reserve	38	30
Retained earnings	30	25
	88	75

Non-current liabilities

Bank loan	13	11

Current liabilities

Trade payables	17	13
Other payables	5	3
Tax payable	5	3
	27	19
	128	**105**

Note 1

Included within Operating Profits are the following items:

	30.06.2009 $m	30.06.2008 $m
Wages and salaries	7	7
Directors' salaries	2	2
Depreciation	3	3
Amortisation	4	3

Note 2

	Land & buildings $m	Plant & machinery $m	Total $m
Cost			
B/fwd at 1 July 2008	70	30	100
Additions	–	5	5
Revaluations	8	–	8
C/fwd at 30 June 2009	78	35	113
Depn			
B/fwd at 1 July 2008	10	23	33
Charge	1	2	3
C/fwd at 30 June 2009	11	25	36
NBV			
At 30 June 2009	67	10	77
At 30 June 2008	60	7	67

The revaluation relates solely to a piece of land.

Plant and machinery are depreciated at 25% using the reducing balance method.

Note 3

Development costs	Total $
Cost	
B/fwd at 1 July 2008	16
Additions	8
C/fwd at 30 June 2009	24
Amortisation	
B/fwd at 1 July 2008	3
Charge	4
C/fwd at 30 June 2009	7

NBV

At 30 June 2009	17
At 30 June 2008	13

During the year significant research and development has taken place with regard.

To a new product, for which commercial production has now commenced.

Note 4

	30.06.2009	30.06.2008
	$m	$m
Inventory	3	2
Raw materials	1	1
WIP	11	7
Finished goods	(1)	(1)
Provision for slow moving stock	14	9

Required:

Prepare a memo for your manager that identifies and explains the key audit risks discovered during your analytical review of the financial statements. Your review should briefly discuss the possible implications for the final audit.

Note: Calculations for materiality are not required.

One professional mark is available.

(12 marks)

Test your understanding 3

(1) Kingston Co operates in the computer games industry, developing new games for sale in retail stores

(2) Portmore Co is currently waiting for confirmation from their bank that their overdraft facility will be extended. The bank have requested a copy of the audited financial statements as soon as they are available

(3) Montego Co has recently begun selling their products into overseas markets

(4) Lucea Co, a manufacturer, has negotiated a contract with a new supplier for all its raw materials

Required:

For each of the scenarios below identify the business risks and state what, if any, impact this might have on your assessment of financial statement risk for the planning of a year-end audit.

Test your understanding 4

Your firm has recently been appointed as the auditor of Holifex Co. The company provides and erects scaffolding on building sites and other industrial locations.

Your client, Stoke Co, has recently expanded its operations overseas. This is Stoke's first venture outside of its home country, where it has operated as a single entity. The venture has been set up by acquiring an entity overseas which is run and operated by its own, recently appointed, management team.

Chantry Co has been your client for many years. In recent years it has experienced rapid growth as its range of bottled water products has become more 'fashionable'. In order to cope with this level of growth, Chantry has introduced a new accounting system and transferred the data from their current software.

Westbourne Co is a major building and construction company focusing mostly on large projects such as the construction of major sporting and entertainment venues. Contracts are usually won through a tender process with construction work on successful tenders taking many years. During the year Westbourne has found itself in dispute with one of its major customers who claim that the concert venue Westbourne has constructed does not meet the specifications per the original contract. As a result the customer is withholding the final completion payment representing 30% of the contract value.

Required:

Identify and explain the financial statements risks to assist with the planning for each of the engagements above.

8 Chapter summary

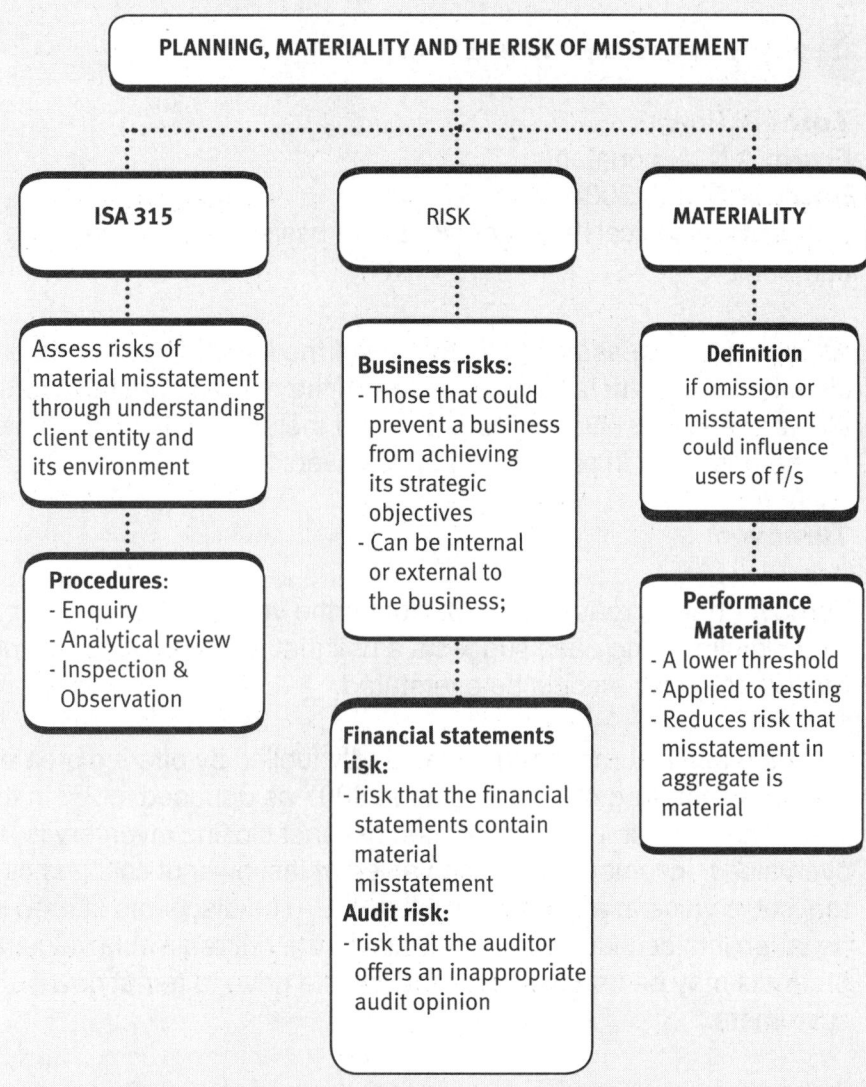

Planning, materiality and assessing the risk of misstatement

Test your understanding answers

Test your understanding 1: 'Ivor'

To: M.R. Partner
From: A.N. Accountant
Date: 24 March 2008
Subject: Analytical review of Ivor Ltd to assist the planning of the year end audit.

As requested, please find a summary of the key audit risks of Ivor Ltd identified during the analytical review of the management accounts for the year ended 31 December 2007 and the audited financial statements for the prior year in preparation of next week's planning meeting.

Turnover

Turnover has increased by 29% during the year to 31 December 2007. This significant increase suggests a risk that turnover – and certain related balances – could be overstated.

The increase in turnover has been partly fuelled by offering greater discounts, totalling 4% of turnover in 2007 as opposed to 2% in the prior year. This could imply an increased risk that closing inventory is overvalued. Inventory should be valued at the lower of cost and net realisable value in accordance with IAS 2. The discounts offered must be taken into account when determining the net realisable value. Some products may be used as loss leaders in a drive to tempt new customers.

It also appears that extended credit terms have been offered due to the lengthening of the receivables collection period from an average 49 days in 2006 to an average 61 days in 2007.

The overall increase in credit sales, coupled with the greater credit period increases the risk of non collection of receivables. However, the bad debt provision has not been adjusted from the previous balance of $70,000, which represented 5% of total receivables in 2006 but only 3% of receivables in 2007. This suggests that the bad debt provision is understated and the trade receivables balance overstated. It also suggests that bad debt expenses in the statement of profit or loss are understated.

The significant increase also suggests that we should pay close attention to the cut-off procedures adopted by the client and our testing of this process. There is no evidence to suggest that cut-off has been incorrectly performed but such a rapid increase in turnover may have put a strain on the company's sales recording system. It is therefore imperative to assess whether there has been any impact on the efficiency of the internal control system.

Distribution costs

These have increased by over 53% during the financial year. It is difficult to identify the cause of this fluctuation without further information. However it is likely that Ivor Ltd has tried to increase their customer base in different geographical locations. Assuming all invoices are made in dollars, this should not greatly affect our assessment of audit risk.

Gas and electricity costs

These have increased by 250% during the financial year. I would have expected such costs to rise directly in comparison with production levels; however this does not appear to be the case. There is a risk that these costs are therefore overstated.

It is unlikely that these balances are material to the financial statements, however enquiries should be made of management during the final audit to identify why the costs have risen so sharply.

Depreciation costs

The statement of profit or loss shows depreciation charges of $42k in 2007 and $49k in 2006 for plant and machinery. However, the reconciling note clearly shows that the depreciation charge for plant and machinery in 2007 is $49k. It appears that depreciation charges have been understated by $7k in the statement of profit or loss. At 0.6% of profits this is clearly immaterial. However, it should still be reported to management/those charged with governance in a comprehensive list of unadjusted audit differences.

Sale of buildings

During the year buildings [they have been depreciated!] with a net book value of $990,000 have been sold for $1,500,000. At the same time the company's rental expenses have increased by 190%. There is no indication elsewhere in the statement of profit or loss that the company has moved premises, such as removal costs, and it is unlikely that the company would be able to increase production so much having sold half of their buildings. It is therefore likely that the company has entered into a sale and leaseback arrangement.

There are no finance lease liabilities on the statement of financial position, hence it appears the lease is being treated as an operating lease. This presents the risk that the lease may have been misclassified and that non-current assets and finance lease liabilities are both understated on the statement of financial position. This would also have the knock on effect that depreciation charges are understated in the statement of profit or loss. This could be as much as $33,000 per annum, which is the disposal proceeds of the building of $1.5mn depreciated over the remaining useful life of 45 years.

Going concern

During the year there appears to have been an improvement in the liquidity of the company, with the current and quick ratios improving from 1.4 and 0.8 in 2006 to 3.9 and 2.3 in 2007 respectively.

However, it should be noted that during the year Ivor Ltd has raised a significant amount of cash from the disposal of buildings and the issuing of new shares. In total $2.2mn has been raised ($1.5mn disposal + $700k share issue) and it appears as though this has been used to pay off significant external debts, most notably the bank loan and trade payables. The result is a healthier statement of financial position.

It should be noted, though, that there is very little residual cash left over and the company appears to be having difficulty generating trading cash balances. Inventory days have increased slightly from 58 to 63 days and, crucially, receivable days have increased from 49 days to 61 days. The increase in the operating cycle could be caused by offering extended credit in an attempt to woo new customers. However, the inability to generate cash balances could indicate problems ahead, particularly if the company is unable to meet loan or lease repayments. A failure to pay trade payables could also lead to a loss of supplier goodwill and have implications for future trade relationships.

Given the nature of the sale and leaseback, and the attempt to keep this debt off the statement of financial position, caution should be used assessing managements' basis of preparing the accounts. If the business is no longer a going concern then the break up basis should be used.

Conclusion

The company has experienced a significant growth in turnover. However, this could come at the expense of greater bad debt risk and slower cash collection. This means the valuation of receivables and associated provisions is crucial. The use of a sale and leaseback mechanism also means the audit of non current assets and leases is a high risk area. Finally, despite a healthy statement of financial position, it appears that Ivor has cash flow problems and this means care needs to be used identifying the appropriate going concern status.

Appendix: Analytical Review

Annual movements

Turnover	2,935/10,160 × 100	28.9%
Purchases	2,320/7,830 × 100	29.6%
Distribution Costs	264/498 × 100	53%
Wages/Salaries	315/960 × 100	32.8%
Directors' Salaries	10/115 × 100	8.7%
Depreciation	(29)/89 × 100	(32.6%)
Amortisation	1/25 × 100	4%
Rent	23/12 × 100	191.7%
Rates	1/4 × 100	25%
Gas/Electricity	5/2 × 100	250%
Insurance	1/15 × 100	6.7%
Cleaning	1/2 × 100	50%
Miscellaneous	5/10 × 100	50%

Planning, materiality and assessing the risk of misstatement

Ratio analysis

	2007		**2006**	
Gross Margin	3,014/13,095 × 100	23%	2,357/10,160 × 100	23.2%
Operating Margin	1,190/13,095 × 100	9.1%	694/10,160 × 100	6.8%
ROCE	1,190/4,094 × 100	29.1%	694/3,004 × 100	23.1%
Asset Turnover	13,095/4,094	3.2	10,160/3,004	3.4
Current	3,994/1,027	3.9:1	2,595/1,796	1.4:1
Quick	2,354/1,027	2.3:1	1,395/1,796	0.8:1
Inventory Days	1,640/9,556 × 365	62.6	1,200/7,603 × 365	57.6
Receivable Days	2,204/13,095 × 365	61.4	1,353/10,160 × 365	48.6
Payable Days	703/10,150 × 365	25.3	1,479/7,830 × 365	68.9

Test your understanding 2

To: M.R.S. Manager

From: A.N. Accountant

Date: 27 September 2009

Subject: Analytical review of Engine Ltd and assessment of key audit risks.

As requested, please find a summary of the key audit risks identified during the analytical review of the financial statements of Engine Ltd and the possible implications for the year end audit.

Profitability

Gross margins have increased during the year from 34% to 36%. Operating margins, however, have increased significantly from 8% to 12%. This has had the overall affect of increasing return on capital employed by 5% during the financial year (from 10% to 15%).

The change in gross margin appears to have been achieved through economies in purchasing, which could be due to bulk purchasing consistent with the increase in turnover.

The gains made due to savings at the operational level appear to be driven through administrative efficiencies. These costs have increased by 11% in the year in comparison to an overall 20% increase in turnover. A review of operating costs suggests that this has been achieved through labour efficiencies, given the stable salary costs.

Salary Costs

There is a risk that salary costs are understated and at the same time intangible development costs are overstated.

During the year Engine Ltd capitalised $8mn of development costs relating to a project which has now begun commercial production. These costs should have been capitalised in line with IAS 38 meaning only those development costs meeting all the capitalisation criteria may be taken to the statement of financial position. All research costs must be expensed.

It is unclear from the financial statements whether any salary costs relating to research have been included in the statement of comprehensive income. However, given the fall in salary as a percentage of turnover it is possible that these costs have been capitalised incorrectly on
the statement of financial position.

Inventory

Closing inventory levels have increased by over 50% since 2008, possibly due to increased demand. This has lead to an increase in inventory days (from 46 to 62). This could, ultimately, have a detrimental effect on cash flows.

There is also a risk that the slow moving inventory provision is understated and, therefore, inventory is overstated. Whilst the inventory balance has increased by 50% in the year the provision has remained static. Increases in inventory increase the risk of damage, obsolescence and theft and consequently IAS 37 suggests the provision should increase in line with this exposure.

Non Current Assets

During the year a piece of land has been revalued by $8m. There does not appear to be any undue concern regarding the recording of this transaction, however care should be taken at the final audit to assess the appropriateness of the revaluation amount and that all appropriate disclosures are made in line with IAS 16.

Of more importance are the additions of plant and machinery. During the year $5m of assets were acquired. However it appears as though these items have not been depreciated during 2009. To this end there is a risk that depreciation charges (and hence profit) are understated and non current assets are overstated.

Using a rough method of calculation (closing NBV x 25%) the depreciation charge for plant and machinery should be $3m, not the $2m presented in the accounts. It therefore appears as though depreciation has not been accounted for as per IAS 16.

Loan

During the year the company has taken out an extra $2m loan, presumably to help finance the purchases of new plant and machinery. This has had a minimal effect on gearing, which has risen from 12.8% in 2008 to 12.9% in 2009. However, if the effect of the revaluation is removed from equity this would mean gearing is actually 14% in 2009.

Whilst this is not a significant amount it will be important to assess the terms of the new loan in case there are any covenants in place. Given the possibility that the directors are excluding salaries, depreciation and inventory provisions from profits there could be a significant adjustment required to the reported profit, which would adversely effect profitability ratios.

Audit Approach

Given the risks identified there will be a need to perform increased substantive tests in these areas because the misstatements appear more likely to be due to misapplication of required accounting standards than breakdowns in accounting controls.

With regard to development costs we will need to identify how pure research time and development time are distinguished. To assist with this goal the audit team should analytically review timesheets and match time spent on both research and development to the capitalisation calculations available.

The revaluation should have been performed by an appropriately qualified specialist (such as a member of the Royal Institute of Chartered Surveyors). We must inspect the revaluation report and confirm that it was performed by an appropriately qualified firm. All the valuations, and necessary disclosures, should be agreed to the financial statements. We must also confirm that the revaluation relates only to land and not to buildings, which would have implications for accumulated depreciation.

With regard to non current assets we will need to re-compute the depreciation charge for plant and machinery to ensure that all additions have been depreciated during the financial year. We will also need to review the non-current asset register to ensure that it has been updated and that it is correctly recognising new assets for the depreciation calculation.

We must also review the calculation for slow moving inventory to ensure that this has been reviewed and recalculated at the year end. Once this has been performed we will need to discuss the basis of the provision with management to ensure that it is appropriate to the level of inventory held. This should be discussed in conjunction with the findings of the inventory count, which should have identified any old or damaged goods in 'quarantine.'

Finally, we must seek a copy of the new loan agreement to identify any covenants. Key performance ratios should be recalculated in light of any proposed audit adjustments. All of the risk areas discussed indicate that profits may be overstated. The cumulative effect of adjustments could be significant. If Engine breach any covenants then the team must assess the impact on the finance agreement and, more importantly, the going concern basis of accounting.

Appendix: Ratio analysis

	2009		2008	
Gross margin	46/128 × 100	35.9%	35/107 × 100	33.6%
Operating margin	15/128 × 100	11.7%	9/107 × 100	8.4%
Return on capital employed	15/101 × 100	14.8%	9/86 × 100	10.5%
Asset turnover	128/101	1.27	107/86	1.24
Current ratio	34/27	1.3:1	25/19	1.3:1
Quick ratio	20/27	0.7:1	16/19	0.8:1
Inventory days	14/82 × 365	62	9/71 × 365	46
Receivables days	17/128 × 365	48	13/107 × 365	44
Payables days	17/87 × 365	71	13/74 × 365	64
Gearing	13/101 × 100	12.9%	11/86 × 100	12.8%

Planning, materiality and assessing the risk of misstatement

Test your understanding 3

Kingston Co

Kingston operates in a rapidly changing industry with constant product developments. They may not have the resources or expertise to keep up with the pace of change. There is a possible risk of overstatement of stock (and WIP) where products become superseded. In the extreme could lead to going concern issues

Portmore Co

Failure of bank to renew overdraft facility may increase risk of insufficient financing or more costly financing. Directors of Portmore will be under pressure to present the financial statements in the best light possible leading to possible manipulation of the F/S.

Lack of confirmation from the bank represents a fundamental uncertainty surrounding the appropriateness of the going concern concept.

Montego Co

The new venture overseas may not be successful; the market may have been overestimated. More complex transactions leading to increased risk of error.

Lucea Co

The new supplier may not deliver the right quality of products or at the right time, disrupting manufacturing and leading to delays in supplying customers. Ultimately this could increase the risk that inventory is overstated due to poor quality items leading to reduced selling prices or provisions for slow goods.

Test your understanding 4

Holifex Co

There is a risk that provisions are understated or that contingencies are undisclosed. Holifex operates in an industry where health and safety is paramount; any breaches in regulations may lead to fines.

There is a further risk of understating provisions and a more serious risk to the going concern assumption because Holifex could be exposed to potential claims by injured parties if they have been negligent in erecting scaffolding.

There is a possible overstatement of non-current assets. These are dispersed across many different locations. To this end controls over the storage and valuation of the assets could potentially be diluted.

There is also a risk that turnover is overstated due to cut off error. Use of scaffolding by customers is likely to span the year end in some instances.

Stoke Co

Lack of experience of recording this type of acquisition increases the risk of error both in recording and measuring transactions.

The new entity will require consolidation into the group accounts. There is a risk that this has not been performed correctly. The overseas operation will require translation prior to consolidation. There is a risk that incorrect rates have been used to translate the statement of financial position and statement of profit or loss.

The overseas entity is operated by its own management team. This increases control risk, as these may not be in line with group controls. This exposes the company to both prevention and detection risk.

Chantry Co

The period of rapid growth could indicate the possibility of increased control risk due to systems and procedures not been able to cope with the expansion.

An external business risk is the 'fashionable' demand of the product. Such items are prone to rapid changes in demand as social attitudes change. As a result the company must not rely solely on this product for future prosperity and ultimately this could affect the going concern assumption.

There is a risk of understatement of provisions/undisclosed liabilities. The bottled water industry has to comply with health and safety regulations and failure to comply could lead to fines and penalties.

Another inherent risk could be that staff may not be familiar/adequately trained re new accounting system, which increases the risk of human error.

Data has been transferred from old accounting system. There is a risk that the transfer was not performed correctly or that the information is in some way incompatible. Either way there is a risk that errors occurred on transfer.

Westbourne Co

Long term contracts in building and construction could present the risk that turnover is overstated and that related balances (WIP, receivables, payables) are also misstated.

The possible over reliance on few customers given size of contracts poses a constant going concern threat if tenders are unsuccessful and new clients are not found. This threat has been heightened by the dispute and the possible negative PR consequences.

The disputed receivable increases the risk that receivables are overstated and provisions (for doubtful debt) are understated.

The dispute also impacts cash flow, which is likely to be significant at 30% of the contract value. The shortfall in cash could lead to problems meeting debt requirements, particularly is liquidity is also an issue. Once again this could threaten going concern.

chapter 10

Group and transnational audits

Chapter learning objectives

When you have completed this chapter you will be able to:

- recognise the matters to be considered before accepting appointment as principal auditor to a group;
- identify and explain the matters specific to planning an audit of group financial statements;
- recognise the audit problems and describe audit procedures specific to a business combination;
- consider how the principal auditor should evaluate the audit work performed by a component auditor;
- justify the situations where a joint audit would be appropriate; and
- explain the implications for the auditor's report where the opinion of a component is modified.

Group and transnational audits

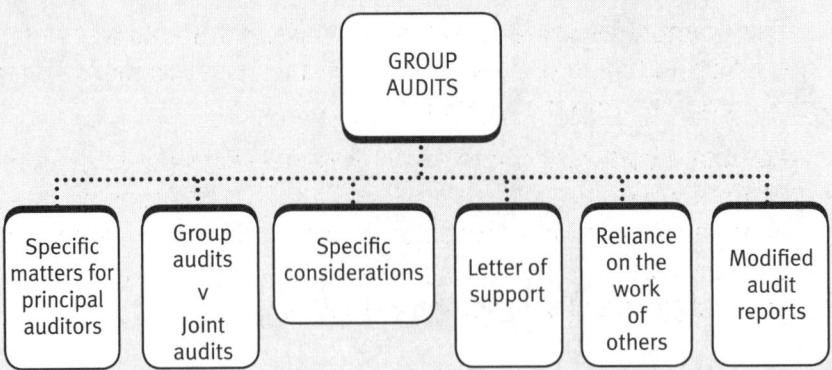

 A group could appear in any question in the exam, and is relevant to all stages of an engagement. You should identify early in the exam whether the scenario is for a single entity or a group, as groups will wither significantly affect your answer or provide you with additional points to make.

1 Group audits – specific considerations

The principles of auditing a group are the same as the audit of a single company and all of the ISAs are still relevant to a group audit. There are, however, some specific considerations relevant to the audit of a group:

- Group financial statements require numerous and potentially complicated consolidation adjustments.

- Specific accounting standards relating to group accounts must be complied with.

- The components of the group (i.e. the subsidiaries) may be audited by firms other than the principal group auditor.

- The organisation and planning of a group audit may be significantly more complex than for a single company.

The objectives of an auditor with regard to these matters are identified in ISA 600 *Special Considerations – Audits of Group Financial Statements (Including the Work of Component Auditors)* as follows:

- To determine whether it is appropriate to act as the auditor of the group financial statements and

- If acting as the auditor of the group financial statements:
  - To communicate clearly with the component auditors about the scope and timing of their work on financial information related to components and their findings.
  - To obtain sufficient appropriate evidence regarding the financial information of the components and the consolidation process to express an opinion on whether the group financial statements are prepared, in all material respects, in accordance with the applicable financial reporting framework.

Any stage of the audit process could be examined in relation to group audit issues.

> **Key terms**
>
> The auditor with the responsibility for reporting on the consolidated group financial statements is referred to as the **principal auditor**.
>
> There may be a wide number of subsidiary or associate companies within the group that have their own audit firms. These firms are referred to as the **component auditors**.
>
> The related subsidiaries, associates, joint ventures and branches etc of the group are referred to as **components**.

2 Acceptance as principal auditor

In addition to the normal acceptance considerations (discussed in chapters 3 and 4) firms should consider whether their own participation is sufficient to enable them to acceot the role of principal auditor. To assist the decision they must consider:

- Whether sufficient appropriate audit evidence can reasonably be expected to be obtained in relation to the consolidation process and the financial information of the components of the group;
- Where component auditors are involved the engagement partner shall evaluate whether the group engagement team will be able to be involved in the work of the component auditors;

If the engagement partner concludes that it will not be possible to obtain sufficient appropriate evidence due to restrictions imposed by group management and that the possible effect of this will result in a disclaimer of opinion then they must not accept the engagement. If it is a continuing engagement, the auditor should withdraw from the engagement, where possible under applicable laws and regulations.

Group and transnational audits

> **Ethics**
>
> Don't forget that in addition to these specific acceptance considerations the auditor must also consider the ethical and professional issues covered in chapters 1 to 7. For example, the auditor must consider their professional competence to accept a group audit engagement.
>
> The addition of a new subsidiary to a group may create additional threats to any of the fundamental principles that will need to be evaluated and managed appropriately.

3 Planning the group audit

Overall audit strategy and plan

The group auditor is responsible for establishing an overall group audit strategy and plan (in accordance with ISA 300). The group engagement partner is ultimately responsible for reviewing and approving this.

In order to fulfil this objective the group auditor has to obtain an understanding of:

- the group structure
- its components (including their significance) and their environments
- group-wide controls
- the consolidation process
- the risk of material misstatement in the component and group financial statements.

If an acquisition is made by the group, this will need to be taken into account when planning the audit. Business understanding will need to be obtained for the new component, and potentially new component auditors liaised with. There will be new transactions and balances to understand and audit.

If a disposal is made by the group, this will also need to be taken into account when planning the audit; the auditor will need to audit the disposal transaction.

Examples of matters to be understood

In order to perform their risk assessment thoroughly the group auditor must obtain a wide ranging understanding of matters relevant to the unique circumstances of the group and its components. Whilst the list below is not exhaustive, it provides a range of common examples to be considered specific to the circumstances of a group:

- Group-wide controls:
  - Regularity of meetings between group and component management;
  - Monitoring process of components operations and financial results;
  - Group management's risk assessment process;
  - Monitoring, controlling, reconciling and elimination of intra-group transactions;
  - Centralisation of IT systems;
  - Activities of internal audit;
  - Consistency of policies across the group; and
  - Group wide codes of conduct and fraud prevention.
- Consolidation process:
  - The extent to which component management understand the consolidation process;
  - The process for identifying and accounting for components;
  - The process for identifying reportable segments;
  - The process for identifying related party transactions;
  - How changes to accounting policies are managed;
  - The procedures for dealing with differing year-ends;
  - The procedures for dealing with differing accounting policies;
  - Group's process for ensuring complete, accurate and timely financial reporting;
  - The process for translating foreign components;
  - How IT is used in the consolidation;
  - Procedures for reporting subsequent events;
  - The preparation and authorisation of consolidation adjustments;
  - Frequency, nature and size of transactions between components; and
  - Steps taken to arrive at fair values.

Materiality

The group auditor is responsible for establishing materiality and performance materiality for the group financial statements as a whole. In addition the group auditor should establish materiality for the components where they are to be audited by other auditors.

Items that are material in individual financial statements may not be material in the consolidated financial statements. This will affect the amount of evidence that needs to be obtained to support the group audit opinion.

Clearly trivial

As well as establishing materiality, the group auditor should define a threshold above which misstatements cannot be regarded as "clearly trivial".

It is important to note that **"clearly trivial" does not mean "not material"**.

The threshold for "clearly trivial" is significantly lower than the threshold for materiality. Matters that are clearly trivial are inconsequential, individually and in aggregate, by nature or by size.

Further implications of materiality

In order to reduce the risk of material misstatement in the group financial statements, materiality for the components should be set at an amount below materiality for the group as a whole.

If the component is considered to be financially significant to the group, then it shall be audited using component materiality. If, however, it is considered to be significant because it is likely to pose risks of material misstatement to the group due to its nature or circumstances, one or more of the following should be performed:

- An audit using component materiality;
- An audit of one or more classes of transaction, account balances or disclosures relating to the risk of misstatement of the group financial statements; and/or
- Specific audit procedures relating to the risk of material misstatement of the group financial statements.

chapter 10

Risk assessment

The group audit team has to determine the type of work to be performed on the financial information of the components, whether performed by the group team or another auditor.

If, however, the audit of a significant component is to be performed by another auditor then the group auditor shall be involved in the component's risk assessment. This includes, as a minimum:

- Discussing with the component auditor or management those components of the business that are significant to the group;
- Discussing with the component auditor the susceptibility of the component to material misstatement; and
- Reviewing the component auditor's documentation of identified risks of material misstatement.

If significant risks of material misstatement of the group accounts have been identified in a component that is audited by another auditor then the group auditor shall evaluate the appropriateness of the further audit procedures performed in response to this assessment.

If the component is not considered significant then the group auditor shall simply perform analytical procedures at group level.

Risk indicators

The following examples, whilst not exhaustive, cover a wide range of conditions or events that could indicate an increased risk of material misstatement of the group financial statements:

- A complex group structure;
- Frequent acquisitions, disposals and/or reorganisations;
- Poor corporate governance systems;
- Non-existent or ineffective group-wide controls;
- Components operating under foreign jurisdictions that may be subject to unusual government intervention;
- High risk business activities of components;
- Unusual related party transactions;
- Prior occurrences of intra-group balances that did not reconcile;
- The existence of complex transactions that are accounted for in more than one component;
- Differing application of accounting policies;
- Differing financial year-ends;

- Prior occurrences of unauthorised or incomplete consolidation adjustments;
- Aggressive tax planning; and
- Frequent changes of auditor.

Relying on component auditors

Principal auditors cannot simply rely on the work of other auditors. The principal may have assessed audit risk and designed their own procedures in accordance with ISAs but they have no guarantee that other auditors have been as prudent. In fact the other auditors may not even follow International Standards on Auditing.

Therefore the principal should obtain and understanding of:

- Whether the component auditor understands and will comply with the code of ethics;
- The professional competence of the component auditor;
- Whether the group auditor will be able to be involved in the work of the component auditor; and
- Whether the component auditor operates in a regulatory environment that actively oversees auditors.

If the group auditor has serious concerns about any of the above issues then they shall obtain sufficient appropriate evidence relating to the financial information of the component, without requesting that the component auditor performs any work.

Dealing with non-coterminous year-ends

The parent and subsidiaries may not have the same year-end.

IFRS 10 *Consolidated Financial Statements*, requires the parent and subsidiaries to have the same year-end or to consolidate based on additional financial information prepared by the subsidiary (or if impracticable, the most recent financial statements adjusted for significant transactions or events). The difference between the parent and subsidiary's year-end must be no more than three months.

This **increases audit risk**, as there may be **transactions and adjustments in the consolidated financial statements that have not been audited** by the component auditor(s).

The group auditor must **plan** to obtain sufficient appropriate evidence about transaction or events that have not been subject to audit.

chapter 10

4 Auditing the consolidated accounts

For many groups the consolidation process will be complicated. There are also significant areas where adjustments and estimations are required. The principal needs to plan to perform sufficient procedures on the consolidation to minimise the risk of material misstatement. These include:

- Ensuring the correct figures are transferred from the component proforma accounts to the consolidation.
- Evaluating the classification of the component (i.e. subsidiary, associate, joint venture etc).
- Reviewing disclosures for related party transactions.
- Reviewing the policies and year-ends applied by the components and any consequent adjustments.
- Reviewing the calculation of specific consolidation adjustments.

Revision of consolidation

At a basic level consolidating a set of group accounts involves taking a number of sets of individual company financial statements and adding them all together to form one combined set. Due to various complications, such as companies using different currencies and intergroup trading, a number of adjustments have to be made before the consolidated set of accounts can be finalised. This is illustrated in the diagram below:

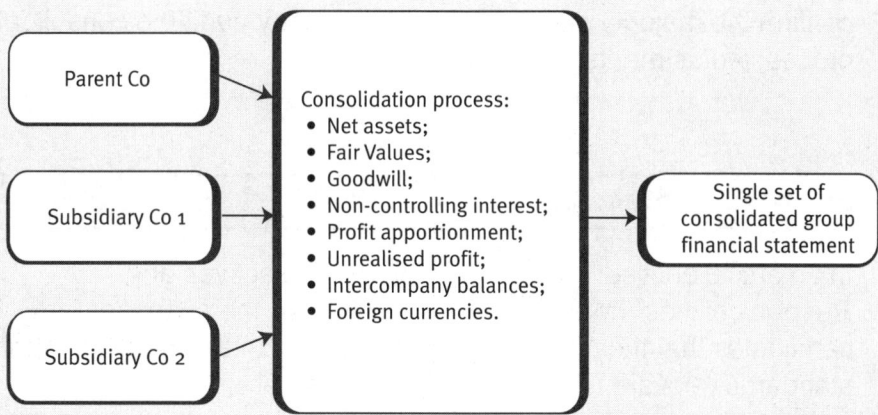

Significantly, these adjustments do not pass through the usual transaction processing systems and, for that reason, may not be subject to the same internal controls as other transactions. Therefore to evaluate the appropriateness, completeness and accuracy of the adjustments the group auditor may:

- Evaluate whether the adjustments appropriately reflect the events and transactions underlying them;

- Determine whether adjustments have been correctly calculated, processed and authorised;
- Determine whether adjustments are supported by sufficient appropriate documentation; and
- Check the reconciliation and elimination of intra-group balances and transactions.

Impact on the auditing process

The impact on the auditing process

Before any group considerations can be made the individual company's financial statements have to be prepared and subjected to audit. In the diagram above this includes Parent Co, Subsidiary Co 1 and Subsidiary Co 2. It is the responsibility of individual company directors/management to prepare their accounts. These may be audited by the group auditor or another firm of auditors.

Once this process is complete the individual sets of accounts are combined and adjusted to create a single set of consolidated financial statements. This process is the responsibility of the group's directors. Once the consolidated accounts have been prepared the group auditor performs an audit of the consolidated financial statements.

As the group is a summary of the trading results and positions of the various components of the group (and is itself not a trading entity) the group auditor does not need to audit the group accounts in the same way. They rely upon the audited figures of the individual accounts to confirm the majority of balances and then they audit the consolidation process/adjustments.

Exam focus: Standards

In an article entitled "Group Audit Issues: Objectives and Responsibilities" (March 2008) Lisa Weaver, the examiner, advises candidates that they must be 'very familiar' with the financial reporting standards relevant to consolidations. These are:

- IFRS 3, Business Combinations;
- IAS 28, Investments in Associates;
- IAS 31, Interests in Joint Ventures;
- IAS 32, Financial Instruments: Presentation; and
- IAS 39, Financial Instruments: Recognition and Measurement.

> In addition to the stated financial reporting standards students would be well advised to consider International Standards on Auditing 540 and 550, which cover accounting estimates, fair value measurements and related party disclosures respectively. In a more recent article entitled, "The Importance of Financial Reporting Standards to Auditors" (October 2008) Lisa indicates that these standards, all of which are relevant to the consolidation process, are highly examinable.

Communication with component auditors

The group auditor is responsible for communicating with the auditors of the components on a timely basis. Communication shall include;

- The work to be performed by the component and the use made of this;
- The form and content of the communications made by the component auditor to the group auditor;
- A request that the component auditor co-operates with the group team;
- The ethical requirements relevant to the group audit;
- Component materiality and the threshold for triviality;
- Identified significant risks of material misstatement of the group financial statements; and
- A list of identified related parties.

As part of the communication process the group auditor should also request that the component auditor communicates matters that are relevant to the group audit on a timely basis. Such matters include:

- Compliance with ethical standards;
- Compliance with audit instructions;
- Identification of financial information upon which the component auditor is reporting;
- Instances of non-compliance with laws and regulations;
- Uncorrected misstatements;
- Indications of management bias;
- Significant deficiencies in internal control;
- Other significant matters to be communicated to those charged with governance;
- Any other matters relevant to the group audit; and
- The component auditor's overall conclusion.

Further communications

As well as the matters identified above, the group auditor should also communicate further matters in a letter of instruction. This is likely to include

- Matters relevant to the planning of the component audit:
  - the timetable for completion;
  - dates of planned visits by the group auditor;
  - a list of key contacts;
  - work to be performed on intra-group balances;
  - guidance on other statutory reporting responsibilities;
  - instructions for subsequent events review.

- Matters relevant to the conduct of component auditor work:
  - The findings of the group auditors tests of controls on common systems;
  - The findings of internal audit relevant to the component;
  - A request for timely communication of evidence that contradicts evidence used in the group risk assessment;
  - A request for written representations on component management's compliance with the applicable financial reporting framework;
  - Matters to be documented by the component auditor.

- Other information:
  - A request that the following be reported in a timely fashion:
    - Significant accounting, financial reporting and auditing matters, including accounting estimates and related judgements;
    - Matters relating to the going concern status of the component;
    - Matters relating to litigation and claims;
    - Significant deficiencies in internal control and information that indicates the existence of fraud
  - A request that the group auditor be notified of any unusual events as early as possible.

5 Completion and review

The group auditor has to review the communications from the component auditors. If any significant matters have arisen they should then engage in a discussion with the component auditor or group management, as appropriate. If necessary the group auditor should then also review other relevant parts of the component auditor's working papers.

If the group auditor is not satisfied with the sufficiency or appropriateness of the component auditor's work they are responsible for determining what additional procedures are required. If it is not feasible for the component auditor to perform this then the group auditor must perform the procedures.

When all procedures on the components have been completed the group engagement partner must consider whether the aggregate effect of any uncorrected misstatements will have a material impact on the group financial statements.

6 Reporting

Modified audit reports

Where one or more of the subsidiaries has a modified audit report (regardless of who audited the subsidiary) the principal auditor must consider the impact of the issue on the group financial statements, according to group materiality levels, as follows:

- If the matter is not material in a group context then it may be ignored.
- If the matter is material to both the component and the group then the modification should be carried through to the group audit report.
- Note that a disclaimer of opinion in a subsidiary, given because the component auditor has not been able to gather sufficient appropriate audit evidence, may be altered to a qualified opinion in the group context.

Letters of support

In certain circumstances, a letter of support from the directors of a group may be required.

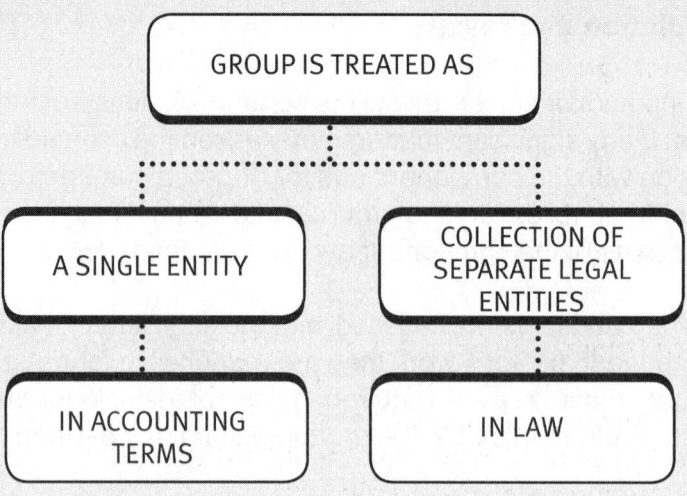

A situation may arise where a subsidiary may not be a going concern. If so, the subsidiaries accounts, which are consequently consolidated into the group accounts, should be prepared on a break up basis.

However, the group may offer support to the subsidiary to enable it to continue trading in the foreseeable future. If this is the case the directors must give the principal auditor formal documentation, usually called a 'comfort' or 'support' letter. This confirms their intention to support the ailing subsidiary.

The auditor will normally accept such a letter as valid audit evidence of the going concern basis for the subsidiary's financial statements. However, the principal auditor should not take this at face value. They should consider the position of the group to help identify whether it has the resources to fulfil its promise of support.

7 Joint audit

What is a joint audit?

This is when two audit firms are appointed to provide an audit opinion on a set of financial statements. They will work together planning the audit, gathering evidence, reviewing the work and providing the opinion.

Benefits

- retention of subsidiary auditor (and therefore their cumulative audit knowledge and experience) following acquisition;
- Availability of a wider range of resources (particularly important across national boundaries);
- Possible efficiency improvements.

Disadvantages

- Cultural clashes;
- Difficulty setting a joint approach – too many cooks!
- Both firms will need to be paid a fee.

> **Recent trends**
>
> Joint auditing allows small and medium sized entities to continue to be involved in an audit once their client has been acquired or merged with another organisation. Given recent trends in globalisation the alternative would likely be the replacement of the existing auditor with a larger firm.
>
> Given the nature of the current economy and the level of acquisition activity this could significantly reduce the pool of business for small and medium sized accountancy practices. Joint audit is therefore considered to be an important tool in combating the increased power of the 'Big 4' and the more significant medium tier firms.

8 What are 'transnational audits'?

Transnational audit means an audit of financial statements which may be relied upon outside the audited entity's home jurisdiction.

Reliance on these audits might be for purposes of significant lending, investment or regulatory decisions.

The differences between a 'normal' audit, conducted within the boundaries of one set of legal and regulatory requirements, and a transnational audit are largely due to variations in:

- Auditing standards;
- Regulation and oversight of auditors;
- Financial reporting standards; and
- Corporate governance requirements.

Auditors must be aware of the different regimes that apply to the audit of a transnational entity because they will be bound by the varying laws and regulations. Given the globalisation of businesses and stock markets this is an increasingly significant concern for many firms of auditors.

Group and transnational audits

Specific differences with transnational audit

Auditing standards

Despite the prevalence of International Standards on Auditing, many countries use modified versions and many continue to use local standards. As a result, in a group audit with components from a wide range of geographical backgrounds, it is possible that the audits of the components will be performed according to different standards. This could lead to inconsistency and poor quality for the group audit as a whole.

Regulation and oversight of auditors

As well as differing audit standards there are many different ways that the auditing profession is regulated. This can also affect the quality of the audit of components from different regimes, which will also lead to inconsistency in the quality of a group audit.

Financial reporting standards

Within a multinational group it is likely that adjustments will be required due to the application of differing financial reporting standards. These standards will be reflected in the component financial statements but, upon consolidation, must be adjusted to reflect the parent's accounting policies. These can lead to some very technically difficult consolidation adjustments, which will most likely increase the risk of material misstatement significantly.

In other countries the corporate governance requirements, particularly with regard to internal controls, are much more relaxed. However, this also affects the audit because this could indicate that internal controls may be less effective than those of a component that operates in a highly regulated environment.

Corporate governance requirements

In some countries there are very strict corporate governance requirements that not only affect the directors of the company but their auditor. Often the auditor is required to perform, and report on, procedures supplementary to the normal audit.

chapter 10

The Transnational Audit Committee

The International Federation of Accountants (IFAC) has a committee with specific responsibilities for transnational audits: the Transnational Audit Committee (TAC).

ROLE OF THE TAC

- Identifying audit practice issues. When the issues suggest changes in auditing or assurance standards may be required, recommend to the appropriate IFAC standard-setting boards that the issue be reviewed.
- Proposing members to the IFAC Regulatory Liaison Group and identifying qualified candidates to serve on IFAC standard-setting boards.
- Providing a forum to discuss 'best practices' in areas including quality control, auditing practices, independence, and training and development.
- Acting as a formal conduit for interaction among transnational firms and international regulators and financial institutions with regard to audit quality, systems of quality control, and transparency of international networks.

9 The impact of globalisation

Globalisation is the movement toward the whole world being the market from which resources are used and to which products are sold. Factories, shops and service organisations in many countries are likely to be foreign-owned or controlled. Goods, services, capital, and people are also more likely to move across national borders.

The problem with global businesses is that they operate in widely different legal and ethical systems. As a result audit firms have to have the resources and expertise to operate in a diverse geographical market and have to know how to audit highly regulated modern businesses; it is likely that only the larger audit firms can acquire the global expertise to handle such audits.

KAPLAN PUBLISHING 243

Advantages	Disadvantages
• Wide ranging expertise • Global facilities • Can invest in expensive systems and necessary IT to meet needs of international clients	• Lack of competition and choice, particularly for large companies

The concentration of the audit market into a few very large firms has come about because of globalisation. The larger firms found that **amalgamations** amongst the audit firms were the way forward leading to a more concentrated audit market:

- **Affiliation** is used by the larger accounting firms to develop an internationally recognised brand name.
- **Co-operation** is used by the mid-tier firms who join international co-operatives of firms who send each other business, but retain their own trading name in their home countries.

Current trends

Current trends still lean towards mergers:

- of firms in the countries where the profession is more highly developed, for example USA and many European countries, and
- between firms in the more developed arenas with practices in less developed locations.

In the mid-tier sector, the fastest way for firms to grow and achieve dominance in the sector is to merge with other similar sized companies.

Due to the debate about audit firms offering other services, and the impact this may have on auditor independence, the trend may be for audit firms to divest themselves of consultancy services.

- The SEC in the USA has drawn up stricter rules on auditor independence which put pressure on large audit firms to sell off their other services, particularly their consultancy divisions.
- As a result, by the end of 2002 each of the Big Four had separated their consultancy divisions from their audit practices, either by sale or by demerger.

The auditing profession is organised much as any other business sector, with a small number of very large, global organisations, a significant number of mid-sized practices, and many smaller firms and sole practitioners.

The dawn of International Standards on Auditing (and accounting/financial reporting) have helped to align the objectives and procedures of auditors across the globe. The aim is to ensure the quality of audits world-wide.

Exam style question: Group audit

You are an audit manager in Ross & Co, a firm of Certified Public Accountants. The principal activity of one of your audit clients, Murray Co, is the manufacture and retail sale of women's fashions and menswear throughout the capital cities of Western Europe.

The following financial information has been extracted from Murray's most recent consolidated financial statements:

	2012 $'000	2011 $'000
Revenue	36,367	27,141
Gross profit	22,368	16,624
Profit before tax	5,307	4,405
Intangible assets		
- goodwill	85	85
- trademarks	52	37
Property, plant and equipment	7,577	4,898
Current assets	13,803	9,737
Total assets	21,517	14,757
Equity	13,226	10,285
Non-current liabilities: provisions	201	87
Current liabilities: trade and other payables	4,385	8,090
Total equity and liabilities	21,517	14,757

Group and transnational audits

In May 2011 Murray purchased 100% of the shareholding of Di Rollo Co. Di Rollo manufactures fashion accessories (for example, jewellery, scarves and bags) in South America that are sold throughout the world by mail order. Murray's management is now planning that clothes manufacture will expand into South America and sold into Di Rollo's mail order market. Additionally, Di Rollo's accessories will be added to the retail stores' product range.

Murray is a member of an ethical trade initiative that aims to improve the employment conditions of all workers involved in the manufacture of its products. Last week Di Rollo's chief executive was dismissed following allegations that he contravened Di Rollo's policy relating to the environmentally-friendly disposal of waste products. The former chief executive is now suing Di Rollo for six months' salary in lieu of notice and a currently undisclosed sum for damages.

Ross & Co has recently been invited to accept nomination as auditor to Di Rollo. Murray's management has indicated that the audit fee for the enlarged Murray group should not exceed 120% of the fee for the year ended 31 March 2011. You have been provided with the following information relating to the acquisition of Di Rollo:

	Carrying amount $'000	Fair value adjustment $'000	Fair value to the group $'000
Di Rollo brand name	–	–	600
Plant and equipment	95	419	514
Current assets	400	–	400
Current liabilities	(648)	–	(648)
Net assets at date of acquisition	(153)	419	866
Goodwill arising on acquisition			859
Cash consideration			1,725

Required:

(a) **Using the information provided, explain the matters that should be considered before accepting the engagement to audit the financial statements of Di Rollo Co for the year ending 31 March 2012.**

(b) **Explain what effect the acquisition of Di Rollo Co will have on the planning of your audit of the consolidated financial statements of Murray Co for the year ending 31 March 2012.**

chapter 10

Test your understanding 1

You are an audit manager in Nailah & Co, a firm of Chartered Certified Accountants. One of your audit clients Chione Co provides satellite broadcasting services in a rapidly growing market. During the current accounting period Chione made the following acquisitions:

(1) Chione purchased Nubia Co, a competitor group of companies. Significant revenue, cost and capital expenditure synergies are expected as the operations of Chione and Nubia are being combined into one group of companies.

(2) Chione purchased Maahes Co, a large cable communications provider in India, where your firm has no representation. The financial statements of Maahes for the year end will continue to be audited by a local firm of Chartered Certified Accountants.

Required:

Explain what effect the acquisitions will have on the planning of the audit of the consolidated financial statements of Chione Co for the current accounting period.

Test your understanding 2

Bellatrix is a carpet manufacturer and an audit client of your firm. Bellatrix has identified a company in the same business, Scorpio, as a target for acquisition in the current year.

As audit manager to Bellatrix and its subsidiaries for the year ended 31 December 2006, you have been asked to examine Scorpio's management accounts and budget forecasts. The chief executive of Bellatrix, Sirius Deneb, believes that despite its current cash flow difficulties, Scorpio's current trading performance is satisfactory and future prospects are good. The chief executive of Scorpio is Ursula Minor.

The findings of your examination are as follows:

Budget forecasts for Scorpio, for the current accounting year to 31 December 2006 and for the following year, reflect a rising profit trend.

Scorpio's results for the first half year to 30 June 2006 reflect $800,000 profit from the sale of a warehouse that had been carried in the books at historical cost. There are plans to sell two similar properties later in the year and outsource warehousing.

KAPLAN PUBLISHING

About 10% of Scorpio's sales are to Andromeda, a limited liability company. Two members of the management board of Scorpio hold minority interests in Andromeda. Selling prices negotiated between Scorpio and Andromeda appear to be on an arm's length basis.

Scorpio's management accounts for the six months to 30 June 2006 have been used to support an application to the bank for an additional loan facility to refurbish the executive and administration offices. These management accounts show inventory and trade receivables' balances that exceed the figures in the accounting records by $150,000. This excess has also been reflected in the first half year's profit. Upon enquiry, you have established that allowances, to reduce inventory and trade receivables' to estimated realizable values, have been reduced to assist with the loan application.

Although there has been a recent downturn in trading, Ursula Minor has stated that she is very confident that the negotiations with the bank will be successful as Scorpio has met its budgeted profit for the first six months. Ursula believes that increased demand for carpets and rugs in the winter months will enable results to exceed budget.

Required:

(a) Identify and comment on the implications of your findings for Bellatrix's plan to proceed with the acquisition of Scorpio.

(10 marks)

(b) Explain what impact the acquisition will have on the conduct of your audit of Bellatrix and its subsidiaries for the year to 31 December 2006.

(15 marks)

(Total: 25 marks)

10 Chapter summary

GROUP AUDITS

Specific matters for principal auditors
- requirement for complex FS adjustments
- group IAS/IFRS's
- involvement of component auditors
- complexity organising a group audit

Specific considerations
- correct classification of investments
- differing accounting policies and frameworks
- fair values on acquisition
- intangibles
- taxation
- goodwill on consolidation
- intra-group balances, transactions and profits
- related parties
- share options
- post balance sheet events

Reliance on the component auditors
- compliance with the code of ethics
- competence of component auditors
- involvement of group auditor in audit of component
- regulatory environment of component auditor
- assess materiality and risk at group and component level
- communications with the component auditors

Group audits
- 1 firm appointed as the principal auditor,
- take full responsibility for f/s
- decide how and when work will be performed

Joint audits
- responsibility is shared jointly
- cooperation is required to divide and plan the work.

Letter of support
- Issued by directors of parent co. where subsid ceases to be going concern
- Auditors accept as evidence of g.c. and audit report not modified

Modified audit reports
Ignore unless material to the group.

Group and transnational audits

Test your understanding answers

Exam style question: Group audit

This question is unusual in that it doesn't ask about risk. However, matters to consider in taking on an engagement includes risk, so it's examined indirectly. This question a good question to revise groups, but make sure you restrict your answer to the planning of the audit, not the whole audit process.

(a) **Matters to consider**

Ross & Co should be sufficiently competent and experienced to undertake the audit of Di Rollo as it has similar competence and experience in auditing the larger Murray Co. However, Ross needs knowledge of conducting businesses in South America including legal and tax regulations.

Any factors that might impair Ross's objectivity in forming an opinion on the financial statements of Di Rollo (and the consolidated financial statements of Murray). For example, if Ross was involved in any due diligence review of Di Rollo, the same senior staff should not be assigned to the audit.

Whether Ross has sufficient, if any, resources in South America (e.g. in representative/associated offices). Ross must have sufficient time to report on Di Rollo within the timeframe for reporting on the consolidated financial statements of Murray.

Ross should not accept the nomination if any limitation imposed by management would be likely to result in the need to issue a disclaimer of opinion on Di Rollo's financial statements.

Whether the proposed restriction in audit fee compromises the quality of the audit of Di Rollo and/or the Murray group. The 20% increase needs to be sufficient to cover the cost of the audit of Di Rollo and the incremental costs associated with auditing Murray's consolidated financial statements (as well as any general annual price increase that might be applied to audit fees).

Di Rollo is material to the Murray group. At acquisition the fair values of Di Rollo's tangible non-current assets, current assets and current liabilities represent 6.8%, 2.9% and 8%, respectively, of those in Murray's consolidated financial statements at 31 March 2011.

It is usual that a parent company should want its auditors to audit its subsidiaries. If Ross were to decline the nomination, Murray's management may seek an alternative auditor for the group.

Murray should give Ross written permission to communicate with Di Rollo's current auditor to enquire if there is any professional reason why they should not accept this assignment.

Murray may provide Ross with additional fee-earning opportunities (e.g. due diligence reviews, tax consultancy, etc) if it continues to expand in future.

(b) Effect of acquisition on planning the audit of Murray's consolidated financial statements for the year ending 31 March 2012.

Group structure

The new group structure must be ascertained to identify all entities that should be consolidated into the Murray group's financial statements for the year ending 31 March 2012.

Materiality assessment

Preliminary materiality for the group will be much higher, in monetary terms, than in the prior year. For example, if a % of total assets is a determinant of the preliminary materiality, it may be increased by 10% (as the fair value of assets acquired, including goodwill, is $2,373,000 compared with $21.5m in Murray's consolidated financial statements for the year ended 31 March 2011).

The materiality of each subsidiary should be re-assessed, in terms of the enlarged group as at the planning stage. For example, any subsidiary that was just material for the year ended 31 March 2007 may no longer be material to the group.

This assessment will identify, for example:

- those entities requiring an audit visit; and
- those entities for which substantive analytical procedures may suffice.

As Di Rollo's assets are material to the group Ross should plan to inspect the South American operations. The visit may include a meeting with Di Rollo's previous auditors to discuss any problems that might affect the balances at acquisition and a review of the prior year audit working papers, with their permission.

Di Rollo was acquired two months into the financial year therefore its post-acquisition results should be expected to be material to the consolidated statement of comprehensive income.

Goodwill acquired

The assets and liabilities of Di Rollo at 31 March 2012 will be combined on a line-by-line basis into the consolidated financial statements of Murray and goodwill arising on acquisition recognised.

Audit work on the fair value of the Di Rollo brand name at acquisition, $600,000, may include a review of a brand valuation specialist's working papers and an assessment of the reasonableness of assumptions made.

Significant items of plant are likely to have been independently valued prior to the acquisition. It may be appropriate to plan to place reliance on the work of expert valuers. The fair value adjustment on plant and equipment is very high (441% of carrying amount at the date of acquisition). This may suggest that Di Rollo's depreciation policies are over-prudent (e.g. if accelerated depreciation allowed for tax purposes is accounted for under local GAAP).

As the amount of goodwill is very material (approximately 50% of the cash consideration) it may be overstated if Murray has failed to recognise any assets acquired in the purchase of Di Rollo in accordance with IFRS 10 Business Combinations. For example, Murray may have acquired intangible assets such as customer lists or franchises that should be recognised separately from goodwill and amortized (rather than tested for impairment).

Subsequent impairment

The audit plan should draw attention to the need to consider whether the Di Rollo brand name and goodwill arising have suffered impairment as a result of the allegations against Di Rollo's former chief executive.

Liabilities

Proceedings in the legal claim made by Di Rollo's former chief executive will need to be reviewed. If the case is not resolved at 31 March 2012, a contingent liability may require disclosure in the consolidated financial statements, depending on the materiality of amounts involved. Legal opinion on the likelihood of Di Rollo successfully defending the claim may be sought. Provision should be made for any actual liabilities, such as legal fees. Group (related party) transactions and balances.

A list of all the companies in the group (including any associates) should be included in group audit instructions to ensure that intra-group transactions and balances (and any unrealized profits and losses on transactions with associates) are identified for elimination on consolidation. Any transfer pricing policies (e.g. for clothes manufactured by Di Rollo for Murray and sales of Di Rollo's accessories to Murray's retail stores) must be ascertained and any provisions for unrealized profit eliminated on consolidation.

It should be confirmed at the planning stage that inter-company transactions are identified as such in the accounting systems of all companies and that inter-company balances are regularly reconciled. (Problems are likely to arise if new inter-company balances are not identified/reconciled. In particular, exchange differences are to be expected.)

Other auditors

If Ross plans to use the work of other auditors in South America (rather than send its own staff to undertake the audit of Di Rollo), group instructions will need to be sent containing:

- proforma statements;
- a list of group and associated companies
- a statement of group accounting policies (see below)
- the timetable for the preparation of the group accounts (see below)
- a request for copies of management letters
- an audit work summary questionnaire or checklist
- contact details (of senior members of Ross's audit team).

Accounting policies

Di Rollo may have material accounting policies which do not comply with the rest of the Murray group. As auditor to Di Rollo, Ross will be able to recalculate the effect of any non-compliance with a group accounting policy (that Murray's management would be adjusting on consolidation).

Group and transnational audits

Timetable

The timetable for the preparation of Murray's consolidated financial statements should be agreed with management as soon as possible. Key dates should be planned for:

- agreement of inter-company balances and transactions
- submission of proforma statements
- completion of the consolidation package
- tax review of group accounts
- completion of audit fieldwork by other auditors
- subsequent events review
- final clearance on accounts of subsidiaries
- Ross's final clearance of consolidated financial statements.

Test your understanding 1

Group structure

The new group structure must be ascertained to identify the entities that should be consolidated into the group financial statements of Chione for the year end.

It will also be imperative to identify the locations of the new subsidiaries and the scale of their operations. This will help to identify the number of team members and the locations they have to visit. This could impact upon the budget for the engagement and, ultimately, on the fee charged.

Materiality assessment

Preliminary materiality will be much higher, in monetary terms, than in the prior year. The materiality of each subsidiary should be assessed, in terms of the enlarged group as at the planning stage. This will identify, for example:

- those entities requiring an audit visit by the principal auditor; and
- those for which analytical procedures may suffice.

If either acquisition is particularly material to the group, Nailah may plan (provisionally) to visit Maahes's auditors to discuss any problems shown to arise in their audit work summary (see group instructions below).

Goodwill arising

The audit plan should draw attention to the need to audit the amount of goodwill arising on the acquisitions and management's impairment test at the reporting date.

The assets and liabilities of Nubia and Maahes, at fair value to the group, will be combined on a line-by-line basis and any goodwill arising recognised.

Significant non-current assets such as properties are likely to have been independently valued prior to the acquisition. It may be appropriate to plan to place reliance on the work of quantity surveyors or other property valuers.

Group (related party) transactions and balances

A list of all the companies in the group (including any associated companies) should be included in group audit instructions to ensure that intra-group transactions and balances (and any unrealised profits and losses on transactions with associated companies) are identified for elimination on consolidation.

It should be confirmed at the planning stage that inter-company transactions are identified as such in the accounting systems of all Chione companies and that inter-company balances are regularly reconciled.

Analytical procedures

Having brought in the operations of a group of companies (Nubia) with similar activities may extend the scope of analytical procedures available. This could have the effect of increasing audit efficiency.

Other auditors

Other auditors will include:

- any affiliates of Nailah in any of the countries in which Chione (as combined with Nubia) operates; and
- unrelated auditors (including those of Maahes).

Nailah will plan to use the work of Maahes's auditors who are Chartered Certified Accountants. Their competence and independence should be assessed (e.g. through information obtained from a questionnaire and evidence of their work).

A letter of introduction should be sent to the unrelated auditors, with Chione's permission, as soon as possible (if not already done) requesting their co-operation in providing specified information within a given timescale.

Group instructions will need to be sent to affiliated and unrelated auditors containing:

- proforma statements;
- a list of group and associated companies;
- a statement of group accounting policies (see below);
- the timetable for the preparation of the group accounts (see below);
- a request for copies of management letters;
- an audit work summary questionnaire or checklist;
- contact details (of senior members of Nailah's audit team).

Accounting policies (Nubia & Maahes)

Whilst it is likely that Nubia has the same accounting policies as Chione (because, as a competitor, it operates in the same jurisdictions) Maahes may have material accounting policies which do not comply with the rest of the group. Nailah may request that Maahes's auditors calculate the effect of any non-compliance with a group accounting policy for adjustment on consolidation.

Timetable

The timetable for the preparation of Chione's consolidated financial statements should be agreed with management as soon as possible. Key dates should be planned for:

- agreement of inter-company balances and transactions;
- submission of proforma statements to Nailah;
- completion of the consolidation package;
- tax review of group accounts;
- completion of audit fieldwork by other auditors ;
- subsequent events review;
- final clearance on accounts of subsidiaries;
- Nailah's final clearance of consolidated financial statements.

Test your understanding 2

(a) **Implications of findings**

$800,000 profit on sale of property

Although the profit on sale of the property arises from ordinary activities, it needs to be separately identified (IAS 1) so that Scorpio's current trading performance can be assessed (by Bellatrix and the bank). It should be excluded from any trading results that are being extrapolated to provide figures for profit forecasts. To include it would result in a distortion of sustainable profits.

Scorpio's properties are being valued at historical cost in its financial statements (IAS 16). Bellatrix should obtain an independent valuation of the properties before finalising a purchase price for the acquisition of Scorpio.

The property sale could have been made to realise cash and so mitigate current cash flow difficulties. The proposed sale of two more properties and outsourcing of warehousing may further improve the cash flow situation in the short-term. However, outsourcing warehousing could place a further burden on cash flow if an agreement is entered into and no buyer can subsequently be found for the properties.

Scorpio's management is seeking (or negotiating with) a suitable organization to provide warehousing. However, one of the synergies to be obtained from acquiring Scorpio may be utilising Bellatrix's spare warehousing capacity. Bellatrix should therefore obtain warranties and indemnities in the purchase contract in respect of any contingent liabilities that could arise. For example, penalties may be incurred if an agreement to outsource warehousing is entered into and subsequently cancelled.

Sales to Andromeda

The two members of the management board of Scorpio will be related parties (IAS 24) if they are key management personnel (i.e. having authority and responsibility for planning, directing and controlling the activities of Scorpio).

Andromeda will be a related party if the management board members have the ability (acting individually or in concert) to exercise influence over Andromeda's financial and operating policy decisions. This seems likely, as 10% of Scorpio's sales constitutes material intercompany transactions. (Control of Andromeda is not an issue as the two members have only a minority interest.)

Sales to Andromeda appear to be related party transactions which should have been disclosed in Scorpio's financial statements for the year to 31 December 2006.

Although prices appear to be on an arm's length basis, the transactions may not be at arm's length if other trading terms (e.g. delivery or payment terms) are more or less favourable than transactions with unrelated parties. If credit terms are not 'normal commercial' these sales could be contributing to Scorpio's current cash flow difficulties.

The sales to Andromeda are material to Scorpio and may be lost after the acquisition (e.g. if the two minority shareholders do not continue to hold positions on the management board of Scorpio). A proportional (i.e. 10%) reduction in gross profit would also be expected (assuming margins on sales to Andromeda are not dissimilar to those on other sales).

Bank loan application

The $150,000 discrepancy between the current asset values per the management accounts and the balances per the accounting records appears to be an irregularity that could constitute a fraud against the bank. It casts serious doubts on the integrity of Scorpio's management. Revising the accounting estimates for allowances against asset values downwards is clearly inappropriate as it is most likely that they should be increased (as stock levels increase with falling demand and customers are more likely to be bad and doubtful).

Refurbishing the offices is unlikely to constitute essential expenditure when the company is experiencing cash flow difficulties. Also it is possible that refurbishment may not be required when Bellatrix acquires Scorpio because the functions of the executive and administration offices may be relocated elsewhere within the Bellatrix group of companies.

Although current trading performance is clearly below budget (after deducting the profit on disposal and reinstating the provisions against stock and debtors), the loan finance is not being sought for a purpose that would increase the company's revenue-earning opportunities. This may cast doubts on the business acumen of Scorpio's management. It is possible that the loan finance would not be forthcoming if the bank were aware of Scorpio's true position.

Bellatrix should seek to have the negotiations with the bank suspended until after the acquisition, when the need for loan finance can be reassessed. Bellatrix should obtain guarantees from Scorpio's executives in the event that they pursue the loan application (which may possibly create charges over Scorpio's assets).

Budget forecast

The profit estimates made by the management of Scorpio appear to be unduly optimistic because the first six month's budget has only been 'met' by the inclusion, in the reported results of:

- a non-sustainable profit on disposal of a warehouse;
- unwarranted reversals of provisions against asset values.

Perhaps it is more likely that the forecast 'rising profit trend' will be achieved (and the annual budget exceeded) through profits arising on the disposals of two more properties rather than increased demand.

Budgeted profits should therefore be disregarded in the determination of the purchase price.

Tutorial note: It is a higher skill to recognise, when planning an answer, that it is not always suitable to address the items in the scenario in the order in which they are presented. For example, in this Q, there is not a lot to be said about the budget forecasts until the other findings have been interpreted.

(b) **Impact of acquisition on audit**

Tutorial notes:

(1) The acquisition will be completed before 31 December 2006 (see 1st para 'acquisition in current year').

(2) Accounting year ends will be coterminous ('first half year to 30 June 2006') – to assume otherwise would be a fabrication.

(3) You will be appointed as auditor to Scorpio ('as audit manager to Bellatrix and its subsidiaries').

(4) The acquisition method will be used to consolidate Scorpio as, under IFRS 3, this is the only permitted accounting treatment.

(5) 'Conduct of your audit' must not be confined to the 'audit testing' phase but consider, within the scope of the given scenario, the whole audit process.

Practice management

It is possible that audit objectivity may appear to have suffered impairment (e.g. due to a closer relationship between Bellatrix's management and the audit team having developed during the acquisition assignment). A second partner review may therefore be required as an appropriate safeguard.

Bellatrix's individual company accounts

The acquisition will constitute an addition, at cost, to Investments in subsidiaries in Bellatrix's own financial statements. The purchase consideration paid (or contingently payable) should also be disclosed.

The cost of acquisition should be verified to the sale agreement. Cash consideration must be agreed to entries in the cash book and bank statements. Company minutes and entries in the share register will evidence consideration in shares.

Bellatrix's consolidated accounts

Statement of financial position

Scorpio's assets and liabilities, at fair value to the group, will be combined on a line-by-line basis and any goodwill arising recognised.

The fair value of such assets as the properties (assuming that they have not yet been sold) may be material to the consolidated statement of financial position. Assuming that the properties were independently valued prior to the acquisition, it will be appropriate to seek to place reliance on the work of the expert valuer.

The calculation of the amount attributed to goodwill must be agreed to be the excess of the cost of the acquisition over the aggregate fair values of the identifiable assets and liabilities existing at the date of acquisition.

The period over which this goodwill is to be amortised must be reviewed for reasonableness. If an amortisation method other than the straight-line approach has been adopted, Bellatrix's management must be able to offer persuasive evidence (which must be subject to audit scrutiny) that it is appropriate.

Statement of profit or loss

As Scorpio is going to have been acquired quite late on in the year (certainly the second half of the year) it is possible that its post-acquisition results are not material to the consolidated statement of profit or loss.

Unless accounting adjustments are required (e.g. to bring any accounting policies of Scorpio into line with Bellatrix) the addition of one more subsidiary into the consolidation working papers is unlikely to have an appreciable impact on the amount of work involved.

Other subsidiaries

The materiality of other subsidiaries, in the group context, should be reassessed in terms of the enlarged group. The existence of another company (Scorpio) in the same business within the group may extend the scope of analytical procedures available.

This could have the effect of increasing audit efficiency.

Scorpio's financial statements

Planning

Much of the collection of background information associated with planning the conduct of a new audit assignment will have already been obtained as a result of the pre-acquisition work.

Materiality assessment

Material matters requiring attention will include:

- sales to Andromeda
- property valuations
- inventory valuations (raw materials, WIP and finished carpets)
- trade receivables balances
- liabilities (including bank loans).

The management accounts for the six months to 30 June should provide information sufficient to make an initial evaluation of materiality. However, as the reliability of certain management information is in doubt, this should be reassessed before detailed work commences.

The materiality of these items should also be assessed in the context of monetary amounts in the consolidated financial statements.

Risk assessment

Specific areas of audit risk have already been identified, thereby reducing the time required to assess the risk of misstatement at the planning stage. In particular:

- inherent risk is high due to Scorpio's management overstating profit (even if the management board has since been replaced);
- inventory may be overstated/allowances understated due to inventory having increased (due to a fall in demand);

- trade receivables may be overstated/allowances for bad and doubtful debts understated due to Scorpio's management having 'massaged' these figures to achieve their profit estimates.

Ascertaining the systems and internal controls

Some systems review work may have already been undertaken (e.g. when considering the source of information used in the preparation of Scorpio budgetary information).

The relevance of Scorpio's current accounting systems and internal controls will depend on Bellatrix's plans for change. For example, a Bellatrix office may account for Scorpio's transactions. If significant changes are proposed it may be more appropriate to adopt a substantive approach to the first audit of Scorpio.

Audit evidence

Some audit evidence should have been obtained for the assignment file (e.g. concerning the sales to Andromeda and the sale of property). This should be copied/referenced to the audit working papers to ensure that work is not unnecessarily reperformed.

As Scorpio is in the same business as Bellatrix, ratio analysis and other substantive analytical procedures should provide a more cost-effective approach to obtaining audit evidence than tests of detail.

Review

The relationship between the two members of Scorpio's management board and Andromeda after the date of acquisition must be established and the extent of transactions between them, if any. (For example, these minority shareholders of Andromeda may no longer hold board positions and/or sales to Andromeda may have ceased.)

The proportion of sales should be disclosed (e.g. 10%) along with factual information concerning the pricing policy. Audit tests must verify, for example, that price is determined based on a published price list.

chapter 11

Evidence

Chapter learning objectives

Upon completion of this chapter you will be able to:

- identify and describe audit procedures to obtain sufficient audit evidence from identified sources;
- apply analytical procedures to financial and non-financial data;
- explain the specific audit problems and procedures concerning related party transactions;
- evaluate the use of written management representations to support other audit evidence;
- demonstrate the use of written management representations as a source of audit evidence;
- recognise when it is justifiable to place reliance on the work of an expert; and
- assess the appropriateness of the work of internal auditors and the extent to which reliance can be placed on it.

Evidence

1 The risk based approach revised

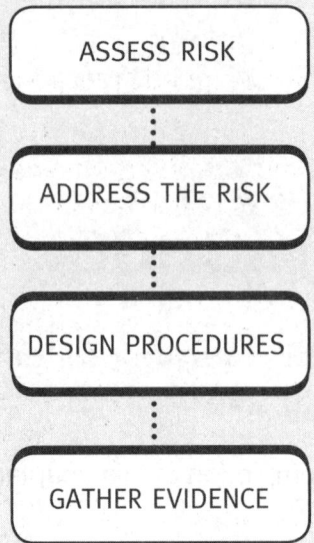

 More than one question in the exam is likely to feature a requirement to design relevant audit or assurance procedures. It is essential that you understand the principles of audit evidence but also that you can apply this knowledge to the scenario and design procedures relevant to the specific financial reporting standard or area of the subject matter being tested.

 ## 2 The principles of evidence

The importance of financial reporting standards

The unmodified audit opinion states:

"In our opinion, the financial statements present fairly, in all material respects (or *give a true and fair view of*) the financial position of ABC Company as at December 31, 20X1, and (*of*) its financial performance and its cash flows for the year then ended **in accordance with International Financial Reporting Standards**."

Therefore, in order to reach this opinion, the auditor must fully understand the relevant financial reporting standards, and must evaluate whether the financial statements comply with these standards. This knowledge and understanding needs to be applied throughout the audit. Chapter 20 summarises the key points from these standards.

During the **evidence gathering** phase of the audit, the auditor must obtain sufficient appropriate evidence that the financial statements are free from material misstatement however caused. This includes obtaining sufficient appropriate evidence that the financial reporting standards are applied correctly and complied with fully.

The fundamental principles laid down in ISA's 315 and 330 for gathering audit evidence are:

- audit procedures are designed in response to the assessment of risk at the planning stage;
- evidence gathered must be sufficient and appropriate enough to reduce assessed risk to an acceptable level.

The risk assessment loop

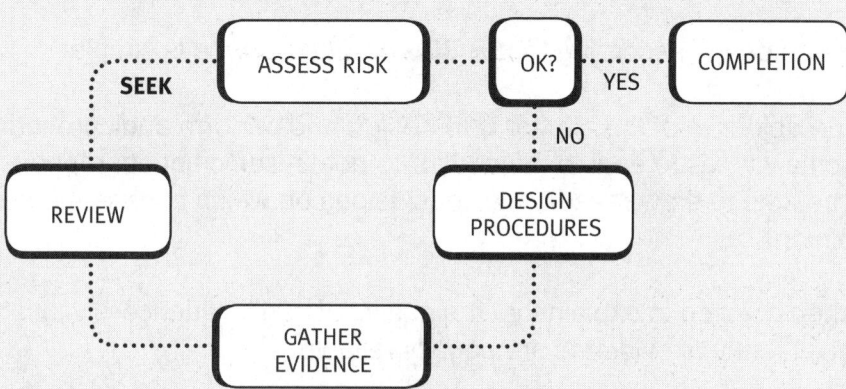

If, at the review stage, the senior audit staff deem that the risk of misstatement has not been reduced to an acceptable level, more evidence will be required.

Exam focus

Part A of the exam, consists of case study type questions that will most likely require you to decide what pieces of evidence should be gathered to address a particular risk. For example: in question 1 "Island Co" on the December 2007 paper, students were requested to suggest tests they would perform in respect of a warranty provision.

More recently Lisa Weaver, the examiner, suggested that she would begin testing more complicated areas of the syllabus (See the article entitled "The Importance of Financial Reporting Standards to Auditors," October 2008). True to her word she followed this up in December 2008 with a question (Bluebell) regarding audit procedures to be performed in respect of:

(i) the **measurement** of share based expenses; and

(ii) the **recoverability** of deferred tax assets.

Note: the question was specific to measurement and recoverability. Responses tailored to the presentation of share based expenses and the valuation of deferred tax assets, for example, were irrelevant and did not score.

Evidence

> Part A is compulsory. Therefore a well prepared student must be able to suggest audit procedures.
>
> It is also possible that in section B students may be asked to identify the evidence they would expect to see with regard to certain technical areas of financial reporting as part of a review of working files. See the self study questions accompanying this chapter as a guide.

3 Getting the right evidence

The guidance according to **ISA 500** *Audit Evidence* is simple:

"The objective of the auditor is to design and perform audit procedures in such a way as to enable the auditor to obtain sufficient appropriate evidence to be able to draw reasonable conclusions on which to base the auditor's opinion."

It then goes on to explain that the quality of audit evidence is vital and that not all forms of evidence are equally reliable:

- Independent, externally generated evidence is better than evidence generated internally by the client;
- Effective controls imposed by the entity, generally improve the reliability of evidence;
- Evidence obtained directly by the auditor is more reliable than evidence obtained indirectly or by inference;
- It is better to get written, documentary evidence rather than verbal confirmations; and
- Original documents provide more reliable evidence than photocopies or facsimiles.

Audit procedures for obtaining evidence

The auditor obtains evidence to draw conclusions on which to base the audit opinion. This is achieved by performing procedures to:

- Obtain an understanding of the entity and its environment, including internal control, to assess the risks of material misstatement;
- Test the operating effectiveness of controls in preventing, detecting and correcting material misstatements; and
- Detect material misstatements.

The methods of obtaining evidence for use in an audit are:

- Inspection of records, documents or physical assets;
- Observation of processes and procedures, e.g. inventory counts;
- External confirmation obtained in the form of a direct written response to the auditor from a third party;
- Recalculation to confirm the numerical accuracy of documents or records;
- Reperformance by the auditor of procedures or controls;
- Analytical procedures; and
- Enquiry of knowledgeable parties.

Financial statements assertions

For an audit test to be relevant it must fulfil the objective of the procedure. The objectives are usually to confirm one, or more, financial statements assertions made by management when preparing the class of transaction, accounting balance or disclosure. The assertions are:

For classes of transaction:

- Occurrence – transactions and events that have been recorded actually occurred and relate to the entity;
- Completeness – all transactions and events that should have been recorded have been recorded;
- Accuracy – amounts have been recorded appropriately;
- Cut-off – transactions and events have been recorded in the correct period; and
- Classification – transactions and events have been recorded in the correct accounts.

For account balances:

- Existence – assets, liabilities and equity interests exist;
- Rights and obligations – the entity controls rights to assets and liabilities are the obligation of the entity;
- Completeness – all assets, liabilities and equity interests that should have been recorded have been recorded; and
- Valuation and allocation – assets, liabilities and equity interests are included in the financial statements at appropriate amounts.

For presentation and disclosures:

- Occurrence and rights and obligations – disclosed events and transactions have occurred and pertain to the entity;
- Completeness – all disclosures that should have been recorded have been recorded;
- Classification and understandability – financial information is appropriately presented and described, and disclosures are clearly expressed; and
- Accuracy and valuation – financial and other information are disclosed fairly and at appropriate amounts.

(ISA 315)

Substantive analytical procedures

The use of analytical procedures as substantive evidence is generally more applicable where:

- there are large volumes of transactions
- relationships exist amongst the data and are believed to be predictable over time.

Their suitability as substantive procedures depends, to a large extent, on the auditor's risk assessment of specific assertions and the reliability of the underlying data used for comparison. It is likely that if an assertion is considered to be high risk then other tests of detail are likely to be performed. Likewise if the data is considered unreliable then further analysis of it will be futile.

If analytical procedures identify fluctuations or relationships that are inconsistent with the auditor's knowledge of the business then the auditor should investigate those peculiarities through:

- Enquiry of management; and
- Other procedures, as deemed necessary, for example: when management's response is considered inadequate.

chapter 11

Substantive procedures vs tests of control

Tests of controls are designed to check that the audit client's internal control systems operate effectively.

A substantive procedure is one designed to detect material misstatement at the assertion level in the financial statements (i.e. designed to detect errors and, possibly, fraud).

We have already seen that analytical procedures can be used to assist with risk assessment. However, they can also be used in conjunction with other tests to detect misstatement.

External confirmations

External confirmations are written responses received from third parties directly by the auditor to help them obtain sufficient appropriate evidence. Examples include: receivables circularisations and bank letters.

As these form external, written evidence they are considered to be reliable sources of evidence. However, in accordance with ISA 505 *External Confirmations* auditors should maintain control over this process to ensure that the evidence sought remains reliable. To do this they should:

- Determine the information to be confirmed;
- Select the appropriate third party;
- Design the confirmation requests and instructions to return directly to the auditor; and
- Send the requests, including a follow up when no response is received.

If management refuses to allow the auditor to send such requests the auditor should consider whether this is reasonable or not in the circumstances. This may affect the auditor's fraud risk assessment and reliance upon written management representations.

If the auditor concludes that management's request is unreasonable and they cannot obtain sufficient appropriate evidence by another means the matter should be communicated to those charged with governance in accordance with ISA 260.

KAPLAN PUBLISHING

269

Evidence

IAASB Practice Alert: Use of External Confirmations

IAASB Practice Alert: Emerging Practice Issues Regarding the Use of External Confirmations in an Audit of Financial Statements was published in November 2009.

It highlighted that external confirmations can be an "effective tool in obtaining relevant and reliable audit evidence **when used properly**".

The Alert notes that the auditor will need to plan **alternative or additional procedures** to ensure that sufficient appropriate audit evidence is obtained, where external confirmations are being used. In particular, to:

- manage the potential for difficulties in obtaining responses to external confirmation requests; and
- to ensure that evidence is obtained specific to all relevant assertions.

The auditor must "**be alert to the risk of interception, alteration or fraud**" and maintain appropriate professional scepticism when evaluating the confirmation responses, in particular considering the additional risks that may affect the reliability of confirmations received through e-mail.

Finally, the Alert notes that the auditor may need to consider "the nature and substance" of "disclaimers and other restrictions included in confirmation responses" when evaluating the response to determine whether they provide sufficient appropriate audit evidence.

Sampling

It is understood that auditors can rarely, if ever, test every transaction, balance and disclosure relevant to a set of financial statements. ISA 530 *Audit Sampling* states that auditors should select appropriate samples for testing that provide a reasonable basis to draw conclusions about the population from which the sample is selected.

When selecting samples auditors should consider the following concepts:

- Materiality and performance materiality;
- Sampling risk: the risk that the conclusions reached based upon testing the sample would be different than the conclusions reached applying the same procedures to the whole population;

- The nature (and risk) of the population being tested, including the number of items within the population, their size relative to the total of the population and the coverage required to reduce audit risk to an acceptable level;
- The need to project, or extrapolate, the results of misstatements identified in the sample to the whole population.

When choosing a sampling method there are two broad approaches:

- Statistical sampling, where items in the population are selected randomly so that probability theory may be used to evaluate the results (through extrapolation to the whole population); and
- Non-statistical, which is a method that does not meet the characteristics of statistical. This is usually employed when the auditor uses judgement to select sample items (e.g. focusing on high value, or known high risk items). Extrapolation cannot be used when bias has been introduced into the sample because the sample is no longer representative of the whole population.

Specific sampling methods include:

- Random: through use of random selectors/number tables;
- Systematic: number of items divided by a specific testing interval (e.g. every 50th balance to be tested). The starting point should be determined haphazardly/randomly;
- Monetary unit: value weighted selection so that conclusions are permitted in monetary amounts;
- Haphazard: no structured technique but avoids bias (not appropriate for statistical analysis); and
- Block: selection of contiguous items (i.e. sequential) (rarely appropriate for statistical analysis)

4 Written representations

The value of written (management) representations

According to **ISA 580** *Written Representations* the auditor should obtain 'appropriate' written representations from management:

- That they have fulfilled their responsibilities for the preparation of the financial statements;
- That they have provided the auditor with all relevant information;
- That all transactions have been recorded and reflected in the financial statements;

- To support other audit evidence relevant to the financial statements or specific assertions if deemed necessary by the auditor; and
- As required by specific ISA's.

However, as a form of evidence representations are low down in the order of reliability because they are internally produced.

ISA 580 clearly states that on their own, written representations "**do not provide sufficient appropriate evidence about any of the matters with which they deal**."

Therefore the auditor cannot delegate responsibility for gathering evidence to management. Moreover, auditors should only use written management representations on matters material to the financial statements when other sufficient appropriate evidence **cannot reasonably be expected to be obtained**.

If, having received the representations considered necessary to gather sufficient appropriate evidence, the auditor concludes that there is sufficient doubt about the integrity of management to the extent that the representations are unreliable, then the auditor shall disclaim an opinion in accordance with ISA 705.

Other written representations

The typical subjects of other representations include:

- Whether the selection and application of accounting policies are appropriate;
- Whether the following matters have been measured, presented and disclosed in accordance with the relevant financial reporting framework:
    - Plans or intentions that may affect the carrying value or classification of assets and liabilities;
    - Liabilities, both contingent and actual;
    - Title to, or control over, assets; and
    - Aspects of laws, regulations and contractual agreements that may affect the financial statements, including non-compliance.
- That the directors have communicated all deficiencies in internal control to the auditor;
- Specific assertions about classes of transactions, accounts balances and disclosures requiring management judgement; and
- That management has considered the effect of uncorrected misstatements and considers them to be immaterial.

chapter 11

> **Exam focus**
>
> **The limitations of management representations**
>
> Quite simply, they do not represent independent evidence, and the auditor is not able to absolve himself from his responsibilities, by obtaining representations.
>
> Students should be careful not to suggest management representations as appropriate evidence for all areas of testing. The examiner has suggested this is a common concern amongst weaker students who do not appreciate the nature of 'appropriate' evidence and that it detracts from the quality of an answer.

5 Relying on the work of others

```
                    RELYING ON THE WORK OF OTHERS

                                              Auditors are
                                              responsible for
    NO DELEGATION OF RESPONSIBILITY ······    obtaining sufficient
                                              appropriate audit
                                              evidence

                                              COMPETENCE
            CONSIDERATIONS           ······   INDEPENDENCE
                                              OBJECTIVITY

       REFERENCE IN AUDIT REPORT?    ······   NO!
```

Relying on the work of an auditor's expert

Occasionally, when the auditor lacks the required technical knowledge to gather sufficient appropriate evidence to form an opinion, they may have to rely on the work of an expert. Examples of such circumstances include:

- The valuation of complex financial instruments, land and buildings, works of art, jewellery and intangible assets;
- Actuarial calculations associated with insurance contracts or employee benefit plans;
- The estimation of oil and gas reserves;

Evidence

- The interpretation of contracts, laws and regulations; and
- The analysis of complex or unusual tax compliance issues.

ISA 620 *Using the Work of an Auditor's Expert* suggests that, whilst this is acceptable, auditor still needs to obtain sufficient appropriate evidence that such work is adequate for the purposes of the audit.

To fulfil this responsibility the auditor must **evaluate whether the expert has the necessary competence, capability and objectivity for the purpose of the audit** procedures required. The auditor also needs to obtain an understanding of the field of expertise of the expert to:

- Determine the nature, scope and objectives of the expert's work for audit purposes; and
- Evaluate the adequacy of that work for audit purposes.

Once the auditor has considered the above issues they must then agree the following matters in writing with the expert:

- The nature, scope and objectives of the expert's work;
- The roles and responsibilities of the auditor and the expert;
- The nature, timing and extent of communication between the two parties; and
- The need for the expert to observe confidentiality.

Once the expert's work is complete the auditor must scrutinise it and evaluate whether it is appropriate for audit purposes. In particular, the auditor should consider:

- The reasonableness of the findings and their consistency with other evidence;
- The significant assumptions made; and
- The use and accuracy of source data.

The competence, capability and objectivity of the expert

Information regarding the competence, capability and objectivity on an expert may come from a variety of sources, including:

- Personal experience of working with the expert;
- Discussions with the expert;
- Discussions with other auditors;
- Knowledge of the expert's qualifications, memberships of professional bodies and licences;

- Published papers or books written by the expert; and
- The audit firm's quality control procedures.

Assessing the objectivity of the expert is particularly difficult, as they may not be bound by a similar code of ethics as the auditor and, as such, may be unaware of the ethical requirements and threats with which auditors are familiar. It may therefore be relevant to:

- Make enquiries of the client about known interests or relationships with the chosen expert;
- Discuss applicable safeguards with the expert;
- Discuss financial, business and personal interests in the client with the expert; and
- Obtain written representation from the expert.

The auditor's responsibilities

Auditors cannot devolve responsibility for forming an audit opinion, or for reaching conclusions with regard to specific assertions, onto an expert. The auditor has to use their professional judgment whether the evidence produced by the expert is sufficient and appropriate to support the audit opinion.

Finally, the auditor should not make reference to the use of an expert in their audit report unless it is required to aid the understanding of a modification to the audit opinion. In such circumstances the auditor shall indicate that the reference to the expert does not diminish the auditor's responsibility for the opinion.

Relying on internal audit

An internal audit department forms part of the client's system of internal control. If this is an effective element of the control system it may well reduce control risk, and therefore reduce the need for the auditor to perform detailed substantive testing. This will obviously be taken into account during the planning phase of the audit.

Additionally, auditors may be able to co-operate with a client's internal audit department and place reliance on their procedures in place of performing their own.

ISA 610 (Revised) *Using the Work of Internal Auditors* (issued March 2012, effective for audits of financial statements for periods ending on or after December 15, 2013) states that before relying on the work of internal auditors, the external auditor must determine whether the work of internal audit can be used and whether that work is adequate for the purposes of the audit.

This involves an evaluation of:

- the extent to which the internal audit function's **organisational status** and relevant policies and procedures support the **objectivity** of the internal auditors);
- the **competence** of the internal audit function; and
- whether the internal audit function applies a systematic and disciplined **approach**, including quality control.

If the auditor considers it appropriate to use the work of the internal auditors they then have to determine the areas and extent to which the work of the internal audit function can be used (by considering the nature and scope of work) and incorporate this into their planning to assess the impact on the nature, timing and extent of further audit procedures.

They also have to plan adequate time to review the work of the internal audit function to evaluate whether:

- The work was properly planned, performed, supervised, reviewed and documented;
- Sufficient appropriate evidence has been obtained;
- The conclusions reached are appropriate in the circumstances; and
- The reports prepared are consistent with the work performed.

Note that the auditor is not required to rely on the work of internal audit. In some jurisdictions, the external auditor may be prohibited or restricted from using the work of the internal auditor by law.

- As when relying on an auditor's expert, responsibility for the auditor's opinion cannot be devolved and no reference should be made in the audit report regarding the use of others during the audit.

chapter 11

The objectivity and competence of internal audit

When evaluating the competence of the internal audit function, the external auditor will consider:

- whether the resources of the internal audit function are appropriate and adequate for the size of the organisation and nature of its operations
- whether there are established policies for hiring, training and assigning internal auditors to internal audit engagements
- whether internal auditors have adequate technical training and proficiency, including relevant professional qualifications and experience
- whether the internal auditors have the required knowledge of the entity's financial reporting and the applicable financial reporting framework
- whether the internal audit function possesses the necessary skills (e.g. industry-specific knowledge) to perform work related to the entity's financial statements
- whether the internal auditors are members of relevant professional bodies that oblige them to comply with the relevant professional standards including continuing professional development.

When evaluating whether the internal audit function applies a systematic and disciplined approach, the external auditor will consider:

- whether there are adequate documented internal audit procedures or guidance
- whether the internal audit function has appropriate quality control procedures.

(ISA 610 (Revised) *Using the Work of Internal Auditors*)

6 Related parties

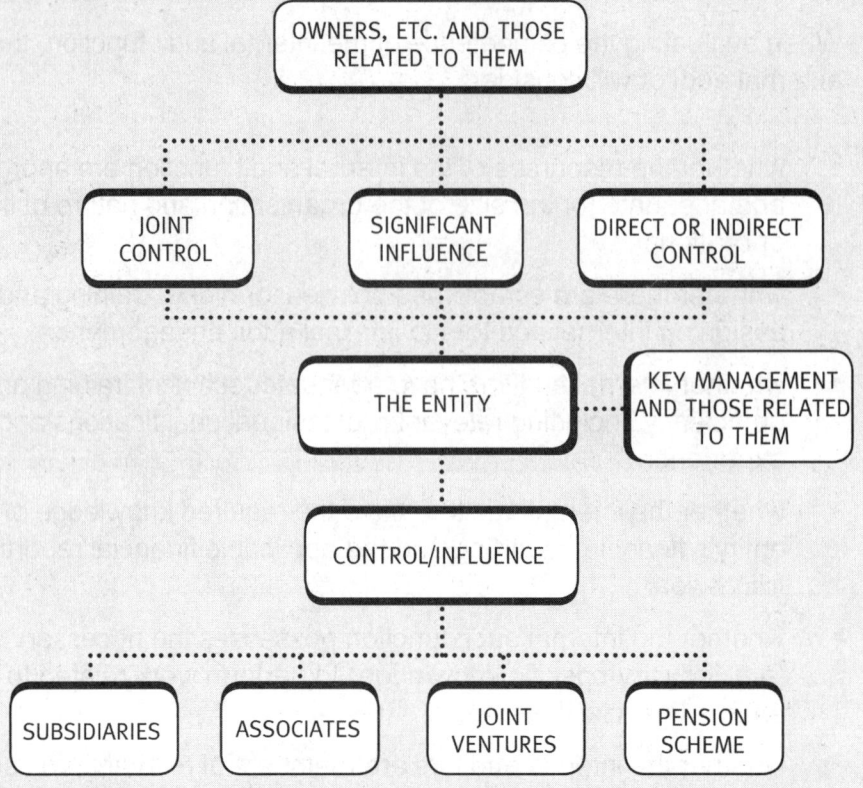

Related parties to a business

- Those who control, directly or indirectly, the entity.
- Those related to those who control the entity.
    - Family
    - Entities under their control (including group entities)
    - Parent company management.
- Those who manage the entity.
- Those related to those who manage the entity.
- Those under the control or influence of the entity.
    - Subsidiaries
    - Associates
    - Joint ventures
    - Pension schemes.

Why are related party transactions potentially significant?

There is nothing wrong with an entity dealing with a related party.

However, dealing with related parties increases the potential for transactions to be carried out on a basis other than 'arms length' and for the financial results to be manipulated. In these circumstances it is appropriate for such transactions to be brought to the attention of shareholders.

The problem with related parties

Related parties are often difficult to identify in practice. It can be hard to establish exactly who, or what, are the related parties of an entity.

Furthermore, once related parties have been identified it can be difficult to spot associated transactions with them:

- Directors may be reluctant to disclose transactions, particularly in the case of family members;
- Transactions may not be easy to identify from the accounting systems because they are not separately identified from 'normal' transactions;
- Transactions may be concealed in whole, or in part, from auditors for fraudulent purposes.

Materiality is a difficult concept to apply to related party transactions. **ISA 550** *Related Parties* states that the auditor should consider the effect of a related party transaction on the financial statements. However, it is likely the transaction could occur at an abnormally small, even nil, value. Determining materiality based on monetary value is therefore irrelevant, and the auditor should instead be alert to the unusual nature of the transaction making it material.

Audit procedures for dealing with related party transactions

The degree of difficulty in identifying undisclosed related parties is recognised by ISA 550 *Related Parties*. However, it states that, regardless of financial reporting requirements with regard to related parties, the auditor should obtain an understanding of related party relationships and transactions sufficient to be able to:

- Recognise fraud risk factors; and
- To conclude whether the financial statements:
    - achieve a fair presentation; or
    - are not misleading.

Evidence

In addition, where there are applicable financial reporting requirements relating to related parties, the auditor should obtain sufficient appropriate evidence that transactions have been identified, accounted for and disclosed in accordance with those requirements.

If transactions have not been accounted for or disclosed in accordance with those requirements, the potentially significant deficiency in the internal control system should be reported to those charged with governance.

Typical procedures auditors use to identify related party transactions include:

- inspecting prior year working papers ;
- assessing the entity's procedures for identifying, authorising and recording related party transactions;
- enquiring about relationships between those charged with governance and management and other entities;
- inspecting shareholder records for details of principal shareholders;
- inspecting minutes of shareholders' meetings and other relevant minutes and records;
- enquiring of other auditors involved with the audit; and
- inspecting the entity's income tax returns and other information supplied to the regulatory authorities.

As a significant area of the audit, the auditor should apply performance materiality when when designing the nature, timing and extent of procedures over related parties.

ISA 550 also states that the engagement team discussion during planning "shall include specific consideration of the susceptibility of the financial statements to material misstatement due to fraud or error that could result from the entity's related party relationships and transactions".

Indicators of related party transactions

- transactions with abnormal terms of trade
- transactions that appear not to have a logical business reason
- transactions where substance and form differ
- transactions that are not processed in the usual or routine way
- where there are high volumes of transactions, or high value or otherwise significant transactions with individual customers or suppliers
- unrecorded transactions such as rent free accommodation, or management or other services provided at no cost.

Members of the audit team need to be aware that they should consider the possibility of undisclosed related party transactions while they carry out audit procedures such as examining documents, inspecting minutes of meetings, etc. If the auditor identifies related parties that were not previously indentified or disclosed they shall:

- Communicate that information to the rest of the engagements team;
- Request that management identifies all transactions with the related party and enquire why they failed to identify them;
- Perform appropriate substantive procedures relating to transactions with these entities;
- Reconsider the risk that other, unidentified, related parties may exist; and
- Evaluate the implications if the non-disclosure by management appears intentional.

If the auditor identifies related party transactions outside the entity's normal course of business they should also:

- Inspect the underlying contracts or agreements to establish: the business rationale; the terms of the transaction; and whether appropriate disclosures have been made; and
- Obtain evidence that the transactions were appropriately authorised.

7 Estimates and fair values

ISA 540 *Auditing Accounting Estimates, Including Fair Value Accounting Estimates and Related Disclosures* merges the old ISA 540 *Audit of Accounting* Estimates and ISA 545 *Audit of Fair Value Measurements* as the principles and techniques applied to each are the same. In accordance with ISA 540 auditors need to obtain sufficient appropriate evidence about whether estimates (including fair values) are reasonable and adequately disclosed in the financial statements.

Consideration should first be made when planning and performing risk assessment. In particular the auditor should consider:

- How management identifies transactions and balances requiring estimation;

- How management makes estimates, including:
  - models used;
  - relevant controls;
  - use of an expert;
  - assumptions underlying the estimates;
  - changes since the prior period; and
  - how management assesses the effect of uncertainty.

To assist with this process the auditor should consider the outcome of estimates made in the prior period.

Responses to risk assessment

In response to the assessed risk of material misstatement due to estimations the auditor is required to perform one or more of the following procedures with regard to estimates:

- Determining whether events up to the date of the audit report provide additional evidence with regard to the appropriateness of estimates;
- Testing how management made their estimates and evaluating whether the method is appropriate;
- Testing the effectiveness of controls over estimations; and
- Developing a point estimate to use in comparison to management's

If there are significant risks associated with estimates the auditor should also identify whether management considered any alternative assumptions and why they rejected them and whether the assumptions used are reasonable in the circumstances.

Ultimately, due to the uncertainty surrounding estimates, the auditor should obtain written representations from management confirming that they believe the assumptions used in making estimates are reasonable.

Challenges auditing fair values

Staff Audit Practice Alert (IAASB – October 2008): Challenges in Auditing Fair Value Accounting Estimates in the Current Market Environment

The practice alert has been prepared in light of difficulties in the credit markets and therefore has a focus on financial instruments. Recent market experience has highlighted the difficulties that arise in valuing financial instruments when market information is either not available or sufficient information is difficult to obtain.

In the current environment obtaining reliable information relevant to fair values has been one of the greatest challenges faced by preparers, and consequently by auditors. The nature and reliability of information available to management to support the making of a fair value accounting estimate vary widely, and thereby affect the degree of estimation uncertainty associated with that fair value.

The alert is a comprehensive and lengthy document. A summary of some of the key points is included below:

- Due to the complex nature of certain financial instruments, it is vital that both the entity and the auditor understand the instruments in which the entity has invested or to which it is exposed, and the related risks;
- The auditor's understanding of the instruments may be developed by understanding the entity's processes for investing in particular instruments;
- Factors that may influence the auditor's risk assessment with regard to financial instruments include:
    - Whether the entity has control procedures in place for making investment decisions;
    - The level of due diligence associated with particular investments;
    - The expertise of those responsible for making investment decisions;
    - Whether the entity has the ability to subsequently value the instruments; and
    - Management's track record for assessing the risks of particular instruments.
- In the case of fair value accounting estimates, it is necessary that the audit engagement team include one or more members sufficiently skilled and knowledgeable about fair value accounting in order to comply with the required quality control procedures.
- Depending on the nature, materiality and complexity of fair values, management representations about fair value measurements and disclosures contained in the financial statements may also include representations about the following:
    - The appropriateness of the measurement methods and the consistency in application of the methods;
    - The completeness and appropriateness of disclosure related to fair values;
    - Whether subsequent events require adjustment to the fair value measurements;

Evidence

Specific considerations

In accordance with ISA 501 auditors are required to obtain sufficient appropriate evidence with regard to three specific matters, as follows:

(1) The existence and condition of inventory
   - Attendance at the inventory count
       - evaluate management's instructions;
       - observe the count procedures;
       - inspect the inventory;
       - perform test counts
   - Perform procedures with regard to final inventory records to ensure they reflect actual inventory count results

(2) The completeness of litigation and claims involving the entity
   - Enquiry of management and in-house legal counsel;
   - Inspecting minutes of board meetings and meetings with legal counsel;
   - Inspecting legal expense accounts
   - If there is a significant risk of material misstatement due to unidentified litigation or claims the audit should seek direct communication with the entity's external legal counsel

(3) The presentation and disclosure of segmental information
   - Understand methods used by management to determine segmental information;
       - evaluate methods;
       - test methods
   - Perform analytical procedures.

chapter 11

Audit documentation

The need for documentation

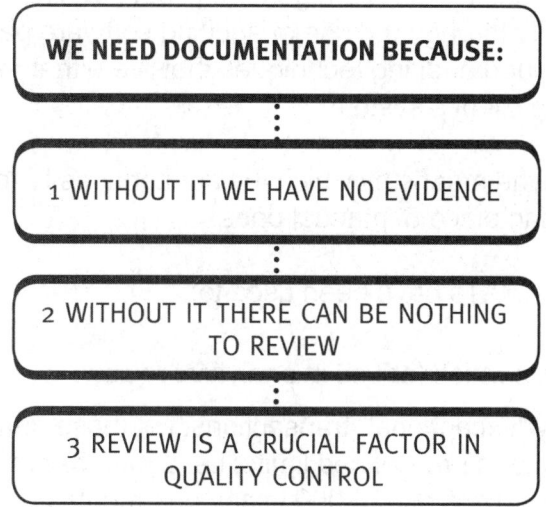

ISA 230 *Audit Documentation* deals specifically with audit documentation and requires:

- timely preparation of audit documentation necessary to provide a sufficient and appropriate record of the basis for the auditor's report, and evidence that the audit was carried out in accordance with ISAs and applicable legal and regulatory requirements

- audit documentation sufficient to enable an experienced auditor, having no previous connection with the audit, to understand the audit work performed, the results and audit evidence obtained, and the significant matters identified and conclusions reached thereon.

Current issue – changing technology

Technological development means that increasingly sophisticated information systems are available to businesses at a steadily decreasing cost. This has led to a demand for reliable and more timely reporting on financial information.

Continuous auditing enables auditors to give assurance on a subject matter (e.g. inventory levels, receivables balances, etc.) by issuing audit reports simultaneously with (or a short time after) the events that underlie the subject matter.

KAPLAN PUBLISHING

285

Continuous auditing clearly increases the frequency of reporting. Where a traditional audit report is issued annually on the year's financial statements, continuous auditing generates audit reports much more frequently, e.g. weekly or daily.

Continuous audit reports are generally (but not exclusively) produced automatically through the use of auditing software packages that use computer aided auditing techniques that are either installed onto or linked to the client's system.

CAATs are the means by which the auditor uses IT to carry out audit procedures in place of manual ones.

Practically CAATs have been used to:

- calculate ratios for use in analytical review;
- identify "exceptional" transactions, i.e. those unusual transactions that exceed pre-defined limits, i.e. a member of management being paid in excess of $20,000 in any one month. This helps identify balances that require further audit testing;
- extract samples in a non-biased fashion;
- check the calculations in client prepared reports; and
- prepare lead schedules for the auditor to use in working papers.

Auditing software has obvious benefits:

- It allows continual auditing of processes and delivery of more frequent reports;
- It can process large volumes of data and perform large volumes of calculations, many more than could reasonably be performed manually;
- CAATs test the underlying system data, rather than copies and prints;
- Once software has been written for a client it can then be applied to their system with few further costs;
- Reduced need for audit staff to perform procedures, hence further cost savings for clients; and
- Reduced need for paper audit trails (hence reduced environmental impact of the audit process).

However, there are many concerns that need to be addressed before an audit firm actually implements computer based auditing techniques:

- There is an initial high cost of designing the software package, although this cost can be recouped over a number of years of use;

- Software may interfere with the client's system and could potentially increase the risk of viruses and data corruption;
- Clients may fear for the security of their data;
- Software generally has to be written for bespoke accounting packages and therefore can only be used on one client;
- They are only usually cost effective if the client's accounting systems are integrated, otherwise auditors would need different software programmes for different systems;
- Lead times tend to be long and the planning has to be carried out well in advance – not just three or four weeks before the start of fieldwork, but perhaps a whole year in advance;
- Audit firms will need to recruit increasingly from an IT, rather than an accounting, background;
- Software has to be tested on a 'live' system before the auditor knows whether it will work or not (i.e. high risk of corrupting that system); and
- If the client wishes to change their system the auditor has to incur further costs changing their CAAT software.

UK syllabus focus

Bank Reports

In February 2011, the FRC issued a revised Practice Note (16) *Bank Reports for Audit Purposes in the United Kingdom*.

ISA 330 *The Auditor's Responses to Assessed Risks* requires the auditor to consider whether external confirmation procedures are to be performed as substantive procedures in order to perform the audit in an effective manner.

Practice Note 16 summarises the process agreed between the UK auditing profession and the British Bankers Association (BBA) regarding the procedures auditors use when requesting confirmation of balances, transactions or arrangements from the bankers of an entity being audited, using bank reports (bank confirmations).

This Practice Note includes templates for the different types of bank reports available and the circumstances in which they should be used:

- **Standard**: in most circumstances, when the auditor is not able to supply sufficient references to identify the bank accounts for which information is required.

- **Fast Track**: in exceptional circumstances, e.g. to meet a reporting deadline within a month or less of the accounting year end.
- **Incomplete Information**: when the auditor is unable to provide the main account sort code and number for all the entities in a group.

Attendance at Stocktaking

In February 2011, the FRC issued a revised Practice Note (25) *Attendance at Stocktaking*.

ISA 501 *Audit Evidence - Specific Considerations for Selected items* includes requirements and application material relating to inventory (stock) and in particular, obtaining audit evidence by attendance at physical inventory counts (stock takes).

The Practice Note contains further guidance including how the requirements of other ISAs may be applied in relation to attendance at stocktaking, in particular in relation to obtaining evidence relating to the existence assertion. The Practice Note covers:

- Assessment of risks and internal controls including factors relating to risk of material misstatement in the context of the existence of stocks (e.g. timing of stocktakes relative to the year-end date)
- Audit evidence obtained from attendance at stocktaking, in particular the principal sources of evidence relating to the existence of stocks (e.g. substantive evidence from physical inspection of stock)
- The principal procedures that should be performed when attending a stocktake, including:
    - the need for procedures to be performed by audit staff who are familiar with the entity's business
    - the need for advance planning
    - procedures before during and after the stocktake
    - inspection of work-in-progress
    - the use of expert valuers and stocktakers
    - the need to obtain sufficient appropriate evidence over stock held by third parties or in public warehouses.

Smaller Entities

In December 2009, the FRC issued a revised Practice Note (26) *Guidance on Smaller Entity Audit Documentation*. The Practice Note provides guidance on the application of documentation requirements contained within ISAs to the audit of financial statements of smaller entities in an efficient manner.

chapter 11

> The guidance is aimed at auditors of smaller, simpler entities, including entities which are exempt from audit but which choose to have a voluntary audit, small subsidiary companies, small charities, and simple larger entities. It excludes smaller entities with complex operations or the audit of complex and subjective matters.
>
> The Practice Note highlights that it is neither practicable nor necessary to document every matter considered, or professional judgement made, in an audit. It encourages:
>
> - the use of structured forms (instead of narrative notes) to document understanding of the entity.
>
> - focusing on how the main transaction cycles operate an highlighting the risks of material misstatement when documenting smaller entitie's accounting systems.
>
> - not documenting matters that would normally have been documented soley to inform or instruct members of the audit team, when the engagement partner is performing the work themselves (as smaller audit teams are common in audits of smaller entities).

Exam focus: Section A-style question

> *Study Note: this is an example of a typical section A case study style question. The examiner has indicated that risk assessment and audit procedures are core areas and will be examined in every sitting. The format below represents how these topics have been examined so far.*
>
> Your firm has recently been appointed as auditor of Queens Cars Ltd, a new and second hand motor vehicle dealer with six sites. You are currently planning the audit for the year ended 29 February 2008. The draft financial statements show turnover of $23.3mn (2007: $18.1mn), profit before tax of $2.6mn (2007: $1.4mn) and total assets of $15.8mn (2007: $12.6mn).
>
> New cars are purchased on a consignment basis from a single supplier. Queens pays the invoice price (plus a 2% display fee) six months after delivery, or on sale of the vehicle if sooner. Currently Queens records the purchase of the vehicles when the invoice is paid because their supplier legally owns the vehicles and may demand their return at any point prior to settlement. Although, the FD has told you that this has yet to happen.
>
> The value of all new cars held across the various sites at the year end, according to management records, was $2.4mn (2007: $1.9mn). The value of used cars held at the year end, according to inventory records, was $0.6mn (2007: $0.6mn).

KAPLAN PUBLISHING

Evidence

Whilst less popular with new cars, many customers like to pay cash, using this as leverage to barter for a "cash discount. In addition, Queens also accept cars in part exchange. One of their current promotions is that they will accept any vehicle for a minimum of $500 trade in value.

The MD of Queens has informed you that he has employed his nephew, a trainee accountant, to manage and record the spare parts inventory across all branches. It was his responsibility to conduct the year end count. However, you have been told that the year end fell during the nephew's reading week and he was on holiday at the time. Therefore he conducted the count the week before the year end and then reconciled the movements on his return. The year end valuation of spare parts inventory was $0.2mn (2007: $0.15mn).

During the year Queens purchased a brand of simple fitting replacement parts that it will now supply on all servicing and repair jobs. As part of this purchase $0.7mn was paid for the brand name "Quick Fit." This has been capitalised as an intangible asset. However, Queens are not amortising the brand following the advice of the MD's nephew, who argued that the brand was so strong that its useful life was indefinite.

All new cars come with a manufacturer's warranty of three years or 30,000 miles, whichever is sooner. Second hand cars are offered with a six month guarantee. At the end of the year the warranty provision was $0.8mn (2007: $0.7mn). The FD believes that despite the increase in the number of cars sold there is no need to increase the warranty provision because the company has focused more heavily on new car sales this year, which – according to him – require less after sales repairs than used cars.

Required:

(a) Prepare a briefing document for the engagement partner that identifies and explains the principal audit risks that need to be considered when planning the final audit of Queens Cars for the year ended 29 February 2008.

Professional marks will be awarded in part (a) for the format of the answer and for the clarity of assessment provided.

(15 marks)

(b) Describe the principal audit procedures that would be carried out in respect of the amortisation of the "Quick Fit" brand.

(5 marks)

chapter 11

Test your understanding 1

Harmonica Ltd owns a portfolio of commercial properties for renting that are valued on an open market basis by a firm of professional valuers of which the senior partner is the brother of Harmonica's Chief Executive. Harmonica's auditors write each year to the valuers and receive confirmation that the market value of the company's properties is as stated in the accounts.

(1) Are there any particular factors the auditors should take into consideration?

(2) If there were reports in the press that property prices were falling in an area where Harmonica owns properties, what implications would there be for the auditors?

(3) If following a visit to some of the company's properties the auditor gained the distinct impression that some were in a poor state of repair, what implications would there be for the auditors?

8 Chapter summary

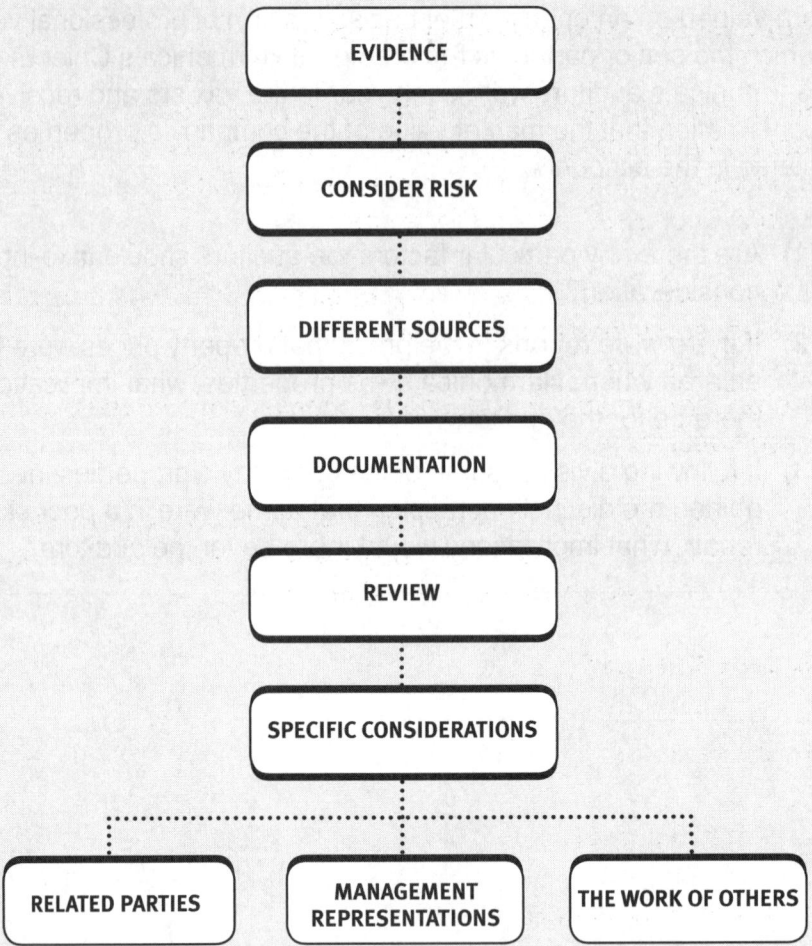

chapter 11

Test your understanding answers

Exam focus: Section A-style question

*Study Note: throughout your answer you must remain specific to the scenario presented in the question. The vast bulk of the marks are for **application** of knowledge. Simple presentation of definitions and facts will not score enough for a pass.*

Note the use of structure (short paragraphs, headings, report format). This generally leads to more succinct answers, which are easier to mark. There are also professional marks available for use of appropriate formats, introductions, conclusions and the quality of the presentation/flow.

Finally: this is a large question! You must plan your time effectively to answer all parts. Do not simply answer the risk section. It is never going to be enough for a comfortable pass.

Queens Cars Ltd

(a) **Audit risk**

To: A. Partner

From: A.N. Accountant

Date: 8 April 2008

Subject: Audit Risks to be Considered During the Planning of the Year End Audit of Queens Cars Limited

The audit risks identified during a review of the operations of Queens Cars Limited have been summarised in this report for consideration at the audit planning meeting.

Materiality

The materiality thresholds are as follows:

Turnover:	½ – 1%	$117k – $233k
Profit before tax:	5 – 10%	$130k – $260k
Total assets:	1 – 2%	$158k – $316k

Evidence

Consignment inventory

In legal terms Queens Cars do not own the consignment inventory held on site at the year end. However, Queens have never returned a vehicle and in substance they should record the purchase of inventory in their accounting records at the point of delivery. There is therefore a risk that new car inventories, and the consequent liabilities, are understated.

There is also an associated risk that finance costs are understated in the statement of profit or loss. The 2% display fee should be treated as a finance cost in the statement of profit or loss.

There is a risk that second hand inventories are overstated. At $0.6mn these are material to total assets. According to IAS 2 inventory should be valued at the lower of cost and net realisable value. The case suggests that it is common for customers to barter for discounts, which could lead to vehicles being sold for less than cost.

Queens also offer a fixed part exchange value for any vehicle and it is therefore likely that they may receive vehicles in part exchange that do not have a resale value of $500 or more. It will be necessary to establish whether such vehicles have a resale value above their part exchange value.

Spare parts inventory total $0.2mn and are therefore material to total assets. There is a risk that these have been incorrectly valued at the year-end due to the fact that the year end count was performed before the year-end. This increases the risk that inventory balances are overstated.

Brand

There is also a risk that the acquired brand, "Quick Fit" is overstated at the year end. The balance of $0.7mn is material to total assets. According to IAS 38 "indefinite" does not mean "infinite." Indefinite suggests the company has sufficient resources to maintain the brand strength. However other factors, such as competition, new technology and substitutes, suggest that this could be difficult to maintain in the long term.

Regardless, according to IAS 38 if Queens Cars rebuts the presumption that the useful life is less than 20 years they must still perform an annual impairment review. Therefore there is further risk that the asset is overstated and impairment charges are understated.

Turnover

There is a risk that turnover is misstated due to discounts for cash sales. There is a risk that the sale may be recorded at the original amount, rather than the renegotiated value. There is also an increased risk of theft by sales persons, who could record a higher cash discount in the accounts and keep some of the cash for themselves.

Provision

There is a risk that the warranty provision is understated on the statement of financial position. $0.8mn is material to total assets. Whereas turnover has increased by 29% the provision has only increased by 14%, which suggests that the provision does not reflect the increased activity of the business. IAS 37 suggests that a provision should be recorded for all probable liabilities and given that all cars are sold with a warranty there is a suggestion that the provision should be increased accordingly.

Other issues

This is our first year of audit. Given our lack of cumulative audit knowledge and experience there is a greater exposure to audit risk. In response it may be prudent to perform increased substantive procedures this year.

Given the multiple sites it will be necessary to visit at least a sample to assess the accounting/control environment. This could increase the time taken to perform the audit and will have consequences for the budget.

(b) **Audit work on useful life**
- Inspect any purchase agreements/invoices available for the purchase of the brand to confirm the cost to be used in any subsequent impairment tests.
- Review the history of the "Quick Fit" brand. Most importantly assess how long the brand has been trading under that name.
- Inspect advertising invoices to confirm the amount spent on marketing the "Quick Fit" brand during the accounting year.
- Consider the amortisation policies of known competitor brands within the same industry. The accounts should be publicly available and an accounting policy note should be included for amortisation of intangibles.
- Inspect any forecasts/budgets available to assess the level of marketing considered necessary to maintain the brand name.

Evidence

- Analytically review the performance of the brand since acquisition in comparison to forecasts to identify if performance is as strong as predicted.

- Analytically review the performance of the brand on a month by month basis since acquisition to the present day to identify if performance continues to improve, or at least remain healthy to confirm management's assumption of brand strength.

- Inspect a breakdown of the repairs and maintenance account after the year-end to identify any possible concerns over the quality of the replacement parts.

- Consider industry factors to identify the risk of new entrants or substitute products to the spare parts industry.

- Inspect any impairment tests carried out by management, or make enquiries of management to the same effect.

- Make enquiries of management about the basis of their assumptions with regard to the strength of the brand and their strategy for maintaining its market position.

- Obtain written management representations to corroborate the results of enquiries with management with regard to areas of judgement and estimation.

Test your understanding 1

(1) The service provided by the valuers is a related party transaction and should be disclosed in the financial statements. In the absence of any evidence to the contrary, there is no reason to doubt the valuation, although the auditors should increase the amount of attention they pay to local property prices, etc.

(2) Here there is a conflict between two sources of evidence, which may be exacerbated because of the increased risk due to the involvement of a related party. The auditor should, in the first instance, discuss the matter with management. It is possible that a further valuation from an independent adviser should be sought.

(3) Here there is prima facie evidence of impairment, which again should be discussed with management and that might lead to another independent valuation.

chapter 12

Completion

Chapter learning objectives

When you have completed this chapter you will be able to:

- explain the use of analytical procedures and checklists in evaluation and review;
- explain the auditor's responsibilities for corresponding figures, comparatives and other information;
- specify audit procedures designed to identify subsequent events;
- identify and explain indicators that the going concern basis may be in doubt;
- recommend audit procedures and assess the appropriateness of the going concern basis; and
- assess the adequacy of disclosures in financial statements relating to going concern and explain the implications for the auditor's report with regard to the going concern basis.

Completion

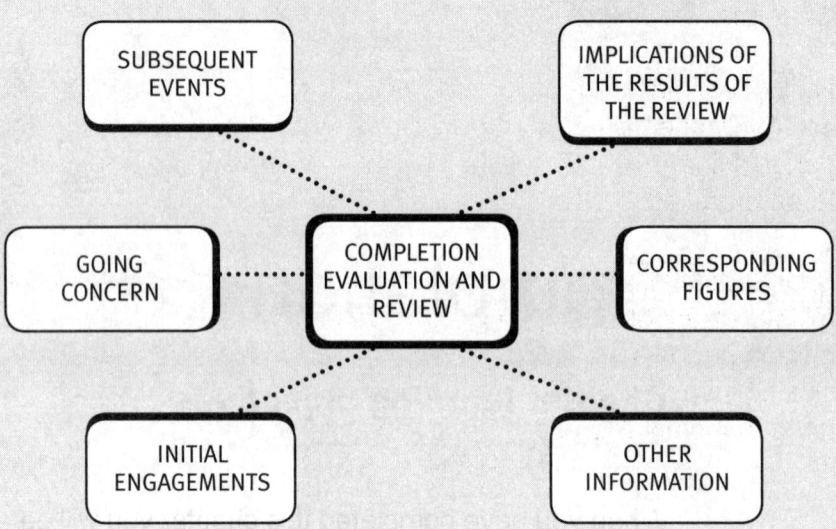

At least one question will examine the completion stage of an engagement. Often the requirement is to explain the "matters to consider" and "evidence you would expect to find" in your review of the engagement files. However, a requirement could also test a specific area of the completion stage in more detail.

1 Initial engagements – audit considerations

ISA 510 *Initial Engagements – Opening Balances* requires that when auditors take on a new client, they must ensure that:

- opening balances do not contain material misstatements;
- prior period closing balances have been correctly brought forward or, where appropriate, restated; and
- appropriate accounting policies have been consistently applied, or changes adequately disclosed.

Considerations:

- Were the previous financial statements audited?
- If the previous financial statements were audited, was the opinion modified?
- If the previous opinion was modified, has the matter been resolved since then?
- Were any adjustments made as a result of the audit? If so, has the client adjusted their accounting ledgers as well as the financial statements?

If auditors are unable to satisfy themselves with regard to the preceding period, they will have to consider modifying the current audit report.

chapter 12

Example

Difficulties may arise where the prior period audit report was modified and the matter remains unresolved. If the matter is material to the current period's financial statements then the current audit report will also need to be modified.

For example; if there was a modification on the grounds of a material misstatement of closing inventory in the prior period, this will affect the current period's statement of profit or loss. This is because last year's closing inventory is this year's opening inventory and the auditor may need to modify this year's audit report on that basis.

Audit procedures

Where the prior period was audited by another auditor or unaudited, the auditors will need to perform additional work in order to satisfy themselves regarding the opening position. Such work would include:

- consulting the client's management
- reviewing records and accounting and control procedures in the preceding period
- consulting with the previous auditor and reviewing (with their permission) their working papers and relevant management letters
- substantive testing of any opening balances where the above procedures are unsatisfactory.

Some evidence of the opening position will also usually be gained from the audit work performed in the current period.

2 Corresponding figures and comparative financial statements

ISA 710 *Comparative Information – Corresponding Figures and Comparative Financial Statements* requires that comparative figures comply with the identified financial reporting framework and that they are free from material misstatement.

The IASB's Framework for the Preparation and Presentation of Financial Statements and IAS 1 Presentation of Financial Statements both require that financial statements show comparatives.

Two categories of comparatives exist:

- *corresponding figures* where preceding period figures are included as an integral part of the current period financial statements; and
- *comparative financial statements* where preceding period amounts are included for comparison with the current period.

Corresponding figures

Audit procedures in respect of corresponding figures should be significantly less than for the current period and are limited to ensuring that corresponding figures have been correctly reported and appropriately classified. This involves evaluating whether:

- accounting policies are consistently applied; and
- corresponding figures agree to the prior period financial statements.

> **Corresponding figures and the audit report**
>
> The audit report only refers to the financial statements of the current period which encompasses the prior period figures. If a matter in respect of which the prior period audit report was modified is unresolved, the current audit report may also have to be modified in respect of corresponding figures.

Comparative financial statements

Sufficient appropriate evidence should be gathered to ensure that comparative financial statements meet the requirements of an applicable financial reporting framework. This involves evaluating whether:

- accounting policies are consistently applied; and
- comparative figures agree to the prior period financial statements.

> **Comparative figures and the audit report**
>
> Where figures are presented as comparative financial statements the auditor should issue a report in which the comparatives are specifically identified because the auditor's opinion is expressed individually on the financial statements of each period presented.
>
> It is therefore possible for the auditor to express a modified opinion with respect to one year of financial statements while issuing a different report on the other financial statements.

3 Review procedures

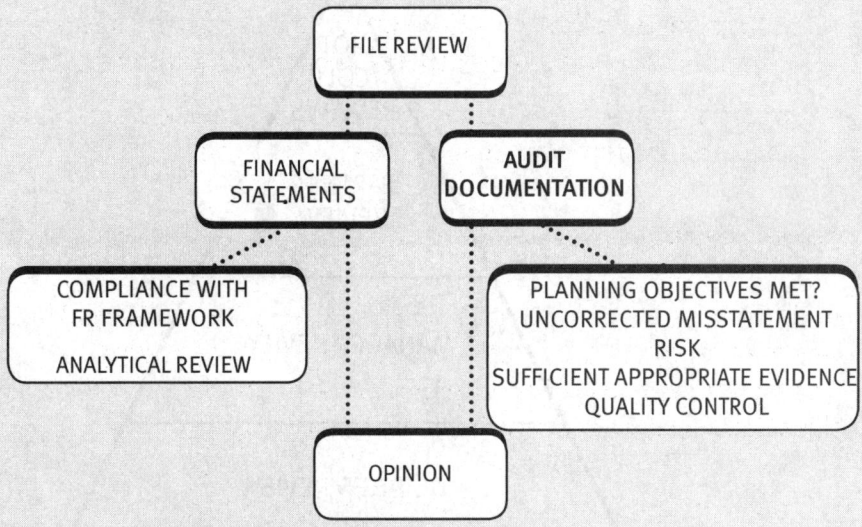

The purpose of review procedures

It is the review process that enables the decision to be taken by the partner, whether:

- the plan was satisfactory in the light of the audit evidence raised
- the plan was properly flexed to meet any new circumstances
- the audit work was carried out properly
- the evidence gathered has reduced the risk of material misstatement to a satisfactory level
- the audit opinion on financial statements is supported by the audit evidence gathered
- the financial statements comply with the appropriate financial framework.

Different levels of review

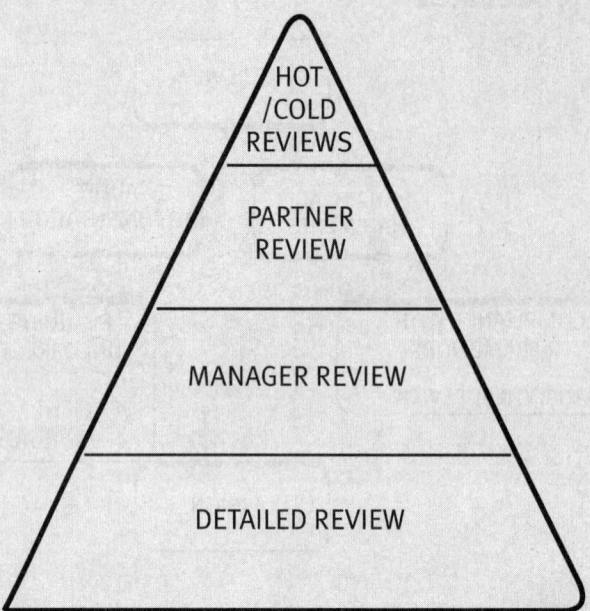

Explanation of types of review

Detailed review

- Carried out by senior staff on all work submitted by more junior team members.
- Concerned with quality control.
  - Are working papers properly prepared? – proper headings, dates, identity of preparer, cross references, meaning of audit symbols etc.
  - Has the right work been done in accordance with the audit plan?
  - Is the amount of work sufficient?
  - Are there any unresolved issues that can and should be resolved by the person carrying out the work – incomplete tests, queries not followed up etc.
- Assessment of matters arising – ensuring that errors found and other issues uncovered are summarised so that they can be brought to the partner's attention.
- Enables a completion memorandum (as recommended by ISA 230) to be produced to facilitate manager and partner reviews.

Manager review

- Some quality control aspects:
  - general review to ensure that working papers are properly prepared
  - checklists and programmes completed properly
  - no obvious omissions or gaps
  - has the detailed review been conducted properly?
  - is the file in a fit state to be reviewed by the partner?
- What matters are arising?
  - Are they fully understood?
  - Can they be resolved by the manager?
  - What course of action does the manager recommend?

Partner/final review

- Top level review, concerned with the significant issues (i.e. those identified as risks during planning) and finalising the firm's opinion on the financial statements.
- Clearly does have a quality control function, but procedural problems should all really have been resolved by this stage.

Cold review

- Takes place after the audit is finished and the audit report is signed.
- Therefore is the one review dealt with here which is purely concerned with quality control.
- Is not concerned with detecting misstatements in the financial statements (because it is too late), but with ensuring that the firm's procedures were applied properly.

"Hot" or "independent" reviews

- Compulsory per ISQC (International Standard on Quality Control) 1 for clients which are:
  - listed
  - public interest
- Conducted **before** the audit report is signed.
- Conducted by a partner who is independent of the main audit team.

- Assesses whether:
  - the firm's independence and objectivity is impaired in any way
  - the planning appears to have been carried out properly
  - the file appears to have been reviewed satisfactorily
  - if, in all the circumstances, the audit opinion has been based on valid evidence
  - if, in all the circumstances, the audit opinion is appropriate.

4 Evaluation of misstatements

The auditor must consider the effect of misstatements on both the audit procedures performed and ultimately, if uncorrected, on the financial statements as a whole. Guidance on how this is performed is given in the revised and redrafted ISA 450 *Evaluation of Misstatements Identified During the Audit*.

In order to achieve this the auditor must accumulate a record of all identified misstatements, unless they are clearly trivial. In the first instance they must consider if the existence of such misstatements indicates that others may exist, which, when aggregated with other misstatements, could be considered material. If so the audit plan and strategy may need to be revised.

The importance of financial reporting standards

The unmodified audit opinion states:

"In our opinion, the financial statements present fairly, in all material respects (or *give a true and fair view of*) the financial position of ABC Company as at December 31, 20X1, and (*of*) its financial performance and its cash flows for the year then ended **in accordance with International Financial Reporting Standards**."

Therefore, in order to reach this opinion, the auditor must fully understand the relevant financial reporting standards, and must evaluate whether the financial statements comply with these standards. This knowledge and understanding needs to be applied throughout the audit. These standards are summarised in Chapter 20.

During the **completion** phase of the audit, if the auditor has identified the incorrect application of or non-compliance with financial reporting standards, the auditor will need to assess the materiality of the matter (both quantitative and qualitative) in determining their audit opinion. This in itself will also require knowledge and understanding of the applicable financial reporting standards, in particular when considering the wider impact on the financial statements as a whole, including the notes.

All misstatements identified during the course of the audit should be reported to an appropriate level of management on a timely basis. Importantly, the auditor should request that **all** misstatements are corrected.

If management refuses to correct some or all of the misstatements the auditor should consider their reasons for refusal and take these into account when considering if the financial statements are free from material misstatement.

Evaluation of uncorrected misstatement

Before misstatements are evaluated the auditor should revisit their assessment of materiality to determine whether, according to their judgement, it is still appropriate in the circumstances. Following this they can then determine whether the unrecorded misstatements, either individually or in aggregate, are material to the financial statements as a whole.

In so doing the auditor must consider both the size and nature of the misstatements and the effect of misstatements related to prior periods (e.g. on corresponding figures, comparatives and opening balances).

Following this consideration the auditor should report the uncorrected misstatements to those charged with governance and explain the effect this will have upon the audit opinion. At the same time they should request a written representation from those charged with governance that they believe the effects of uncorrected misstatements are immaterial.

5 Overall review of the financial statements

Before forming an opinion on the financial statements and deciding on the wording of the audit report, the auditor should conduct **an overall review**.

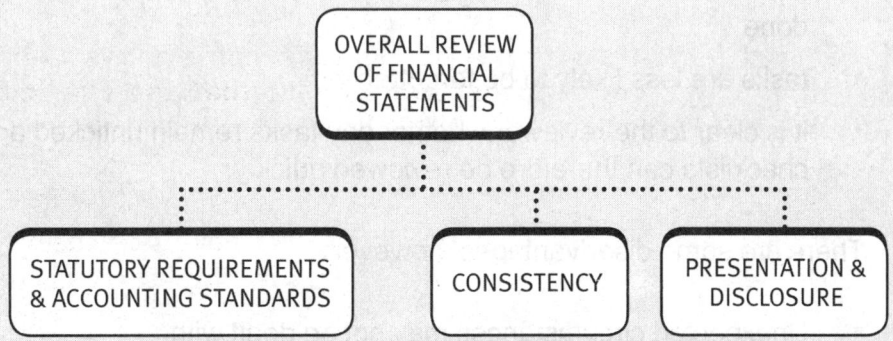

Key methods used to carry out final review include:

- final analytical procedures; and
- checklists.

6 Final analytical procedures

The need for final analytical procedures

Final analytical procedures have to be carried out because:

- they are compulsory according to ISA 520
- they assist the auditor when forming an overall conclusion as to whether the financial statements are consistent with the auditor's understanding of the entity.

What should be done?

Analytical procedures at the final stage of the audit focus on:

- the relationships between figures within the financial statements
- comparisons with figures from previous years
- comparisons with budgets and management information

> **Checklists**
>
> Many of the procedures to be dealt with at the completion stage of the audit are set out in checklists. These are basically long lists of questions that the auditor must answer to ensure that the financial statements are appropriately prepared. They usually concern financial reporting, regulatory and administrative matters.
>
> The main advantages of this approach are:
>
> - it is clear to the person completing the checklist what needs to be done
> - tasks are less likely to be forgotten
> - it is clear to the reviewer whether any tasks remain unticked and checklists can therefore be reviewed quickly.
>
> There are some disadvantages, however:
>
> - Unexpected circumstances may not be dealt with
> - Checklists are sometimes completed by rote in an unthinking way.
>
> **Example of key checklists at the completion stage:**
>
> - Financial statements disclosures.
> - Subsequent events review.
> - Going concern review.

- Management Representations.
- Communication with those charged with governance.

Statutory requirements and accounting policies

- The auditor will review the compliance with statutory requirements in relation to the presentation of the financial statements.
- Usually focused on disclosures made within the financial statements.
- A checklist approach is often used by the auditor to ensure all areas have been considered.
- The auditor should review the **accounting policies** adopted by the enterprise to determine whether they:
  - comply with relevant accounting standards
  - are consistent with those of the previous period
  - are consistently applied throughout the enterprise.

7 Other Information

'Other information' refers to documents and reports contained within the annual report and financial statements that are not subject to audit. For example:

- the Chairman's Report;
- the Operating and Financial Review;
- employee reports; and
- five-year summaries.

ISA 720 *The Auditor's Responsibilities Relating to Other Information in Documents Containing Audited Financial Statements* requires that auditors should read the other information to identify:

- areas of **material inconsistency** between the unaudited information and the audited financial statements; and
- obvious **misstatements of fact** to other information, unrelated to matters appearing in the audited financial statements.

Completion

> **Further definitions**
>
> A material inconsistency is a statement in the unaudited reports that contradict and therefore undermine the contents of the audited financial statements.
>
> Misstatements of fact are statements in the unaudited reports that the auditor knows to be untrue, whether intended or erroneous.

Material inconsistency

Upon discovering a material inconsistency the auditor should determine if the audited accounts or the other information needs amending.

The auditor should seek to resolve the matter with those charged with governance.

If, upon further examination, amendment is necessary to the audited financial statements and the entity refuses to make the amendment, the auditor should consider the implication on the audit opinion and whether a modification is necessary. If so this would usually be in the form of a qualified opinion.

If, however, the other information is incorrect and the entity refuses to amend it then the auditor should consider including an **Other Matter paragraph** in the audit report describing the inconsistency, in accordance with ISA 706.

Material misstatement of fact

If the auditor concludes that the other information contains a material misstatement of fact then once again they should seek to resolve the matter with those charged with governance.

If, following such discussions, the auditor still considers that there is an apparent material misstatement of fact the auditor shall request management consult with a qualified third party.

If the auditor eventually concludes that there is a material misstatement of fact that management refuses to correct the auditor shall notify those charged with governance and take appropriate further action, which is likely to include seeking legal counsel.

chapter 12

What next?

Depending on the circumstances, the significance of the issue in question and the advice of any legal counsel sought, the auditor may take further, more severe action, such as:

- Not issuing the auditor's report;
- Withdrawing/resigning from the engagement and making an appropriate statement; and
- Enforcing the auditor's right to be heard at a general meeting of the members.

When taking such action the auditor must consider the severity of the action and the possible financial and reputational repercussions.

8 Events after the reporting period

The term 'events after the reporting period' refers to both events occurring between the period end and the date of the auditor's report, and facts discovered after the date of the auditor's report.

To adjust or not to adjust?

IAS 10 identifies two types of event after the reporting period:

- adjusting; and
- non-adjusting.

Discussion of adjusting and non-adjusting events

Adjusting events

These are events that provide additional evidence relating to conditions existing at the reporting date. Such events cast doubt on whether the period end accounts are correct and, hence, require adjustment.

Non-adjusting events

These are events concerning conditions which arose after the reporting date, but which may be of such materiality that their disclosure is required to ensure that the financial statements are not misleading. Such events, therefore, will not have any effect on items in the statements of financial position or comprehensive income for the period.

Completion

> However, in order to prevent the financial statements from presenting a misleading position, some form of additional disclosure is required, by way of note, indicating what effect the events may have.

Illustration 1 Auditor's responsibilities

Examples of **adjusting** events include:

- provisions for damaged inventory and doubtful debts
- amounts received or receivable in respect of insurance claims which were being negotiated at the reporting date
- the determination of the purchase or sale price of non-current assets purchased or sold before the year end
- agreement of a tax liability
- discovery of errors/ fraud revealing that the financials are incorrect.

Illustration 2 Auditor's responsibilities

Examples of **non-adjusting** events include:

- the issue of new share or loan capital
- major changes in the composition of the group (for example, mergers, acquisitions or reconstructions)
- financial consequences of losses of non-current assets or inventory as a result of fires or floods
- strikes, government action such as nationalisation, and declines in the value of non-current assets or investments
- purchases/sales of significant non-current assets

Auditor's responsibilities

Active duty – up to the date of the audit report:

- the auditor should perform procedures to identify events that might require adjustment or disclosure in the year-end financial statements;

- if the identified adjustments or disclosures are necessary but not adjusted in the financial statements then the auditor should consider the impact on the audit report and whether a modification is necessary to the audit report.

chapter 12

Passive duty – after the date of the audit report:

- the auditor does not have a duty to search for evidence of events after the reporting period;
- however, if after the audit report is signed and the auditor becomes aware of information which might have led him to give a different audit opinion, he should discuss the matter with the directors and take appropriate action;
- this will normally be in the form of amending the accounts, reviewing the amendments and re-issuing the audit report;
- if, however the directors refuse to make necessary amendments the auditor should take necessary steps to prevent reliance on their report. Such action depends upon the advice given by the auditor's lawyer but could involve:
  - resigning from the engagement and issuing a statement;
  - using the auditor's right to make a statement at a general meeting of the members.

Procedures

Procedures include:

- enquiring into management procedures/systems for the identification of events after the reporting period;
- reading minutes of members' and directors' meetings;
- reviewing accounting records including budgets, forecasts, cash flows, management accounts and interim information;
- reviewing the progress of known 'risk' areas and contingencies;
- making enquiries of directors to ask if they are aware of any events, adjusting or non-adjusting, that have not yet been included or disclosed in the financial statements;
- considering relevant information which has come to the auditor's attention, from sources outside the enterprise, including public knowledge, or competitors, suppliers and customers
- obtaining a letter of representation.

9 Going concern

ISA 570 *Going Concern* states that the objectives of an auditor are:

- To obtain sufficient appropriate evidence regarding the appropriateness of management's use of the going concern assumption;
- To conclude, based on the audit evidence obtained, whether a material uncertainty exists; and
- To determine the implications for the audit report.

Responsibilities

Management

The going concern is a fundamental principle in the preparation of financial statements, which management are responsible for preparing.

Some financial reporting standards (for example IAS 1) contain an explicit requirement for management to make a specific assessment of the entities ability to continue as a going concern.

This requires management to make judgements about the future outcome of events or conditions which are inherently uncertain.

The auditor

The auditor's responsibilities are:

- To consider the appropriateness of management's use of the going concern assumption;
- To consider whether there are adequate disclosures regarding the going concern basis in the financial statements;
- To consider the entity's ability to continue for the foreseeable future.

Procedures

The auditor should consider whether there are, and remain alert for evidence of, any events, conditions or risks that cast significant doubt on the entity's ability to continue as a going concern.

When events or conditions have been identified which may cast significant doubt on the entity's ability to continue as a going concern, the auditor should:

- review management's plans for future actions based on its going concern assessment
- gather sufficient appropriate audit evidence to confirm or dispel whether or not a material uncertainty exists – this is done by carrying out procedures considered necessary, including considering the effect of any plans of management and other mitigating factors
- seek written representations from management regarding its plans for future action.

Example procedures

- analysing and discussing cash flow, profit and other relevant forecasts with management
- analysing and discussing the entity's latest available interim financial statements
- reviewing the terms of debentures and loan agreements and determining whether any have been breached
- reading minutes of the meetings of shareholders, the board of directors and important committees for reference to financing difficulties
- enquiring of the entity's lawyer regarding the existence of litigation and claims and the reasonableness of management's assessments of their outcome and the estimate of their financial implications
- confirming the existence, legality and enforceability of arrangements to provide or maintain financial support with related and third parties and assessing the financial ability of such parties to provide additional funds
- considering the entity's plans to deal with unfilled customer orders
- reviewing events after the period end to identify those that either mitigate or otherwise affect the entity's ability to continue as a going concern.

Completion

Indicators of going concern risk

Auditors should consider the following indicators as possible reasons for doubt over the going concern presumption:

- rapidly increasing costs;
- shortages of supplies;
- adverse movements in exchange rates;
- business failures amongst customers or suppliers;
- loan repayments falling due in the near future;
- high gearing;
- nearness to present borrowing limits;
- companies financed by loans from directors;
- loss of key staff;
- loss of key suppliers/customers;
- technical obsolescence of product range.
- impact of major litigation; and
- other fundamental uncertainties.

The foreseeable future

The auditor should remain alert to the possibility of events or conditions that will occur beyond management's period of assessment that may bring into question the appropriateness of the going concern assumption. However, due to the uncertainty surrounding such distant events, the indicator needs to be significant to prompt the auditor into further action. If such an event is identified the auditor should request that management consider the significance of the event of condition.

Other than enquiry, the auditor has no other responsibility to perform any other procedures to identify events or conditions beyond the period assessed by management (i.e. at least 12 months from the financial statements date).

UK syllabus focus

ISA 570 (UK & Ireland) Going Concern requires management to assess going concern for a period of at least one year from the (expected) date of approval of the financial statements (rather than 12 months from the reporting date).

chapter 12

Audit conclusions and reporting

As seen previously, representations do not relieve the auditor of any responsibility. Based on the audit evidence obtained, the auditor should determine if, in their judgement:

(a) the basis of preparing the financial statements is or is not appropriate in the circumstances; and

(b) a material uncertainty exists that may cast significant doubt on the entity's ability to continue as a going concern.

If, in the auditors opinion, the going concern assumption is inappropriate then the accounts should be re-stated on an alternative ('break up') basis. Under this basis of accounting all assets and liabilities are re-classified as 'current' and revalued at net realisable value. Further provisions for liquidation, such as redundancy and legal costs, may also be required.

If management were to refuse then a modified opinion would be issued. Given the severity and pervasiveness of the potential misstatements it is likely that an adverse opinion would be issued in these circumstances.

Where there is a material uncertainty (but the going concern basis is still considered appropriate) then the financial statements should contain disclosures describing the conditions that give rise to the significant doubt. If those disclosures are adequate then the auditor should express an **unmodified opinion** but **modify the audit report** by including an emphasis of matter paragraph that highlights the disclosure of uncertainty in the financial statements to users of the financial statements.

According to ISA 570 the auditor should consider the same period reviewed by management as required by financial reporting requirements. If that period is less than twelve months from the statement of financial position date then the auditor should request that management extend their review to cover that period. If management is unwilling to do so, a qualified opinion or a disclaimer of opinion in the auditor's report may be appropriate, because it may not be possible for the auditor to obtain sufficient appropriate audit evidence regarding the use of the going concern assumption.

Exam focus

In the exam you may be asked to consider issues that are likely to have some or all of the following conditions in common:

- a critical area of the financial statements
- the subject of an accounting standard which has specific disclosure requirements and recognition and measurement principles
- a contentious or subjective accounting area which has alternative treatments

KAPLAN PUBLISHING 315

- a high risk matter
- an area involving a high degree of judgement
- an area where the main source of evidence is that from management.

Many of these conditions will draw upon your detailed knowledge of financial reporting standards from P2. You should use the financial reporting revision chapter at the end of this text to recap the basic principles.

In her article entitled "The Importance of Financial Reporting Standards to the Auditor" (October 2008) Lisa Weaver lists the technical areas that are likely to be tested in detail. She followed this up in the December 2008 exam with questions regarding share options and deferred tax, two of the areas referred to in the article. A well prepared student would be advised to read this article and prepare for the technical areas identified.

The questions at the end of this chapter and in your exam kit provide good practice for this topic area.

Test your understanding 1

You are the manager responsible for the audit of Phoenix, a private limited liability company, which manufactures super alloys from imported zinc and aluminium. The company operates three similar foundries at different sites under the direction of Troy Pitz, the chief executive. The draft accounts for the year ended 31 March 2007 show profit before taxation of $1.7m (2006 – $1.5m).

The audit senior has produced a schedule of 'Points for the Attention of the Audit Manager' as follows:

(a) A trade investment in 60,000 $1 ordinary shares of Pegasus, one of the company's major shipping contractors, is included in the statement of financial position at cost of $80,000. In May 2007, the published financial statements of Pegasus as at 30 September 2006 show only a small surplus of net assets. A recent press report now suggests that Pegasus is insolvent and has ceased to trade. Although dividends declared by Pegasus in respect of earlier years have not yet been paid, Phoenix has included $15,000 of dividends receivable in its draft accounts as at 31 March 2007.

(6 marks)

chapter 12

(b) Current liabilities include a $500,000 provision for future maintenance. This represents the estimated cost of overhauling the blast furnaces and other foundry equipment. The overhaul is planned for August 2007 when all foundry workers take two weeks annual leave.

(7 marks)

(c) All industrial waste from the furnaces ('clinker') is purchased by Cleanaway Ltd, a government-approved disposal company, under a five-year contract that is due for renewal later this year. A recent newspaper article states that 'substantial fines have been levied on Cleanaway for illegal dumping'. Troy Pitz is the majority shareholder of Cleanaway.

(7 marks)

Required:

For each of the above points:

(i) comment on the matters that you would consider; and

(ii) state the audit evidence that you would expect to find, in undertaking your review of the audit working papers and financial statements of Phoenix.

(Total: 20 marks)

Test your understanding 2

Briefly describe the various criteria against which the effectiveness of a written representation letter may be assessed.

Completion

Test your understanding 3

You are the manager responsible for the audit of Aspersion, a limited liability company, which mainly provides national cargo services with a small fleet of aircraft. The draft accounts for the year ended 30 September 2006 show profit before taxation of $2.7 million (2005 – $2.2 million) and total assets of $10.4 million (2005 – $9.8 million).

The following issues are outstanding and have been left for your attention:

(a) The sale of a cargo carrier to Abra, a private limited company, during the year resulted in a loss on disposal of $400,000. The aircraft cost $1.2 million when it was purchased in October 1997 and was being depreciated on a straight-line basis over 20 years. The minutes of the board meeting at which the sale was approved record that Aspersion's finance director, Iain Joiteon, has a 30% equity interest in Abra.

(7 marks)

(b) As well as cargo carriers, Aspersion owns two light aircraft which were purchased in 2003 to provide business passenger flights to a small island under a three year service contract. It is now known that the contract will not be renewed when it expires at the end of March 2007. The aircraft, which cost $450,000 each, are being depreciated over 15 years.

(7 marks)

(c) Deferred tax amounting to $570,000 as at 30 September 2006 has been calculated relating to tangible fixed assets at a tax rate of 30% using the full provision method (IAS 12, Income Taxes). On 1 December 2006, the government announced an increase in the corporate income tax rate to 34%. The directors are proposing to adjust the draft accounts for the further liability arising.

(6 marks)

Required:

For each of the above points:

(i) comment on the matters that you should consider; and

(ii) state the audit evidence that you should expect to find, in undertaking your review of the audit working papers and financial statements of Aspersion.

(Total: 20 marks)

Test your understanding 4

You are the manager responsible for the audit of Visean, a limited liability company, which manufactures health and beauty products and distributes them through a chain of 72 retail pharmacies. The draft accounts for the year ended 31 December 2006 show profit before taxation of $1.83 million (2000 – $1.24 million) and total assets $18.4 million (2005 – $12.7 million).

The following issues are outstanding and have been left for your attention:

(a) Visean owns nine brand names of fragrances used for ranges of products (e.g. perfumes, bath oils, soaps, etc), four of which were purchased and five self-created. Purchased brands are recognised as an intangible asset at cost amounting to $589,000 and amortised on a straight-line basis over 10 years. The costs of generating self-created brands and maintaining existing ones are recognised as an expense when incurred. Demand for products of one of the purchased fragrances, 'Ulexite', fell significantly in January 2007 after a marketing campaign in December caused offence to customers.

(8 marks)

(b) In December 2006 the directors announced plans to discontinue the range of medical consumables supplied to hospital pharmacies. The plant manufacturing these products closed in January 2007. A provision of $800,000 has been made as at 31 December 2006 for the compensation of redundant employees and a further $450,000 for the three years' unexpired lease term on the plant premises.

(7 marks)

(c) Historically the company's cash flow statement has reported net cash flows from operating activities under the 'indirect method'. However, the cash flow statement for the year ended 31 December 2006 reports net cash flows under the 'direct method' and the corresponding figures have been restated.

(5 marks)

Required:

For each of the above issues:

(i) comment on the matters that you should consider; and

(ii) state the audit evidence that you should expect to find, in undertaking your review of the audit working papers and financial statements of Visean.

(Total: 20 marks)

chapter 12

10 Chapter summary

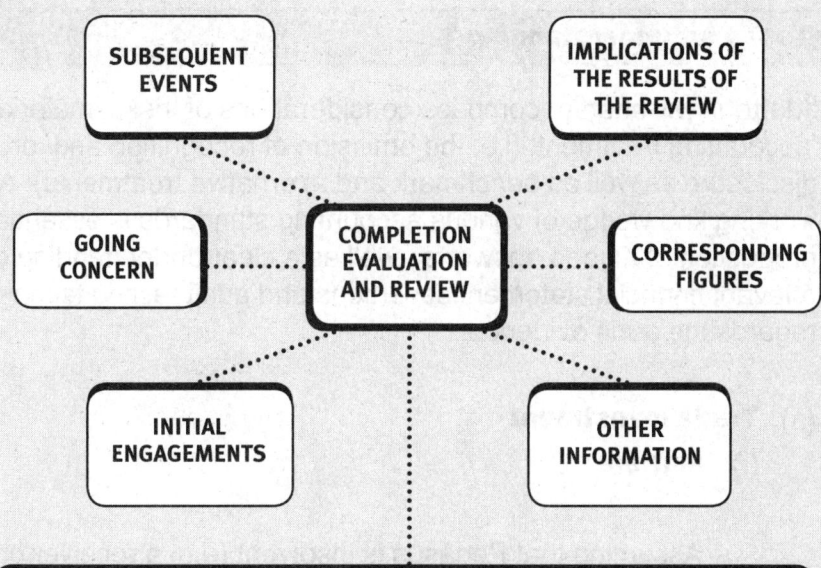

Completion

Test your understanding answers

Test your understanding 1

'Matters' will often encompass considerations of 'risk', 'materiality' and 'accounting treatment' (i.e. the omission of recognition and/ or disclosure as well as benchmark and alternative treatments). A good working knowledge of various accounting standards is essential to the production of a good answer as well as a clear understanding of the relevant financial statement assertions and audit testing techniques as regards the audit evidence.

(a) **Trade investment**

    (i) **Matters**

        Assuming that Pegasus is insolvent (e.g. a receiver or liquidator has been appointed) this is an adjusting event (IAS 10).

        As the recoverable amount is likely to be $nil, $80,000 impairment loss should be recognised in the statement of profit or loss for the year to 31 March 2007 (IAS 36).

        As the likelihood of any distribution of the declared dividends is remote, the $15,000 dividends receivable should be written off.

        The total expense of $95,000 represents 5.6% of draft profit before tax and is therefore material. As is it not expected to recur, separate disclosure (IAS 1) may be appropriate to explaining Phoenix's performance for the year.

        Before deciding whether or not an 'except for' modified opinion would be reported, if adjustments are not made, materiality should also be assessed in relation to the statement of financial position.

        The subsequent event may also be described in the directors' report with a cross-reference to the investments note.

    (ii) **Audit evidence**

        – A copy of the press report.

        – The audited accounts of Pegasus for the year ended 30 September 2006 showing whether there are assets with market values in excess of book values.

- The receiver's (or liquidator's) statement of affairs indicating whether any distribution is possible.
- If a meeting of the shareholders of Pegasus has been held to consider the company's state of affairs, a copy of the minutes (may be obtained by Phoenix).
- Discussion with client who, if anyone, has replaced Pegasus as one of their major shipping contractors. Also, whether any consignments have been held up while negotiating for an alternative shipping contractor.
- Discussion with client who, if anyone, has replaced Pegasus as one of their major shipping contractors. Also, whether any consignments have been held up while negotiating for an alternative shipping contractor.

(b) **Future maintenance**

(i) **Matters**

The provision represents 29% of draft profit before tax and is therefore material.

The accounting treatment of maintenance costs should be consistent with prior years. However, IAS 37 does not permit the recognition of a provision that does not meet the recognition criteria for liabilities.

Overhaul expenditure to restore or maintain the future economic benefits expected from the plant and equipment should normally be recognised as an expense when it is incurred. However, blast furnaces are of a type of plant and equipment that require relining after a specified period. The components (blast furnace interiors) which require replacement are separate assets that should be depreciated over the replacement cycle. To the extent that the $500k includes the cost of replacing separate assets, it represents future capital cost.

Prudence does not permit the creation of hidden reserves and excessive provisions. This 'provision' does not meet the IAS 37 definition:

- there is no uncertainty about the timing (August);
- there may be relatively little uncertainty about the amounts involved;
- there is no liability as at 31 March 2007.

If the provision is not 'unmade', as being unnecessary, the audit opinion should be qualified 'except for' on grounds of non-compliance with IAS 37.

Draft profit before tax ($1.7m) shows a 13% increase on the previous year. If adjustments are made for points (1) and (2), profit will be increased by at least $400,000 (i.e. (1) $95k decrease plus (2) $500k increase). Profit before tax of $2.1m would be a 40% increase on the prior year.

The management of Phoenix may have decided that $1.7m is what is to be reported. Management may have made the future maintenance provision (which may have been permitted in previous years) as a way of 'setting aside' a reserve. For example, in anticipation of increased costs expected to arise in respect of waste disposal in (3).

Tutorial note: It is a 'higher skill' to be able to demonstrate an ability to stand back from the individual items and take an overall view – in this part of the question, considering the overall impact on the draft PBT.

(ii) **Audit evidence**

- Client's schedule showing make-up of provision.
- Discussion with senior management their reasons for having made the provision and whether any costs have been contracted for.
- External tenders or quotes for sub-contracted work (and/or internal costings).
- Prior year working papers (and/or the permanent audit file) showing the cost and frequency of overhauls in previous periods (whether all sites done at once or on a cyclical basis).

(c) **Cleanaway**

(i) **Matters**

The matter is likely to be material as ALL Phoenix's industrial waste is disposed of by Cleanaway.

Whether Phoenix has been implicated in Cleanaway's illegal dumping (e.g. by Phoenix's clinker having been dumped, or by Troy Pitz's relationship with the two companies).

Whether the integrity of Troy Pitz has been questioned (either by the media or other key personnel in Phoenix) and, if so, its impact on the audit. For example, any assessment of control risk as less than high should be reassessed in the light of his role in the control environment.

Possible consequences for Phoenix of the contract not being renewed:

- a legal alternative will need to be found for disposal of clinker, e.g.:
- another approved provider of waste disposal services
- a suitable landfill site (taxes may be substantial), otherwise
- there may be doubts about going concern.

Possible consequences for Phoenix of the contract being renewed:

- a substantial increase in costs of disposal, e.g. because:
- terms were last agreed five years ago
- Cleanaway will need to pass on the costs of penalties to its customers
- loss of customers' goodwill through associations with Cleanaway
- risk of investigation by a government agency into the company's environmental practices.

Even if doubts about the going concern assumption are resolved, whether or not the contract is renewed in the future amounts to a 'significant uncertainty'. An emphasis of matter paragraph in the auditor's report is likely to be appropriate. The matter must therefore be adequately disclosed (e.g. in the notes to the financial statements).

Cleanaway is a related party. Troy Pitz has authority and responsibility for Phoenix's operational activities (as chief executive) and a controlling interest in Cleanaway. The financial statements of Phoenix should disclose (IAS 24):

- the nature of the related party relationship;
- an indication of the services received including:
- amount (or proportion) of costs involved

- pricing policy (per contract)
- amount outstanding (trade creditor balance)
- credit terms, etc.

(ii) **Audit evidence**

- The terms of the contract, in particular whether:
- early termination could be an option for Phoenix (in the light of Cleanaway's illegal activities);
- any clauses are relevant to its renewal (e.g. restricting price increases).
- Newspaper articles, including any editorial comment or letters from Cleanaway or Troy Pitz.
- Discussions with senior management (Troy Pitz and others) whether a suitable alternative service provider exists.
- Concerning related parties and related party transactions:
- prior year working papers and financial statements;
- review of Phoenix's procedures (e.g. keeping of registers and requiring board approval of certain transactions)
- inquiries of directors, key management and the company secretary
- an extract of principal shareholders from the share register
- minutes of shareholder and board meetings;
- relevant statutory books and records (e.g. register of directors' interests)
- relevant returns supplied to regulatory agencies (e.g. income tax returns)
- extracts from all significant contracts
- third party replies (e.g. bank reports for audit purposes and loan confirmations identifying guarantees).
- A post-year-end review, up to the date of signing the auditors' report, must support the validity or otherwise of the going concern assumption. In particular:
- board minutes should indicate what action, if any, management propose to take to mitigate the adverse publicity surrounding Cleanaway
- order books may reveal the loss of major customers (e.g. if delays experienced consequent on the demise of Pegasus)

- successful negotiations with existing or new shipping contractors, to take on the work of Pegasus, should result in signed contracts

- discussions with management, to ascertain their plans to secure Phoenix's future, may be confirmed by written management representations (assuming there is neither corroborative nor conflicting alternative evidence).

Tutorial note: Taking an overall view on something like the going concern assumption is another example of the higher skill of 'standing back' from the individual items.

Test your understanding 2

- A suitable structure – for example 'tiered', where the report contains matters of varying levels of significance. By directing different classes of matters to the appropriate level or area of responsibility action by management can be taken more speedily and constructively.

- Inclusion of staff responses – both to advise senior management of action proposed/ being taken by their staff and to give credit to recommendations for improvements where it is due (e.g. where client's staff have proposed recommendations).

- Inclusion of management's response – an indication of the actions that management intends to take is more likely to result in action being taken. Discussing findings with management first should also ensure their factual accuracy.

- Client's perspective – implications from the client's viewpoint (e.g. in terms of cost savings) are more likely to be acted on than those expressed from an audit perspective (e.g. in terms of lowered audit risk).

- Professional tone – should not be offensive. Comments that fault management's knowledge, competence, motives or integrity are likely to provoke defensive reactions. Comments should be positive/constructive by emphasising solutions/benefits.

Written representation letter effectiveness criteria

- **Timeliness** – a management letter should be issued as soon as possible after completion of the audit procedures giving rise to comment. This is particularly important when audit work is carried out on more than one audit visit and where it is a matter of urgency that management make improvements to their procedures (e.g. where there is evidence of serious weakness).

- **Clarity** – wording must be clear so that recipients understand the significance of weaknesses that are being drawn to their attention. It is particularly important that implications are explained clearly in terms that will prompt management to respond positively (e.g. drawing attention to the risks of financial loss arising).

- **Illustrative** – specific illustrative examples (e.g. of where controls have not been evidenced) should aid management in understanding the nature of the problem(s).

- **Constructive comments/advice** – recommendations for improvements must be practicable (i.e. appropriate and cost effective in the light of the client's resources) if the client is to take corrective action.

- **Conciseness** – unnecessary volume will distract management from new/additional matters that require their attention. For example, matters adequately dealt with in the internal auditor's report should not be repeated.

- **Factual accuracy** is essential. Inaccuracies will not only aggravate the client and appear unprofessional but could, in rare circumstances, result in liability. Similarly, the letter should not criticize (or 'cast aspersions') on individual staff members if it is the system that is inadequate.

Test your understanding 3

(1) 'Matters' will often encompass considerations of 'risk', 'materiality' and 'accounting treatment' (i.e. the omission of recognition and/or disclosure as well as benchmark and alternative treatments).

(2) Many points can only be made as either 'matters' or 'audit evidence' (and there is no 'one-for-one' relationship between the two that would warrant a columnar approach). However, some points could be made as either (or both) although the emphasis would need to be different. For example, a matter to consider is the audit program for the identification of related parties and RPTs, whilst the evidence will include copies of extracts from minutes and company registers and written management representation.

(a) **Related party transaction – sale of cargo carrier**

Matters

The cargo carrier was in use for 8/9 years and would have had a carrying value of $720,000 at 30 September 2005 (assuming nil residual value and a full year's depreciation charge in the year of acquisition and none in the year of disposal). Disposal proceeds were only therefore $300,000 (say).

The $400,000 loss represents 15% of profit before tax and is therefore material. Disclosure as a separate line item may therefore be appropriate (IAS 1).

Abra appears to have a related party with Aspersion as Iain:

- is one of the key management personnel of Aspersion (being the finance director); and
- has an equity interest in Abra which is presumed to constitute significant influence (being greater than 20%).

This relationship will be further strengthened/closer/more apparent if:

- Iain is also a shareholder of Aspersion and/or a director of Abra;
- any close members of Iain's family are also shareholders of Abra (being a private company).

The reason for the sale e.g. whether this aircraft was:

- surplus to operating requirements (i.e. not being replaced) and
- being replaced with a new model (perhaps more likely as total assets have increased by $600,000 during the year).

The reason for the loss on sale e.g. whether the:

- sale was at an under-value (if the sale to the related party was not at arm's length)
- aircraft had a bad maintenance history (or was otherwise impaired)
- useful life of a cargo carrier is less than 20 years.

If the latter, it is likely that non-current assets are materially overstated in respect of cargo carriers still in use.

How selling price was determined. For example, whether the asset was independently valued or whether this was Abra's best offer. Also whether there were any other unrelated potential purchasers or offers made.

The principal terms of the sale e.g. for settlement of the purchase price.

The board was aware of the related party relationship (as it was minuted) when the sale was approved.

Whether RPTs have been identified and disclosed in prior period financial statements.

The related party relationship and the sale of the cargo carrier to Abra should be disclosed in a note to the financial statements for the year to 30 September 2007. The elements of such a material transaction which are likely to be necessary (for an understanding of the financial statements) are:

- the amount(s) involved (i.e. sale proceeds and loss)
- any outstanding balance of amounts due from Abra
- how price was determined (e.g. by an independent valuation).

If suitable disclosure is not made, the audit opinion would be modified on an 'except for' basis due to a material misstatement with regard to non-compliance with IAS 24 Related Party Disclosures.

(b) **Impairment – light aircraft**

(i) **Matters**

The annual depreciation charge for each of these two aircraft is $30,000 (1/15 450,000). The aircraft have been depreciated for only 2½ years to 30 September 2006 (assuming time apportionment in 2004 when the aircraft were brought into use) and have a total carrying amount of $750,000 (2 [450,000 – (2½ 30,000)]). This represents 7.2% of total assets (and some greater % of tangible fixed assets) and is therefore material.

Tutorial note: Alternatively it could be assumed (though less appropriate) that a full year's depreciation was charged in the year to 30.9.04 (i.e. three years' accumulated depreciation to 30.9.06).

The aircraft were purchased for a specific use which will cease six months after the reporting date. The value of the aircraft may be impaired and Aspersion should have made a formal estimate of their recoverable amount (IAS 36).

Whether management has estimated net selling price and/or value in use.

Whether Aspersion prepares management accounts and budgets and has experience in projecting cash flows (for determining value in use).

Management's intentions, for example:

- to sell the aircraft
- to find an alternative use (e.g. providing other business or pleasure flights).

Completion

The amount of any impairment loss identified and whether or not it is:

- material (say $100,000)
- to be recognised in the financial statements.

Additional point: If the passenger business constitutes a business segment (IAS 14), cessation of the contract may result in a discontinued operation (IFRS 5).

(ii) **Audit evidence**

- A copy of the service contract confirming expiry in March 2007.
- Physical inspection of aircraft (evidence of existence and condition at 30 September 2006).
- Notes of discussions with Aspersion's management concerning negotiations for:
- the sale of the aircraft or
- obtaining new service contracts.
- Extracts from any correspondence.
- A copy of any (draft) agreement for:
- the sale of the aircraft after the contract expires;
- new business or pleasure contracts.
- Discounted cash flow projections for any proposed new venture/contracts (i.e. value in use).
- Comparison of projected cash flows with budgets and assumptions (e.g. aircraft days available and average daily utilisation per aircraft).

(c) **Deferred tax – change in tax rate**

(i) **Matters**

The total provision amounts to 21% of PBT and is therefore material. (However the deferred tax expense/income for the year may not have been material.)

Under IAS 12 deferred tax should be provided for if the transactions or events that give rise to an obligation to pay more tax in the future have occurred by the reporting date. Accelerated capital allowances are a timing difference calculated as the difference between the tax written down value and the net book value of assets.

The increase in liability if calculated at 34% ($570,000 (34/30 – 1) = $76,000) represents 2.8% of PBT. Considered in isolation, this amount is not material.

The tax rate that should be used is the rate that is expected to apply to the period when the liability is settled, based on tax rates that have been (substantively) enacted by the reporting date (IAS 12). The increase in tax rate announced on 1 December is a non-adjusting event (IAS 10).

Also, the extra 4% does not meet the definition of a liability ('a present obligation arising from past events') and no provision should be recognised (IAS 37).

If the directors adjust the draft accounts there will be non-compliance with IASs 10, 12 and 37 which may be regarded as material 'by nature'.

(ii) **Audit evidence**

- A copy of the computations of:
- deferred tax liability (sofp)
- current tax expense (sopl)
- deferred tax expense/income.
- Agreement of tax rate(s) to tax legislation.
- A numerical reconciliation between tax expense and accounting profit multiplied by the applicable tax rate.
- Schedules of carrying amount (i.e. cost of revalued amounts net of accumulated depreciation) of fixed assets agreed to:
- the asset register (individual assets and in total)
- general ledger account balances (totals).
- Completed audit program for non-current assets (e.g. inspecting invoices for additions, agreeing depreciation rates to prior year account policies, etc).
- Client's schedules of tax base agreed, on a test basis, to:
- the asset register (for completeness)
- prior year working papers (completeness and accuracy of brought forward balances).

Completion

Test your understanding 4

(1) 'Matters' will often encompass considerations of 'risk', 'materiality' and 'accounting treatment' (i.e. the omission of recognition and/or disclosure as well as benchmark and alternative treatments).

(2) Many points can only be made as either 'matters' or 'audit evidence' (and there is no 'one-for-one' relationship between the two that would warrant a columnar approach). However, some points could be made as either or both – although the emphasis would need to be different. For example, a matter to consider in (1) is the fall in demand which may provide evidence of impairment, whilst the evidence will include the level of after-date sales, by month, by fragrance.

(a) **Brand names**

   (i) **Matters**

   'Ulexite' is one of the four purchased brands and therefore has a net book value in the statement of financial position.

   The cost of the purchased brands represents 3.2% of total assets and 32% of PBT (net book value will be less). Annual amortisation amounts to 3.2% of PBT. Brands as a whole are therefore material. If the net book value of 'Ulexite' at the year end is greater than $91,500 (i.e. 5% PBT) its total write-off (e.g. due to impairment) is likely to be regarded as material.

   The fall in demand in January 2007 is an adjusting event (IAS 10) providing evidence about the valuation of assets as at 31 December 2006 as a result of the marketing campaign.

   In particular:

   – the net realisable value of inventory of 'Ulexite' products may be less than cost

   – the value of the brand name 'Ulexite' itself may be impaired

   – by association, the value of other brand names and their associated products may be similarly affected

   – there could be loss of customer goodwill to Visean as a whole if, by the association of 'Ulexite' with Visean, there is a boycotting of Visean's products (as has been the case with Benetton and Nestlé).

Each purchased brand is likely to be regarded as a cash-generating unit as the revenues flowing from each brand are largely independent of each other (IAS 36). Also, decisions can be made about individual fragrances (e.g. to discontinue use of the 'offending' fragrance). It is likely that the recoverable amount of an individual purchased brand name can be assessed.

Whether management consider the 'Ulexite' brand value to be impaired and, if so:

- the amount they propose to recognise as an impairment loss and
- how the recoverable amount (the higher of net selling price and value in use) has been determined.

Net book value of 'Ulexite' as at the year-end will provide a 'ceiling' for the amount of any impairment loss recognised.

What action, if any, management propose to take (e.g. to discontinue the fragrance, sell the name or promote it).

If management is taking legal action against the advertising consultants (if external to Visean) – there may be a disclosable contingent gain.

Whether 10 years is a reasonable period over which to amortise purchased brand names. It is appropriate that the straight line method should be used (as an alternative pattern of consumption of economic benefits cannot be determined reliably) – IAS 38

(ii) **Audit evidence**

Year-end cost/net book value of 'Ulexite' agreed to prior year working papers, less current year's amortisation charge.

Analytical review of actual after-date sales (and/or inventory turnover) against budget, month on month, and by fragrance to identify:

- the significance of the fall in demand of 'Ulexite'
- whether other fragrances have been similarly affected
- if demand is 'picking up' again (in February to June).

Monthly sales analysis returns received from retail pharmacies.

The advert, promotional literature or 'slogan' relating to 'Ulexite' which caused the offence. (And media reports, if any, arising from bad publicity.)

If the 'Ulexite' brand name has been written down:

- to net selling price – a binding agreement to sell 'Ulexite'
- to value in use – cash flow projections for the next five years (or the remaining useful life of 'Ulexite' if shorter).

Board minutes reflecting any decisions taken (e.g. to discontinue the fragrance).

Expenses, if any, incurred since April (reflected in the cash book and/or after-date invoices) to rectify the damage done (e.g. a new marketing campaign).

Amortisation rates and periods used in the 'cosmetics' industry.

Copy correspondence and notes concerning any pending legal action and possible quantified outcomes.

(b) **Discontinued operation**

(i) **Matters**

The provisions have reduced PBT by 40% (i.e. 1.25 ÷ [1.83 + 1.25]) and now represent 68% of PBT and are therefore considered to be material.

The plan to close the plant facility is likely to result in a discontinued operation if hospital medical consumables are a separate line of business which can be distinguished operationally and for financial reporting purposes (IFRS 5).

If hospital medical consumables were reported as a business segment in the notes to the financial statements for the prior year (under IAS 14) this will satisfy the 'separate line of business' criterion.

The initial disclosure event will be the earlier of:

- the directors' announcement in December (that the factory closed in January strongly suggests that a formal detailed plan existed and was approved before it was announced);
- a binding sale agreement for substantially all the related assets (i.e. equipment and inventory – not the plant itself, as it is leased).

Tutorial note: The announcement is the more likely in the context of the given scenario.

The disposal of any assets (e.g. equipment) arising from the plant closure in January is a non-adjusting event (IAS 10) which may require disclosure in the financial statements (if material).

No provision should be made for the loss on sale of related assets after the year end unless a binding sale agreement was entered into before the year end. However:

- plant assets (plant and equipment) should be reviewed for impairment (IAS 36); and
- inventory of hospital consumables should be measured at the lower of cost and net realisable value (IAS 2).

Assuming that the announcement in December raised valid expectations (in employees and customers) that a detailed formal restructuring plan would be carried out, a constructive obligation to restructure arises (IAS 37). The provision made should include:

- redundancy costs (but not any costs of retraining or relocating continuing staff);
- present obligations under onerous contracts (e.g. for the unexpired lease term on the factory premises).

If products other than medical consumables were supplied to hospitals, Visean may lose hospital customers altogether (as the hospitals turn to other suppliers for the medical consumables).

Tutorial note: Presumably this was taken into account when making the decision to discontinue the activity.

Further provision may be necessary for onerous contracts with customers (and possibly suppliers). For example, hospitals (as public sector bodies) are likely to have contracts with Visean containing penalty clauses for non-performance (breach of contract, etc).

Completion

(ii) **Audit evidence**

Segmental information in the prior year financial statements showing hospital medical consumables to be a business segment (e.g. if this activity accounted for 10% or more of Visean's turnover, result or net assets).

Initial disclosure of:

- carrying amounts of assets being disposed of (if any) and
- revenue, expenses, pre-tax profit (or loss) and income tax expense attributable to the discontinuing of medical consumable supplies.

Agreement of initial disclosure to underlying financial ledger accounts (management reports, etc).

Comparison of separate disclosure with budgeted amounts and prior year.

Board minutes approving the formal plan to discontinue the product range, close the factory and make staff redundant.

Copies of announcements (e.g. press releases and letters to hospitals (i.e. as customers) and employees).

The binding sale agreement (if any) for plant, equipment and stock.

The contractual terms of the factory lease and correspondence with the lessor (e.g. to negotiate the surrender of the lease, sub-leasing, etc).

Penalty clauses, if any, in contracts with hospitals (also contracts with suppliers).

Calculations of the provisions (and assumptions made).

Redundancy terms for employees (both contractual and statutory).

Past redundancy settlements (as compared with statutory and contractual obligations).

After-date sales of hospital medical consumables.

(c) **Cash flow statement**

   (i) **Matters**

   The cash flow statement should be prepared in accordance with IAS 7, Cash flow statements i.e. reporting cash flows classified under the standard headings (including operating activities, returns on investments, taxation, capital expenditure, etc). IAS 1 requires comparative figures for all items in the primary statements (and therefore for the cash flow statement).

   Cash flows from operating activities may be reported using either:

   – the 'direct' method (i.e. showing relevant constituent cash flows) or
   – the 'indirect' method (i.e. calculating operating cash flows by adjustment to the operating profit reported in the profit and loss account).

   IAS 7 encourages reporting under the direct method because it provides information which is not available under the indirect method. Because the provision of such additional information may be more time-consuming and costly, the direct method is not required – however, the change from indirect to direct is clearly permitted.

   It is appropriate, in the interest of comparability that the corresponding figures have been restated. The reason for reclassification should also be disclosed.

   The restatement only affects the amounts which make up cash generated from operating activities (i.e. a part of 'Net cash inflow from/outflow for operating activities').

   The auditor's responsibility for corresponding figures (ISA 710) is to obtain sufficient appropriate audit evidence that they have been correctly reported and appropriately classified.

   The auditor's report should not specifically identify the comparatives because the audit opinion is on the current period's financial statements as a whole, including the corresponding figures.

There should be no specific reference to the corresponding figures in the auditor's report merely because they have been restated (ISA 710). However, if the corresponding amounts have not been properly restated (or appropriate disclosures have not been made – e.g. the reason for restatement) the report should be modified with respect to the corresponding figures.

(ii) **Audit evidence**

Agreement of 'Net cash from operating activities' downwards in the cash flow statement corresponding amounts to the prior year cash flow statement in the financial statements.

For the prior year, agreement (or reconciliation) of net PBT as adjusted for non-cash items (e.g. depreciation) and working capital changes to cash receipts from customers less cash paid to suppliers and employees.

Schedules of cash receipts (per analysis of cash book receipts) agreed to the debtors ledger control a/c.

Schedules of cash payments to suppliers and employees (per analysis of cash book payments) agreed to the creditors ledger and payroll control a/cs (respectively).

Analytical procedures such as the comparison of trade debtor (and creditor) days (i.e. average credit periods given to customers and received from suppliers) with prior year.

chapter 13

Auditors' reports

Chapter learning objectives

When you have completed this chapter you will be able to:

- critically appraise the form and content of an auditor's report in a given situation;
- recognise and evaluate the factors to be taken into account when forming an audit opinion and justify audit opinions;
- assess whether or not a proposed audit opinion is appropriate;
- advise on the actions which may be taken by the auditor in the event that a modified audit report is issued; and
- recognise when the use of an emphasis of matter paragraph and other matter paragraph would be appropriate.

Auditors' reports

Reporting could appear in section A or B in the exam, and could also appear as a requirement within more than one question. The importance of making sure you are fully comfortable with both unmodified and modified reports cannot be underemphasised! Common requirements include critical evaluation of draft audit report extracts or suggested modifications.

1 The objectives of the auditor

According to ISA 700 *Forming an Opinion and Reporting on Financial Statements,* the auditor's objectives are:

- To form an opinion on the financial statements based on an evaluation of the conclusions drawn from the audit evidence obtained; and
- To express clearly that opinion through a written report that also describes the basis for that opinion.

2 The written report

To ensure consistency and clarity in the reporting of the audit opinion, ISA 700 prescribes the following structure for the audit report:

chapter 13

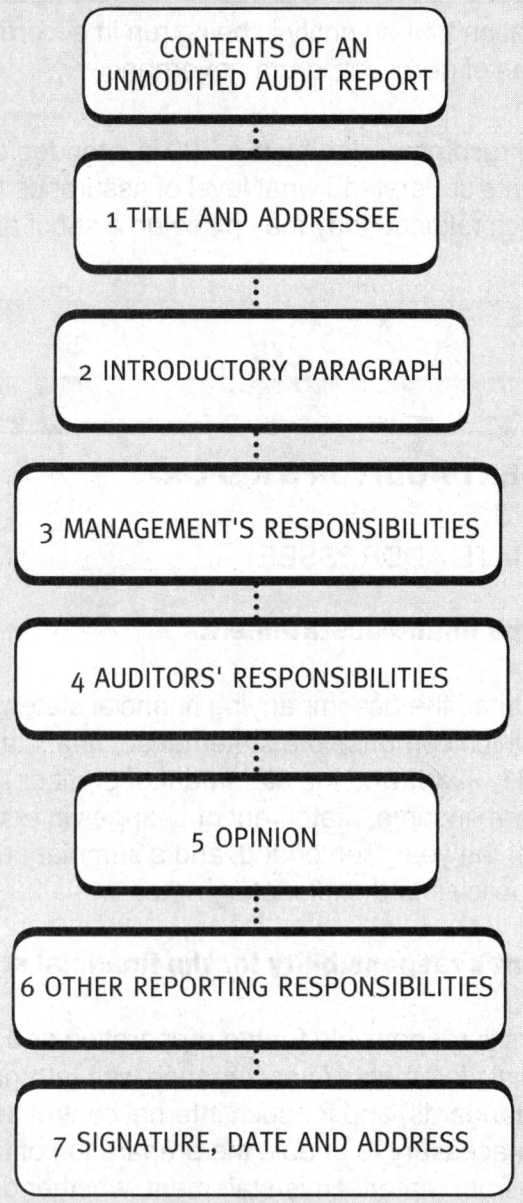

The 'expectations gap'

Background

The seven sections of the audit report are set out in **ISA 700**.

Over time the wording of the audit report has grown longer in an attempt to counteract what has become known as the **expectation gap**, i.e. the difference between what an auditor's responsibility actually is (and can reasonably be expected) and what the public perceives the auditor's responsibility to be.

The audit report is not:

- a certificate of the accuracy of the contents of financial statements;
- a guarantee against fraud; and/or

- confirmation that an entity is being run in accordance with the principles of good corporate governance.

The wording recommended by ISA 700 is intended to ensure that users of the accounts understand what level of assurance they are being given and how much reliance they may place on a set of audited financial statements.

Example of an unmodified audit report

INDEPENDENT AUDITOR'S REPORT

(APPROPRIATE ADDRESSEE)

Report on the financial statements

We have audited the accompanying financial statements of the ABC Company, which comprise the statement of financial position as of December 31, 20X1, and the statement of profit or loss and other comprehensive income, statement of changes in equity, and cash flow statement for the year then ended, and a summary of significant accounting policies and explanatory notes.

Management's responsibility for the financial statements

Management is responsible for the preparation and fair presentation of these financial statements in accordance with International Financial Reporting Standards, and for such internal control as management determines necessary to enable the preparation of financial statements that are free from material mis-statement, whether due to fraud or error.

Auditor's responsibility

Our responsibility is to express an opinion on these financial statements based on our audit. We conducted our audit in accordance with International Standards on Auditing. Those Standards require that we comply with ethical requirements and plan and perform the audit to obtain reasonable assurance about whether the financial statements are free from material mis-statement.

An audit involves performing procedures to obtain audit evidence about the amounts and disclosures in the financial statements. The procedures selected depend on the auditor's judgment, including the assessment of the risks of material mis-statement of the financial statements, whether due to fraud or error.

In making those risk assessments, the auditor considers internal control relevant to the entity's preparation and fair presentation of the financial statements in order to design audit procedures that are appropriate in the circumstances, but not for the purpose of expressing an opinion on the effectiveness of the entity's internal control. An audit also includes evaluating the appropriateness of accounting policies used and the reasonableness of accounting estimates made by management, as well as evaluating the overall financial statement presentation.

We believe that the audit evidence we have obtained is sufficient and appropriate to provide a basis for our audit opinion.

Opinion (UK & Ireland: **Opinion on Financial Statements**)

In our opinion, the financial statements present fairly, in all material respects (or *give a true and fair view of*) the financial position of ABC Company as at December 31, 20X1, and (*of)* its financial performance and its cash flows for the year then ended in accordance with International Financial Reporting Standards.

Report on other legal and regulatory requirements

(Form and content of this section of the auditor's report will vary depending on the nature of the auditor's other reporting responsibilities.)

Auditor's signature

Date of the auditor's report

Auditor's address

The illustration above is provided by ISA 700 as an example of the wording of an unmodified report, i.e. when the auditor concludes that the financial statements are prepared, in all material respects, in accordance with the applicable financial reporting framework. In essence, this is the report an auditor gives when there are no concerns about the financial statements prepared by management.

Current Issues: Improving the Auditor's Report

In June 2012, the IAASB released an invitation to comment on suggested improvements to the auditor's report.

These changes have been suggested in order to increase the transparency of the audit and significant matters in the financial statements.

The proposed changes include:

- mandating the wording and ordering of matters to be addressed in the auditor's report (currently it is recommended but not required);
- increasing the prominence of the auditor's opinion, by presenting it first in the auditor's report along with the description of the financial statements;
- including a 'basis for opinion' paragraph in reports with modified opinions as well as unmodified opinions (instead of within the auditor's responsibility section);
- adding auditor's commentary on entity specific matters that are likely to be most important to users' understanding of the financial statements or the audit;
- including the auditor's conclusion on the appropriateness of management's use of the going concern assumption and an explicit opinion on whether material uncertainties in relation to going concern have been identified;
- including an auditor's statement on whether any material inconsistencies between the audited financial statements and other information have been identified.

Purpose of sections within an audit report

Title and addressee

- The title differentiates the audit report, from the rest of the financial statements and other matter included.
- The word 'independent' in the title reminds the reader of the value of the audit.
- Specifying the addressee of the report, clarifies its purpose.
- This may also be regarded as an attempt to restrict to a defined category, those people to whom the auditor acknowledges a duty of care.

Introductory paragraph

- Identifying the financial statements on which the auditor is reporting.
- It may also serve to restrict the scope of the auditor's implied responsibility.
- There is often a reference to the accounting convention or the applicable financial reporting framework in the introductory paragraph, which clarifies the basis on which the financial statements are prepared.

Management's responsibilities

- This is clearly an attempt to manage the expectation gap, by making it clear to the reader what management is responsible for.

Auditor's responsibility

- Principally aimed at managing the expectation gap.
- Includes information regarding:
  - ethical requirements
  - reasonable assurance
  - the risk-based approach
  - true and fair (see below)
  - no opinion on the effectiveness of internal control.
- Clear statement that the auditor believes that sufficient, appropriate evidence has been obtained.

Opinion

- The only issue here is the meaning of 'true and fair' (or present fairly).

Signature, date, and address

- Further emphasis on who has responsibility for what.
- There is some debate currently about whether the report should be signed by the firm, or whether the individual taking responsibility for the audit within the firm should be identified.
- There is clearly scope for debate about the relative merits of collective v personal responsibility:
  - Collective responsibility puts the whole weight of the firm behind the audit opinion.
  - Collective responsibility arguably allows an individual to hide behind the anonymity of the firm's name.
  - Personal responsibility of the individual potentially allows 'scapegoating.'

The meaning of 'fair presentation'

'Fair presentation' (or 'true and fair') has never been defined as a concept by the courts and yet it appears in legislation, financial reporting standards, and auditing standards throughout the world.

Possible definitions

Auditors should attempt to ensure that the financial statements that are the subject of the audit present clearly and equitably the financial state of affairs of the enterprise. This suggests that in order to achieve fair presentation it is necessary to:

- present information impartially (i.e. without bias);
- present information equitably; and
- present information that is clear, plain and clearly understood by the users.

3 Forming an opinion

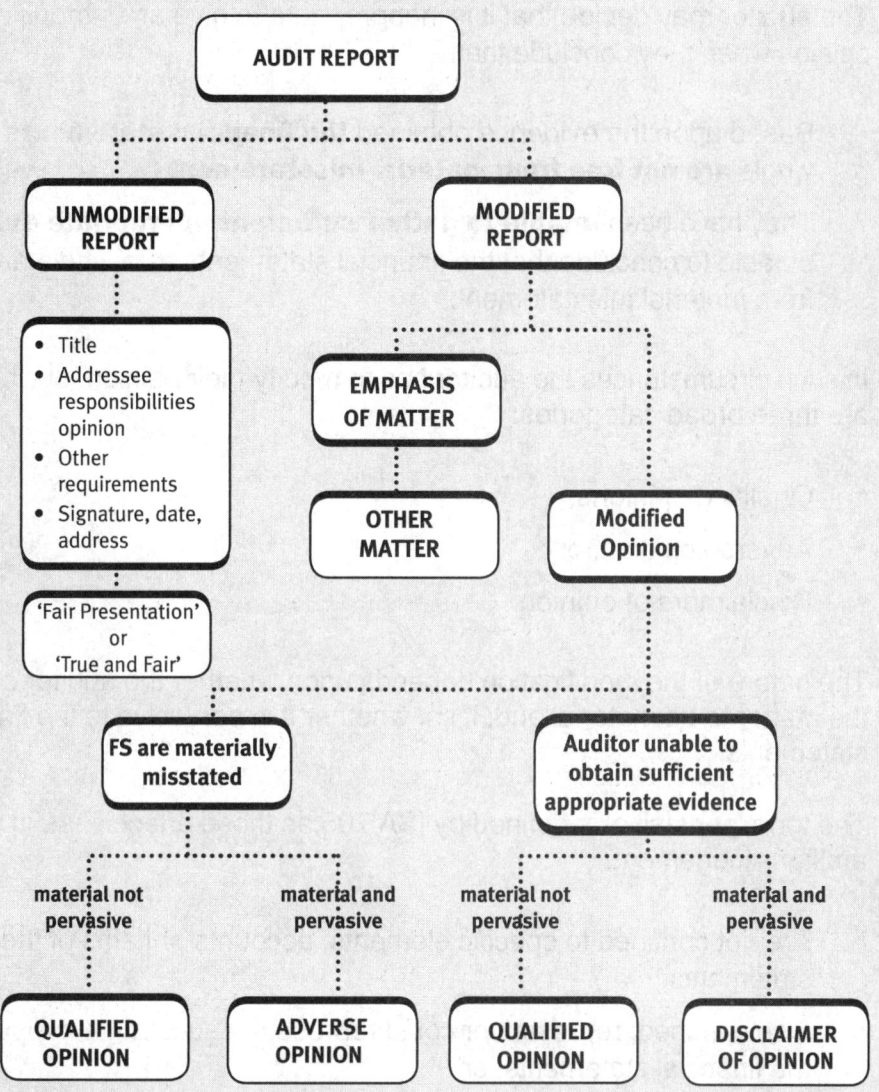

Recap from earlier studies

ISA 700 provides illustrations of the wordings of the standard, or unmodified, audit report. There are two ways that the audit report can be modified:

- By modifying the audit opinion; or
- By drawing users' attention to certain issues by way of an additional communication.

To clarify the reasons for and the impacts of the above departures from the standard, unmodified audit report, guidance has been split into two further ISA's, namely: 705 *Modifications to the Opinion in the Independent Auditor's Report* and 706 *Emphasis of Matter Paragraphs and Other Matter Paragraphs in the Independent Auditor's Report.*

Modifications of the audit opinion

The auditor may decide that it is inappropriate to give an unmodified opinion when they conclude that:

- Based upon the evidence obtained **the financial statements** as a whole **are not free from material misstatement**
- They have been **unable to gather sufficient appropriate evidence** to be able to conclude that the financial statements as a whole are free from material misstatement.

In such circumstances the auditor has to modify their opinion, of which there are three broad categories:

- Qualified opinions;
- Adverse opinion; or
- Disclaimers of opinion.

The nature of the modification depends upon whether the auditor considers the matter to be material and, if so, whether it is pervasive to the financial statements.

The term 'pervasive' is defined by ISA 705 as those effects that, in the auditor's judgement:

- Are not confined to specific elements, accounts or items of the financial statements;
- If so confined, represent or could represent a substantial proportion of the financial statements; or
- In relation to disclosures, are fundamental to users' understanding of the financial statements.

In brief, a pervasive matter must be fundamental to the financial statements, therefore rendering them unreliable as a whole. A simple material matter, whilst itself significant to users' decision making, can be isolated whilst the remainder of the financial statements may be relied upon.

The following table illustrates how the auditor's judgement about the nature of the matter affects the type of opinion to be given in the audit report:

chapter 13

	Material but Not Pervasive	Material & Pervasive
Financial statements are materially misstated	Qualified Opinion	Adverse Opinion
Inability to obtain sufficient appropriate audit evidence	Qualified Opinion	Disclaimer of Opinion

Audit report: University of Oxford

The auditors of the University of Oxford, Deloitte, have issued a **Qualified Opinion** due to material misstatement for a number of years. The results of Oxford University Press (OUP), a department of the University, are not consolidated in the financial statements of the University because the financial regulations of the Council of the University do not apply to OUP. The financial statements do not comply with UK GAAP in this respect, and are therefore materially misstated.

Example wording of a Qualified Opinion (a)

Below is an example of a qualified opinion where the auditor concludes that inventories have been materially misstated but the matter is not pervasive to the financial statements:

Basis for Qualified Opinion (UK & Ireland: *Basis for Qualified Opinion on Financial Statements*)

The company's inventories are carried in the statement of financial position at xxx. Management has not stated the inventories at the lower of cost and net realisable value but has stated them solely at cost, which constitutes a departure from International Financial Reporting Standards. The company's records indicate that had management stated the inventories at the lower of cost and net realisable value, an amount of xxx would have been required to write the inventories down to their net realisable value. Accordingly, cost of sales would have been increased by xxx, and income tax, net income and shareholder's equity would have been reduced by xxx, xxx and xxx respectively.

Qualified Opinion (UK & Ireland: *Qualified Opinion on Financial Statements*)

KAPLAN PUBLISHING

In our opinion, except for the effect on the matter described in the Basis for Qualified Opinion paragraph, the financial statements present fairly in all material respects (*or give a true and fair view of*) … (remaining words are the same as illustrated in the opinion illustrated by ISA 700).'

(ISA 705)

Example wording of a Qualified Opinion (b)

Below is an example of a qualified opinion where the auditor was unable to obtain sufficient appropriate evidence regarding an investment in a foreign affiliate. The possible effects are deemed to be material but the matter is not pervasive to the financial statements:

Basis for Qualified Opinion (UK & Ireland: *Basis for Qualified Opinion on Financial Statements*)

ABC Company's investment in XYZ Company, a foreign associate acquired during the year and accounted for by the equity method, is carried at xxx on the statement of financial position as at December 31, 20X1, and ABC's share of XYZ's net income of xxx is included in ABC's income for the year then ended. We were unable to obtain sufficient appropriate evidence about the carrying amount of ABC's investment for the year because we were denied access to the financial information, management, and the auditors of XYZ. Consequently we were unable to determine whether any adjustments to these amounts were necessary.

Qualified Opinion (UK & Ireland: *Qualified Opinion on Financial Statements*)

In our opinion, except for the possible effects of the matter described in the Basis for Qualified Opinion paragraph, the financial statements present fairly in all material respects (*or give a true and fair view of*) … (remaining words are the same as illustrated in the opinion illustrated by ISA 700).'

(ISA 705)

chapter 13

Example wording of an Adverse Opinion

Below is an example of an adverse opinion where the auditor has concluded that the financial statements are misstated due to the non-consolidation of a material subsidiary that was deemed pervasive to the financial statements:

Basis for Adverse Opinion (UK & Ireland: *Basis for Adverse Opinion on Financial Statements*)

As explained in Note X, the company has not consolidated the financial statements of subsidiary XYZ Company it acquired during 20X1 because it has not yet been able to ascertain the fair values of certain of the subsidiary's material assets and liabilities at the acquisition date.

The investment is therefore accounted for on a cost basis. Under International Financial Reporting Standards, the subsidiary should have been consolidated because it is controlled by the company. Had XYZ been consolidated, many elements in the accompanying financial statements would have been materially affected. The effects on the consolidated financial statements of the failure to consolidate have not been determined.

Adverse Opinion (UK & Ireland: *Adverse Opinion on Financial Statements*)

In our opinion, because of the significance of the matter discussed in the Basis for Adverse Opinion paragraph, the consolidated financial statements do not present fairly (or *do not give a true and fair view*) of the financial position of ABC Company and its subsidiaries as at December 31 20X1, and their financial performance and their cash flows for the year then ended in accordance with International Financial Reporting Standards.

(ISA 705)

Audit report: NASA

The auditors of the National Aeronautics and Space Administration (NASA, an agency of the United States government), PwC, issued a **Disclaimer of Opinion** on the 2003 financial statements because (in part) NASA were unable to provide documentary evidence for nearly $565 billion year-end adjustments relating to data conversion errors. The auditors were unable to complete further audit procedures to obtain sufficient appropriate evidence on which to form their audit opinion.

Auditors' reports

> PwC issued a Disclaimer of Opinion for the following six years for similar reasons.

Example wording of a Disclaimer of Opinion

Below is an example of a disclaimer of opinion where the auditor was unable to obtain sufficient appropriate evidence about a single element of the financial statements. The auditor has concluded that the possible effects of this matter are both material and pervasive to the financial statements:

Basis for Disclaimer of Opinion (UK & Ireland: *Basis for Disclaimer of Opinion on Financial Statements*)

The company's investment in its joint venture XYZ (Country X) Company is carried at xxx on the company's statement of financial position, which represents over 90% of the company's net assets as at December 31 20X1. We were not allowed access to the management and the auditors of XYZ, including XYZ auditor's audit documentation. As a result, we were unable to determine whether any adjustments were necessary in respect of the company's proportional share of XYZ's assets that it controls jointly, its proportional share of XYZ's income and expenses for the year, and the elements making up the statement of changes in equity and cash flow statement.

Disclaimer of Opinion (UK & Ireland: *Disclaimer of Opinion on Financial Statements*)

Because of the significance of the matter described in the Basis for Disclaimer of Opinion paragraph, we have not been able to obtain sufficient appropriate audit evidence to provide a basis for an audit opinion. Accordingly, we do not express an opinion on the financial statements.

(ISA 705)

4 Additional communications in the audit report

In certain circumstances auditors are required to make additional communications in the audit report. Issues requiring communication include:

- Matters already communicated in the financial statements that are of fundamental importance to users' understanding of the financial statements; and
- Any other matters relevant to the users' understanding of the audit, the auditor's responsibility and the auditor's report.

These matters are communicated either through use of an 'Emphasis of Matter' paragraph or an 'Other Matter' paragraph.

It is important to note that these **do not impact the wording of the opinion** and do not constitute either a qualified, adverse or disclaimer of opinion.

The Emphasis of Matter Paragraph

Emphasis of matter is used to refer to **a matter that has been adequately presented or disclosed in the financial statements** by directors. The auditor's judgement is that these matters are **of such fundamental importance to the users' understanding** of the financial statements that the auditor should emphasise the disclosure.

Examples of such fundamental matters include:

- An uncertainty relating to the future outcome of exceptional litigation or regulatory action;
- Early application of a new accounting standards; and
- Major catastrophes that have had a significant effect on the entity's financial position.

For P7, fundamental matters tend to be uncertainties that, if and when they crystallise, could damage the entity's ability to continue as a going concern. ISA 570 *Going Concern,* in fact, requires the auditor to include an emphasis of matter paragraph in certain circumstances.

Auditors' reports

Audit report: Ocado

The auditors of Ocado (an online supermarket in the UK), PwC, issued a modified audit report on the 2009 financial statements, with an **Emphasis of Matter** paragraph due to a material uncertainty. The company was seeking new funding through an initial public offering of shares in Ocado Group plc. If the initial public offering did not proceed, Ocado may have needed to renegotiate existing banking arrangements and seek alternative sources of finance.

Example wording of an 'Emphasis of Matter' paragraph

Below is an example of the wording of an emphasis of matter paragraph included in an otherwise unmodified audit report in response to exceptional pending litigation:

Emphasis of Matter

We draw attention to Note X to the financial statements which describes the uncertainty related to the outcome of the lawsuit filed against the company by XYZ Company. Our opinion is not modified in respect of this matter.

(ISA 706)

Other Matter Paragraphs

If the auditor considers it necessary to communicate to the users regarding **matters that are not presented or disclosed in the financial statements** that, in the auditor's judgement, are **relevant to understanding: the audit; the auditor's responsibilities; or the audit report**, the auditor includes an "Other Matter" paragraph in the audit report.

Examples of its use include:

- To explain why the auditor has not resigned, when a pervasive inability to obtain sufficient appropriate evidence is imposed by management (e.g. denying the auditor access to books and records) but the auditor is unable to withdraw from the engagement due to legal restrictions;

- Where an entity prepares one set of accounts in accordance with a general purpose framework and another set in accordance with a different one (e.g. one according to UK and one according to International standards) and engage the auditor to report on both sets;

- When restricting the use of the auditor's report when the financial statements are prepared for a specific purpose;

- When law, regulation or generally accepted practice requires or permits the auditor to provide further explanation of their responsibilities; and

- When the auditor has identified a material inconsistency between financial statements and the 'Other Information' in the annual report (in accordance with ISA 720).

An Other Matter paragraph would not be used where the material misstatement in the 'other information' does not contradict the financial statements, e.g. a company materially mistating the volume of carbon dioxide emissions. This would be described as a material misstatement of fact. The auditor would need to seek legal advice on an appropriate course of action if management refuse to amend the mistatement (note the UK differences, in the UK syllabus focus below).

IAASB: Q&A XBRL

In January 2010, the IAASB issued a Questions & Answers publication called 'XBRL: The Emerging Landscape' to "highlight the growing interest in, and use of, XBRL".

XBRL (eXtensible Business Reporting Language), is a language for the electronic communication of business and financial data. XBRL assigns all individual disclosure items within business reports a unique, electronically readable tags (like a barcode). The IAASB Q&A publication explains that "These tags are mapped to taxonomies that have been and are being developed by market constituents (such as regulators, accounting standard setters, and others)... Taxonomies are, in essence, dictionaries that contain the terms used in financial statements and other business reports and their corresponding XBRL tags. The use of XBRL is expected to provide benefits in the preparation, analysis and communication of business information. It offers potential cost savings and improved accuracy of information for those involved in supplying or using financial data."

As we have seen, ISA 720, sets out the auditor's responsibilities relating to other information in documents containing audited financial statements. XBRL-tagged data does not represent "other information" as referred to in ISA 720.

Auditors are not required to provide assurance on XBRL data in the context of an audit of financial statements.

However, auditors may be able to provide other services in relation to XBRL data, including:

- Agreed-upon procedures engagements (see "Other Assignments" chapter)

Auditors' reports

- Assurance engagements (e.g. assurance on the controls over the XBRL-tagging process or over the accuracy of the XBRL-tagged data).
- Preparation of the XBRL-tagged data (after having carefully considered the implications on their independence of course!).

UK syllabus focus

ISA 700 (UK & Ireland) The Auditor's Report on Financial Statements

In the UK & Ireland, the auditor's responsibilities are not required to include the scope of the audit. Instead, the auditor's report must:

- cross reference to a "Statement of the Scope of an Audit" on the FRC's website,
- cross reference to a "Statement of the Scope of an Audit" elsewhere within the annual report, or
- include a description of the scope of an audit in the auditor's report.

ISA 720A (UK & Ireland) The Auditor's Responsibilities Relating to Other Information in Documents Containing Audited Financial Statements

In the UK & Ireland the auditor is also required to identify any information contained within any of the financial or non-financial information in the annual report that is apparently materially incorrect based on, or materially inconsistent with, the knowledge acquired by the auditor in the course of performing the audit.

If on reading the other information, the auditor becomes aware of a material misstatement of fact that management refuses to correct, they may include a description of this misstatement of fact in an Other Matters paragraph.

ISA 720(b) (UK & Ireland) The Auditor's Statutory Reporting Responsibility in Relation to Directors' Reports

In the United Kingdom legislation (i.e. the Companies Act 2006) requires the auditor of a company to state in the auditor's report whether, in the auditor's opinion, the information given in the directors' report is consistent with the financial statements.

This would appear in a paragraph headed "Opinion on other matters", immediately after the "Opinion on the Financial Statements"

Objectives

The objective of the auditor is to form an opinion on whether the information given in the directors' report is consistent with the financial statements and to respond appropriately if it is not consistent.

Requirements

The auditor shall read the information in the directors' report and assess whether it is consistent with the financial statements.

The auditor is not required to verify, or report on, the completeness of the information in the directors' report. If, however, the auditor becomes aware that information that is required by law or regulations to be in the directors' report has been omitted the auditor communicates the matter to those charged with governance.

If the auditor identifies any inconsistencies between the information in the directors' report and the financial statements the auditor shall seek to resolve them.

If the auditor is of the opinion that the information in the directors' report is materially inconsistent with the financial statements, and has been unable to resolve the inconsistency, the auditor shall state that opinion and describe the inconsistency in the auditor's report.

If an amendment is necessary to the financial statements and management and those charged with governance refuse to make the amendment, the auditor shall express a qualified or adverse opinion on the financial statements.

Exam style question: Reporting

This question is typical of the style and wording of an audit reporting question. In order to ensure a good mark you must discuss relevant accounting guidance, why there appears to be a departure from that guidance, whether you are able to gather sufficient appropriate evidence to support an opinion and how these issues affect your opinion.

Ultimately you will have to suggest an opinion. You must reach a specific conclusion (i.e. the wording of your report) based upon your discussion. Do not offer a range of possible solutions as there is very rarely a range of possible opinions to these questions. The examiner has indicated that she would like to see students be able to draw conclusions from their work.

Auditors' reports

You are a partner of Finbar & Sons, a firm of accountants. You are conducting a review of the draft financial statements of a major client, Holly & Ivy Ltd, for the year ended 30 April 2008. According to the draft accounts turnover for the year was $125mn, profit before tax was $9mn and total assets were $100mn. You also identify the following issues:

(1) The accounting policies note state that all development costs are expensed as incurred. The audit work performed shows that these costs totalled $6mn during the year and that of these $1.3mn should have been capitalised as development assets in accordance with relevant financial reporting standards.

The audit senior has suggested a qualified audit opinion with a disclaimer paragraph, given the highly material nature of the matter above in comparison to profit before tax. She has also included and emphasis of matter paragraph, due to the perceived significance of the issue.

(2) The directors of Holly & Ivy have, for the first time, stated their intention to publish the annual report on the company's website.

Required:

Identify and comment upon the implications of the above matters and the impact they will have on the final audit report for the year ended 30 April 2008.

(10 marks)

Test your understanding 1

(a) Explain the importance of comparatives to the conduct of an audit.

(5 marks)

(b) Libra & Leo, a small firm of certified accountants, has provided audit services to Delphinus Ltd for many years. The company, which makes hand-crafted beds, is undergoing expansion and has recently relocated its operations. Having completed the audit of the financial statements for the year ended 31 December 2006 and issued an unmodified opinion thereon, Libra & Leo have now indicated that they do not propose to offer themselves for re-election.

The chief executive of Delphinus, Mr Pleiades, has now approached your firm to audit the financial statements for the year to 31 December 2007. However, before inviting you to accept the nomination he has asked for your views on the following extracts from an auditors' report:

'However, the evidence available to us was limited because we were not appointed auditors of the company until (date 2007) and in consequence we were not able to attend the inventory count at 31 December 2006. There were no satisfactory alternative means that we could adopt to confirm the amount of inventory and work-in-progress included in the preceding period's financial statements at $ ....

'In our opinion, the financial statements give a true and fair view of the state of the company's affairs as at 31 December 2007 and, except for any adjustments that might have been found to be necessary had we been able to obtain sufficient evidence concerning inventory and work-in-progress as at 1 January 2007, of its profit [loss] for the year then ended ....

'In respect alone of the limitation on our work relating to inventory and work-in-progress:

we have not obtained all the information and explanations that we considered necessary for the purpose of our audit, and we were unable to determine whether proper accounting records had been maintained.'

Mr Pleiades has been led to understand that such a qualified opinion must be given on the financial statements of Delphinus for the year ended 31 December 2007, as a necessary consequence of the change in audit appointment. He is anxious to establish whether you would issue anything other than an unmodified opinion.

Required:

Comment on the proposed auditors' report. Your answer should consider whether and how the chief executive's concerns can be overcome.

(10 marks)

(Total: 15 marks)

Test your understanding 2

(a) Explain, with reasons, how a member of The Association of Chartered Certified Accountants should respond to a request to provide a 'second opinion'.

(5 marks)

(b) Avid, a limited liability company, is a wholly-owned subsidiary of Drago. As a result of Drago divesting its non-core activities, Avid ceased to trade in the year to 31 March 2006 when its trade and assets were sold to a competitor.

At 31 March 2006, Avid's remaining assets (including amounts due to group companies, current investment, cash and cash equivalents) were sufficient to meet Avid's provisions which totalled $9.7 million in respect of:

– year 2000 product liability;
– staff redundancies;
– claims for unfair dismissal;
– property leases;
– breach of contracts with distributors and suppliers.

The audit opinion on the financial statements for the year ended 31 March 2006 was unmodified.

All known claims and liabilities have since been settled. The draft financial statements for the year ending 31 March 2007 show the balance on the provisions account to be $3.9 million.

Avid's finance director, Marek, has approached you, as a personal friend, to discuss the following extract from the draft auditor's report which he received yesterday.

'As more fully explained in note 7 an amount of $3.9 million has been included in 'Provisions' in respect of general risks facing the Company. The directors consider that such a provision is prudent in the light of the impending liquidation of the Company. In our opinion future liabilities should be recognised in accordance with the International Accounting Standard 37 Provisions, Contingent Liabilities and Contingent Assets. If liabilities had been so recognised, the effect would have been to increase the profits brought forward in the financial statements to 31 March 2007 by $3.9 m.

'In our opinion, because of the effects of the matters discussed above, the financial statements do not give a true and fair view of the financial position of the Company as at 31 March 2007, and of the results of its operation and its cash flows for the year then ended …'

Required:

Comment on the suitability or otherwise of the proposed auditor's report. Your answer should discuss the appropriateness of alternative audit opinions.

(10 marks)

(Total: 15 marks)

5 Chapter summary

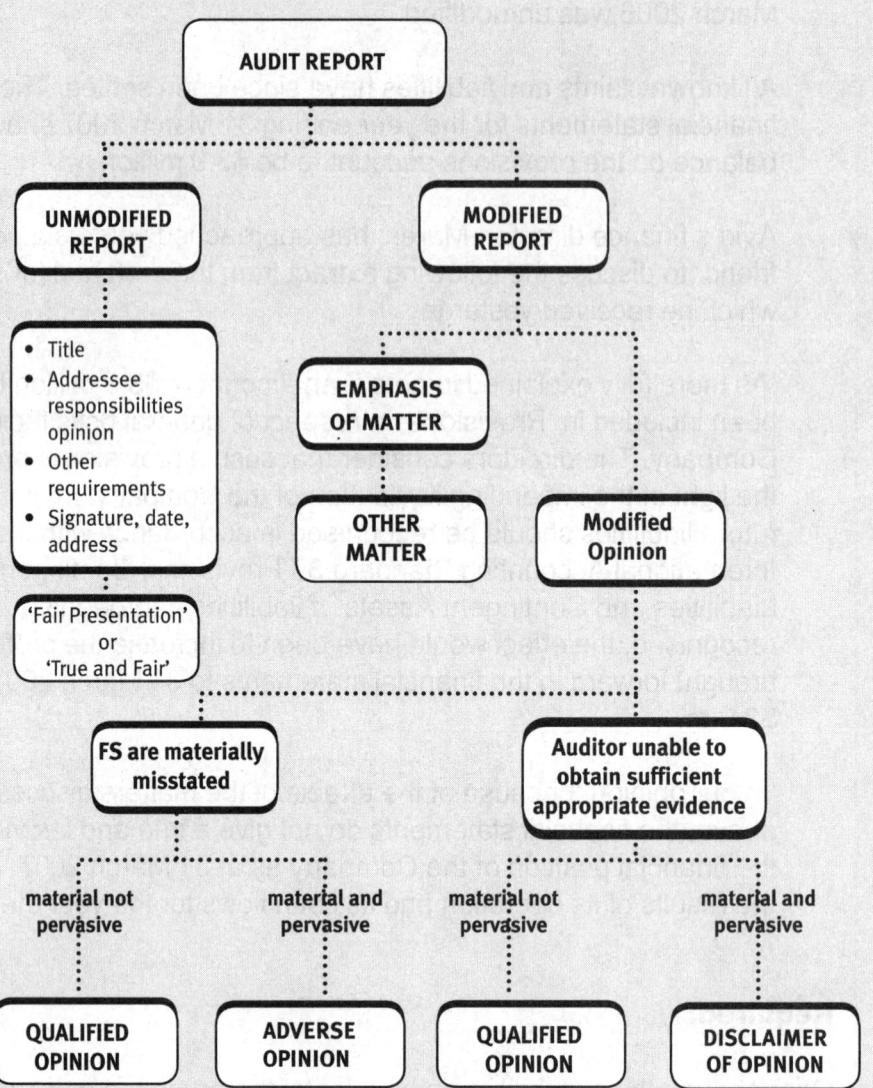

chapter 13

Test your understanding answers

Exam style question: Reporting

Development costs

The expensing of development costs is in direct contravention of IAS 38 "Intangible Assets." According to the standard if the costs of a project can be measured separately and reliably, if the project is commercially viable and technically feasible and if an overall profit is expected then the development costs MUST be capitalised.

It is the auditor's responsibility to express an opinion on whether the financial statements are prepared, in all material aspects, in accordance with an identified financial reporting framework.

In this instance the error of $1.3mn represents 14.4% of profit before tax and is clearly material to the financial statements. Therefore an adjustment should be proposed and the director's of Holly & Ivy should be given the opportunity to amend the financial statements. To achieve this the directors must restate the accounts, removing the $1.3mn from the statement of profit or loss and capitalising them as intangible development costs on the statement of financial position, as per IAS 38.

In addition the directors will be required to update the accounting policy notes. If this policy were adopted in the prior year, and development costs expensed again, then a restatement of opening reserves may be required. This would require an explanatory note in the accounts discussing the nature of the prior year adjustment.

With regard to the audit opinion the first matter is that disclaimers of opinion are given when the auditor is unable to gather sufficient appropriate audit evidence, which is not the case here. In this instance the auditor has identified a material misstatement in the financial statements.

The second matter is that the use of a disclaimer suggests that the matter is being treated as a pervasive issue. This means that the misstatement is so significant to the users' understanding of the financial statements that it renders them unreliable on the whole. If this were the case then an adverse opinion would be given.

However, whilst the error represents 14% of profit before tax and 1.3% of total assets and is clearly material, it is unlikely to be pervasive. With full knowledge of the error the users should still be able to rely on the other information contained in the financial statements as there is no indication of further misstatement.

KAPLAN PUBLISHING

365

Therefore, in this instance, an 'except for' qualification would be made on the basis of a failure to comply with relevant financial reporting guidelines for capitalising development costs.

The emphasis of matter paragraph is not required in these circumstance. These are usually required when uncertainty exists that is so fundamental it could cast doubt on the entity's ability to continue trading as a going concern in the future. That is clearly not the case here. Emphasis of matter paragraphs should not be used to refer to the nature of a modification to the audit opinion. That information is contained in the 'Basis of Opinion' paragraph.

Internet report

There is no extension to the auditor's duty of care simply because the report is being published electronically as well as in hard copy. All accounts are publically available. The main concern is the extent to which audited information is published on the web. The directors may choose to exclude some parts of the financial statements and there will need to be some sort of upload onto the internet, where information may be corrupted.

The auditor must check the following:

(a) that the information uploaded is derived from the information contained in the manually signed financial statements (e.g. conversion to PDF or HTML);

(b) that the electronic copy agrees to the hard copy, by proof reading;

(c) that the auditor's signature copied onto the electronic document is protected from modification;

(d) that the conversion has not distorted the information in any way.

Most importantly, the auditor needs to make it clear in the audit opinion which information has and has not been audited (e.g. by use of page numbers if PDF version).

A point should be raised in the management representation letter that the directors sign asking them to acknowledge their responsibility for implementing a security system that prevents the deliberate corruption or manipulation of the electronic financial statements.

chapter 13

Test your understanding 1

It is important that you should not make issues out of information given in a question which is not relevant to answering the question set. For example, this question requires a predecessor auditor.

Addressing or speculating upon the reasons for the change will not earn marks because (i) it is not relevant; (ii) the tone of the introductory paragraph ('expansion', 'relocation', 'unqualified opinion') does not suggest anything untoward about the change.

(a) **Corresponding figures**

Amounts and disclosures derived from preceding financial statements are included with (and are intended to be read in relation to) the current period figures. When comparatives are presented as corresponding figures they are not specifically identified in an auditor's report because the auditor's opinion is on the current period financial statements as a whole, including the corresponding figures. (ISA 710)

For initial engagements (ISA 510) the auditor seeks to obtain sufficient, appropriate audit evidence to confirm that:

- opening balances do not contain misstatements that materially affect the current period's financial statements;

- prior period's closing balances have been properly brought forward as the current period's opening balances;

- accounting policies have been consistently applied (or changes properly accounted for per IAS 8).

An auditor must be satisfied with the opening position, in particular, to form an opinion on the current year's profit (or loss). A new auditor, however, does not have previously obtained audit evidence to support transactions and accounting policies of the prior period.

To obtain the necessary assurance on the opening position, additional procedures can be performed, for example:

- a review of working papers and accounting records for the previous year end kept by the client's management;

- audit work on the current year's transactions and balances will also provide some evidence to support the completeness, valuation, existence and rights or obligations of the opening balances.

Also, a predecessor auditor may make their audit working papers available to a new auditor.

KAPLAN PUBLISHING

In rare circumstances, if these procedures are unsatisfactory, some of the opening balances may need to be substantively tested in order to form an opinion on them.

If the scope of a new auditor's work (with respect to the opening position) is effectively limited, the lack of audit evidence may result in a modification.

(b) Proposed auditors' report

If it is not possible to form an opinion on a material matter, due to lack of evidence, a modified opinion ('except for' qualification or disclaimer) will be required.

The mere fact that an auditor was not previously appointed to perform procedures on the prior period closing balances is not grounds for modification. For example, a new auditor does not obtain direct confirmations in respect of prior period trade receivable balances, but that does not mean that he cannot form an opinion about the opening trade receivables balance.

ISAs 510 and 710 both use inventory as an example of an opening balance where lack of evidence may result in a qualified 'except for' opinion – such as the one proposed – or a disclaimer.

Inventory is certainly likely to be a very significant balance in a manufacturing business such as Delphinus. It will be more difficult to form an opinion on the opening balance if:

- inventory is not accounted for in the double-entry bookkeeping system
- inventory records are not maintained
- quantities are ascertained by a year-end physical count and
- values of work-in-progress, slow-moving and damaged items are a matter of judgement.

Where a modification is warranted (e.g. because sufficient evidence regarding opening stock quantities cannot be ascertained by alternative means) the 'except for' opinion is a modification of the opinion on the current period's result (i.e. profit or loss) only and not its financial position.

For Delphinus, it is likely that sufficient evidence will be available to a new auditor in respect of inventory. In particular:

- stock quantities as at 31 December 2006 and the valuation thereof should be available from Delphinus (if Delphinus does not have, Mr Pleaides would be able to request a copy from Libra and Leo);
- hand-crafted beds are not small, inexpensive items and the auditor will be able to compare quantities as at 31 December 2007 with those of the prior year;
- gross profit margins might be expected to be relatively stable, so if opening stock was materially overstated (say) the current year margin would be deflated (and the prior year inflated).

How to overcome chief executive's concerns

Such audit procedures (as outlined above) should be undertaken, as necessary, to confirm the opening position. In particular:

- reviewing prior year end inventory sheets and comparing quantities of raw materials, WIP and finished beds
- analytically reviewing key ratios (e.g. gross profit percentages and inventory turnover) and the relative proportions of raw materials, WIP and finished beds.

Such analytical procedures would take into account known fluctuations which, in the case of Delphinus, would arise through recent acquisitions.

It is highly unlikely that there would be a need to substantively test opening stock or make specific enquiries of the prior year auditors, Libra & Leo.

To assist the audit, Mr Pleaides should ensure that the following information is readily available:

- records of physical inventory taking at 31 December 2006
- full details of write-downs and provisions
- adjustments, if any, requested to be made by Libra & Leo
- statements of inventory acquired on purchase of unincorporated businesses
- an analysis of turnover by business segment.

Auditors' reports

Although Libra & Leo have no legal or ethical obligation to make their working papers, or other information, available to their successor, they may do so as the reason for the change in audit appointment (re-location of client) should not affect reasonable co-operation.

Whether the chief executive's concerns can be overcome

The change in audit appointment does not necessitate a modified auditor's report. For a company such as Delphinus, minimal additional procedures should confirm, to the auditor's satisfaction, the opening position including that of inventory.

However, it is not possible to state, unequivocally, that an unmodified opinion will be issued (since the audit has yet to be performed). If, for example, a matter of material misstatement were to arise in respect of the current year, the auditor would be duty-bound to report this to the members.

Tutorial note: To agree that the proposed modification is unavoidable or, at the other extreme, promising an unmodified opinion without any reservation would not be a professional stance.

Test your understanding 2

(a) **Responding to a request**

How?

When asked to provide a 'second opinion' (i.e. concerning the application of accounting standards or principles to specific circumstances or transactions of an entity which is not an audit client) a member should seek to minimise the risk of giving inappropriate guidance, by ensuring that they have access to all relevant information.

The member should therefore:

– ascertain why their opinion is being sought
– contact the auditor to provide any relevant facts
– with the entity's permission, provide the auditor with a copy of their opinion.

If asked to give an opinion in a hypothetical situation the member should make it clear that their response is not based on specific facts or circumstances relating to a particular organisation.

Reasons

The member who is not the entity's auditor must be alert to the possibility that their opinion – if it differs from that of the auditor – may create undue pressure on the auditor's judgement and so threaten the objectivity of the audit.

The member's opinion is more likely to differ if it is based on information which is different (or incomplete) as compared with that available to the auditor. The member should decline to act if permission to communicate with the auditor is not given.

(b) **Comment on suitability**

The proposed auditor's report gives an adverse opinion on the grounds of a material and pervasive misstatement. The financial statements appear not to have complied with IAS 37 and that $3.9 million shown as a liability does not meet the criteria for recognition as a provision.

The auditor agreed with the setting up of the provision (as the prior year audit opinion was not modified). However, in reviewing the unutilised provision at 31 March 2007, it should be adjusted to reflect the current best estimate. This appears to be zero (as all known claims, etc have since been settled). As a provision should only be used for expenditure for which the provision was originally recognised, the balance on the provision should be reversed (IAS 37) and disclosed separately within profit from ordinary activities (as it is likely that the expenses for which the provision was originally set up were disclosed separately per IAS 1).

The directors' argument of prudence does not appear to be justified. That the proposed audit modification is one of misstatement means that the auditor has sufficient evidence to support his opinion that the provision is not required. If the directors wish to draw the users of financial statements attention to uncertainties and possible contingent liabilities (e.g. for claims not received) they should do so by way of disclosure in a note to the accounts.

The provision is an accounting estimate. $9.7 million should have been the directors' best estimate at 30 March 2006. Assuming it is now nil, the $3.9 million balance should be included in the determination of profit or loss in the year to 31 March 2007 (IAS 1).

However, the auditor is proposing a prior period adjustment (i.e. restating the opening balance of retained earnings) which is covered by IAS 8. This suggests that the auditor considers that there was a fundamental error in the determination of the prior period provision (and not merely that the approximation was inaccurate). For example, mathematical mistakes may have occurred in estimating the Y2K product liability or facts about the contracts or leases may have been misinterpreted (to suggest that liabilities existed which did not). In proposing a prior period adjustment the auditor is implying that they would have modified their previous year's opinion (had they known of the error before they issued it).

As 40% of the provision was not utilised and should be written back (in some way) it is clearly material (as the statement of financial position contains relatively little else).

In proposing an adverse opinion the auditor is concluding that the non-compliance (with IAS 37) is 'so material and persuasive' that a qualified opinion is not adequate to disclose the misleading nature of the financial statements. However, the adjustment proposed is to restate the retained profits brought forward which has no impact on the results of operation or cash flows for the current year.

Alternative audit opinions

It is unlikely, given the amount involved, that Avid can avoid modification without adjusting for the provision. Therefore, an unmodified opinion would NOT be appropriate.

A disclaimer of opinion would also be inappropriate (as there is nothing to suggest a lack of evidence).

It is not certain from the information available whether the audit opinion should be modified on grounds of non-compliance with IAS 37 and/or IAS 8. In either case provisions (in current liabilities) should be reduced and either:

- profit for the year increased by $3.9 million (if non-compliance with IAS 37) or

- retained profit brought forward increased by $3.9 million (as per the proposed report if non-compliance with IAS 37).

In either case the matter is material but not pervasive and the auditor should express an 'except for' opinion.

chapter 14

Reports to management

Chapter learning objectives

Upon completion of this chapter you will be able to:

- critically assess the quality of a report to those charged with governance and management; and
- advise on the content of reports to those charged with governance and management in a given situation.

Reports to management

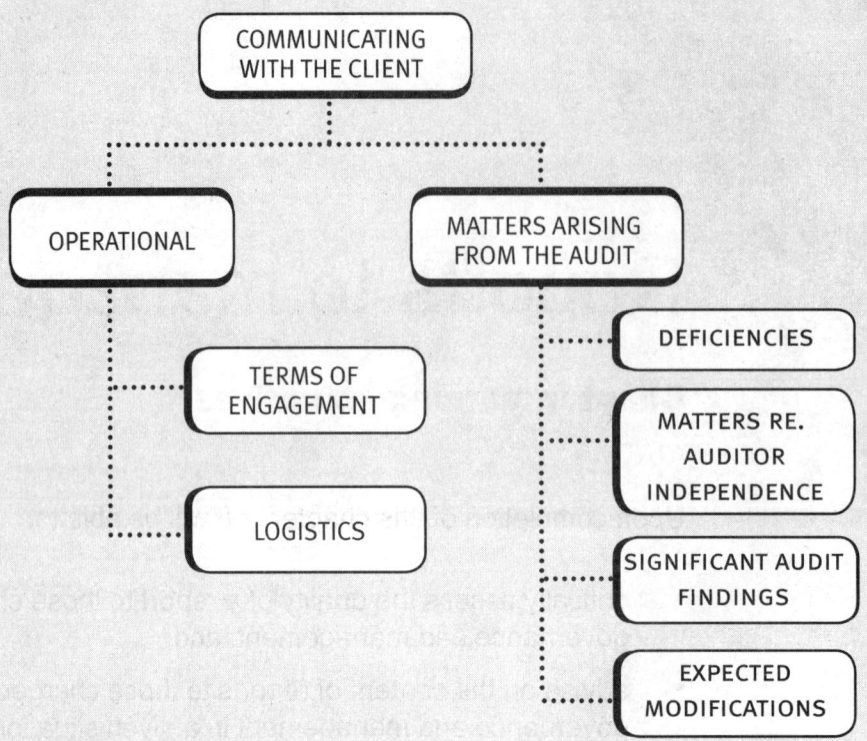

Reporting to management and those charged with governance does not appear in every exam. A typical requirement might incorporate identification of the matters to be reported from a scenario.

1 Management and those charged with governance

According to ISA 260 'those charged with governance' can be defined as

"The persons with responsibility for overseeing the strategic direction of the entity and obligations related to the accountability of the entity."

In contrast management are defined as:

"The persons with executive responsibility for the conduct of the entity's operations."

ISAs

There are two standards requiring the auditor to engage in communication with the client, other than the audit report. These are:

- ISA 260 *Communication With Those Charged With Governance;* and

- ISA 265 *Communicating Deficiencies in Internal Control to Those Charged with Governance and Management.*

chapter 14

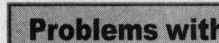

Problems with these definitions

One of the areas of difficulty with ISA's 260 and 265 is that they assume that there is a distinction between management and those charged with governance. For small and medium-sized entities and particularly for owner-managed businesses, this is often not the case.

There is a possibility, therefore, that the auditor could find themselves reporting to the owners of the business, matters already discussed with them in their capacity as management.

2 Communicating with those charged with governance

According to ISA 260 the matters that should be reported to those charged with governance include:

- The auditor's responsibilities in relation to the financial statements audit;
- The planned scope and timing of the audit including, for example;
  - the auditor's approach to internal control relevant to the audit;
  - the extent to which the auditor is planning to use the work of internal audit and the arrangements for so doing;
  - business risks that may result in material misstatements;
  - communications with regulators.
- Significant findings from the audit, such as:
  - the auditor's views about qualitative aspects of the entity's accounting practices/policies;
  - significant difficulties encountered during the audit;
  - significant matters arising during the audit that were discussed with management;
  - written representations the auditor is requesting;
  - other matters that, in the auditor's opinion, are significant to the oversight of the reporting process.
- Matters of auditor independence.

Reports to management

> **Matters to be communicated (in detail)**
>
> Ultimately what constitutes a matter requiring the attention of those charged with governance is a matter of professional judgement. However, typical examples include:
>
> - Expected limitations on the audit, either imposed by management or other circumstances'
> - The selection of, or changes in, significant accounting policies and practices that have, or could have, a material effect on the entity's financial statements;
> - The potential effect on the financial statements of any material risks and exposures, such as pending litigation, that are required to be disclosed in the financial statements;
> - A summary of identified errors, whether corrected or not by the entity;
> - Material uncertainties related to events and conditions that may cast significant doubt on the entity's ability to continue as a going concern.
> - A request that uncorrected material misstatements be adjusted in the financial statements;
> - The nature and wording of expected modifications to the auditor's report;
> - Any other matters agreed upon in the terms of the audit engagement.

3 Communicating deficiencies in internal control

The clarity project included one new standard, addressing communication of deficiencies in internal control, ISA 265. According to ISA 265 the auditor should also communicate identified deficiencies in internal control that, in the auditor's judgement, are of sufficient importance to merit attention by the entity.

The first task of the auditor, therefore, is to distinguish between simple deficiencies, which do not require communication, and significant ones that do. This is a matter of judgement. Deficiencies, however, have been defined as occurring when:

- A control is designed, implemented or operated in such a way that it is unable to prevent, or detect and correct misstatements in the financial statements on a timely basis; or

- A control necessary to prevent, or detect and correct, misstatements in the financial statements on a timely basis is missing.

In their communication the auditor includes:

- A description of the deficiencies and their potential effects;
- An explanation of the purpose of the auditor (i.e. to express an opinion on the financial statements, not to help redesign internal systems);
- An explanation of why consideration of internal control is relevant to the audit; and
- An explanation that the matters being reported are only those identified during the audit and considered to be significant enough to report.

As well as reporting to those charged with governance, ISA 265 requires auditors to communicate deficiencies to management on a timely basis (including those significant ones reported to those charged with governance and other, less significant ones, meriting the attention of management).

UK syllabus focus

ISA 260 *Communication with those charged with governance* (UK & Ireland) Revised:

- Clarifies that those charged with governance are both executive and non-executive directors (or equivalent), including members of the audit committee, whereas management would not normally included non-executive directors.
- Sets out additional information that the auditors are required to report to those charged with governance:
  - information relevant to compliance with the UK Corporate Governance Code for relevant entities
  - business risks relevant to financial reporting
  - significant accounting policies
  - management's valuation of material assets and liabilities and related disclosures
  - effectiveness of internal controls relevant to financial reporting
  - other business risks and effectiveness of other internal controls where the auditor has obtained an understanding of these matters.

Reports to management

Exam focus

Management letters formed the basis of a 17 mark question in June 2008. To clarify the examination perspective on such audit outputs Lisa Weaver published an article entitled "Auditor's Reports to Those Charged with Governance" (April 2008).

This can be found on the P7 section of the ACCA website.

Test your understanding 1

The following issues have been highlighted by the audit team during the audit of Mandolin Limited, an unlisted medium-sized company. It has eight directors including two non-executives. The directors together own 60% of Mandolin's share capital.

For each issue draft suitable paragraphs for inclusion in the management letter or, if appropriate, explain what other action, if any, you would take.

(1) The passwords that enable the finance director to access the accounting system when Ms Z needs to are written on a sticky label on the inside of the top right-hand drawer of Ms Z desk. Ms Z office is usually locked and access to Ms Z office is usually observable by the two personal assistants who assist the directors.

(2) The person who runs the payroll each month has access to all aspects of the payroll system and is responsible for processing changes to salary rates, tax deduction codes, and all other payroll items. No one reviews the payroll in detail, although the directors do review the management accounts that are produced promptly each month. The finance director is an experienced, qualified accountant and the CEO and one of the non-executive directors also have financial expertise.

(3) The company has used the same freight company for despatching its goods to customers for many years. The audit team has noticed that freight costs have increased considerably as a proportion of sales revenue over the past two years.

(4) The company's inventory includes a material amount of spares inventory against which provisions are made based on a formula calculated on the basis of the period since the last inventory movement. Broadly, the longer the period since the last movement, the higher the provision. It has emerged that any adjustments to the inventory files, whether or not they represent valid sales, are interpreted by the system as if the inventory is active and therefore current. Such adjustments might include changes of location, the scrapping of small amounts of damaged inventory, or the correction of errors.

(5) The audit team, when testing purchases, found it difficult to locate particular invoices because once approved for payment, they are scanned and held digitally in a sequence which depends upon when they were scanned. The originals are kept for the statutory period, off site in a remote location and there is no reason to believe that access there would be any easier. The client's staff very rarely need to have access to the original invoices because all the necessary checks to validate the invoice happen prior to approval for payment, and in the event of any dispute, copies can be obtained from the supplier.

(6) The client's system for segregating expenditure on non-current assets from repairs is haphazard. The client's staff are happy to correct mistakes uncovered by the audit team, but seem unconcerned by the distinction between capital and revenue expenditure.

4 Chapter summary

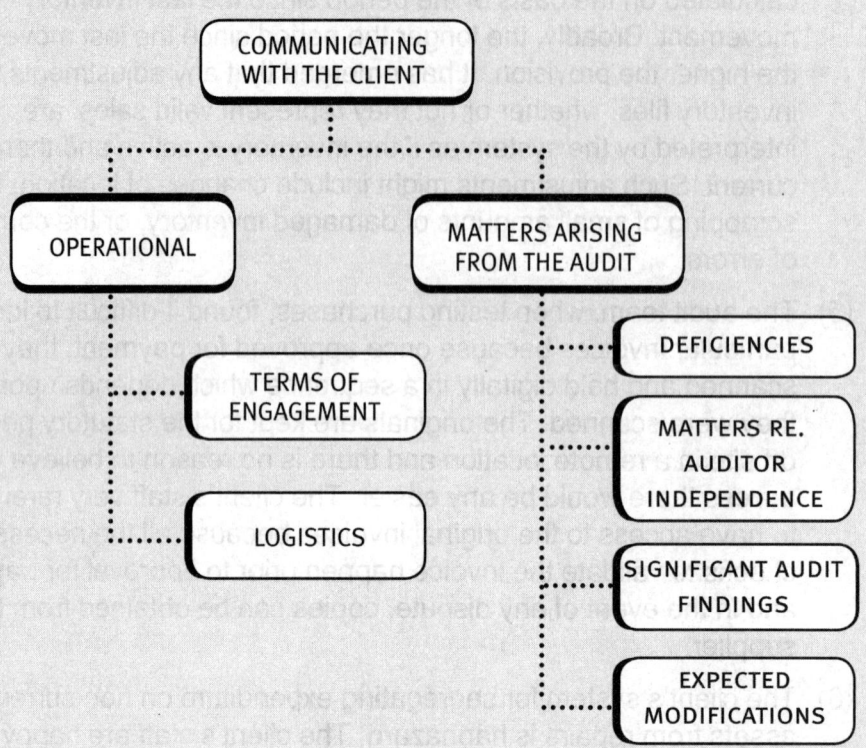

chapter 14

Test your understanding answers

Test your understanding 1

(1) This issue should initially be addressed by discussion with the finance director.

It is probable that due to the apparent reasonable security of the director's office, the risk of unauthorized use of her passwords is minimal.

If there is a real risk of abuse, this may be an example of lax controls throughout the company, which should be brought to the attention of the non-executive directors.

A possible paragraph for the management letter might be:

'We found a number of instances where the passwords giving access to the company's accounting systems were written down and kept in relatively accessible locations.

We recommend that passwords should always be kept confidential to the intended user. Ideally passwords should be memorized. If this is not feasible and a written record of the password needs to be kept, such a record should be locked in a safe.'

(2) It is possible that the budgetary controls operated by the board in reviewing the management accounts are sufficient for the detection of possible abuse of the payroll system. If not the following might be appropriate.

'Mr X has sole control of the payroll system and puts all changes into effect. While we have no reason to doubt Mr X's integrity in any way, he or his successors in post have the capability to introduce dummy employees onto the payroll or manipulate their own or other staff members' rates of pay.

In our view, the monthly review of the management accounts conducted by the board is insufficiently detailed to detect modest abuses of the system, which, although unlikely to be material on an individual basis, could amount, over time, to substantial sums.

We recommend that before the instruction to make the monthly transfers is given to the bank, the payroll should be reviewed in detail by either Mr Y the financial controller or Ms Z the finance director.'

KAPLAN PUBLISHING

Reports to management

(3) 'We draw your attention to the fact that ABC Ltd has been the sole contractor for the company's outward freight business for a number of years.

We have noted that freight charges as a proportion of sales revenue have increased at the rate of x% per annum on average over the past five years and may not be giving best value for money.

We recommend that you should consider asking ABC Ltd to review their charges, or else invite tenders for the business from other companies.'

(4) We have identified a flaw in the operation of the spares inventory provisions system, which has led to an overstatement of spares inventory that we estimate to be $Xm at the year-end (PY $Ym). The impact on net profit for the current year was $Ak (PY $Bk).

The errors have arisen because the system recognizes any adjustment to spares inventory as a movement on inventory and therefore treats the relevant inventory lines as being current, even though the movements may be minor technical adjustments or, even, write downs.

Although the impact of profits is not material year on year, it is possible that the cumulative overstatement of spares inventory values is material.

We recommend that the company should investigate further the actual level of the overstatement of spares inventory, and should take immediate steps to ensure that only valid sales of inventory are recognized as movements for the purpose of deciding whether or not a particular line of inventory is current.

(5) It is possible that the company is in breach of statutory rules concerning the accessibility of accounting records, but may well not be.

If not, this should almost certainly not be dealt with in the management letter.

Instead, the impact on the audit fee should be explained to the client. It is possible that the client will agree to give administrative assistance in retrieving relevant invoices, and the precise terms of these arrangements should be set out in the engagement letter.

The auditors will need to take care that such arrangements do not limit the scope of the audit in some way.

(6) Misallocations between capital and revenue expenditure tend to have tax implications, so the concept of audit materiality may not be relevant.

Possible wording might be:

'We have identified $Xk of capital expenditure which has been incorrectly treated as repairs. Such errors have an equal impact on the company's profits for the year, which in turn affects its tax liability.

We recommend that your accounts staff should receive training about the impact of tax sensitive expenditure so that such misallocations do not occur in the future.'

chapter 15

Other assignments

Chapter learning objectives

When you have completed this chapter you will be able to:

- describe the nature of audit-related services and the comparative levels of assurance provided by professional accountants;

- plan review engagements, for example: interim reviews and due diligence;

- explain the importance of and apply enquiry and analytical procedures in review engagements;

- describe the main categories of assurance services that audit firms can provide;

- justify a level of assurance for an engagement; and

- recognise the ways in which different types of risk may be identified and analysed.

Other assignments

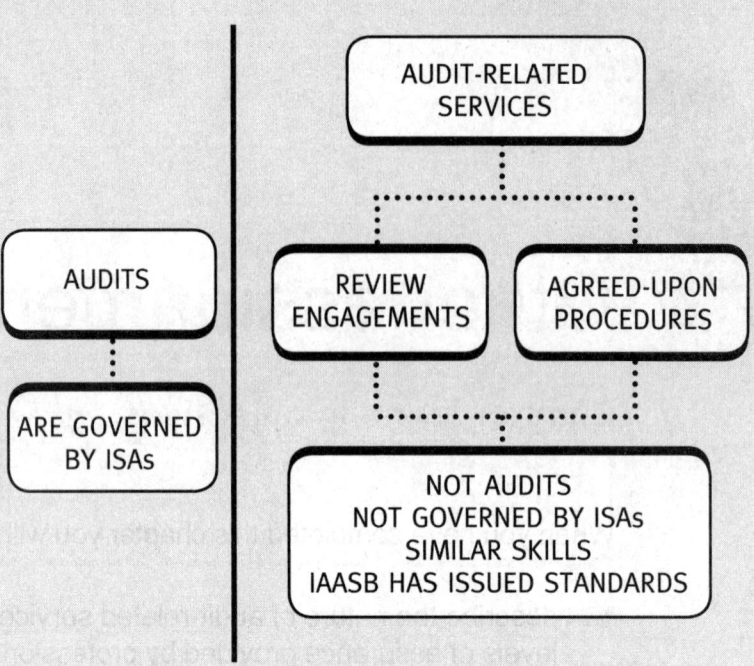

At least one question in the exam will test your ability to apply your knowledge to a non-audit engagement. The question could cover any area of the engagement process.

1 Audit-related services

What are audit-related services?

Audit-related services are those services that professional accountants offer but which are not statutory audits, although they are conceptually related and use similar skills.

You must be familiar with two types of audit-related services.

(1) review/assurance engagements; and
(2) agreed-upon procedures.

chapter 15

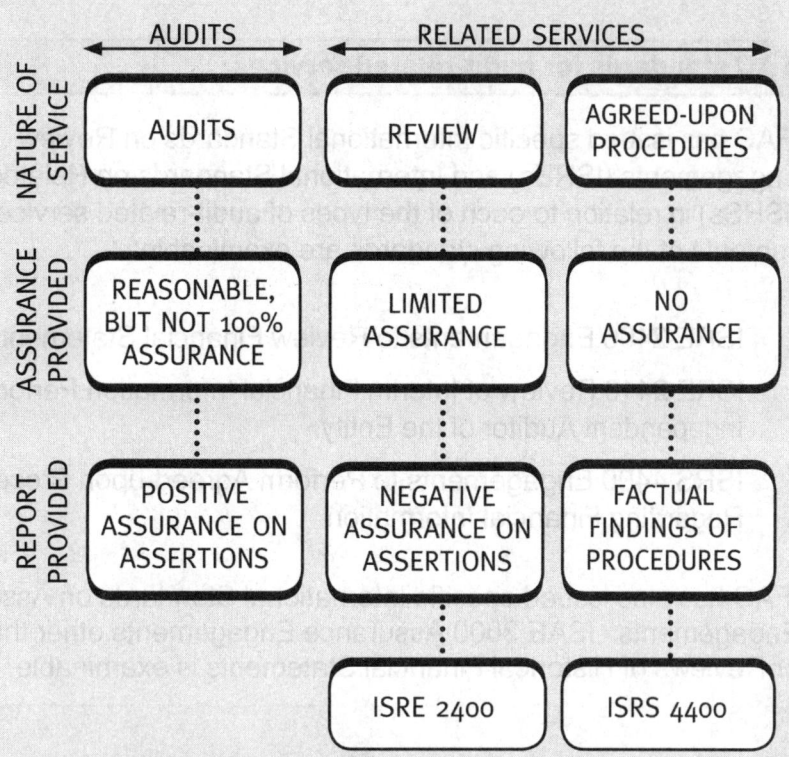

	An Audit	**Audit-related Services**
Level of assurance	Reasonable assurance	Either limited or no assurance
Scope of work	Established by the auditor in accordance with auditing standards.	Established in consultation with client, in accordance with assurance and related services standards.
Wording of assurance/other reports	positive assurance	Negative or no assurance
Required by	Law in many countries	Usually not required by law

Other assignments

IFAC standards for audit-related services

IFAC has issued specific International Standards on Review Engagements (ISREs) and International Standards on Related Services (ISRSs) in relation to each of the types of audit-related service. The key contents of the following standards are examinable:

- ISRE 2400 Engagements to Review Financial Statements.
- ISRE 2410 Review of Interim Financial Information Performed by the Independent Auditor of the Entity.
- ISRS 4400 Engagements to Perform Agreed-upon Procedures Regarding Financial Information.

IFAC has also issued specific International Standards on Assurance Engagements. ISAE 3000 Assurance Engagements other than Audits or Reviews of Historical Financial Statements is examinable.

The circumstances in which audit-related services are required

The usual types of audit-related work are:

Reviews/assurance engagements	Agreed-upon procedures
• Financial statements review (e.g. for small companies). • Interim financial statements reviews. • 'Due diligence' assignments. • Benchmarking/KPI reviews.	• Forensic audit. • Verifying insurance claims. • 'Due diligence' assignments.

Agreed-upon procedures

ISRS 4400 *Engagements to Perform Agreed-upon Procedures Regarding Financial Information* governs occasions when an accountant is engaged to carry out procedures of an audit nature but is only required to report their factual findings. For example, reports on insurance claims to insurance companies.

chapter 15

Procedures are agreed upon between the accountant and the client, and the accountant reports on factual findings; no assurance is expressed. The accountant simply reports their findings in a pre-defined manner.

Ultimately, the users of the accountant's report assess for themselves the findings reported by the accountant and draw their own conclusions.

An assurance engagement is an engagement in which a practitioner expresses a conclusion designed to enhance the degree of confidence of the intended users other than the responsible party about the outcome of the evaluation or measurement of a subject matter against criteria.

The International Framework for Assurance Engagements (the Framework) provides the overall guidance for carrying out assurance engagements. It states that the objective of an assurance engagement is:

"for a professional accountant to evaluate or measure a subject matter, that is the responsibility of another party, against identified suitable criteria and to express a conclusion that provides the intended user with a level of assurance about that subject matter."

The elements of an assurance engagement

The five elements of an assurance engagement are:

- A 'tripartite' relationship between the practitioner (i.e. accountant), the responsible party (usually directors) and the users of the report.
- A subject matter (the items about which assurance is being sought, e.g. compliance with environmental requirements).
- Suitable criteria (the benchmarks against which the subject matter is being evaluated, e.g. compliance with International Financial Reporting Standards).
- Sufficient appropriate evidence.
- A written assurance report.

The engagement process usually involves:

- agreeing the terms of the engagement in an engagement letter;
- deciding on a methodology for evidence gathering, and evaluation and measurement to support a conclusion; and
- agreeing on the type of report to be produced at the end of the engagement.

KAPLAN PUBLISHING

389

Other assignments

Levels of assurance provided

The Framework provides the overall guidance for carrying out assurance engagements such as audits and reviews. It permits only two types of assurance engagement to be performed; either a 'reasonable assurance' or a 'limited assurance' engagement.

- The objective of a '**reasonable assurance engagement**' is to obtain sufficient appropriate evidence to conclude that the subject matter conforms in all material respects with identified suitable criteria. The accountant expresses their conclusion in a positive form, giving an opinion on whether the subject matter is free from material misstatement, e.g. statutory audit.

- The objective of a '**limited assurance engagement**' is to obtain sufficient appropriate evidence to be satisfied that the subject matter 'appears reasonable' in the circumstances. The accountant expresses their conclusion in a negative form, stating that their procedures have not identified any material misstatement of the subject matter, e.g. a review engagement.

The procedures for a limited assurance engagement are therefore more limited than for a reasonable assurance engagement.

- In agreed-upon procedures engagements the reporting accountant **does not provide assurance**.

Types of assurance engagements

The framework also permits assurance engagements to be performed as either an **attestation** (or **assertion based**) engagement or a **direct reporting** engagement.

In an **attestation engagement**, the accountant's conclusion relates to an assertion made by the party who is responsible for the subject matter. The accountant can either express a conclusion about this assertion, or can provide a conclusion about the subject matter.

In a **direct reporting engagement**, the accountant expresses a conclusion on the subject matter based on identified criteria, regardless of whether the responsible party has made a written assertion on the subject matter.

For example: a professional accountant may be engaged to report on a company's internal financial controls.

Structured as an attestation engagement:

- management would first make a written assertion about the effectiveness of the company's control structure; and
- the accountant would then give an opinion on management's assertion.

Care must be taken to ensure that management's assertion is clearly understandable and is not subjective. For example, an assertion that the control structure is 'very effective' would be unacceptable since this is a subjective opinion.

Alternatively the engagement could be structured as a direct reporting engagement and the accountant would simply report directly on the effectiveness of the control structure in accordance with pre-determined performance criteria.

ISAE 3000: Assurance Engagements other than Audits or Reviews

ISAE 3000 *International Standard on Assurance Engagements other than Audits or Reviews of Historical Financial Information* provides guidance as to the conduct of assurance engagements. Accordingly, practitioners should:

- comply with the ethical requirements of IFAC and ACCA's codes of conduct;
- apply appropriate quality controls;
- record and agree the terms of engagement in an engagement letter;
- plan the engagement so that it will be performed effectively including considering materiality and engagement risk;
- obtain sufficient appropriate evidence on which to base the conclusion; and
- provide a clear written expression of their conclusion about the subject matter information.

As such, the approach and work may be similar to an audit, although the context is different.

Other assignments

Current issues: Exposure Draft ISAE 3000 (revised)

In April 2011 the IAASB released an **exposure draft** for a proposed **ISAE 3000 (revised)** Engagements other than Audits or Reviews of Historical Financial Information. The revised standard is due to be finalised and published in 2012. Corresponding changes have also been proposed to the International Framework for Assurance Engagements (the Framework).

The original standard was released in 2003, and the assurance field has evolved (and continues to evolve) since its release. The revised standard aims to clarify how some of the core underlying concepts of assurance should be applied in practice.

- In particular the revised standard aims to clarify the differences and similarities between a limited assurance engagement and a reasonable assurance engagement. Specifically:
  The revised definition of a limited assurance engagement states that it is: "a **level of assurance** that is, in the practitioner's professional judgment, **meaningful to the intended users**". The revised standard also recognises that the level of assurance is not quantifiable.

- The terms "positive form" and "negative form" in order to differentiate between reasonable and limited assurance conclusions expressed by a practitioner, have been removed. This is in order to avoid any perceived reduction in the value of a limited assurance engagement. Instead, the standard explains that in a **reasonable assurance engagement** "the practitioner's **conclusion** is expressed in a form that **conveys the practitioner's opinion** on the outcome of the measurement or evaluation of the underlying subject matter". Whereas in a **limited assurance engagement** "the practitioner's **conclusion** is expressed in a form that **conveys that**, based on the procedures performed, **nothing has come to the practitioner's attention** to cause the practitioner to believe the subject matter information is materially misstated".

- The revised standard also clarifies what is **not affected by the level of assurance**, namely:
  - The suitability of the underlying criteria
  - The appropriateness of the subject matter
  - The users; and
  - Materiality, as this is based on the information needs of the users

> Finally, the revised standard aims to clarify the difference between a **direct engagement** and **attestation engagement** ("direct reporting" engagements are renamed "direct" engagements), and how the standard should be applied to direct engagements.
>
> It defines an **attestation engagement** as: "An assurance engagement in which **a party other than the practitioner measures or evaluates the underlying subject matter against the criteria**"; and
>
> A **direct engagement** as: "An assurance engagement in which **the practitioner measures or evaluates the underlying subject matter against the criteria and** the practitioner **presents the resulting subject matter information** as part of, or accompanying, the assurance report".

2 Review engagements

ISRE 2400 *Engagements to Review Financial Statements* states that:

'The objective of a review of financial statements is to enable an auditor to state whether, **on the basis of procedures that do not provide all the evidence that would be required in an audit**, anything has come to the auditor's attention that causes the auditor to believe that the financial statements are not prepared, in all material respects, in accordance with an identified financial reporting framework.'

A review involves less work than an audit and the review report is worded to offer negative assurance.

Other assignments

The work required for a review engagement

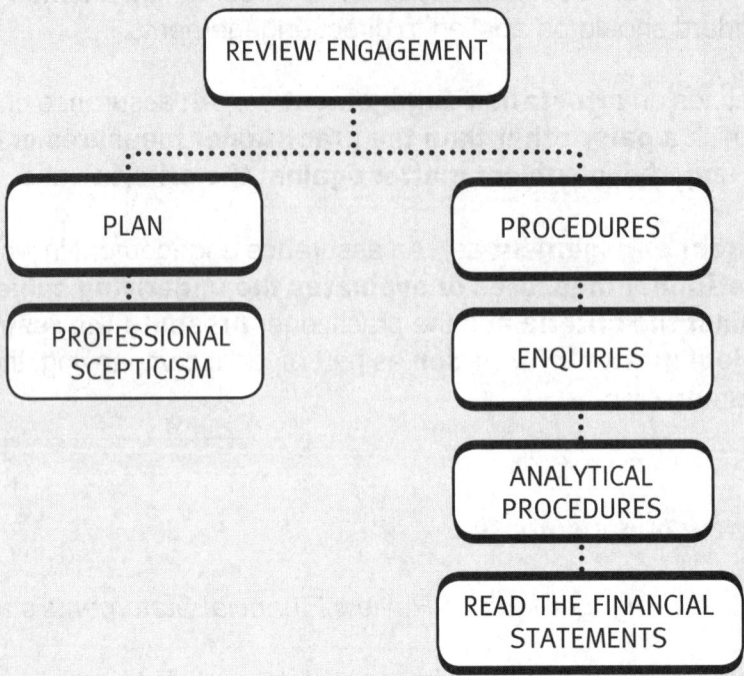

Engagement terms and planning considerations

- Once the terms of the engagement have been agreed, the accountant should send an engagement letter to the client to confirm their acceptance of the appointment and to avoid misunderstandings over the scope of the work to be done and the extent of the accountant's responsibilities.

- The engagement letter is the starting point for planning the engagement.

- In planning the engagement, the accountant should update their knowledge of the business including the client's:
  - organisational structure
  - accounting systems
  - operating characteristics
  - assets, liabilities, revenues, and expenses.

Appropriate procedures in review engagements

The accountant must carry out sufficient work to enable them to express negative assurance on the financial statements.

In deciding on the scope of the review (i.e. the procedures deemed necessary in the circumstances), the accountant will consider:

- any knowledge acquired previously about the client;
- the nature of the accounting systems;
- the extent to which items are affected by management judgment; and
- the materiality of transactions and balances.

Procedures concentrate primarily on:

- enquiries of relevant parties (usually management); and
- analytical procedures.

Analytical procedures during a review engagement

Analytical procedures should be designed to identify relationships and individual items that appear unusual. Such procedures might include:

- Current financial statements vs. prior periods.
- Current financial statements vs. forecasts.
- Review for any relationships within the financial statements that would be expected to conform to a predictable pattern based on previous patterns for the entity or industry norms.

Other assignments

Work performed during a review engagement

The work of the review should incorporate the following features:

- The auditor should plan and perform the review with an attitude of professional scepticism, obtain knowledge and obtain sufficient appropriate evidence on which to base conclusions.

- Detailed procedures will comprise:
    - making enquiries concerning the entity's accounting principles, practices, recording procedures, and material financial statement assertions
    - performing analytical procedures designed to identify relationships and individual items that appear unusual
    - enquiries concerning actions taken at meetings of shareholders, the board of directors, and other meetings that may affect the financial statements
    - reading the financial statements to consider whether they appear to conform with the basis of accounting indicated
    - obtaining reports from other auditors who have been engaged to audit or review the financial statements of components of the entity
    - enquiries of persons having responsibility for financial and accounting matters concerning such matters as, for example, completeness of recording transactions, basis of preparation of financial statements, accounting policies, etc.
    - enquiries into subsequent events
    - suspected mis-statements should be further investigated.

The review report

The review report must contain a clear written expression of negative assurance.

chapter 15

Illustration 1: Example of an unmodified review report

REVIEW REPORT TO ... ...

We have reviewed the accompanying statement of financial position of Company X at December 31 20XX, and the related statements of profit or loss and cash flows for the year then ended.

These financial statements are the responsibility of the company's management. Our responsibility is to issue a report on these financial statements based on our review.

We conducted our review in accordance with the International Standard on Review Engagements 2400 (or refer to relevant national standards or practices applicable to review engagements). This Standard requires that we plan and perform the review to obtain moderate assurance as to whether the financial statements are free of material mis-statement. A review is limited primarily to enquiries of company personnel and analytical procedures applied to financial data and thus provides less assurance than an audit. **We have not performed an audit and, accordingly, we do not express an audit opinion.**

Based on our review, nothing has come to our attention that causes us to believe that the accompanying financial statements are not presented fairly, in all material respects, (or 'do not give a true and fair view') in accordance with International Financial Reporting Standards.

AUDITOR

Date

Address

Current issues: Exposure Draft ISRE 2400 (revised)

In January 2011 the IAASB released an **exposure draft** for a proposed **ISRE 2400 (revised)** Engagements to Review Historical Financial Statements. The revised standard is due to be finalised and published in 2012.

Exemptions from a statutory audit have been expanded in many jurisdictions and this has increased the number of entities seeking assurance from a voluntary 'audit'. The revised ISRE 2400 aims to provide a benchmark for undertaking such limited assurance engagements, and promote better clarity for users about the nature of a review engagement.

KAPLAN PUBLISHING

Other assignments

> The objective of a review of financial statements has therefore been amended slightly to "**conclude, through performing primarily inquiry and analytical procedures, and evaluating the sufficiency and appropriateness of evidence obtained**, whether anything has come to the practitioner's attention that causes the practitioner to believe the financial statements are not prepared, in all material respects, in accordance with an applicable financial reporting framework."
>
> The key revision is the requirement for the practitioner's report to place more emphasis on the nature of the procedures performed and the limited assurance that results from performing those procedures in order to promote better clarity for users.
>
> In addition, the standard requires the practitioner to obtain an understanding of the entity and its environment sufficient to identify areas in the financial statements where material misstatements are likely to arise, so that procedures can be designed to address those areas. However, unlike the current version, the proposed standard does not contain a list of illustrative procedures, in order to avoid such a list being misunderstood as a set of default procedures for every review engagement. The revised standard does set out more clearly the circumstances where additional procedures are needed.

Review of interim financial information

ISRE 2410 *Review of Interim Financial Information Performed by the Independent Auditor of the Entity* gives guidance to the accountant in carrying out a review of interim financial information.

- In many countries, listed companies are required to publish a half-yearly interim report containing a summarised statement of profit or loss for the first six months of the financial year as well as certain statement of financial position information and notes.

- Companies may choose to, or be required to, have this report reviewed by professional accountants (normally the company's auditors).

- Where a review has been performed, the review report must typically be published with the interim report.

- The review report will offer negative assurance, i.e. the reviewer reports that he is not aware of any material modifications that should be made to the financial information as presented.

chapter 15

3 Other assurance services

The main categories of assurance services

As well as statutory audits and review engagements audit firms offer assurance services in the following areas:

- due diligence
- business performance measurement
- social and environmental audit
- risk assessment
- systems reliability (including e-commerce).

The benefits of assurance services

Businesses need to know if their systems are reliable and their business procedures are sound. They may need to demonstrate this to third parties, e.g. a company may wish to persuade influential shareholders that their business plans are sensible and are supported by sound infrastructures. It would be desirable if a third party with the necessary skills and reputation reassured the shareholders.

The assurance services listed above bridge the gap between traditional audit and the problem solving activities of management consultancy. This recognises that decisions are not based on financial information alone, but incorporate a wide range of commercial factors.

The incumbent auditor is in a strong position to carry out these additional assurance services for their clients. They are professionally trained and already familiar with the business systems in operation at the company. Although this does raise a number of questions regarding the objectivity of the reporting accountant.

In practice, the skills required to offer a comprehensive suite of assurance services mean that it is only the largest firms that can straddle the market to offer a complete range of services to clients. Other firms still offer these services and many specialise in certain areas, such as due diligence.

Other assignments

Auditors providing other assurance services

The implications of assurance services being provided by auditors are wide-ranging.

- There will be further pressures on the audit firm to maintain its independence as the proportion of fees earned from non-audit work continues to grow and as the incidence of self-review risk increases.

- Practitioners specialising in a range of disciplines (e.g. IT systems, public sector specialists, etc.) will be needed in the firm as well as traditional financial auditors.

- Many assurance services involve reporting on risk (operational, financial, environmental, etc.). Reporting on such matters will increase the auditor's exposure to professional liability claims.

- The pressures on traditional audit fees will continue to drive them down, since clients will be willing to pay for value-adding assurance services but correspondingly less willing to pay for the statutory audit where they perceive less value for their money.

Article focus

In October 2007 Lisa Weaver published an article entitled "Continue to be Rest Assured."

The purpose of the article was to identify how assurance has been examined in the past. Lisa indicates that similar methods will be adopted in future exam sittings.

In addition, the articles "How to Tackle Audit and Assurance Case Study Questions 1 & 2" provide vital guidance regarding the practical implications of answering assurance questions in the exam.

All of these articles can be found on the ACCA website.

Due diligence assignments

Due diligence is a "fact finding exercise" and is usually conducted to reduce the risk of poor investment decisions.

Assurance services are an evolving field, and due diligence is one of the more increasingly common forms of assurance engagements. Due diligence is an example of a **direct reporting engagement**.

The term can be used to describe a wide range of services, including financial, legal and operational investigations. They are **normally voluntary** investigations, but there can be a legal obligation to carry out due diligence investigations, such as with customer due diligence requirements under Money Laundering regulations.

Depending upon the client's requirements a professional opinion may be expressed, although in practice it is more likely that such investigations result in the presentation of factual findings. Therefore it may **either be conducted as an assurance assignment or an agreed upon procedures assignment**.

Whilst it has a range of applications it is normally conducted in relation to potential company mergers and acquisitions. Most commonly, an advisor is engaged by the potential acquirer of a company to undertake a comprehensive survey of the target, in order to make sure the potential acquirer enters into the transaction with "open eyes".

Example of a due diligence assignment

Due diligence prior to a flotation

Company A has decided to float part of its share capital on the stock market, so it engages its auditors to conduct a due diligence review. The auditors will investigate:

- the structure of the business – how it is currently owned and constituted
- the financial health of the business – looking at past financial statements
- the credibility of the senior management of the business – looking at the career histories of the directors and ensuring that a balance of skills is available
- the future potential of the business – planned products and likely future earnings
- the risk involved in the business
- the business plan – whether it is realistic.

Due diligence provides the directors of an acquiring company with the information they need to decide whether or not to go ahead with an acquisition; when to go ahead with the acquisition; and how much should be paid for the target company.

Due diligence is a risk management tool that can increase stakeholder confidence in the acquisition decision.

Other assignments

Types of due diligence

This type of due diligence can be categorised into three areas:

(1) **Financial due diligence**: analysing and validating the target's revenue; maintainable earnings; future cash flows; and financial position including identification and valuation of contingent liabilities and key assets.

(2) **Operational due diligence**: investigation of the operational risks; cost base; asset base; capex requirements; quality of IT and other systems; key customers and suppliers; and performance gaps of the target company.

(3) **Commercial and market due diligence**: a comprehensive review of the target's business plan in the context of the industry and market conditions; including compliance with relevant legal, taxation, and regulatory frameworks.

The advisor will investigate and advise on post-acquisition issues such as consideration of staffing requirements, including the roles of management and key personnel to identify who will need to be retained post-acquistion as well as redundancy, training and other restructuring costs; and identification of potential synergies. The advisor may also provide practical recommendations regarding the acquisition process.

Purposes of due diligence

The main purpose of due diligence is **information gathering**: gathering of financial, operational, commercial and market information to ensure the acquirer has full knowledge of the operations, financial performance and position, commercial and market position of the target company. The aim is to reveal any potential problems before a decision regarding the acquisition is made.

Other purposes of engaging an advisor to carry out a due diligence review are:

– **Reduce management time spent assessing the acquisition decision**: Due diligence reviews can be performed internally, by the management of an acquiring company. However, this can be time consuming and the directors may lack the knowledge and experience necessary to perform the review adequately. Engaging an external advisor to carry out the review allows management to focus on strategic matters and running the existing group as well as ensuring an impartial review;

- **Evaluation of operational issues and risk assessment of the target company**: For example, possible contractual disputes following a takeover; potential breaches of covenants attached to any finance; the adequacy of the skills and experience of key management within the target company; operational issues such as high staff turnover; or issues with supplies/suppliers or the retention of key customers. The acquiring company may decide the issues and risks identified are so significant they do not want to go ahead with the acquisition; they may use the issues to negotiate a reduced price; or require the vendor to resolve the issues before the acquisition completes;

- **Contingent liabilities, other liabilities and assets will need to be identified**: It is particularly important that the potential acquirer identifies internally generated intangibles (i.e. those not included on the statement of financial position but vital to purchasing decisions, such as internal brands) and contingent liabilities that may crystallise in the future, and considers the likelihood of them crystallising and the potential financial consequences. These will affect the price the acquirer wishes to pay for the target as well as the value of the goodwill acquired;

- **Identification of possible post-acquisition synergies and economies of scale and potential further costs** such as redundancy/restructuring;

- **Planning the acquisition**: The due diligence provider can advise on change management following the acquisition, including integrating the new company into the group, help with any restructuring as well as the more immediate issues of determining an appropriate price and reviewing the terms of the sale and purchase agreement;

- **Enhance the credibility of the investment decision**: Engaging an external advisor to carry out the due diligence will ensure an independent, objective view is obtained on the investment decision, including the price to be paid; and

- **Substantiate claims made by the vendor:** For example: future order levels and current finance agreements.

Due diligence procedures will concentrate primarily on:

- enquiries of relevant parties; and
- analytical procedures.

Other assignments

Comparison to external audit

The objective of an audit is to form an opinion regarding whether the financial statements are free from material misstatement.

In contrast, the main aim of due diligence is fact finding to assist a specific decision. Therefore due diligence tends to draw upon wider informational resources that include: historical financial statements; management accounts; business plans; profit and cash flow forecasts; and the results of enquiries with management, employees and third parties. The aim of due diligence is not to form an opinion on the financial statements, but instead to provide the acquirer with sufficient information to make an informed decision about the acquisition.

Unless there are specific issues that cause concern, or specific tests have been requested by the client, no detailed audit procedures will be performed on a due diligence investigation. The type of work conducted tends to focus primarily on analytical procedures and enquiry. It will also focus more heavily on forecasts and projections, rather than just historical data. An audit will primarily review forecasts in order to form an opinion on whether the going concern basis is appropriate, but they are not the focus of an audit. Finally, it is unlikely that any internal control assessment/testing will be performed on a due diligence exercise unless specifically requested by the client.

Business performance measurement

Key Performance Indicators (KPI's)

KPIs or business performance measures are financial and non-financial statistical measures that are chosen and monitored to determine the strategic performance of an organisation, including those factors of performance that are critical for the continued success of the organisation.

KPIs should be:

- Specific
- Measurable
- Achievable
- Realistic
- Timely

Monitoring KPIs is part of the information system that management should establish; it enables performance to be evaluated in comparison to benchmark performance criteria or progress to be compared to the results of competitors.

> ### Example KPIs
>
> KPIs can be both financial (e.g. ratios based on the Financial Statements) and non-financial. Remember KPI's have to be SMART. Examples include:
>
> **Operational**
>
> - To despatch, over a twelve month average, 95% of customer orders within 1 day of receipt of the order.
> - To reduce waste raw materials from the production process by 10% over the next twelve months.
>
> **Financial**
>
> - To increase gross profit margin by 5% every year over the next three years.
> - To reduce total wages and salary costs to 50% of total costs in the next two years.
>
> **Social**
>
> - To increase spending on staff training by 10% in the next twelve months.
> - To increase the monetary valuation of charitable donations by 10% over the next twelve months.
>
> **Environmental**
>
> - To reduce energy consumption by 10% over the next two years.
> - To increase the recycling of waste by 10% over the next twelve months.

Providing assurance on KPIs

Many organisations are choosing to disclose KPIs as part of their annual reporting process, largely in response to stakeholder expectations.

Auditors may be engaged to report on the fairness and validity of KPI benchmarking exercises. This will add credibility to the data published and give assurance to external users that the progress claimed by a company's management is in fact real progress.

This poses a number of problems for the reporting accountant though and it is unlikely that auditors will ever be able to offer anything other than limited assurance – and even this may not be feasible. Reasons include:

- KPI's may not be specific enough to measure accurately. Take, for example: "To increase the monetary value of charitable donations by 10% over the next 12 months."

    Although this appears easy enough to assess in principle, what would happen if the company chose to donate goods and human resources? How would you value donated goods (cost vs. sales price) and how would you value human resources (i.e. wage cost vs. value of skills contributed)? This becomes much more difficult to measure in practice.

- The concepts involved may lack precise definition.

    Consider the concepts of 'sustainability,' 'being green,' 'customer satisfaction,' and 'serious workplace accidents.' All of these are common terms for KPI's but none of them have a standard definition and for that reason may lack credibility.

- Evidence may not be sufficient or appropriate for the purposes of providing an assurance opinion.

    It is unlikely that companies will establish sophisticated measuring and recording systems to gather the data used for all KPI's. For example: if a company donates goods to charity it is unlikely that there will be invoices, orders, goods despatched notes, remittances, cash transactions etc. In this case how does the auditor determine the quantity and value of goods donated?

- The potential for manipulation to achieve the desired result.

chapter 15

Planning the engagement: providing assurance on KPIs

There are a number of issues that should be considered when planning an engagement to provide assurance over an entity's business performance measures and sustainability indicators. These include:

- Understanding and agreeing the scope of the engagement, i.e. is assurance to be provided on the outcome and measurement of the KPIs only, or on the fairness and validity of the entire KPI benchmarking exercise (e.g. including the appropriateness (and completeness) of the measures chosen).

- Obtaining an understanding of the entity.

- Considering the appropriateness of the KPIs chosen in the light of this understanding, ensuring the KPIs chosen represent the priorities of the company.

- Evaluating the KPIs to ensure that each measure is quantifiable and to ensure that evidence will be readily available to support the stated KPI.

- Reviewing and agreeing the KPI's over which assurance is to be provided, flagging any KPIs that are not specific enough to measure accurately (and over which assurance can therefore not be provided).

- Identifying the evidence that should be available in relation to each KPI in order to provide an assurance opinion.

- Considering the potential for manipulation of each KPI, to achieve the desired result (i.e. identifying those KPIs which present the highest engagement risk).

Other assignments

Environmental and social auditing

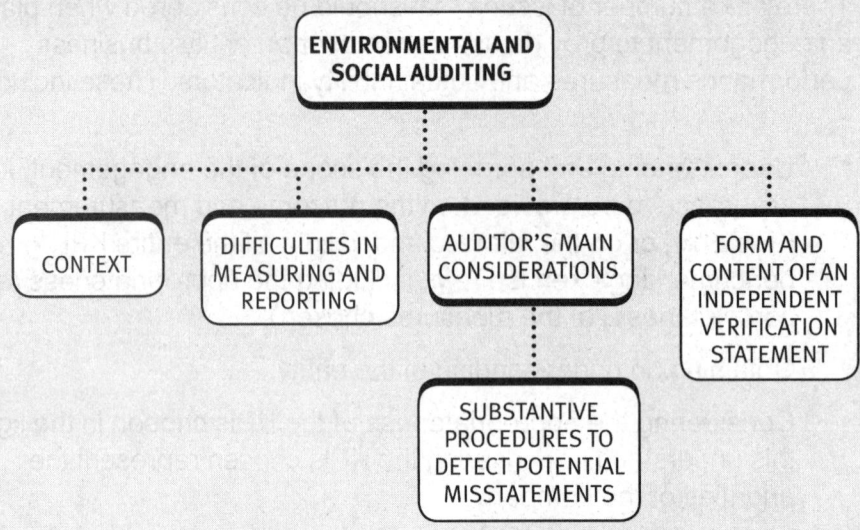

Socio-environmental policies

Today's heightened interest in the role of businesses in society has been promoted by increased sensitivity to and awareness of environmental and ethical issues. Consequently, in addition to reporting on the use of shareholder funds, businesses are now expected to account for their impact on the social and natural environment. Performance in this area is often a factor affecting the decision of employees, customers, and suppliers to engage with an organisation.

The importance of society and the environment

- Issues like environmental damage, improper treatment of workers, and faulty production that inconveniences or endangers customers are highlighted in the media.

- In some countries government regulation regarding environmental and social issues has increased.

- Some investors and investment fund managers have begun to take account of a corporation's social and environmental policies in making investment decisions.

- Some consumers have become increasingly sensitive to the social and environmental performance of the companies from which they buy their goods and services.

- These trends have contributed to the pressure on companies to operate in an economically, socially, and environmentally sustainable way.

The problem of measurement

There is obviously a great deal of skill and experience required to derive measures for social and environmental responsibility.

- Two possible approaches (which are not mutually exclusive):
    - comply with an externally defined set of standards; and/or
    - define one's own set of relevant targets and indicators and monitor progress towards achieving these.
- Many companies adopt a benchmarking approach where they work with a market leader in order to derive performance standards that will lead to improvement.
- For example in the plastics industry, the Du Pont corporation is often used as a benchmarking partner for such issues as waste disposal and energy conservation.

Many companies now develop and maintain social, ethical and environmental policies that can vary from highly generalised statements of ethical intention to more detailed corporate guidelines.

Sometimes there is a marked difference between a company's code of ethics and their actual practices, giving rise to the opinion that such policies may be more of a marketing tool than a serious statement of intent.

In addition, environmental and social reporting is normally voluntary although stakeholder pressure demands it in many industries (and organisations in some industries are required to report on specific targets by law); therefore the extent and selection of reporting measures varies significantly from company to company. Each company is likely to have differing views on what to measure and how to measure it, making comparison very difficult.

For these reasons environmental and social reporting is quite a controversial area.

Environmental and social auditing – reporting and measurement

Due to the complex and often subjective nature of environmental and social benchmarking and performance, measurement, and therefore reporting, upon these matters is a difficult task.

Generally an organisation will set an overall goal, with specific targets to meet in relation to that goal and a number of sustainability indicators to measure performance against each target. They may also report on compliance or variances between the sustainability indicator and target, including narrative explaining measures taken to achieve or improve their performance.

Other assignments

For example, an organisation with a goal to improve their contribution to environmental sustainability may set the following targets and sustainability indicators:

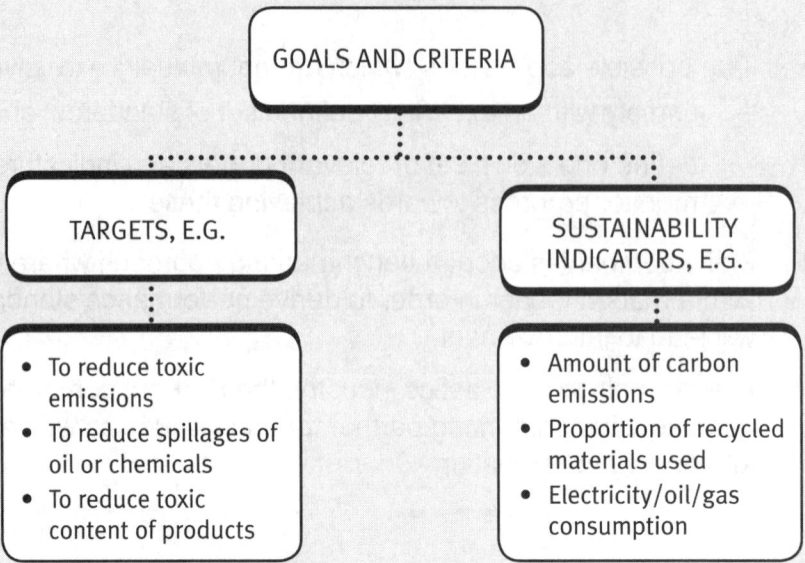

Environmental and social reporting

McDonald's is a large international chain of fast food restaurants, established in 1940.

In 1990 McDonald's established a Global Environmental Commitment. McDonald's has three core goals in relation to its environmental commitment:

- Energy conservation - to increase energy efficiency in order to reduce costs and reduce its impact on the environment.

- Sustainable packaging and waste management - to reduce the impact on the environment of its packaging and customer waste.

- Green building design - to increase the use of environmentally efficient measures in the design and construction of its restaurants.

McDonald's has set targets for each goal. For example, in relation to the second goal of sustainable packaging, the targets set include:

— Maximising the use of recycled materials

Sustainability indicators for these targets are then reported. For example McDonald's reports that around 30% of its consumer packaging is made from recycled materials.

However, it is not always possible to identify appropriate sustainability indicators. For example, in relation to McDonald's third goal of green building design, one target is to promote natural lighting in the design and construction of new restaurants. It would be very difficult to quantify the promotion of natural lighting.

Many companies now publish social and environmental reports. However, without independent audit and given public scepticism with regard to the aims of such reports they tend to lack credibility.

Therefore more companies are seeking to have some form of independent review of the validity of the social and environmental data they publish. This type of review is an example of an attestation engagement and is often referred to as an environmental audit.

Example of testing in environmental and social reporting

In order to test McDonald's assertion that it has used 30% recycled materials in its packaging, the steps that the assurance provider would take might include:

- Inspect a copy of McDonald's Global Environmental Commitment policy to confirm the target set
- Obtain an understanding of how the 30% outcome was calculated through enquiries with management including how the outcome was quantified e.g. is it by weight, value, or volume
- Re-perform the calculation to ensure its mathematical accuracy
- Obtain an understanding of how the underlying data was compiled through enquiries with management
- Test a sample of the underlying data compiled to the original source, and vice versa, to ensure its completeness and accuracy
- Obtain an understanding of how materials used in packaging are categorised as recycled and non-recycled through enquiries with management
- Test a sample of the underlying data to ensure the correct categorisation of materials as recycled/non-recycled
- Obtain an understanding of how McDonald's obtains assurance that the materials used are recycled (or not)

Problems auditing social and environmental reports

- Accountants lack the specific skills and experience needed to assess many environmental/social matters. For example, it appears unlikely that an auditor would be able to measure carbon emissions or energy consumption.
- There is a significant amount of subjectivity with regard to social and environmental reports, for example; the use of the term 'environmentally friendly.'
- There are no formally agreed and globally mandatory standards of reporting on such matters, which means directors can be selective in the reports they make (although it is worth noting that voluntary reporting codes do exist, see above).

Despite these concerns accountants can still provide a relevant service.

Namely, auditors can review internal processes and systems for measuring and reporting social and environmental data. They can provide recommendations for improvement and, if required, can provide assurance reports regarding the operation of those systems.

Such systems might include controls to ensure legislation is complied with or as a minimum would include measures to ensure that social and environmental matters are embedded into the culture of the organisation (e.g. with the use of targets).

Independent verification statements

Where a review is carried out by an independent third party into the environmental matters of an organisation, an **independent verification statement** may be issued.

- Some companies conduct an internal audit on environmental matters and have the internal audit verified by external assessors.
- Some companies may contract for a third party independent review of their environmental matters.

Regardless of the type of review undertaken, the report will have some common features:

- the methodology is stated
- the matters reviewed are spelled out precisely
- reference is made to other documents where applicable
- an opinion is given.

chapter 15

Current issue: Investor demand for ESG disclosures

In February 2012, IFAC published a report on *Investor Demand for Environmental, Social and Governance (ESG) Disclosures.*

The report made five recommendations, which are summarised below:

- The performance measures communicated should **reflect the information needs of investors**; professional accountants should work with their clients to ensure that investors are engaged in the process to determine the appropriate ESG disclosures.

- Performance in relation to **ESG measures should be embedded in the reporting process** of organisations; professional accountants should work with their clients to ensure that management information and systems incorporate ESG reporting.

- **Financial performance and sustainability are directly linked**; professional accountants should work with their clients to **increase** their **understanding** of the link between financial and non-financial drivers of performance and value.

- ESG reporting should be useful and transparent; professional accountants should work with their clients to **ensure material, timely, consistent and comparable information** is reported.

- Integrated reporting will enable organisations to deliver the above recommendations; professional accountants should work with their clients to ensure greater **collaboration** between internal client functions and third parties (e.g. suppliers) **when managing and reporting ESG information**.

Illustration of an independent verification statement

Here is an example of a report by an external assessor who might be a Registered Environmental Impact Assessor and/or a member of the Institute of Environmental Assessment or other recognised bodies.

External verification statement

AB & Company has conducted a formal independent verification of the internal audit undertaken by CD Construction plc.

Other assignments

Method and scope of the verification

The verification was conducted by reviewing the internal audit report and by interviewing the senior staff responsible for the audit. The verification examined the audit findings against 50 of the 64 targets in detail. The targets selected were those that had been awarded a maximum score for target achievement (10/10).

Internal audit's role related to auditing progress against targets reported by CD Construction plc's businesses and internal audit's findings are included in the section on Environmental Performance Targets (we have not verified other sections of this report).

Opinion

We are satisfied that the internal audit was conducted against an appropriate methodology. We have reviewed the statements made about progress against targets and confirm that they accurately reflect the audit findings.

Signed

AB & Company

Wolverhampton erh

March 3 20X6.

Risk assessment engagements

Corporate governance best practice requires that boards of directors conduct, at least annually, a review of the effectiveness of the group's system of internal controls.

The entity's risk assessment process is an essential component of an effective internal control system.

Management must therefore have a process for identifying and responding to business risks. Possible responses are:

- **transfer** the risk to someone else, e.g. by insurance or by outsourcing the risky activity or by requiring third parties to sign indemnities
- **avoid** the risk, e.g. terminate the risky operation and move the resources to a less risky activity
- establish controls to **manage** the risk
- **accept** the risk, particularly if it is of low impact and/or low likelihood.

The auditor may be engaged to report on the effectiveness of the company's internal controls, especially where evident criteria exist such as the company applying a specific control framework.

Article focus

Risk audit is also an integral element of P1 *The Professional Accountant*. The P1 examiner, David Campbell, has published an article entitled "Risk and Environmental Auditing" that may also be of use to candidates studying P7.

Risk management procedures for e-commerce

Many companies engage in e-commerce, and by doing so expose themselves to new risks which did not arise with traditional data processing. These risks need to be managed effectively.

Risk management procedures for e-commerce may include:

- risk assessment – essential
- creating a good control environment – there should be an information systems security policy
- subscribing to nationally set standards
- having an internal audit facility
- maintaining systems access control, such as passwords, and physical security
- using encryption
- backups for data but also for service providers and other links in the e-commerce chain
- having good website design – many websites are still in their infancy and are difficult to navigate or are not kept up to date. Loss of customers and/or reputation can follow
- minimising exposure to risk of legal liability in some areas of web page design
- maintaining audit trails – it should be possible (and service level agreements should provide this) to have the ability to retrieve and review audit trails/logs on demand for a date or range of dates
- registering with WebTrust or a similar organisation.

Other assignments

Systems reliability (including e-commerce)

All businesses/organisations begin life with a specific objective (or objectives) in mind: to make profit; to exploit a technological niche in a market; to provide free health care to the population; to provide free education to the population etc. In order to achieve these objectives businesses and organisations have to establish systems to enable:

- the sourcing of required resources;
- the application of those resources to producing relevant goods and services; and
- the production of information for monitoring of performance.

In an audit of financial statements the auditor assesses the effectiveness of those internal systems for measuring, recording and reporting financial data. This is only a small part of the overall systems of internal control of an organisation. Therefore further assurance engagements may be provided to assess the effectiveness of other systems of internal control relevant to achieving the objectives of a business.

Systems reliability and assurance

Practitioners may be engaged to provide assurance about the nature of internal systems. This usually involves considering:

- whether the design of the system is appropriate for meeting its objectives; or
- whether current systems are being operated effectively.

The nature of the assurance report depends upon the requirements of management. However it is likely to include some discussion of:

- The effectiveness of controls within the system;
- Any deficiencies identified in the system;
- The risks applicable to those deficiencies;
- Cost vs. benefit analysis; and
- Whether the overall design of the system is sufficient to meet its objectives.

ISAE 3420 Reporting on Financial Information included in a

ISAE 3420 *Assurance Engagements to Report on the Compilation of Pro Forma Financial Information Included in a Prospectus* is a new standard effective for assurance reports dated on or after March 31 2013.

The standard deals with reasonable assurance engagements to report on the compilation of pro forma financial information included in a prospectus where it is required by relevant law or regulation (note, it does not cover situations where a practitoner is engaged to compile the information).

- A **prospectus** is a document that provides details of an entity's securities (debt or equity) offered for sale to the public, containing the information that potential investors need to make an informed investment decision.
- **Pro forma financial information** models the impact of a significant event or transaction, as though the event had occurred or the transaction had been undertaken at an earlier date (selected for the purpose of the illustration) for example:
    - to illustrate the impact of a recent acquistion on the financial position of the entity
    - to illustrate what the results entity might have been if the acquisiton was made earlier.
- Pro forma financial information is normally presented alongside the unadjusted financial information, with the adjustments made in arriving at the pro forma financial information also shown separately.
- Pro forma financial information does not represent the entity's actual financial position, financial performance, or cash flows.
- Pro forma financial information is necessary because the most recent financial statements would not show the impact of the event or transaction, and the prospective investors would not be able to made an informed investment decision without this information.

The objectives of the engagement are:

- to obtain reasonable assurance about whether the pro forma financial information has been compiled, in all material respects, by the responsible party on the basis of the applicable criteria and
- to report on the above.

In performing the engagement, the practitioner must determine that:

- the unadjusted financial information has been obtained from and agrees to an appropriate source (e.g. the audited financial statements)
- the pro forma adjustments are:
    - directly attributable to the event or transaction
    - factually supportable, and
    - consistent with the entity's applicable financial reporting framework and accounting policies

Other assignments

- the information is presented appropriately, and appropriate disclosures are made to enable the intended users to understand the information conveyed
- all necessary pro forma adjustments have been included
- the calculations within the pro forma financial information are arithmetically accurate.

The other information within the prospectus should be read to identify any inconsistencies with the pro forma information.

Exam style question: Due Diligence

Plaza, a limited liability company, is a major food retailer. Further to the success of its national supermarkets in the late 1990s it has extended its operations throughout Europe and most recently to Asia, where it is expanding rapidly.

You are a manager in Andando, a firm of Chartered Certified Accountants. You have been approached by Duncan Seymour, the chief finance officer of Plaza, to advise on a bid that Plaza is proposing to make for the purchase of MCM. You have ascertained the following from a briefing note received from Duncan. MCM provides training in management, communications and marketing to a wide range of corporate clients, including multi-nationals. The 'MCM' name is well regarded in its areas of expertise. MCM is currently wholly-owned by Frontiers, an international publisher of textbooks, whose shares are quoted on a recognised stock exchange. MCM has a National and an International business.

The National business comprises 11 training centres. The audited financial statements show revenue of $12·5 million and profit before taxation of $1·3 million for this geographic segment for the year to 31 December 2012. Most of the National business's premises are owned or held on long leases. Trainers in the National business are mainly full-time employees.

The International business has five training centres in Europe and Asia. For these segments, revenue amounted to $6·3 million and profit before tax $2·4 million for the year to 31 December 2012. Most of the International business's premises are held on operating leases. International trade receivables at 31 December 2012 amounted to $3·7 million. Although the International centres employ some full-time trainers, the majority of trainers provide their services as freelance consultants.

chapter 15

Required:

(a) Define 'due diligence' and describe the nature and purpose of a due diligence review. (4 marks)

(b) Explain the matters you should consider before accepting an engagement to conduct a due diligence review of MCM. (10 marks)

(c) Illustrate how:

   (i) inquiry; and (4 marks)

   (ii) analytical procedures, (6 marks)

   might appropriately be used in the due diligence review of MCM.

   (Total: 24 marks)

Test your understanding 1

You are the manager responsible for the audit of The National Literary Museum (NLM), a museum focusing on famous literary works. Entry to the museum is free for all visitors and many visitors make repeat visits to the museum.

NLM receives funding from government departments for culture and education, as well as several large charitable donations. The amount of funding received is dependent on three key performance indicator (KPI) targets being met annually. All three of the targets must be met in order to secure the government funding.

Extracts from NLM's operating and financial review are as follows:

	KPI target	Draft KPI 2007	Actual KPI 2006
Number of annual visitors:	100,000	102,659	103,752
Proportion of total visitors of school age:	25%	29%	27%
Number of educational programmes run:	4	4	4

Your firm is engaged to provide an assurance opinion on the KPIs disclosed in NLMs operating and financial review.

Required:

Discuss why it may not be possible to provide a high level of assurance over the stated key performance indicators?

KAPLAN PUBLISHING

419

4 Chapter summary

	Audits	Reviews	Agreed-upon procedures
Assurance provided	Reasonable but not absolute assurance	Limited assurance	No assurance
Guidance given in ...	ISAs	ISRE 2400	ISRS 4400
Scope of work decided by ...	Auditor, as much as he deems necessary to give positive opinion	Reviewer, as much as he deems necessary to give negative opinion	The party engaging the accountant's services (to carry out the procedures)
Type of report provided	Positive assurance	Negative assurance	Factual findings of the procedures carried out

chapter 15

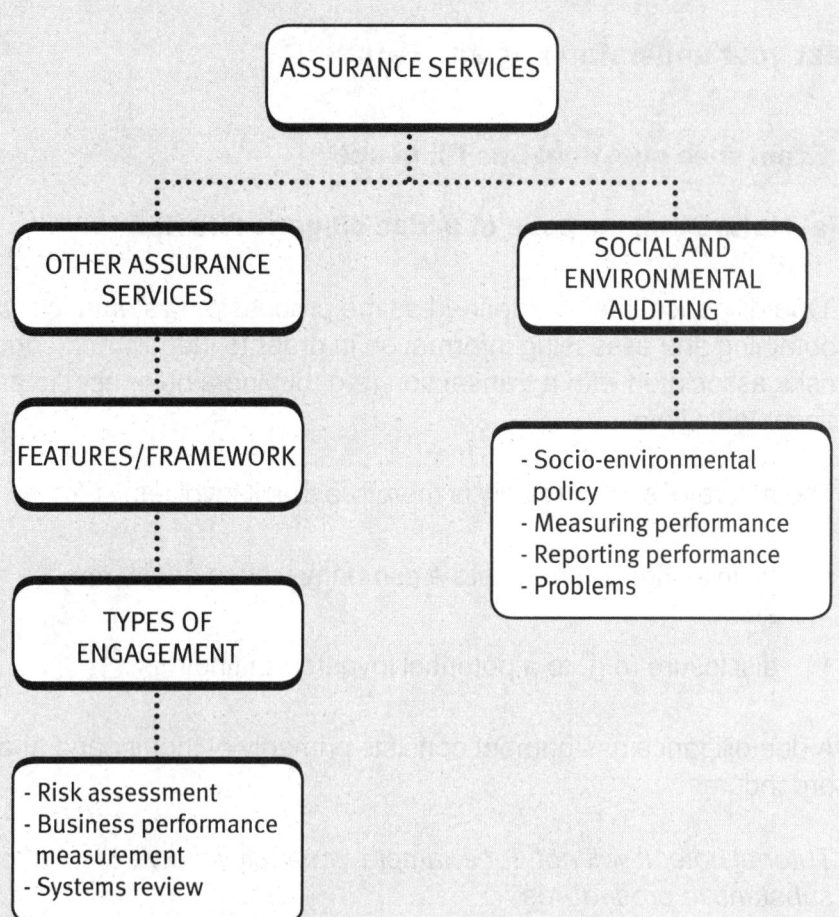

Other assignments

Test your understanding answers

Exam style question: Due Diligence

(a) Nature and purpose of a 'due diligence' review

'Due diligence' may be defined as the process of systematically obtaining and assessing information in order to identify and contain the risks associated with a transaction (e.g. buying a business) to an acceptable level.

The nature of such a review is therefore that it involves:

- an investigation (e.g. into a company whose equity may be sold); and
- disclosure (e.g. to a potential investor) of findings.

A due diligence assignment consists primarily of inquiry and analytical procedures.

Tutorial note: It will not, for example, routinely involve tests of control or substantive procedures.

Its purpose is to find all the facts that would be of material interest to an investor or acquirer of a business. It may not uncover all such factors but should be designed with a reasonable expectation of so doing.

Professional accountants will not be held liable for non-disclosure of information that failed to be uncovered if their review was conducted with 'due diligence'.

(b) Matters to be considered (before accepting the engagement)

Tutorial note: Although candidates may approach this part from a rote-learned list of 'matters to consider' it is important that answer points be tailored, in so far as the information given in the scenario permits, to the specifics of Plaza and MCM. It is critical that answer points should not contradict the scenario (e.g. assuming that it is Plaza's auditor who has been asked to undertake the assignment).

- Information about Duncan Seymour – What is the relationship of the chief finance officer to Plaza (e.g. is he on the management board)? By what authority is he approaching Andando to undertake this assignment?

chapter 15

- The purpose of the assignment must be clarified. Duncan's approach to Andando is 'to advise on a bid'. However, Andando cannot make executive decisions for a client but only provide the facts of material interest. Plaza's management must decide whether or not to bid and, if so, how much to bid.

- The scope of the due diligence review. It seems likely that Plaza will be interested in acquiring all of MCM's business as its areas of operation coincide with Plaza's. However it must be confirmed that Plaza is not merely interested in acquiring only the National or International business of MCM.

- Andando's competence and experience – Andando should not accept the engagement unless the firm has experience in undertaking due diligence assignments. Even then, the firm must have sufficient knowledge of the territories in which the businesses operate to evaluate whether all facts of material interest to Plaza have been identified.

Tutorial note: Candidates should be querying their competence and experience in the fields of retailing and training as though they were dealing with highly regulated or specialist industries such as banking or insurance.

- Whether Andando has sufficient resources (e.g. representative/associated offices), if any, in Europe and Asia to investigate MCM's International business.

- Any factors which might impair Andando's objectivity in reporting to Plaza the facts uncovered by the due diligence review. For example, if Duncan is closely connected with a partner in Andando or if Andando is the auditor of Frontiers.

Tutorial note: Candidates will not be awarded marks for going into 'autopilot' on independence issues. For example, this is a one-off assignment so size of fee is not relevant. Andando holding shares in MCM is not possible (since whollyowned).

- Plaza's rationale for wishing to acquire MCM. Presumably it is significant that MCM operates in the same territories as Plaza. Plaza may be wanting to provide extensive training programs in management, communications and marketing to its workforce.

- The relationship, if any, between Plaza and MCM in any of the territories. Plaza may be a major client of MCM. That is, Plaza is currently out-sourcing training to MCM. Acquiring MCM would bring training in-house.

Tutorial note: Ascertaining what a purchaser hopes to gain from an acquisition before the assignment is accepted is important. The facts to be uncovered for a merger from which synergy is expected will be different from those relevant to acquiring an investment opportunity.

Other assignments

- Time available – Andando must have sufficient time to find all facts that would be of material interest to Plaza before disclosing their findings.

- The acceptability of any limitations – whether there will be restrictions on Andando's access to information held by MCM (e.g. if there will not be access to board minutes) and personnel.

- The degree of secrecy required – this may go beyond the normal duties of confidentiality not to disclose information to outsiders (e.g. if unannounced staff redundancies could arise).

- Why Plaza's current auditors have not been asked to conduct the due diligence review – especially as they are responsible for (and therefore capable of undertaking) the group audit covering the relevant countries.

- Andando should be allowed to communicate with Plaza's current auditor:
    - to inform them of the nature of the work they have been asked to undertake; and
    - to enquire if there is any reason why they should not accept this assignment.

- In taking on Plaza as a new client Andando may have a later opportunity to offer external audit and other services to Plaza (e.g. internal audit).

(c) Due diligence review

(i) Inquiries

Tutorial note: These should be focused on uncovering facts that may not be revealed by the audited financial statements (e.g. off balance sheet finance, contingencies, commitments and contracts) especially where knowledge may be confined to management.

- Do any members of MCM's senior/executive management have contractual terms that will result in significant payouts to them (e.g. on change of ownership of the company or their being made redundant)?

- What contracts with clients, if any, will lapse or be made void in the event that MCM is purchased from Frontiers?

- Are there any major clients who are likely to be lost if MCM is purchased by Plaza (e.g. any competitor food retailers)?

- What are the principal terms of the operating leases relating to the International business's premises?

- What penalties should be expected to be incurred if operating leases and/or contracts with training consultants are terminated?

- Has MCM entered into any purchase commitments since 31 December 2012 (e.g. to buy or lease further premises)?
- Who are the best trainers that Plaza should seek to retain after the purchase of MCM?
- What events since the audited financial statements to 31 December 2012 were published have made a significant impact on MCM's assets, liabilities, operating capability and/or cash flows? (For example, storm damage to premises, major clients defaulting on payments, significant interest/foreign-exchange rate fluctuations, etc.)
- Are there any unresolved tax issues which have not been provided for in full?
- What effect will the purchase have on loan covenants? For example, term loans may be rendered repayable on a change of ownership.

(ii) **Analytical procedures**

Tutorial note: The range of valid answer points is very broad for this part.

- Review the trend of MCM's profit (gross and net) for the last five years (say). Similarly earnings per share and gearing.
- For both the National and International businesses compare:
    - gross profit, net profit, and return on assets for the last five years (say);
    - actual monthly revenue against budget for the last 18 months (say). Similarly, for major items of expenditure such as:
    - full-time salaries;
    - freelance consultancy fees;
    - premises costs (e.g. depreciation, lease rentals, maintenance, etc);
    - monthly revenue (also costs and profit) by centre.
- Review projections of future profitability of MCM against net profit percentage at 31 December 2012 for:
    - the National business (10·4%);
    - the International business (38·1%); and
    - overall (19·9%).
- Review of disposal value of owned premises against book values.
- Compare actual cash balances with budget on a monthly basis and compare borrowings against loan and overdraft facilities.

- Compare the average collection period for International's trade receivables month on month since 31 December 2012 (when it was nearly seven months, i.e. $3·7/$6·3 × 365 days) and compare with the National business.

- Compare financial ratios for each of the national centres against the National business overall (and similarly for the International Business). For example:
  - gross and net profit margins;
  - return on centre assets;
  - average collection period;
  - average payment period;
  - liquidity ratio.

- Compare key performance indicators across the centres for the year to 31 December 2011 and 2012 to date. For example:
  - number of corporate clients;
  - number of delegates
  - number of training days;
  - average revenue per delegate per day;
  - average cost per consultancy day.

Test your understanding 1

The main reason why it may not be possible to provide a high level of assurance are:

- the museum's entry system may not record the total number of visitors each day and, given that entry is free, it may be difficult to identify relevant data from any accounting or financial systems of the museum.

- It is unclear whether multiple visits by one person should be counted as separate 'annual visitors'

- the museum's entry system is unlikely to identify the age of all visitors

- the KPI relating to educational programmes is poorly defined – what constitutes and educational programme? How long does it have to run? How many users have to benefit from it running?

chapter 16

Prospective financial information

Chapter learning objectives

Upon completion of this chapter you will be able to:

- define PFI and distinguish between a forecast, a projection, a hypothetical illustration, and a target;
- explain the principles of useful PFI;
- identify and describe the matters to be considered before accepting an engagement to report on PFI;
- discuss the level of assurance that the auditor may provide and explain the other factors to be considered in determining the nature, timing, and extent of examination procedures;
- describe examination procedures to verify forecasts and projections; and
- compare the content of a report on an examination of PFI and reports made in providing audit-related services.

Prospective financial information

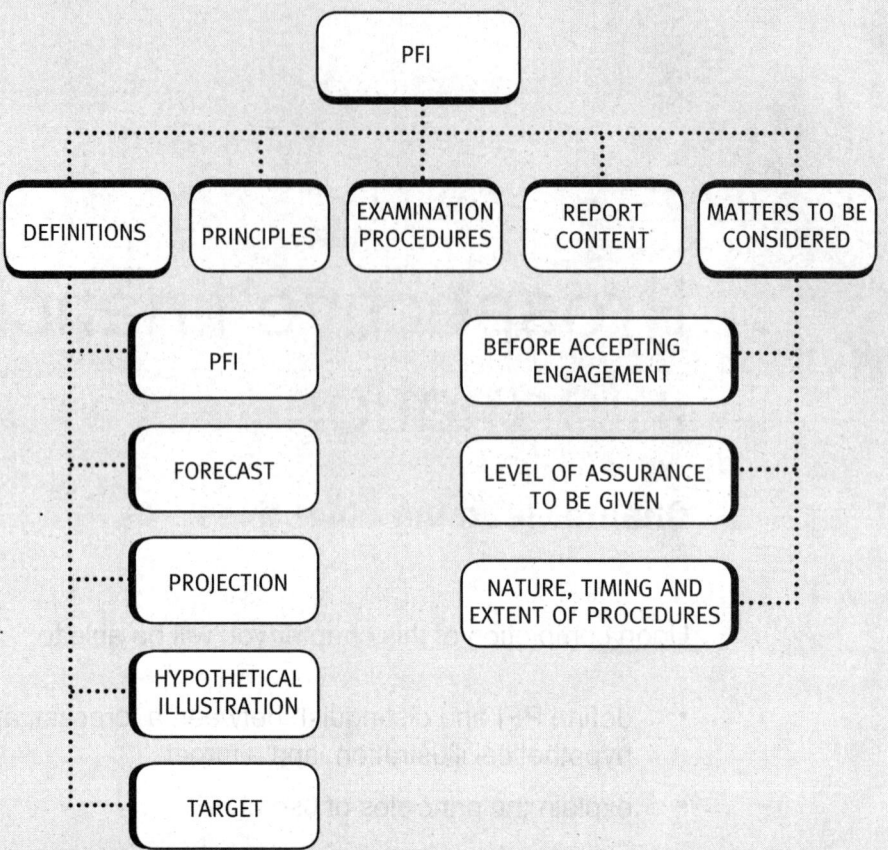

Assurance engagements to review projections and forecasts, often to support an application for a loan, are very common in real life and also feature regularly in the exam.

1 What is 'prospective financial information'?

A reporting accountant may be asked to give an assurance opinion on prospective (i.e. future) financial information. The authoritative source covering this activity is **ISAE 3400** *The Examination of Prospective Financial Information*.

Definitions

Prospective financial information (PFI) means financial information based about events that may occur in the future and possible actions by an entity. It may be in the form of a forecast or a projection, or a combination of both.

A forecast is:

- PFI prepared on the basis of assumptions as to future events that management expects to take place and the actions management expects to take (best-estimate assumptions).

A projection is:

- PFI prepared on the basis of hypothetical assumptions about future events and management actions that are not necessarily expected to take place.

A hypothetical illustration is a depiction of anticipated outcomes based on uncertain future events and actions.

A target is a desired future outcome aimed for by an organisation.

Principles of useful PFI

PFI can be issued:

- as an internal management tool, e.g. to support a possible capital investment; or
- for distribution to third parties, for example:
    - in a prospectus
    - in an annual report
    - to inform lenders or to support an application for finance.

Ultimately the usefulness of PFI depends on the informational requirements of the end user. Consider, for example, the different decisions and information needs of a prospective lender and shareholder. The unifying qualities of good PFI are that reports must:

- address the specific needs of the user; and
- be prepared on a timely basis to enable decisions to be taken.

2 Acceptance of PFI engagements – matters to consider

In general, like an audit engagement, the reporting accountant must consider the risk of involvement with the PFI. The greater the risk of giving an inappropriate report, the greater the risk of legal claims and loss of reputation. Ultimately, if the risk profile is too high the engagement should be politely declined.

More specifically the reporting accountant should consider the following:

Matter under consideration	Reason
The intended use of the information, such as internal management or external users	Information for external use will be relied upon by third parties, potentially for making investment decisions. This makes it riskier for the accountant because the consequences of inappropriate reports will be more severe.
Whether the information will be for general or limited distribution.	Information for general distribution will result in the assignment being potentially more risky to the accountant as a larger audience will be relying on it.
The nature of the assumptions (e.g. best-estimate or hypothetical).	Forecasts and projections cannot be verified with any certainty – because the outcome is unknown, however: • If information is best-estimate, it should be a reasonable approximation as to what might actually happen. • Where the assumptions are hypothetical, they will be much more difficult for the auditor to validate – as there is likely to be little to support them – and therefore the assignment holds higher risk.
The elements to be included in the information.	Inclusion of elements that the auditor has little knowledge of, that are extremely complex or highly subjective increase the risk to the accountant of accepting the engagement.
The period covered by the information.	Short-term forecasts are likely to be more easily verified than projections looking out over a longer period.

3 Level of assurance

Due to the uncertainty surrounding forecasts and projections, and due to the limited nature of the procedures performed during the accountant's review, only **limited assurance** can be offered for PFI engagements.

The terms of engagement

An engagement to report on PFI does not constitute an audit. However, it is unlikely that prospective clients will appreciate this fact. Agreeing the terms of engagement is therefore critical in the avoidance of conflict with the client. Typically the terms should specify:

- The type of assurance offered, i.e. limited;
- The nature of procedures performed, i.e. predominantly enquiry and analytical review;
- The form of opinion given, i.e. negative;
- Management's responsibilities, which are, mainly, to prepare the PFI report and to establish appropriate assumptions;
- Restrictions on the use and distribution of the assurance report; and
- The basis of setting the fees.

4 Planning

In order to provide assurance that forecasts and projections are reasonable, the auditor will need to determine the timing, nature and extent of procedures.

As PFI is a form of limited review engagement and due to the lack of evidence to support forecasts and assumptions, the bulk of procedures will be limited to **analytical review and enquiry**. More detailed testing will normally only be required if potential misstatements are identified.

Some areas of a projection/forecast are capable of more specific procedures, for example: verifying that loan or lease repayments agree to existing contractual terms.

Prospective financial information

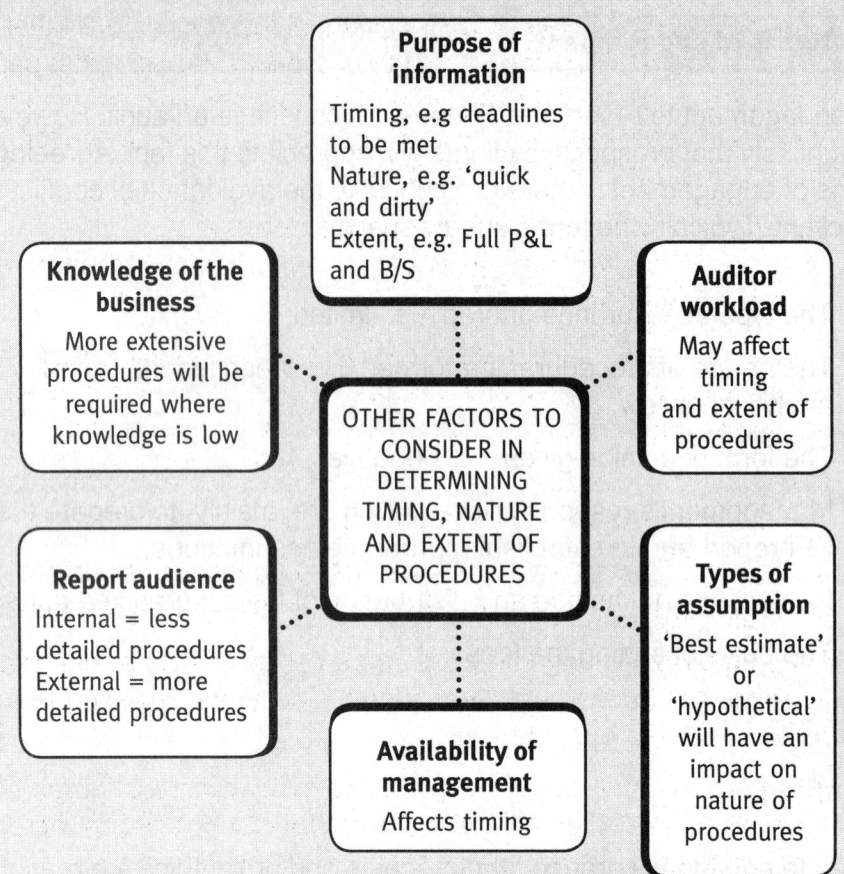

It should be noted that all forecasts and projections are underpinned by management's assumptions. It is these assumptions that must form the basis of the practitioner's investigation. As forecasts/projections are inherently uncertain it will be difficult to obtain anything other than persuasive evidence. For this reason a significant number of management representations will be sought.

However, it is not appropriate for the practitioner to rely solely on such representations and they cannot delegate responsibility for their opinion in so doing. The practitioner must appropriately plan, perform and review a range of procedures to enable them to obtain sufficient appropriate evidence for the purposes of offering limited assurance that the reports under scrutiny are plausible in the circumstances.

PFI procedures: Specific examples

The specific procedures performed on an engagement will depend on the unique nature and informational requirements of the users and the report under scrutiny. However, examples of general procedures include:

- Comparison of forecast amounts to historic performance to ensure consistency. Whilst future results will not always follow previous trends historical patterns give an indication of the capacity of the business. It is also important to consider that rapid growth is unlikely and potentially damaging to a business (overtrading!!).

- Comparison of forecast amounts to actual results. It is likely that by the time that a PFI review is actually conducted some of that period may have elapsed. Internally produced management accounts may therefore be available to use to assess actual performance for the first few months of the forecast period.

- Forecasts for previous periods may also be assessed in comparison to actual results to assess how accurately management have forecast in the past.

- Reasonably certain incomes and costs (such as loan interest) may be verified by comparison of forecast amounts to documents such as orders, contracts, loan agreements, lease contracts etc.

- Comparison of accounting policies/estimates used in forecasts in comparison to financial statements, e.g. depreciation method;

- Inspection of the non-current asset note to identify if assets are approaching the end of their useful lives and require replacement;

- Comparisons of working capital amounts/liquidity to assess whether liabilities can be met and the company can finance its short term resourcing requirements.

- Comparison of the relationships between the reported figures, for example is a significant increase in revenue supported by increased production costs, advertising costs and distribution costs?

- Typical enquiries may include:
  - whether the client requires investment in non-current assets;
  - when loan agreements expire;
  - whether further forms of finance are being sought;
  - whether any new customer/supplier contracts have been agreed since the year-end;
  - have any new capital purchases been agreed;
  - have the company invested in any product research/development and if so what are the results;
  - have they conducted any market research and again what are the results;
  - have there been any new competitors/products in the market place.

This list is by no way exhaustive and is very general in nature. The purpose of the examples is that they all consider events or circumstances that will have an impact on the business in the future. Note that none of the enquiries are vague, such as "how do you forecast sales?" They try and identify issues that will directly impact management's forecasts.

> In the exam you will be required to suggest procedures that are relevant to the specific financial forecasts in the scenario.

5 Final report

The report following an examination of PFI will be significantly different to a traditional audit report. The key elements are summarised below:

- Title, date and addressee
- Reference to any applicable laws or standards (e.g. ISAE 3400)
- Basis of opinion
- Identification of what is included in the prospective forecast information;
- A statement that it is management's responsibility to prepare the PFI;
- A reference to the purpose and distribution of the report;
- A clear written expression of limited (or negative) assurance as to whether anything has come to light to suggest that:
  - the assumptions are not a reasonable for the purposes of the PFI;
  - the report is not prepared on the basis of those assumptions; and
  - the report is not in accordance with a relevant financial reporting framework;
- Appropriate caveats about the nature of assumptions and the inherent limitations in the forecasting process
- Reporting accountant's name, signature, and address.

Test your understanding 1

Imperiol, a limited liability company, manufactures and distributes electrical and telecommunications accessories, household durables (e.g. sink and shower units) and building systems (e.g. air-conditioning, solar heating, security systems). The company has undergone several business restructurings in recent years. Finance is to be sought from both a bank and a venture capitalist in order to implement the board's latest restructuring proposals.

You are a manager at Hal Falcon, a firm of Chartered Certified Accountants. You have been approached by Paulo Gandalf, the chief finance officer of Imperiol, to provide a report on the company's business plan for the year to 31 December 2010.

From a brief telephone conversation with Paulo Gandalf you have ascertained that the proposed restructuring will involve discontinuing all operations except for building systems, where the greatest opportunity for increasing product innovation is believed to lie. Imperiol's strategy is to become the market leader in providing 'total building system solutions' using new fibre optic technology to link building systems. A major benefit of the restructuring is expected to be a lower on-going cost base. As part of the restructuring it is likely that certain of the accounting functions, including internal audit, will be outsourced.

You have obtained a copy of Imperiol's Interim Report for the six months to 30 June 2009 on which the company's auditors, Discorpio, provide a conclusion giving negative assurance. The following information has been extracted from the Interim Financial Report:

(1) **Chairman's statement**

The economic climate is less certain than it was a few months ago and performance has been affected by a severe decline in the electrical accessories market. Management's response will be to gain market share and reduce the cost base.

(2) **Statement of Financial Position**

	30 June 2009 (unaudited) $m	31 December 2008 $m
Intangible assets	83.5	72.6
Non-current assets	69.6	63.8
Inventory	25.2	20.8
Trade receivables	59.9	50.2
Cash	8.3	23.8
Total assets	246.5	231.2
Non-current liabilities – borrowing	65.4	45.7
Current liabilities	55.6	57.0
Equity and liabilities:		
Share capital	30.4	30.4
Reserves	6.0	9.1
Accumulated	89.1	89.0
	246.5	231.2

(3) Continuing and discontinuing operations

	Six months to 30 June 2009 (unaudited) $m	Year to 31 December 2008 $m
Turnover		
Continuing operations		
Electrical and telecommunication accessories	55.3	118.9
Household durables	37.9	77.0
Building systems	53.7	94.9
Total continuing	146.9	290.8
Discontinued	–	65.3
Total turnover	146.9	356.1
Operating profit before interest and taxation – continuing operations	13.4	32.2

Required:

(a) Identify and explain the matters Hal Falcon should consider before accepting the engagement to report on Imperiol's prospective financial information.

(8 marks)

(b) Describe the procedures that a professional accountant should undertake in order to provide an assurance report on the prospective financial information of Imperiol for the year to 31 December 2010.

(10 marks)

(Total: 18 marks)

6 Chapter summary

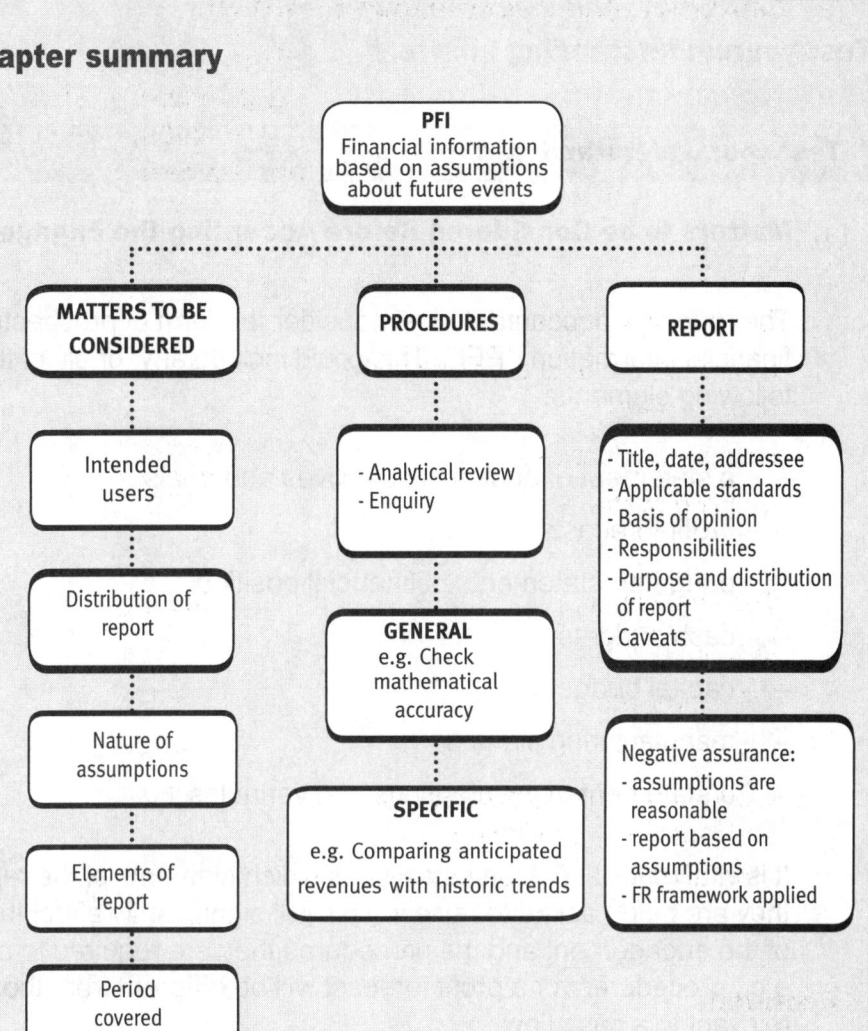

Test your understanding answers

Test your understanding 1

(a) Matters to be Considered Before Accepting the Engagement

The reporting accountant must consider the form of prospective financial information ('PFI'). This could include any, or all, of the following elements:

- a statement of business objectives and goals
- profit forecasts
- budgeted statements of financial position
- cash budgets
- capital budgets
- manufacturing plans
- a statement of assumptions and variables.

It is vital that Hal Falcon establishes which elements of the report they are being asked to review. This will significantly affect the risk of the engagement and the procedures they are required to perform, e.g.; procedures for a profit forecast will be different from those relevant to a cash flow.

It is also vital to establish what sort of report Imperiol require. It is likely that they will want some form of assurance engagement. If so, it must be clarified that only limited assurance can be offered and that this will be based on less thorough procedures than a normal audit of historical financial information, namely analytical review and enquiry. The opinion will be worded negatively, i.e. that the subject matter is 'plausible' and that nothing has come to light during testing to suggest otherwise.

The opinion is focused on whether:

- the assumptions are reasonable and consistent with the purpose of the information;
- the PFI is properly prepared on the basis of the assumptions; and
- the PFI is prepared on a consistent basis with historical financial statements, using appropriate accounting principles.

To enable this to be performed efficiently Imperiol must ensure that access to all relevant information and staff (for enquiry) is made available. Any restrictions would lead to a breach of engagement terms and a potential disclaimer of opinion. Hal Falcon should also request permission to communicate with Discorpio, in the form of a professional etiquette letter.

Paulo Gandalf has requested a review of the forecasts to 31 December 2010. This does not appear to be particularly extensive and it is likely that a provider of significant finance would seek a longer period of review. Before accepting the engagement Hal Falcon should confirm in the engagement letter that the only period under review (and requested by the financiers) is to 31 December 2010.

The report is likely to be used to raise some form of finance. However the source of finance is unclear. The information given simply states that finance is being sought from "both a bank and a venture capitalist." Hal Falcon must agree the distribution of the report prior to accepting. The greater the number of parties that place reliance on the report, the greater the risk involved. Therefore Hal Falcon must seek to reduce this risk by reducing distribution to specific parties and by writing appropriate caveats/disclaimers in the final report.

It may be that specific banks and/or venture capitalists have been selected. If so, they may require business plans and reports in a prescribed form. Hal Falcon should also establish what authority Paulo Gandalf has to appoint them. He may not be empowered by the board and if he is responsible for the preparation of the PFI it may appear to impair Hal Falcon's objectivity if Paulo makes the appointment. Having never audited Imperiol Hal Falcon should consider whether they have the competence and experience to successfully review the PFI. If they have little knowledge of the building system's industry they would have to seriously question their ability to assess the assumptions about future performance. In particular, if the reporting deadlines are tight there will be little room for extensive planning and knowledge gathering. Under those circumstances the existing auditor may be better placed to assign a team.

It appears as though Imperiol have undertaken a number of restructuring initiatives. They discontinued some businesses in 2008 and it appears in the future they will continue to strip away operations until they are left with nothing but 'building systems.' This may suggest that Imperiol is unstable, which increases the risk that forecasts will be inappropriate. Hal Falcon could also consider the following before deciding whether to proceed or not:

- The nature of assumptions underlying the preparation of the PFI: i.e. best-estimate or extrapolation.
- Why Discorpio, Imperiol's auditors, have not been asked to report on the plans.
- Whether there may be an opportunity to offer other services to Imperiol, e.g. internal audit.

(b) **Procedures to be Performed**

General Procedures

In order to assess management's competence at preparing PFI Hal Falcon could review the forecasts for 2008 and 2009. They could then compare these to the results achieved in 2008 and the first 6 months of 2009.

The forecasts should be compared to previous performance to identify if they are in keeping with historical trends. For example: the building systems turnover has increased by 13.2% (annualised for 2009), the increase in finance costs compared with the increase in loans. Any significant distortions from historical trends would require explanation. During this review care should be taken to ensure that the same accounting policies applied to the historical accounts have been applied to the PFI.

Meet with Paulo and the management accounts team and discuss how the assumptions that underpin the PFI are prepared, including the role of internal audit.

Check the arithmetic accuracy of PFI (i.e. reperform calculations).

Specific Procedures

Further Disposals

- Enquire of management how soon the remainder of the operations to be discontinued will be wound down or sold.
- Analytically review the forecasts in comparison to historic performance. There should be sufficient provisions for the costs of all related redundancies, professional costs and impairments of scrap.
- Critically assess the reasonableness of the value of intangible assets. The 15% ($10.9m) increase to June 2009 may reflect development in fibre optic technology. However, intangible assets for those activities which are discontinuing may be significantly impaired. The reduction in profitability should also give rise to indication of impairment.

- Consider the reasonableness of disposal proceeds (in the cash forecast) and the consistency of gains/losses on disposals in the profit forecast. There may already be sale agreements in place. If so, agree the proceeds to the agreements. The forecast profits/losses may then be recalculated.

New Structure

- Enquire whether anticipated new forms of finance have been included in the forecast, in particular relevant interest charges. If negotiations are underway enquire whether any amounts or rates have been discussed. If there is documentary evidence (for example, an agreement that is contingent upon the PFI) review this to ensure it is accurately reflected in the PFI.

- Enquire of management whether the expected increase in fibre optic products has been reflected in the forecast purchases of inventory.

- Analytically review the forecasts in comparison to actual performance in 2008 and 2009. The PFI should reflect a reduction in staff costs and an increase in professional fees due to the outsourcing of accounts.

- Enquire of directors what they believe the extent of the benefit will be from outsourcing accounting functions. Compare the forecast service costs to any quotes received from professional firms.

Changing Performance

- Enquire of management what they consider to be the key variables which underpin building systems revenue. Note that the turnover for the six months (unaudited) to 30 June 2009 annualised indicates a fall in activity for both electrical and household lines. This is compensated only by an increase in building systems revenue. Therefore any assumptions of growth for building systems will require close scrutiny.

- Analytically review forecast sales to be used for the PFI with any internal management accounts or marketing based forecasts to ensure that the amounts are consistent with the key assumptions of future profitability.

- Analytically review depreciation, amortisation and provisions for slow moving inventory and bad/doubtful debt. Given the movement on the statement of financial position it is reasonable to assume that these provisions should also rise. The increases should be reflected in expense forecasts.

Prospective financial information

- Enquire of management what their sales terms are. The receivables days at the end of June 2009 are 74 days. This is considerably higher than 2008 (51 days) and the effect of this should be discussed with management. In particular, the cash flow forecast should be reviewed to ensure that it is consistent with the worsening in credit control.

- Cash flow, in general, should be closely scrutinised. In the 6 months to 30 June 2009 there has been a $15.5 million reduction in cash assets. Coupled with falling sales and profits and rising inventory and receivables balances there could be significant cash flow difficulties ahead. Hal Falcon should discuss what might happen if Imperiol only manages to raise part of the finance. They may not have sufficient resources to develop the newer fibre optic technology, which could lead to reservations about going concern.

- The cash flow forecast needs to be reviewed to ensure that all related interest charges and extensions in receivables days are adequately reflected. Investors will want to see healthy cash flows to safeguard their returns. As such there is an obvious incentive for directors to manipulate this area of the forecast.

chapter 17

Forensic audits

Chapter learning objectives

Upon completion of this chapter you will be able to:

- define the terms 'forensic accounting', 'forensic investigation' and 'forensic audit;'
- describe the major applications of forensic auditing and analyse the role of the forensic auditor as an expert witness;
- apply the fundamental ethical principles for professional accountants engaged in forensic audit assignments;
- plan a forensic audit engagement; and
- select investigative procedures and evaluate evidence appropriate to determining the loss in a given situation.

Forensic audits

Forensic engagements require a much broader range of skills than other typical non-audit engagements that feature in the P7 exam. However, it is the application of traditional auditing skills and techniques that will be examined in detail from this chapter. It could appear as a question in its own right or as a small part of a question.

1 What is 'forensic accounting'?

The field of forensic accounting is a specialist branch of the profession carried out by forensic accountants and encompassing forensic auditing and investigation.

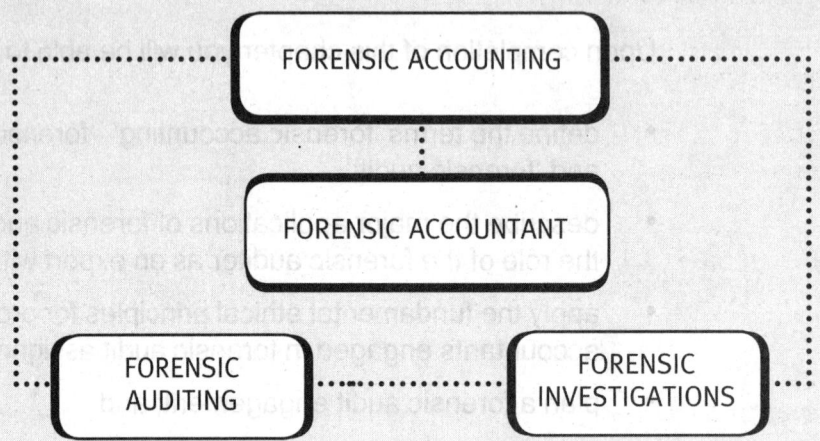

Forensic accounting

- Uses accounting, auditing, and investigative skills to conduct an examination into a company's financial affairs.
- It is often associated with investigations into alleged fraud.
- It involves the whole process of conducting an investigation, including acting as an expert witness.

Forensic investigations

- This refers to the practical steps that the forensic accountant takes in order to gather evidence relevant to the alleged fraudulent activity.
- Such investigations involve a planning phase, a phase of gathering evidence, a review phase and a report to the client.

Forensic audit

- This refers to the specific procedures adopted in order to produce evidence.
- From an accountancy perspective, this usually requires the adoption of traditional financial auditing skills and techniques.

2 What do forensic accountants do?

Forensic accountants become involved in a wide range of investigations, spanning many different industries. Some of the major applications of forensic auditing are shown below.

Application	Examples	Type of work performed
Fraud investigations	Theft of company funds, tax evasion, insider dealing	Funds tracing, asset identification and recovery, forensic intelligence gathering, due diligence reviews, interviews, detailed review of documentary evidence
Insurance claims	Business interruptions, property losses, motor vehicle incidents, personal liability claims, cases of medical malpractice, wrongful dismissal	Detailed review of the policy from either an insured or insurer's perspective to investigate coverage issues, identification of appropriate method of calculating the loss, quantification of losses
Professional negligence	Loss suffered as a result of placing reliance on professional adviser	Advising on merits of a case in regards to liability, quantifying losses
Shareholder, partnership and matrimonial disputes	Determination of funds to be included in settlements, as benefits or distributions	Detailed analysis of numerous years accounting records to quantify the issues in dispute, tracing, locating and evaluation of assets

As part of their assignments forensic accountants will:

- communicate their findings in the form of reports, exhibits and collections of documents; and
- assist in legal proceedings, including testifying in court as an expert witness and preparing visual aids to support trial evidence.

The forensic accountant may be used as an expert witness where:

- it is relevant to a matter that is in dispute between the parties;
- it is a reasonable requirement to resolve proceedings;
- they have the expertise relevant to the issue on which an opinion is sought; and
- they have experience, expertise, and training appropriate to the value, complexity, and importance of the case.

3 Fundamental ethical principles

Implications for forensic assignments

Integrity

Given the nature of their work forensic professionals are likely to deal frequently with individuals who lack integrity, or may even be involved in criminal behaviour. It is imperative that the investigator recognises this, and does nothing to damage their own reputation, such as accepting bribes or giving in to other forms of coercion/intimidation.

Objectivity

The professional accountant must always be – and be perceived to be – entirely neutral.

This is particularly important if the forensic report is going to be submitted to a court of law. Any threat to objectivity could undermine the credibility of the evidence provided.

In particular the accountant must safeguard against self-review and advocacy threats.

- Advocacy threat arises because the firm may feel pressured into promoting the interests and point of view of their fee paying client, which breaches the concept of objectivity in court proceedings.
- Self-review threat arises when an auditor also becomes involved in some form of forensic work because the investigation is likely to involve some form of fraud or potential misstatement to the accounts.

Professional competence and due care

Forensic investigations involve very specialist skills, including:

- Detailed knowledge of the relevant legal framework,
- An understanding of how to gather specialist evidence,
- Skills in the safe custody of evidence, including maintaining a clear 'chain' of evidence, and
- Strong personal skills: interview techniques, presentation of material in court.

Confidentiality

During legal proceedings the court will require the investigator to reveal information discovered during the investigation. There is an overriding requirement for the investigator to disclose all of the information deemed necessary by the court.

Outside of the court, the investigator must maintain confidentiality, especially because much of the information they have access to will be highly sensitive.

Professional behaviour

Fraud investigations can become a matter of public interest, and much media attention is often focused on the work of the forensic investigator. A highly professional attitude must be displayed at all times in order to avoid damage to the reputation of the firm, and of the profession. Any lapse in professional behaviour could undermine the credibility of the investigator, especially when acting in the capacity of expert witness.

4 Gathering and evaluation of evidence

Forensic engagements are general conducted as 'agreed upon procedures' assignments and, as seen above, cover a wide variety of scenarios. The nature of the procedures are therefore entirely dependent upon the requirements of the client. However, the auditor can select from the normal variety of available procedures used in traditional audits.

With most fraud investigations the basic objectives of a forensic engagement include:

- identification of:
    - the type of fraud that has occurred;
    - how long it has been occurring for;
    - how the fraud was concealed;
    - the main suspects.

- quantification of the financial losses;
- gathering of evidence to support legal action/recovery of losses; and
- providing advice to prevent fraud.

The most common procedures include:

- enquiries/interviews of key staff, including the ultimate interview with the suspect/s;
- detailed inspections and analysis of documentary evidence;
- substantive procedures including reconciliations and cash counts;
- control tests to identify weaknesses and, hence, opportunity to commit fraud;
- analytical procedures to compare trends over time or between business segments; and
- computer assisted audit techniques, for example to identify the timing and location of alterations.

To evaluate the results of procedures the forensic auditor can use a range of techniques including:

- recalculation of economic damages;
- regression and sensitivity analysis;
- summarising of large volumes of data;
- present value calculations;
- computerised analysis of large volumes of data; and
- charts/graphs to aid analysis/explanation.

5 The report

Once a forensic investigation is complete, the forensic accountant will write and submit a report of their findings.

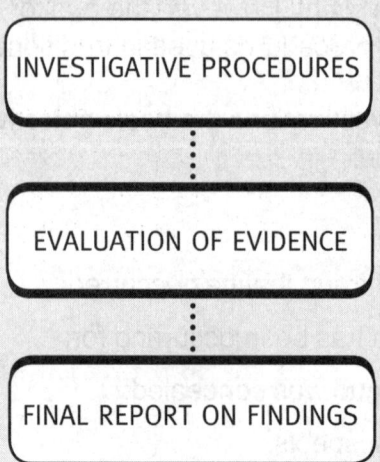

As an agreed upon procedures the most important factor of a forensic report is that the practitioner adequately addresses the requirements of the client, as established in the engagement letter.

A basic report will include:

- a summary of the procedures performed;
- a summary of the results of procedures;
- any limitations in the scope of the engagement; and
- a conclusion regarding the amount of any losses suffered.

It is also likely that the report will discuss how the fraudster set up the scheme, and which controls, if any, were circumvented. In addition, the reporting accounting may provide recommendations to improve the controls within the organisation to prevent any similar frauds occurring in the future.

It is possible that an investigation will lead to legal proceedings. If so it is important to note that the accountant's findings may be used as evidence and the accountant may be required to act as an expert witness.

Forensics: Exam focus

Forensic investigation is a new area of the syllabus. To date there have been a number of questions on the topic:

- the Paper 7 pilot contained a 30 mark case style question based upon a forensic investigation ('Efex Engineering')
- the December 2007 paper contained 5 marks with regard to forensic audit; and
- the December 2008 paper contained a 26 mark compulsory case style question about a payroll fraud investigation ('Crocus').

In order to enhance understanding of this new topic Lisa Weaver has published an article entitled "Forensic Auditing" (September 2008). This can be downloaded from the P7 section of the ACCA website.

Consequent to this the examiner wrote a second article entitled "Massaging the Figures" (April 2009). This focuses on the increasingly common topics of earnings management, creative accounting and fraudulent misstatement of the financial statements.

Forensic audits

Test your understanding 1: Forensic audit

(a) Define the following:
   (i) Forensic accounting
   (ii) Forensic investigations
   (iii) Forensic audit

(3 marks)

(b) You have been asked by the management of The Marvellous Manufacturing Company to carry out an investigation into a suspected expenses fraud within the marketing department.

During a routine annual spend review, management noticed that the expenses budget for year ended 30 June 2007 of $300,000 had been exceeded by nearly $30,000, with no known increase in activity.

Required:

(i) Set out the matters you would consider and procedures you would carry out in planning such an audit

(10 marks)

(ii) Identify the preliminary tests you might carry out to determine whether or not an expenses fraud has taken place.

(7 marks)

(Total: 20 marks)

6 Chapter summary

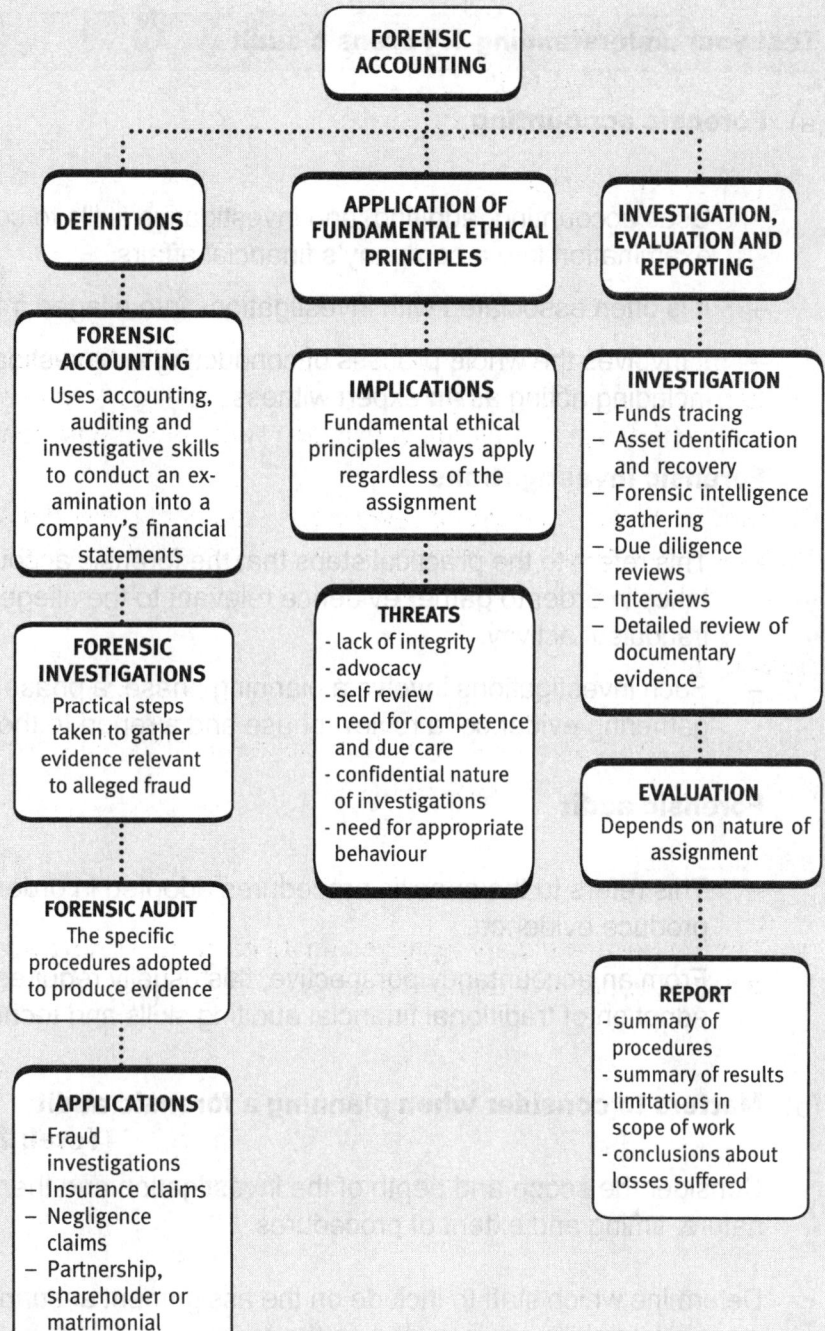

Test your understanding answers

Test your understanding 1: Forensic audit

(a) **Forensic accounting**

- Uses accounting, auditing, and investigative skills to conduct an examination into a company's financial affairs.
- It is often associated with investigations into alleged fraud.
- It involves the whole process of conducting an investigation, including acting as an expert witness.

Forensic investigations

- This refers to the practical steps that the forensic accountant takes in order to gather evidence relevant to the alleged fraudulent activity.
- Such investigations involve a planning phase, a phase of gathering evidence, a review phase and a report to the client.

Forensic audit

- This refers to the specific procedures adopted in order to produce evidence.
- From an accountancy perspective, this usually requires the adoption of traditional financial auditing skills and techniques.

(b) **Matters to consider when planning a forensic audit**

Consider the scope and depth of the investigation and therefore the nature, timing and extent of procedures

Determine which staff to include on the assignment ensuring the appropriate skills are included on the team.

Consider the availability of the staff and whether any other work needs to be rescheduled and whether this is possible.

Prepare the budget for the assignment of hours, grades of staff and costs.

Calculate the fee for the assignment based on the budget.

Discuss with management why they believe the overspend is through fraudulent behaviour

Consider who the intended users of the report will be as this will affect risk and liability levels and therefore the amount of work undertaken.

Identify risk areas that would provide opportunities for fraud to take place e.g. lack of segregation of duties, poor control environment, etc

Develop an assignment plan that focuses on the areas where fraud could have taken place.

Ensure the team are fully briefed on the client and the assignment.

Preliminary tests to determine whether an expenses fraud has taken place

Obtain management accounts and perform analytical procedures to see if any other significant variances have occurred.

Speak with the marketing director to identify if there have been more trips required this year that could explain the reason for the increase.

Enquire if any new customers/contracts have been won in the year that might explain an increase in marketing expenses e.g. entertaining to win new business.

Enquire with the marketing director whether expenses are authorised and what the authority limits are.

Enquire if there has been any change in expenses policy that might explain the increase e.g. an increase in the standard of hotels used, meal allowances, etc.

Enquire when the spending increase was first identified and what measures were taken by the client to find reasons why.

Analyse expense claims by individual to try to identify who might be the culprit.

Analyse expenses by type to identify which category of expenses has seen the biggest rise. For example, if fuel costs the rise might be due to fuel price increases rather than fraud.

chapter 18

Outsourcing

Chapter learning objectives

Upon completion of this chapter you will be able to:

- explain the different approaches to 'outsourcing' and compare with 'insourcing;'
- discuss and conclude on the advantages and disadvantages of outsourcing finance and accounting functions;
- recognise and evaluate the impact of outsourced functions on the conduct of an audit;
- explain the benefits and drawbacks of outsourcing internal audit; and
- consider the ethical implications of the external auditor providing an internal audit service to a client.

Outsourcing

Outsourcing could feature as a requirement in its own right or within a scenario for a risk assessment requirement or requirement relating to gathering audit evidence.

1 What is 'outsourcing'?

- Outsourcing is the practice of contracting out business functions or processes to an external service provider.

- The opposite of outsourcing is 'insourcing.' This is where a business performs functions and processes internally that would ordinarily have been performed by external contractors. This shifts control of the function back to the organisation but often leads to skill shortages internally. This often leads to the employment of subcontractors.

Examples

Common examples of outsourcing arrangements include:

- Data processing
    - Company advises external service organization of the transactions it has undertaken (e.g. sales made).
    - Service organization operates a transaction processing system on the company's behalf, raising invoices, etc. for the company.

- Pensions
    - Many businesses offer a pension scheme to their employees.
    - Rather than employ pension specialists in a human resources department, many companies will select an external pension scheme provider and advise employees to join that provider's scheme if they wish.

- Information technology
    - As an extension of outsourcing the transaction processing, a company could outsource the entire IT function.
    - This would allow the company access to all the latest technological advances without having to buy the hardware itself.
    - Would also provide expertise to deal with one-off projects, such as systems implementation or software upgrades.

- Internal auditing
    - Rather than setting up its own internal audit department, a company could buy in the service from an external provider such as a firm of accountants.

- Due diligence work
  - A Stock Exchange will typically require listed companies to obtain due diligence (special investigations undertaken by professional firms) assurance when they are considering large transactions, e.g. buying another company.
  - This is specialist work where the necessary high level of expertise can be bought in from an external provider.
  - Additional benefits are increased independence and objectivity, professional cachet and indemnity for negligence.
- Tax management
  - Main benefit would be the availability of skilled expertise without having to pay the ongoing employment costs for such an individual.

Reasons for outsourcing

There are many reasons for outsourcing. Ultimately the need or desire to contract services to external providers depends upon the unique circumstances of a particular organisation. However, typical reasons include:

- Freeing up internal resources to concentrate on more "core" business functions;
- Reducing the amount of top management time spent administering "non-core" business functions;
- There is a lack of technical expertise internally;
- The cost of keeping up-to-date with changes is seen to be prohibitive (e.g. tax law, health and safety regulations);
- It allows the business to be more flexible and adaptive to changing industry factors; and
- It may lead to cost savings (particularly if the function does not require continual processes).

Outsourcing

Benefits and limitations

Typically accountancy and IT functions are amongst the most widely outsourced business services. This provides the following benefits:

- Services should be provided by suitably competent professionals who specialise in those services;
- It reduces the cost of wastage to the organisation. This now becomes a cost to the service provider;
- It can help transfer risk to another party (e.g. the risk associated with fraud);
- It helps organisations manage the peaks and troughs of working cycles; and
- It will lead to a fixed fee, thus helping cash flow management.

However, outsourcing can lead to problems. These include:

- The cost involved in changing to an outsourced provider (information transfer, redundancy, "teething problems");
- The loss of control of a business process/function;
- The potential for conflict with the service provider should the quality of service not match expectations;
- The inflexibility of contracts with service providers; and
- The need (potentially) for new systems to be implemented to ensure appropriate information is transferred to the service provider on a timely basis.

chapter 18

2 Impact of outsourcing on audit practice

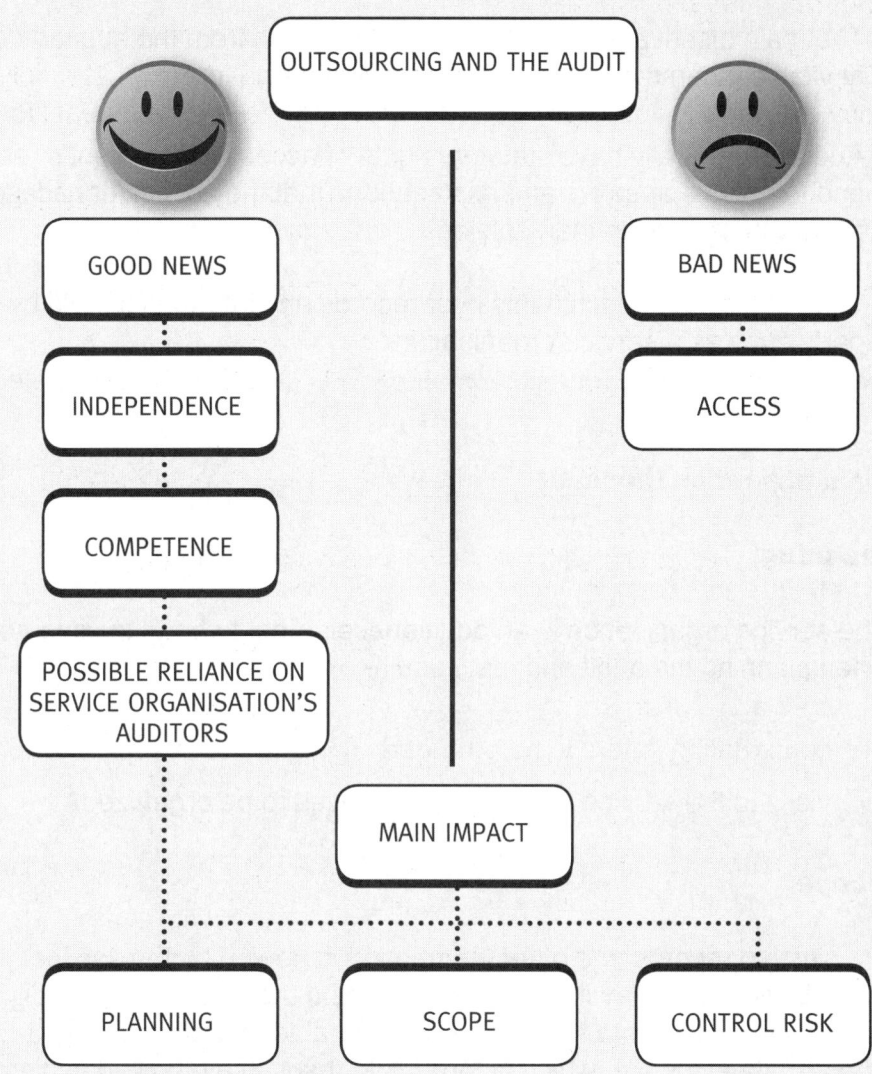

Discussion of the 'Good News'

- Independence – because the service organisation is external to the client, the audit evidence derived from it is regarded as being more reliable than evidence generated internally by the client.

- Competence – because the service organisation is in business to provide the services it provides, it may be more competent in executing its role than the client's internal department.

- Possible reliance on the service organisation's auditors – it may be possible for the client's auditors to confirm balances directly with the service organisation's auditors.

KAPLAN PUBLISHING 459

Outsourcing

Discussion of the 'Bad News'

The main disadvantage of outsourced services from the auditor's point of view concerns access to records and information.

Auditors generally have statutory rights of access to the client's records and to receive answers and explanations that they consider necessary to enable them to form their opinion.

They do not have such rights over records and information held by a third party such as a service organisation.

Main impact on the audit

Planning

The service organisation is an additional element to be taken into account when planning the audit and may require:

- confirmation letters to be arranged
- visits to the service organisation's offices to be organized.

Scope

If access to records and other information is denied by the service organisation, this may impose a limitation on the scope of the auditor's work. This may lead to the auditor being unable to gather sufficient appropriate evidence, which in turn could result in a modified audit report.

Control risk

The use of a service organisation may well result in reduced control risk, and a reduction in the amount of detailed substantive testing required.

ISA 402: Outsourcing and the audit

ISA 402 *Audit Considerations Relating to an Entity Using a Service Organisation* provides guidance to auditors on the audit impact of outsourcing.

Use of service organisations

The auditor should identify whether the client uses service organisations and assess the effect of such use on the procedures necessary to obtain sufficient appropriate audit evidence to determine with reasonable assurance whether the user's financial statements are free from misstatement.

Procedures

The auditor should, as always, obtain a knowledge and understanding of the client's business. They should consider how an entity's use of a service organisation affects the entity's internal control so as to identify and assess the risk of material misstatement and to design and perform further audit procedures. Specifically they should perform the following procedures:

- Obtain a Type 2 report, if available. This is a report on the description, design and operating effectiveness of controls at the service organisation. It contains a report prepared by management of the service organisation and a reasonable assurance report by the service auditor;
- Perform tests of control at the service organisation;
- Use another auditor to perform tests of control at the service organisation on their behalf.

If the auditor intends to use a report from a service auditor they should perform procedures to ensure they are satisfied with the competence and independence of the service auditor and that the service auditor's report provides sufficient appropriate evidence about the effectiveness of controls.

Contractual terms

The auditor should obtain and document an understanding of:

- the contractual terms that apply to the relevant activities;
- the way the user monitors those activities so as to ensure that it meets is fiduciary duty.

Relevant points here include the following:

- right of access to records held by the outsourcer;
- whether the terms take proper account of statutory requirements (e.g. proper accounting records) or regulatory body requirements;
- performance standards; and
- the extent of reliance on controls operated by the service organisation.

Lack of access to records may mean that the auditor has to modify their opinion due to a lack of sufficient appropriate evidence.

The auditor should determine the effect on their assessment of inherent and control risk. The following issues should be considered.

Outsourcing

Inherent risk

- The reputation of the service organization.
- The existence of external supervision.
- The extent to which indemnities offered by the outsourcer can be honoured.

Control risk

- the extent of controls operated by service provider
- the experience of errors and omissions
- the degree of monitoring by the user
- the extent of information on controls provided by the outsourcer
- the quality assurance in the outsourcer, e.g. ISOs or internal audit.

ISAE 3402: Reporting on Controls at a Service Organisation

ISAE 3402 *Assurance Reports on Controls at a Service Organisation* deals with assurance engagements undertaken to provide a report for use by entities engaging the services of another organisation and the user entities' auditors.

It provides guidance to the assurance provider to ensure that where the service is relevant to the user entity's internal controls relating to financial reporting, the reports prepared provide sufficient appropriate audit evidence, as required by ISA 402.

In order to provide sufficient appropriate evidence, these assurance engagements are required to provide **reasonable assurance**. The engagements are performed as attestation engagements.

The objective of the engagement is to obtain reasonable assurance that:

- the service organisation's description of its system fairly presents the system as designed and implemented
- the controls were suitably designed
- the controls operated effectively

throughout the specified period, and

- to report on the above matters.

The evaluation of the suitability of the design and operating effectiveness of the controls would need to be performed to the same standard as an evaluation performed by the external auditor in order to provide reasonable assurance on which the external auditor of the user entity can rely.

The assurance provider can rely on the service entity's internal audit function, in the same way that the external auditor would, where the work of the internal audit function is relevant to the engagement and the work is adequate for the purposes of the engagement - the assessment of the internal audit function required is the same as that required by ISA 610 *Using the Work of Internal Auditors*.

Internal audit engagements

Definition

'Internal audit' is an appraisal activity established by management for the review of accounting and internal control systems as a service to the entity.

Internal audit activities

The function may perform many different activities, many of which might also be the focus of assurance engagements.

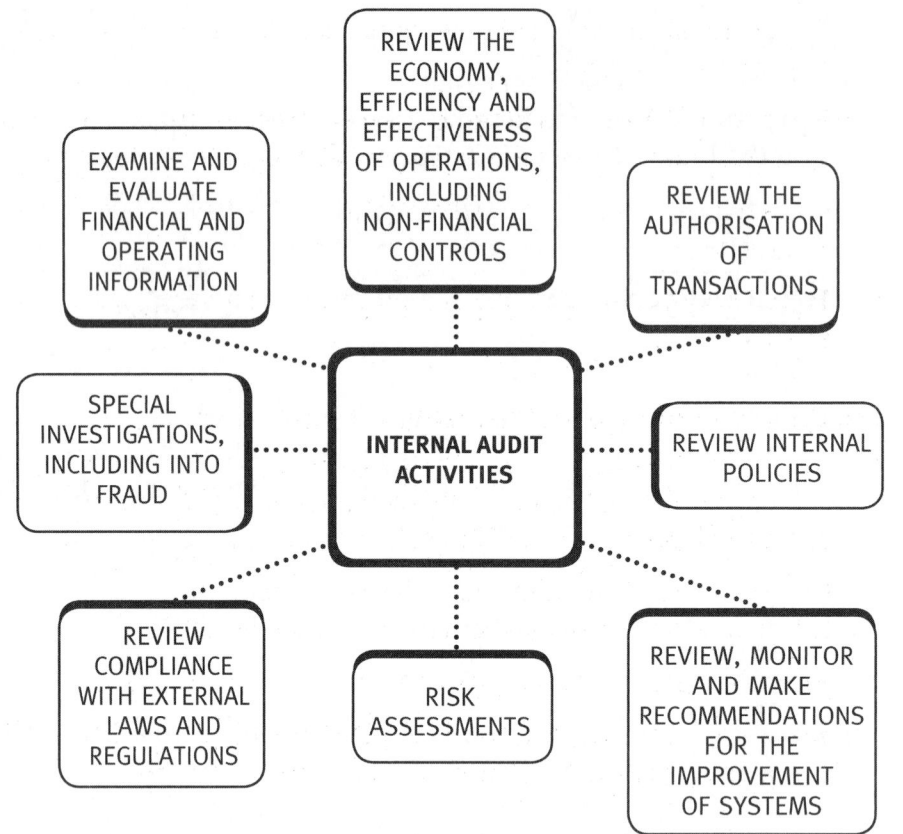

It should be noted that many of the activities performed by internal audit are similar to, or the same as, those activities discussed in chapter 15. Risk assessment, benchmarking, value for money audits and e-commerce assessments are all important tools for internal performance analysis and decision making. These are also fundamental aspects of corporate governance and, therefore, the primary responsibility to perform these assessments rests with internal management.

3 Outsourcing internal audit

Many companies now outsource their internal audit work to professional firms, whose experience of different company systems and procedures provides added benefit to the client.

The advantages of outsourcing internal audit

- Professional firms follow an ethical code of conduct and should therefore be independent of the client and their management;
- Accountancy service providers have specific, professional skills;
- Professional firms should have qualified, competent staff who receive regular development;
- Professional firms can be employed on a flexible basis, i.e. on an individual engagement basis rather than full time employment;
- Professional firms are responsible for their activities and hold insurance.
- The flexibility and expertise of a professional firm may prove more cost effective.

The disadvantages of outsourcing internal audit

- Professional firms cannot have the same intimate knowledge of a company that internal staff have;
- Engagements with professional firms are constrained by contractual terms. Internal terms can be deployed more flexibly;
- Professional fees tend to be high;
- Companies may wish to use their external auditor to provide internal audit services, which can lead to ethical problems (see below).

Current issue: External and internal auditor?

In 2009 KPMG in the UK became the external auditor to a company called Rentokil Initial, a FTSE 250 (and sometime 100) pest control and delivery company. This in itself is not unusual; the audit market is extremely competitive and high profile client wins are becoming increasingly common. However, the circumstances of the contract "win" have caused a number of eyebrows to be raised within the auditing profession and by a number of corporate governance commentators. Some of the reasons include:

- The deal with KPMG has allowed Rentokil Initial to reduce their audit fees by a massive 30%; and
- KPMG are to provide external audit services and to provide internal audit services alongside Rentokil's own internal audit function.

Outsourcing

This creates two significant ethical threats:

- Self-review; and
- Management.

If the auditor were to rely on its own internal audit work as part of the audit it would undoubtedly scrutinise its own work. Given the costs savings identified it is likely that KPMG will use this relationship to streamline the audit process and avoid duplication of procedures.

There is also a significant management threat for one simple reason: external auditors work on behalf of investors and internal auditors work for management. Therefore KPMG would be contributing to the management process it is supposed to be scrutinising.

In the UK this relationship is obviously not outlawed, however this case has created a significant amount of interest and it is suggested that this could be a blueprint for further similar arrangements.

This is contradictory to developments in the profession post Enron, where a significant amount of effort has been spent in attempting to reduce the non-audit services provided by auditors of listed clients. In fact the relationship KPMG has with Rentokil is actually not permitted in the US and a handful of other nations.

At the time of writing the engagement is still coming under heavy scrutiny and, whilst no official action has been taken yet, it is likely that the debate will rage on for some time to come.

Exam focus: Other engagements – 'Thomas Trends'

Please note that with questions of this nature there is usually a more straight forward element coupled with a tougher, more scenario specific, element. Simpler questions tend to focus on definitions, pros and cons and common sense discussions. The more scenario specific question usually focuses on issues you would consider during a planning meeting, what evidence you would gather during the engagement and what the impact on your report might be.

You are a partner of Finbar & Sons, a firm of accountants. You have been approached by a potential client, Thomas Trends Ltd. They recently notified you of their intention to outsource their internal audit function. The company operates a small, high street based, chain of clothes outlets.

chapter 18

They set up the internal audit department some years ago based on advice given them by their external auditors, Suckit & Sea. However, given that most employees use internal audit as a springboard to management positions, the staff turnover is high and the FD believes it may be more effective to use an external provider of this service.

They are interested in some form of evaluation of organisational risks, financial compliance, IT systems and fraud risks. He has asked you if you would be interested in offering this service and, with this in mind, has set up a breakfast meeting with you to discuss the role.

Required:

(a) **Briefly describe the advantages and disadvantages of outsourcing an accounting function.**

(6 marks)

(b) **Describe the principal matters relating to the assignment to be discussed during you meeting with the FD of Thomas Trends Ltd.**

(10 marks)

Test your understanding 1

Your client uses a payroll bureau to operate its payroll. Describe the benefits this may have in the auditors assessment of inherent and control risk. What potential additional risks or pitfalls does this arrangement present to the auditor?

4 Chapter summary

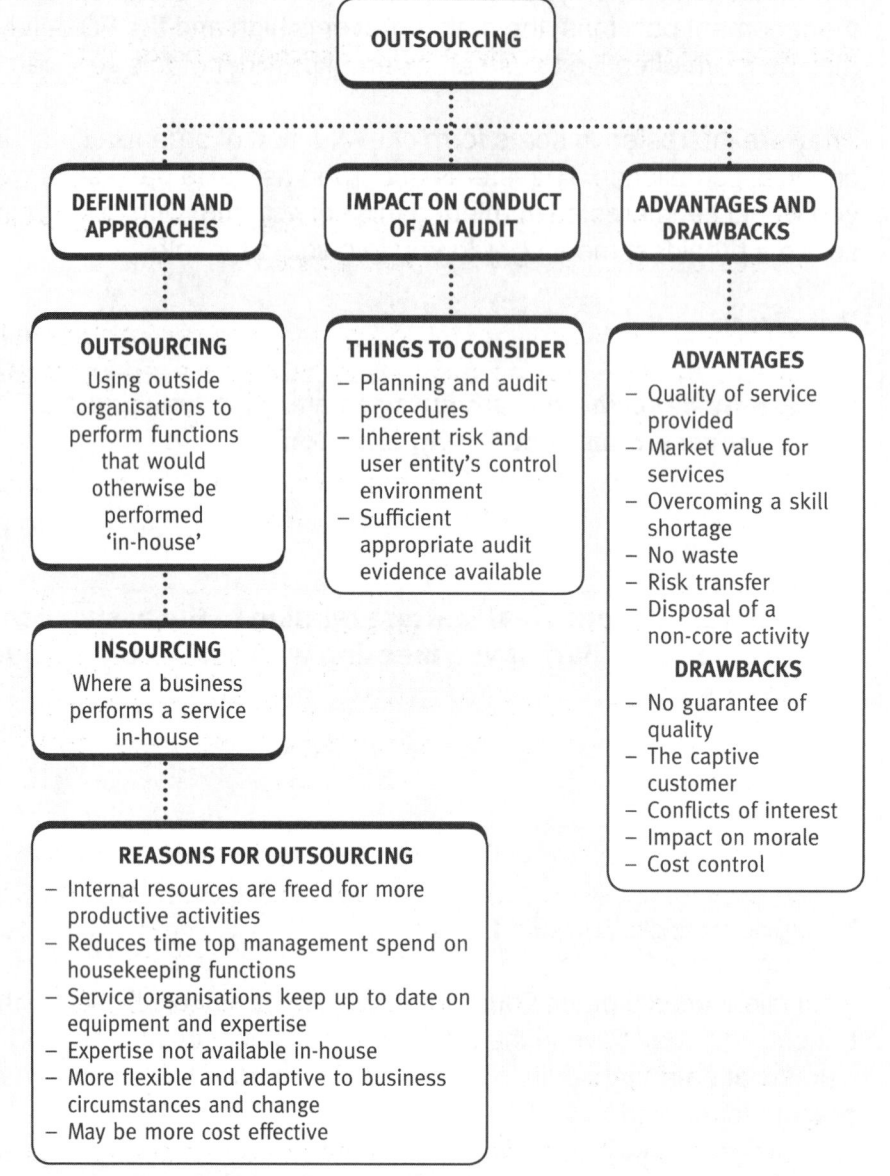

Test your understanding answers

Exam focus: Other engagements – 'Thomas Trends'

(a) **Advantages**

There should be some form of time or cost efficiency made when outsourcing a previously 'in-house' function.

An outsourced internal audit function may improve controls in the eyes of the external auditors, thus reducing the need for substantive testing.

Reduce turnover of staff for Thomas Trends and improve continuity – and perhaps morale – of human resource.

An external source should provide a wider range of industry knowledge. They will also provide an independent perspective. This should lead to recommendations that improve internal procedures. Outsourcing should provide more flexibility in terms of access to experienced staff at all times throughout the year, even busy periods.

The outsourced firm will be technically up to date and will therefore be able to update management about changes in financial reporting requirements.

Management will be able to focus on core competencies.

Disadvantages

Loss of 'springboard' for junior managers trying to work their way in to more senior managerial positions. Future "stars" will have to be identified and trained in other ways.

Over time the outsourced function may increase their charges if they perceive the company is becoming reliant on their expertise.

Whilst the outsourced company may have relevant industry knowledge they will lack understanding of Thomas Trends' internal processes and policies. This issue will be further exaggerated if the audit team used by the outsourced company changes each year.

The outsourced audit staff will not have any allegiance to the Thomas Trends. Therefore the management of Thomas Trends may not buy into any suggestions made as readily.

(b) **Principle matters to be discussed**

Firstly you would introduce your firm, including details of the functions undertaken, the office locations and the experience of the internal audit department and its partners. You would discuss which office would be responsible for providing the services and who the main points of contact would be.

You would incorporate a discussion of how Finbar & Sons services relate to the specific functions requested, namely: organisational risk analysis; financial compliance; IT systems analysis; and fraud risk analysis.

You would discuss Finbar & Sons' approach to assessing the needs for audit and the approach involved. For example:

- Preliminary – review of business and industry characteristics;
- Planning – needs analysis and co-ordination with external auditors;
- Post audit – assurance that activities were effectively executed;
- Review – of services provided, reports and management's responses.

You would discuss the tools/methods adopted for internal audit tasks. Most importantly you would discuss the use of any computer aided audit techniques, namely embedded audit software.

The installation of embedded audit software could require some training for the staff/management of Thomas Trends. You would discuss the provision of any training services offered.

You might discuss any insurance taken out covering, for example, public liability and professional indemnity.

You would probably discuss how your firm ensures quality, namely through the use of the standards you follow (such as the Institute of Internal Auditors).

You might provide sample report templates to help Thomas Trends understand the nature of the reports they will receive in return. Examples might include: risk analysis reports and reports to the audit committee.

You might offer a list of current clients who you provide internal audit services to so that Thomas Trends can take up references if they so wish.

Although Thomas Trends is not an audit client you would discuss any potential conflicts of interest. An important area would be identifying any possible competitors to Thomas Trends that are also clients.

You would also have to discuss fee levels. You would identify the charge out rates for different levels of staff and the firm's policy with regard to recharging travel and others expenses. You would give an indication of possible future increases (e.g. inflationary) and invoicing/credit terms offered, e.g. payable on demand or 30 days credit.

Finally you would discuss performance targets to be met, such as deadlines for completing fieldwork and submission dates for the various reports.

Test your understanding 1

The auditors may also decide that:

- inherent risk in this area is reduced, because of the service organization's experience and competence
- control risk is also reduced because of the independence of the service organization.

Possible pitfalls

- Independence may not be all it seems if the client's business represents a major contract to the service organization.
- Similarly, it may not always be safe to assume competence on the part of the service organization. There may be a possibility that the organization may give misleading responses to the auditors' enquiries to cover up its own failures.

chapter 19

UK syllabus only: Auditing aspects of insolvency

Chapter learning objectives

Upon completion of this chapter you will be able to:

- explain the meaning of and describe the procedures involved in placing a company into voluntary or compulsory liquidation or administration;

- explain procedures and consequences of compulsory liquidation and how it may affect company stakeholders;

- advise on the differences between fraudulent and wrongful trading and the consequences for the company directors;

- examine the financial position of a company and determine whether it is insolvent;

- identify the circumstances where administration could be adopted as an alternative to winding up; and

- explain and apply the priority for the allocation of company assets.

UK syllabus only: Auditing aspects of insolvency

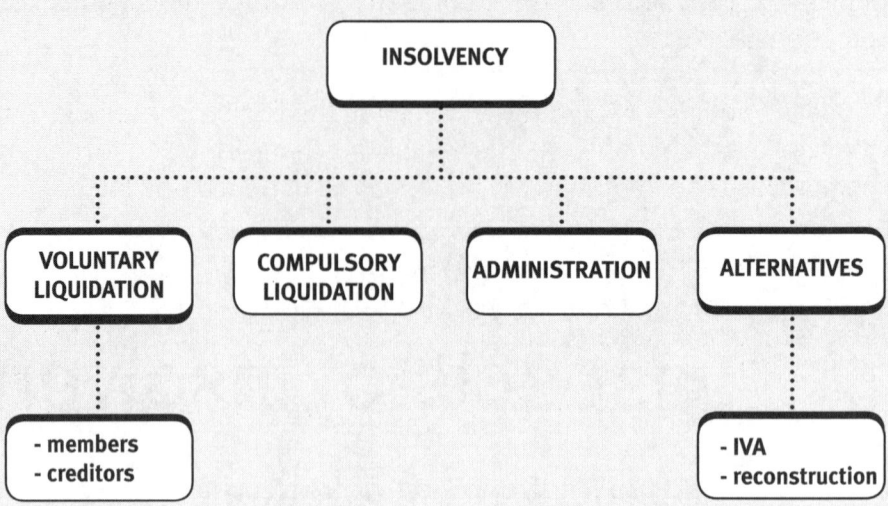

This chapter is relevant to students taking the UK variant of the exam only. Insolvency will not appear in every exam. It is a non-audit area of the syllabus similar in weighting to a topic such as forensic accounting.

1 Voluntary liquidation

Introduction

Liquidation is the process of terminating a company, thus ending its life. The assets of the company are physically liquidated, i.e. they are sold, so that cash can be used to pay off company creditors and equity holders.

There are two forms of voluntary liquidation (Insolvency Act 1986):

- a members' voluntary liquidation; and
- a creditors' voluntary liquidation.

Members' voluntary liquidation

This form of liquidation is used when a company is solvent. In order to facilitate this the members must pass one of two resolutions:

- an ordinary resolution, where the articles provide for liquidation on the expiry of a fixed date or a specific event; or
- a special resolution, for any other reason.

Once this has been passed the directors must make a **declaration of solvency** stating that they are of the opinion that the company will be able to pay its debts within twelve months. A false declaration would constitute a criminal offence.

The company will then appoint a named insolvency practitioner to act as the liquidator. They will realise the company's assets and distribute the proceeds accordingly.

Once the liquidation process is complete the liquidator presents a report at the final meeting of the members, which is then submitted to the registrar of companies. The company will be dissolved three months later.

Creditor's voluntary liquidation

This form of liquidation is used if a company intends to liquidate voluntarily but is insolvent. Once again a resolution of members must be passed (as with a members' voluntary liquidation). However, no declaration of solvency can be made.

Instead a meeting of creditors must be held within fourteen days of passing the resolution. At least seven days written notice must be given for this meeting. During the meeting the directors must present a full statement of the company's affairs and a list of all creditors and amounts owed to them.

Both the members and the creditors are entitled to appoint a liquidator. However, the creditors' choice must prevail over the members' choice. In addition the creditors may appoint up to five people to sit on a liquidation committee.

The liquidator will realise the company's assets and distribute the proceeds accordingly. Once the liquidation process is complete the liquidator presents a report at the final meeting of the members, which is then submitted to the registrar of companies. The company will then be dissolved.

2 Compulsory liquidation

Introduction

Companies may be obliged to liquidate if a winding up order is presented to a court, usually by a creditor or member. Such a petition may be made for a number of reasons, which include (Insolvency Act 1986):

- the company being unable to pay its debts; and
- it is just and equitable to wind up the company.

If a member petitions on the latter basis this will only be considered if the company is solvent and the member has been a registered shareholder for at least six of the prior eighteen months.

Consequences

If successful the court will appoint an official receiver (an officer of the courts) as liquidator. They may be replaced by a practitioner at a later date. The receiver investigates the company's affairs and the cause of its failure. The petition also has the following effects:

- all actions for the recovery of debt against the company are stopped;
- any floating charges crystallise;
- all legal proceedings against the company are halted and none may start unless the courts grant permission;
- the company must cease trading activity, unless it is necessary to complete the liquidation, e.g. completing work-in-progress;
- the directors relinquish power and authority to the liquidator, although they may remain in office; and
- employees are automatically made redundant. The liquidator may choose to re-employ them to help complete the liquidation process.

Procedures

Within twelve weeks of being appointed the official receiver will call a meeting of creditors in order to agree the appointment of a licensed insolvency practitioner and to appoint a liquidation committee.

The liquidator will realise the company's assets and distribute the proceeds accordingly. Once the liquidation process is complete the liquidator presents a report at the final meeting of the members, which is then submitted to the registrar of companies. The company will then be dissolved.

3 Allocation of company assets

Liquidators in a compulsory liquidation must pay debts in the following order:

- fixed charge holders;
- expenses of liquidation, including liquidator's remuneration;
- preferential creditors, including employee's wages and accrued holiday pay;
- floating charge holders;
- unsecured creditors (ranked equally);
- deferred debts, including dividends declared but not paid and interest accrued on debts since liquidation; and
- members.

It is likely that liquidators will also adhere to these principles in a voluntary liquidation as well.

4 Administration

Introduction

Administration is the process whereby an insolvency practitioner is appointed to manage the affairs of a business (Enterprise Act 2002). It is often used as an alternative to liquidation with a view to:

- rescuing a company in financial difficulty;
- achieving better results for creditors than could be achieved through liquidation; or
- realising property to pay off secured creditors.

Appointment

Administrators can be appointed by any one of the following:

- the courts, in response to a petition;
- the holder of a qualifying floating charge over company assets; or
- members or directors, providing that liquidation has not already begun.

Courts will only appoint an administrator if the company is, or is likely to become, unable to pay its debts and if it feels that administration will help meet the objectives listed above.

Consequences

The administrator takes over control of the management of the company. They must follow any proposals approved at any meeting of creditors or dictated by the courts. However, particular powers include:

- removal or appointment of directors;
- calling meetings of creditors and/or members;
- making payments to secured or preferential creditors;
- making payments to unsecured creditors, if it is felt that this will assist the objectives of the administration; and
- presenting or defending a petition for liquidating the company.

Upon appointing an administrator certain protections are afforded to the company, namely:

- the rights of creditors to enforce security over the company's assets are suspended;

- petitions for liquidation are dismissed;
- no resolutions to wind up the company may be passed; and
- the directors continue in office, although their powers are suspended.

5 Alternatives to winding up

Introduction

Often businesses have no alternative but to face up to administration or, in the worst case scenario, liquidation. However, there are alternatives that exist to help both incorporated and non-incorporated businesses survive, namely:

- individual voluntary arrangements; and
- reconstructions.

Individual Voluntary Arrangements ("IVA's")

An IVA is an arrangement available to individuals, sole traders and partnerships to help them reach a compromise with creditors with the aim of avoiding the closure of their business and, perhaps, bankruptcy. Such an arrangement usually facilitates lower payments of debt over an extended period, usually five years.

Once an individual (or their insolvency practitioner) submits a proposal to the courts for an interim order creditors may no longer take action against the individual (referred to as a moratorium on actions). A creditors meeting must be held within fourteen days of the order to include the proposals made by the individual with regard to their debt. The creditors may accept the proposals with a 75% majority (by value of creditors present) vote.

The main benefit is obviously that the individual may continue in business and work towards the payment of their debt in a more flexible manner. They are also not penalised by bankruptcy laws, such as restrictions on becoming a director. Creditors also benefit as it is likely that they will receive more under the terms of an IVA than they would if liquidation was enforced upon a company that is potentially insolvent anyway.

Reconstructions

It may be possible for companies facing problems to survive by taking up new contracts or exploiting market opportunities. However, such ventures usually require cash injections and when faced with liquidity problems than can pose quite a problem, not least because such businesses many not appear attractive to external investment.

Typical traits of such companies include:

- accumulated losses;
- debenture interest arrears;
- cumulative preference shares dividend arrears;
- no payment of ordinary dividends;
- share price below nominal value; and
- share price decline.

To become more attractive to investment the company could reorganise or reconstruct.

Permitted reconstructions

Capital structures protect stakeholders' interests. Therefore changes to these structures are restricted by company law. However, under various mechanisms of the Companies Act 2006 companies are able to:

- write off unpaid share capital;
- write off share capital which is not represented by available assets;
- write off paid up share capital which is in excess of requirements;
- write off debenture interest arrears;
- replace existing debentures with a lower interest debenture;
- write off preference dividend arrears; and
- write off amounts owing to trade creditors.

By altering the capital structure of the business and by removing some of the debt of the business companies may be able to reduce their accumulated losses to the point that they have profits available to begin paying debts and dividends in the future. The reduction in the debt burden also frees up resources for investment in future opportunities and new growth.

Of course, to do this the company must ask its stakeholders to surrender some or all of their existing rights and amounts due. They do this in exchange for new rights under a new or reformed company and a share of the benefits that could arise due to future investment. This may be more appealing than the alternatives, which include:

- to remain as they are, with the prospect of no return from their investment and no growth in their investment; or
- to accept whatever return they could be given in a liquidation.

6 Wrongful and fraudulent trading

Fraudulent trading

Fraudulent trading is where a company carries on a business with the **intention of defrauding creditors** or for any other fraudulent purposes. This would include a situation where the director(s) of a company continue to trade whilst insolvent, and enter into debts knowing that the company will not be in a position to repay those debts.

The Insolvency Act 1986 (s.213) governs situations where, in the course of a winding up, it appears that the business has been carried on with the intent to defraud creditors, or for any other fraudulent purpose.

Fraudulent trading is also a criminal offence under the Companies Act 2006.

Wrongful trading

Wrongful trading (s214 1a of the Insolvency Act 1986) is when the director(s) of a company have **continued to trade** when they: "knew, or ought to have concluded that there was **no reasonable prospect of avoiding insolvent liquidation**".

A director can defend an action of wrongful trading if they can prove that they have taken sufficient steps to minimise the potential loss to creditors.

Wrongful trading is an action that can be taken only by a company's liquidator, once it has gone into insolvent liquidation (either voluntary or compulsory liquidation).

Unlike fraudulent trading, wrongful trading needs no finding of 'intent to defraud'. In addition, because wrongful trading is a civil offence (fraudulent trading is a criminal offence), it only needs to be proven "on the balance of probabilities" (i.e. it is more likely than not that the director(s) are guilty of wrongful trading). Fraudulent trading needs to be proven "beyond reasonable doubt" (i.e. it is almost certain that the director(s) are guilty of fraudulent trading).

For these reasons, wrongful trading is more common than fraudulent trading.

Penalties

A director who is found guilty of fraudulent trading can be made **personally liable** for the debts of the company (a civil liability under the Insolvency Act); be **disqualified as a director for between two and 15 years**, and can be **imprisoned for up to ten years**.

A director who is found guilty of wrongful trading can be made **personally liable** for the debts of the company; and be **disqualified as a director for between two and 15 years**.

Insolvency

There are two tests for insolvency defined in the Insolvency Act 1986.

(1) if assets are exceeded by liabilities; or
(2) if a company is failing to discharge its debts as and when they fall due.

If a company meets **either** criteria then it is technically insolvent.

Test your understanding 1

Tommy Co is in compulsory liquidation. The insolvency practitioner has liquidated the company's assets and has $1.125mn available for distribution. The following points are relevant:

- the company has an issued share capital of 2.5mn $1 shares;
- the directors declared, but have not paid, a dividend of 10c per share six months ago;
- the insolvency practitioner's costs total $50,000;
- Tommy Co's bank have a floating charge over the company's stock, which has now crystallised. The value is $400,000;
- the company's employees have been paid, with the exception of $275,000 of accrued holiday pay; and
- unsecured creditors total $500,000.

Required:

Identify and explain how the available funds will be distributed to the stakeholders of Tommy Co by the insolvency practitioner.

Test your understanding 2

Compare and contrast the characteristics of a members' voluntary winding up and a creditors' voluntary winding up.

UK syllabus only: Auditing aspects of insolvency

Test your understanding 3

Poppy and Rosie registered their petfood business as a private limited company, Wag Ltd, in January 2006. They injected £1,000 of share capital of £1,000 into Wag Ltd, and appointed themselves as directors of Wag Ltd.

Wag Ltd made a small profit in its first few years of trading, after the salaries paid to Poppy and Rosie. However, following difficult economic conditions, Wag Ltd made a loss of £15,000 in the year ended 31 December 2009.

In early 2010, Poppy said she thought the company should cease trading and be wound up. Rosie, however, insisted that the company would be profitable in the long-term so they agreed to carry on the business, although Poppy was no longer involved in the day-to-day running of the business and stopped drawing a salary (although she retained her position as company director).

During 2010 and 2011, Rosie falsified Wag Ltd's accounts to disguise the fact that the company had continued to suffer losses, until it became obvious that they could no longer hide the company's debts and that it would have to go into insolvent liquidation, with debts of £75,000.

Required:

Advise Poppy and Rosie as to any potential liability they might face as regards:

- fraudulent trading, under both criminal and civil law; and
- wrongful trading under s.214 of the Insolvency Act 1986.

7 Chapter summary

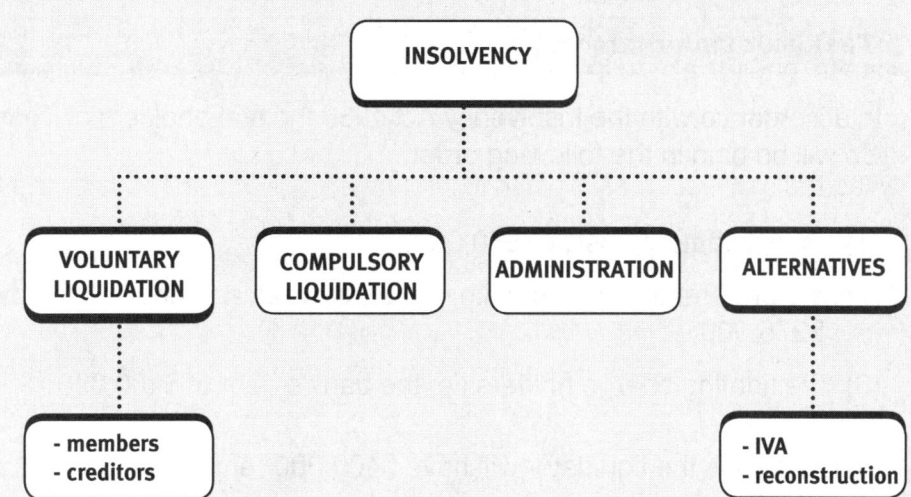

Test your understanding answers

Test your understanding 1

In accordance with the Insolvency Act 1986 the stakeholders of Tommy Co will be paid in the following order:

(1) the liquidators costs of $50,000;

(2) the preferential creditors: i.e. the employees accrued holiday pay of $275,000;

(3) the floating charge holders i.e. the bank's debt of $400,000.

Following this the liquidator will have $400,000 remaining. This will be paid in full to the unsecured creditors who must forfeit the other $100,000 owed to them.

The members' declared but not paid dividends rank below the above stakeholders and will therefore not be paid. Likewise there will be no residual assets left to distribute to the members, who will receive nothing at all upon the liquidation of Tommy Co.

Test your understanding 2

A voluntary winding up takes place when the company resolves by special resolution to be wound up for any cause whatsoever, or by ordinary resolution where the articles provide for liquidation on the expiry of a fixed date or a specific event.

In the case of a members' voluntary winding up, the directors make a declaration of solvency stating that after full inquiry into the company's affairs they are of the opinion that the company will be able to pay its debts within twelve months of the commencement of the winding up.

In a creditors' voluntary winding up, such a declaration is not possible owing to the circumstances leading to the winding up.

In a members' voluntary winding up, the liquidator is appointed by the members and is accountable to them.

In a creditors' voluntary winding up, both members and creditors have the right to nominate a liquidator and, in the event of dispute, subject to the right of appeal to the courts, the creditors' nominee prevails. Here the liquidator is primarily accountable to the creditors.

In a creditors' voluntary winding up, the resolution is followed by a creditors' meeting where it is possible for a liquidation committee to be appointed. Such meetings form no part of a members' voluntary winding up.

Test your understanding 3

The Insolvency Act 1986 governs situations where, in the course of a winding up, it appears that the business of a company has been carried on with intent to defraud creditors, or for any fraudulent purpose.

In such cases, the court, may declare that any persons who were knowingly parties to such carrying on of the business are liable to make such contributions (if any) to the company's assets as the court thinks proper. There is a high burden of proof involved in proving dishonesty on the part of the person against whom it is alleged.

It should be noted that there is also a criminal offence of fraudulent trading under the Companies Act 2006, which applies to anyone who has been party to the carrying on of the business of a company with intent to defraud creditors or any other person, or for any other fraudulent purpose.

Given that it is stated that Rosie hid the fact that Wag Ltd was insolvent it is possible that she might be liable under the fraudulent trading provisions both civil and criminal. As a consequence she may well be liable for a maximum prison sentence of 10 years and may have to contribute to the assets of the company to cover any loss sustained by creditors as a result of her actions.

There is no evidence to support either action against Poppy.

Wrongful trading does not involve dishonesty but it still makes particular individuals potentially liable for the debts of their companies. Where a company is being wound up and it appears that, at some time before the start of the winding up, a director knew, or ought to have known, that there was no reasonable chance of the company avoiding insolvent liquidation, they would be guilty of wrongful trading.

UK syllabus only: Auditing aspects of insolvency

> In such circumstances, then, unless the directors took every reasonable step to minimise the potential loss to the company's creditors, they may be liable to contribute such money to the assets of the company as the court thinks proper.
>
> It is clearly apparent that Rosie will be personally liable under s.214 for the increase in Wag Ltd's debts from £15,000 to £75,000. However, as a director of the company Poppy will also be liable to contribute to the assets of the company under s.214.

chapter 20

Financial reporting revision

Chapter learning objectives

This chapter is designed to assist you with revision of key financial reporting topics. Given the inter-relationship between financial reporting and auditing it is inevitable that the auditing exam will encompass many aspects of financial reporting that you have encountered in previous studies.

For further clarification with regard to the importance of financial reporting standards please refer to Lisa Weaver's article entitled "The Importance of Financial Reporting Standards to Auditors" (Nov 2008).

This can be found on the P7 section of the ACCA website.

Financial reporting revision

IAS 1 Presentation of financial statements

IAS 1 provides standard formats for the statement of profit or loss and other comprehensive income, statement of financial position, statement of cash flows and statement of changes in equity as well as setting out six overall accounting principles that should be applied:

- going concern
- accruals
- consistency of presentation
- materiality and aggregation
- offsetting
- comparative information.

Accounting policies should be selected so that the financial statements comply with all international standards and interpretations.

An entity must make an explicit statement in the notes to the accounts that the financial statements comply with IFRS.

IAS 1 also requires classification of items of other comprehensive income between those which:

- will not be reclassified to profit or loss; and
- which may be reclassified to profit or loss in future reporting periods.

IAS 2 Inventories

IAS 2 Inventory valuation requires that inventories should be valued at the lower of cost and net realisable value.

At this level, the examiner might be more interested in your ability to determine cost in a complex case than to be able to describe the rules.

Cost includes all of the costs associated with bringing items of inventory to their present condition and location.

Cost includes:

- purchase price including import duties, transport and handling costs
- any other directly attributable costs, less
- trade discounts, rebates and subsidies

- costs which are specifically attributable to units of production, e.g. direct labour,
- direct expenses and subcontracted work
- production overheads (which must be based on the normal level of activity)
- other overheads, if any, attributable in the particular circumstances of the business to bringing the product or service to its present location and condition.

Cost excludes:

- abnormal waste
- storage costs
- administrative overheads which do not contribute to bringing inventories to their present location and condition
- selling costs.

Some entities can identify individual units of inventory (e.g. vehicles can be identified by a chassis number). Those that cannot should keep track of costs using either the first in, first out (FIFO) or the weighted average cost (AVCO) assumption.

Some entities may use standard costing for valuing inventory. IAS 2 permits the use of standard cost for convenience, where it is a close approximation to actual cost, and is regularly reviewed and revised in the light of current conditions.

The main disclosure requirements of IAS 2 are:

- accounting policy adopted, including the:
    - cost formula used
    - total carrying amount, classified appropriately
    - amount of inventories carried at NRV
    - amount of inventories recognised as an expense during the period
    - details of any circumstances that have led to the write-down of inventories to their NRV.

IAS 7 Statement of cash flows

The statement of cash flows provides an important insight into the ways in which the entity has created and applied cash during the period. The fact that a business generated profit during a period means that it has created wealth, but wealth is not necessarily reflected by cash. The fact that a business is liquid according to the statement of financial position at the year-end does not say a great deal about the cash movements that occurred during the year.

IAS 7 requires the provision of a statement of cash flows that classifies cash flows into:

- operating activities
- investing activities
- financing activities

This approach to calculating cash generated from operations is known as the "indirect method". It starts with profit before tax from the statement of profit or loss and:

- adjusts for interest to get back to profit from operations
- adjusts for non-cash items such as depreciation
- adjusts for increases and decreases in working capital.

It is possible to get the same result by means of the 'direct method', which states the actual cash flows associated with operations:

- cash received from customers
- cash paid to suppliers
- cash paid for expenses
- cash paid for wages and salaries.

This approach works equally well to the other operating figures.

The balancing figure approach can also be invaluable in obtaining figures for any of the other cash flows under other headings (transactions involving non-current assets, tax paid, etc).

Interpreting statements of cash flow

The statement of cash flows is a vital supplement to the other financial statements.

Arguably, there is no point in a business existing if it cannot produce an adequate profit. However, cash can be more important in the short term because a business that runs short of cash could fail even if it has the capacity to generate profits and even return to a cash surplus in the longer term.

The statement provides another dimension to the liquidity position spelt out in the statement of financial position.

IAS 8 Accounting policies, changes in ....

.... accounting estimates and errors.

IAS 8 is an important standard because it clarifies the accounting treatment of a variety of accounting issues, including:

- selection of accounting policies
- changes in accounting policies
- changes in accounting estimates
- correction of prior period errors.

Accounting policies

Accounting policies are the principles, bases, conventions, rules and practices applied by an entity which specify how the effects of transactions and other events are reflected in the financial statements.

IAS 8 requires an enterprise to select and apply appropriate accounting policies complying with International Financial Reporting Standards (IFRSs) and Interpretations to ensure that the financial statements provide information that is:

- relevant to the decision-making needs of users

- reliable in that they:
  - represent faithfully the results and financial position of the enterprise
  - reflect the economic substance of events and transactions and not merely the legal form
  - are neutral, i.e. free from bias
  - are prudent
  - are complete in all material respects.

Changes in accounting policies

Changes in accounting policies are rare. However, on occasions changes in policy are enforced due to changes/updates to financial reporting standards or if it results in the financial statements providing reliable and more relevant information. It can be difficult to introduce these into a question. Take care not to treat a simple change in an estimate as a rather more complicated change in accounting policy.

Accounting policies should remain the same from period to period in order to allow for consistency of treatment.

In order to preserve the appearance of consistency, a change in accounting policies is accounted for as follows: the new policy will be applied retrospectively, with the opening balance on retained earnings recalculated on the basis that the new policy had always been in force the resulting change in the retained earnings brought forward will be shown as a prior period adjustment in the statement of changes in equity comparatives will be restated as if the new policy had been in force during the previous period.

The change and its effects must be described in the notes to the accounts.

Accounting estimates

Many of the figures in the financial statements rely on estimates.

Inevitably, some estimates will be revised in the light of unfolding events and new information. For example, a change in the method of charging depreciation, e.g. from reducing balance to straight line method is a change of estimate.

Changes in accounting estimates are recognised in the statement of profit or loss in the same period as the change occurs and included under the same classification as for the original asset. If the change is material then it should be disclosed in the notes to the financial statements.

Prior period errors

Prior period errors are omissions from, and misstatements in, the financial statements for one or more prior periods arising from a failure to use, or misuse of, reliable information. The errors must be ones that were reasonably identifiable when the financial statements were authorised for issue.

Prior period errors are dealt with by:

- restating the opening balance of assets, liabilities and equity as if the error had never occurred, and presenting the necessary adjustment to the opening balance of retained earnings in the statement of changes in equity
- restating the comparative figures presented, as if the error had never occurred.

These adjustments should be disclosed in full in the notes to the accounts.

IAS 10 Events after the reporting period

- Events after the reporting period are those events, favourable and unfavourable, that occur between the statement of financial position date and the date when the financial statements are authorised for issue.
- Adjusting events after the reporting period are those that provide evidence of conditions that existed at the statement of financial position date.
- Non-adjusting events after the reporting period are those that are indicative of conditions that arose after the reporting period.

Accounting treatment

- Adjusting events affect the amounts stated in the financial statements so they must be adjusted.
- Non-adjusting events do not concern the position at the statement of financial position date so the accounts are not adjusted. If the event is material then the nature and its financial effect must be disclosed.

Examples of adjusting events

- The sale of inventory after the date which gives evidence about the inventory's net realisable value at the reporting date.
- The bankruptcy of a customer after the date that confirms that a provision is required against a receivable balance at the reporting date.
- The discovery of fraud or errors that show that the financial statements are incorrect.
- The settlement after the reporting period of a court case that confirms that the entity had a present obligation at the statement of financial position date. This would require a provision to be recognised in the financial statements (or an existing provision to be adjusted).

Examples of non-adjusting events that would require disclosure

- A major business combination after the date or disposing of a major subsidiary.
- Announcing a plan to discontinue an operation.
- Major purchases and disposals of assets.
- Destruction of a major production plant by a fire after the reporting date.
- Announcing or commencing a major restructuring.
- Abnormally large changes after the reporting date in asset prices or foreign exchange rates.

Dividends

- Ordinary dividends declared after the date are not recognised as liabilities at the reporting date.
- If the liability did not exist at the reporting date, then it cannot be recognised.
- This is consistent with IAS 37 and the definition of a liability in the Framework.

IAS 11 Construction contracts

IAS 11 Construction contracts deals with the recognition of revenues and balances associated with long-term projects carried out for clients.

The logic behind IAS 11 is that long term contracts are deemed to be "sold" to clients throughout the course of each contract.

If, say, 75% of a potentially profitable contract has been completed to date then 75% of the profit anticipated on that contract should have been recognised during the statement(s) of profit or loss covering the period(s) since work on the contract commenced.

Cumulative revenues and costs that have already been recognised are deducted from the total as at the year end to give the revenue and cost for the year.

Any expected losses on contracts should be recognised as expenses immediately.

Contract revenue comprises:

- the initial revenue agreed with the client.
- any additional variations or claims that are probably going to result in revenue and that can be measured reliably.

Contract costs comprise:

- costs that relate directly to the specific contract;
- costs that are attributable to contract activity in general and can be allocated to the contract; and
- such other costs as are specifically chargeable to the customer under the terms of the contract.

Costs that relate directly to a specific contract include (amongst other things), the estimated costs of rectification and guarantee work, included expected warranty costs.

The statement of financial position will include the gross amount due from/to customers as an asset/ liability. This can be determined as:

	$
Costs incurred	X
Add: recognised profit	X
Less: recognised losses	(X)
Less: progress billings	(X)
Gross amount due to/from customers	X

Any unpaid progress billings will be treated as trade receivables.

IAS 12 Income taxes

- IAS 12 covers both current and deferred tax, but deferred tax is the most examinable and will be reviewed here.
- Temporary differences are differences between the carrying amount of an asset or liability in the statement of financial position and its tax base.
- Tax base is the amount attributed to an asset or liability for tax purposes.

Temporary differences can be either:

(i) taxable temporary differences, when the carrying amount of an asset exceeds its tax base and deferred tax must be provided for - a deferred tax liability is created.

(ii) deductible temporary differences, when the tax base of an asset exceeds the carrying value of that asset - a deferred tax asset is created.

Sources of taxable temporary differences.

- Depreciation of an asset is accelerated for tax purposes.
- Development costs that were capitalised and amortised in the accounts, but deducted as incurred for tax purposes.

- Losses in the statement of profit or loss where tax relief is only available against future profits.
- Intra-group profits in inventory that are unrealised for consolidation purposes but taxable in the individual company that made the unrealised profit.
- A revaluation surplus on non-current assets as the carrying value of the asset increases but the tax base of the asset has not changed. Deferred tax is provided on the revaluation.
- Interest revenue received in arrears, which is accounted for on an accruals basis in the statement of profit or loss but taxable on a cash basis.
- Short term timing differences where amounts are included in the statement of profit or loss on an accruals basis but only allowed for tax on a cash basis (e.g. royalty income or prepayments).

Sources of deductible temporary differences

- Accumulated depreciation of an asset in the statement of financial position is greater than the cumulative depreciation for tax purposes
- Pension liabilities that are recognised in the financial statements but only allowable for tax when the contributions are made to the scheme in the future
- Research expenses are recognised as an expense in determining accounting profit but not deductible for tax until a later period
- Income is deferred in the statement of financial position but has already been included in taxable profit.

Other points

- Unremitted earnings of group companies: a temporary difference arises when the carrying value of subsidiaries, associates and investments is different from the tax base. The accounting base for subsidiaries and associates will be based on net assets value, whilst the tax base will be cost of investment. A deferred tax liability should be recognised unless the investor can control the timing of the reversal of the temporary difference or it is probable that the temporary difference will not reverse. As an associate is not controlled, a deferred tax liability should be recognised. It would be unlikely that deferred tax would be recognised for a subsidiary. A trade investment would only give rise to deferred tax if it was revalued.
- Business combinations: temporary differences can arise on acquisition if assets or liabilities are increased to fair value but the tax base of the asset remains at cost. Deferred tax is recognised on these differences and is included as part of net assets acquired. The exception is for non tax-deductible goodwill.

Accounting treatment

- IAS 12 requires full provision for all taxable temporary differences (except for goodwill) using the statement of financial position liability method.

- Deferred tax assets can be recognised for all deductible temporary differences to the extent it is probable that taxable profits will be available for these differences to be utilised.

- IAS 12 does not permit the discounting of deferred tax liabilities.

- The charge for deferred tax is recognised in the statement of profit or loss unless it relates to a gain or loss that has been recognised in equity e.g. revaluations, in which case the related deferred tax is also recognised in equity.

- Deferred tax should be measured at the rates expected to be in force when the temporary differences reverse, although usually the current tax rate is used.

IAS 16 Property, plant and equipment

An asset's cost is its purchase price, less any trade discounts or rebates, plus any further costs directly attributable to bringing it into working condition for its intended use.

- IAS 23 Borrowing costs (revised 2007) requires finance costs to be capitalised providing they are directly attributable to the asset being constructed. Capitalisation commences when construction expenditure is being incurred and ceases when substantially all of the activities required to bring the asset into use have been completed.

- Subsequent expenditure on non current assets may be capitalised if it:
  - enhances the economic benefits of the asset e.g. adding an new wing to a building
  - replaces part of an asset that has been separately depreciated and has been fully depreciated; e.g. furnace that requires new linings periodically
  - replaces economic benefits previously consumed, e.g. a major inspection of aircraft.

- The aim of depreciation is to spread the cost of the asset over its life in the business.

- The depreciation method and useful life of an asset should be reviewed at the end of each year and revised where necessary in accordance with IAS 8. This is not a change in accounting policy, but a change of accounting estimate.
- If an asset has parts with different lives, (e.g. a building with a flat roof), the component parts of the asset should be capitalised and depreciated separately. It is not acceptable to provide for the cost of replacing the asset.

Revaluation of tangible non-current assets

- Revaluation of non-current assets is optional.
- If one asset is revalued, all assets in that class must be revalued, i.e. no cherry-picking.
- Where an entity adopts a policy of revaluation it need not be applied to all classes of tangible non-current assets held by the entity
- Valuations should be kept up to date to ensure that the carrying amount does not differ materially from the fair value at each statement of financial position date.
- Revaluation gains are credited to the revaluation reserve in equity unless the gain reverses a previous revaluation loss of the same asset previously recognised in the statement of profit or loss.
- Revaluation losses are debited to the statement of profit or loss unless the loss relates to a previous revaluation surplus, in which case the decrease should be debited to the revaluation reserve to the extent of any credit balance existing in the revaluation reserve relating to that asset.

Accounting for revaluations

Steps:

(1) Restate asset from cost to valuation amount: Dr Non-current asset (valuation – cost)

(2) Remove any existing depreciation: Dr Accumulated depreciation provision

(3) Include increase in revaluation reserve: Cr Revaluation reserve (valuation – old carrying value)

Depreciation is charged on the revalued amount less residual value (if any) over the **remaining useful life** of the asset.

An entity may choose to make an annual transfer of excess depreciation from revaluation reserve to retained earinings. If this is done, it should be applied consistently each year.

Note that assets **held for sale** are recognised at fair value less costs to sell in accordance with IFRS 5.

IAS 17 Leases

IAS 17 Leases deals with a complicated area that was frequently used to disguise liabilities in the statement of financial position.

The point of IAS 17 is to identify those leases that are effectively financial instruments used to acquire substantially all of the rights and benefits associated with a particular asset. These are then classified as liabilities in the statement of financial position.

Not all leases have to be treated in this way. Some leases do not give the lessee substantially all of the rights and benefits of ownership (e.g. when a business hires a van for a week).

A **finance lease** is a lease that transfers substantially all the risks and rewards incidental to ownership of an asset to the lessee.

An **operating lease** is any lease other than a finance lease.

Questions incorporating leases will ask you to explain why a particular agreement should be treated as a finance lease or an operating lease.

The question will imply one or the other in terms of whether the lessee has the risks and rewards of ownership.

In general, a lease is a finance lease if:

- the leased asset is likely to become the property of the lessee at the end of the agreement (either automatically or because there is an option that is likely to be exercised)
- the lease (including any secondary term that is likely to be taken up) is likely to run for most of the asset's useful life
- the present value of the minimum lease payments is close to the fair value of the asset at the commencement of the lease
- the asset is of a specialised nature that makes it particularly suited to the lessee.

This list is not intended to be exhaustive.

Substance over form

The treatment required by IAS 17 effectively accounts for the economic substance of finance leases rather than their legal form.

The economic substance is that the lessee has borrowed an amount equivalent to the fair value of the asset and used that sum to purchase the asset itself. The fact that the lessee may never become the legal owner of the asset is ignored.

Accounting for finance leases

At the start of the lease:

- the fair value (or, if lower, the present value of the minimum lease payments) should be included as a non-current asset, subject to depreciation
- the same amount (being the obligation to pay rentals) should be included as a loan, i.e. a liability.

In practice, the fair value of the asset or its cash price will often be a sufficiently close approximation to the present value of the minimum lease payments and therefore can be used instead.

The asset is depreciated over the shorter of the asset's useful life and the term of the lease (including any secondary term that is likely to be taken up).

Each lease payment is split between:

- a repayment of the lease liability
- a finance charge.

IAS 17 developments

In August 2010 the IASB published an exposure draft (ED) for a revised IAS 17, with a new approach to lease accounting. Following some extended deliberation, a revised IAS 17 was re-exposed in 2012.

The proposals remove the distinction between operating and finance leases, combatting 'off-balance sheet liabilities' arising through classification of a lease as an operating lease.

Instead, a 'right-of-use' model would be used, under which an asset would be recognised when an entity has the right to use it and a liability would be recognised for an entity's obligation to meet the lease payments.

IAS 18 Revenue recognition

Revenue is the gross inflow of economic benefits during the period arising from the ordinary activities of the entity.

The standard relates to revenue arising from:

(i) the sale of goods;
(ii) the rendering of services; and
(iii) the use by others of entity assets yielding interest, royalties and dividends.

The primary issue is determining when to recognise revenue. Revenue is recognised when:

– it is probable that future economic benefits will flow to the entity; and
– these benefits can be measured reliably.

It may be necessary to apply the recognition criteria to the separately identifiable components of a single transaction, to two or more transactions together, or (more normally) to a single transaction in its entirety.

Recognition

In addition to the recognition criteria described above:

- Revenue from the sale of goods can be recognised when the seller transfers the risks and rewards of ownership to the buyer.

- Revenue from the rendering of services is recognised by reference to the stage of completion at the statement of financial position date. When the outcome of the transaction cannot be estimated reliably, revenue shall be recognised only to the extent of the expenses recognised that are recoverable.

- In both cases above, the amount of revenue and costs incurred must able to be measured reliably.

- Revenue from interest, royalties and dividends should be recognised, as follows:
    - interest is recognised using the effective interest method;
    - royalties are accrued in accordance with the relevant contract;
    - dividends are recognised when the shareholders right to receive payment is established.

Measurement

- Revenue should be measured at the fair value of consideration received or receivable. Fair value is the amount for which an asset could be exchanged, or liability settled between knowledgeable parties on an arm's length basis.
- In most cases this will be the amount agreed between the two parties as the price, adjusted for discounts if necessary.

If the time value of money is material, then the revenue should be discounted to present value and the unwinding of the discount treated as interest income in the statement of profit or loss. In this case, there are effectively two transactions – the sale of the goods and the provision of finance.

IAS 19 Employee benefits (revised)

Standards covering more complex accounting issues such as IAS 19 (and for example, IFRS 2, IFRS 8 etc.) are likely to be examined in P7.

IAS 19 (revised) deals with accounting for pensions and other employee benefits in the employer's accounts.

- The accounting issues lie with defined benefit schemes where an employer guarantees that an employee will have a specific pension on retirement, usually a percentage of final salary.
- To estimate the fund required, an actuary will have to calculate the contributions required to ensure the scheme has enough funds to pay out its liabilities.
- This involves estimating what may happen in the future, such as the age profile of employees, retirement age etc.
- A pension scheme consists of a pool of assets (cash, investments, shares etc) and a liability for pensions owed to employees when they are at retirement age. The assets are used to pay out the pensions.

Measurement and recognition

Profit or loss	Other comprehensive income	Statement of Financial Position
Service cost components: current and past service costs, including any gains or losses arising on curtailments and settlements	Remeasurement component	Net scheme asset or liability, where assets are measured at fair value and liabilities measured at present value
Net interest component	Remeasurement component: actuarial gains and losses on scheme assets and liabilities, plus any income, gains etc. not taken to profit or loss as part of the net interest component.	

Definitions

- **Current service cost** is the increase in the actuarial liability (present value of the defined benefit obligation) resulting from employee service in the current period. This is part of the service cost component.

- **Past service cost** is the increase in the actuarial liability relating to employee service in previous periods but only arising in the current period. Past service costs usually arise because there has been an improvement in the benefits to be provided under the plan. This will apply whether or not the benefits have vested (i.e. whether or not employees are immediately entitled to those enhanced benefits), or whether they are obliged to provide additional work and service to become eligible for those enhanced benefits. In the revised standard, they are part of the service cost component and are now recognised when the plan amendments occur, rather than when vested.

- A **curtailment** occurs when an entity is demonstrably committed to making a material reduction in the number of employees covered by a plan, or amends the terms of a plan such that a material element of future service by current employees will qualify for no or reduced benefits. This may occur, for example if an entity closes a plant and makes those employees redundant. Any gain or loss on curtailment is part of the service cost component.

- A **settlement** occurs when an entity enters into a transaction to eliminate the obligation for part or all of the benefits under a plan. For example, an employee may leave the entity for a new job elsewhere, and a payment is made from that pension plan to the to the pension plan operated by the new employer. Any gain or loss on settlement is part of the service cost component.

- **Net interest** is computed by applying the discount rate to the net liability (or asset) at the start of the reporting period. This is charged (or credited) to profit or loss for the year. This is a separate component included in profit or loss for the year. Net interest expense (or income) is determined by applying the discount rate used to measure the defined benefit obligation, irrespective of whether the is a net interest expense or net interest income.

- **Remeasurement component** comprises actuarial gains and losses arising during the reporting period, including the actual returns on plan assets less any amount taken to profit or loss as part of the net interest component. Actuarial gains and losses are increases and decreases in the pension asset or liability that occur either because the actuarial assumptions have changed or because of differences between the previous actuarial assumptions and what has actually happened (experience adjustments). This component is recognised in Other Comprehensive Income for the year and is not recycled to profit or loss.

IAS 20 Accounting for government grants and disclosure of ....

Government grants are assistance by government in the form of transfers of resources to an entity in return for past or future compliance with certain conditions.

Government assistance is action by government designed to provide economic benefit to a specific entity.

Government grants exclude:

1. assistance which cannot reasonably have a value placed upon it; and
2. normal trading transactions of the entity.

Accounting treatment

Grants shall not be recognised until there is reasonable assurance that:

(i) the conditions attached to the grant will be complied with; and

(ii) the grant will be received.

- Grants shall be recognised in the statement of profit or loss so as to match them with the expenditure towards which they are intended to contribute.
  - Income grants given to subsidise expenditure should be matched to the related costs.
  - Income grants given to help achieve a non-financial goal (such as job creation) should be matched to the costs incurred to meet that goal.
- Grants which contribute towards past expenditure, with no related future costs, shall be recognised immediately in the period in which they are received.
- Grants related to income should be presented separately in the statement of profit or loss, or under a general heading, or alternatively deducted from the related expense.
- Grants for purchases of non-current assets should be recognised over the expected useful lives of the related assets.

There are two acceptable accounting treatments for grants related to non-current assets:

- deduct the grant from the cost of the asset and depreciate the net cost; or
- treat the grant as deferred income. Release the grant to the statement of profit or loss over the life of the asset. This is the method most commonly used.

Grants that become repayable

A government grant that becomes repayable shall be accounted for as a change in accounting estimate.

Disclosure

The following matters should be disclosed:

- the accounting policy adopted;
- the nature and extend of government grants recognised;
- unfulfilled conditions attaching to government grants.

chapter 20

IAS 21 The effects of changes in foreign exchange rates

Provides the accounting guidance on foreign currency transactions.

The main points are summarised below:

Functional and presentation currencies

A company must determine both its functional and presentation currency. Presentation currency is the currency in which the entity presents its financial statements.

In determining **functional currency**, the following must be considered.

- The currency that mainly influences sales prices for goods and services.
- The currency of the country whose competitive forces and regulations mainly determine the sales price of goods and services.
- The currency that mainly influences labour, material and other costs of providing goods and services.

If the company is a foreign owned subsidiary, the following must be considered to determine whether it is has the same functional currency as the parent.

- Whether the activities of the foreign operation are carried out as an extension of the parent, rather than with a significant degree of autonomy.
- Whether transactions with the parent are a high or low proportion of the of the foreign operation's activities.
- Whether cash flows from the foreign operation directly affect the cash flows of the parent and are readily available for remittance to it.
- Whether cash flows from the activities of the foreign operation are sufficient to service existing debt obligations without funds being made available by the parent.

Once determined, functional currency should not be changed.

Presentation currency can be any currency and can be different from functional currency.

This is particularly the case if the company is foreign-controlled as the presentation currency may be that of the parent. If the presentation currency is different from the functional currency, then the financial statements must be translated into the presentation currency.

Individual transactions in foreign currency

If a company enters into **foreign currency transactions** the results of these transactions should be translated and recorded in the accounting records in the functional currency:

- at the rate on the date the transaction occurred; or
- using an average rate over a period of time providing the exchange rate has not fluctuated significantly.

At subsequent statement of financial position dates, the following process must be applied.

- At subsequent statement of financial position dates, the following foreign currency monetary items (receivables, payables, cash, loans) must be translated using the closing rate.
- The closing rate is the exchange rate at the statement of financial position date.
- Foreign currency non-monetary items (non-current assets, investments, inventory) are not retranslated. They are left at the exchange rate that was used at the date of the transaction (called the historic rate).
- Exchange differences on settlement of monetary items or on retranslating monetary items are recognised in the statement of profit or loss.

Hedging loans

It is not unusual for entities making overseas equity investments to raise the funds locally, in an overseas currency. Such a loan is known as a hedging loan as it will **hedge** against foreign currency movements.

- The investing entity holds both an asset (the investment) and a liability (the loan) denominated in foreign currency. As the exchange rate moves, so the values of the asset and liability will move.
- If the functional currency value of the loan increases, this exchange loss is set off by an increase in the functional currency value of the asset (and so an exchange gain).

The hedging provisions of IAS 39 state that the exchange differences arising on a foreign currency hedge of an entity's investment in a foreign entity should be recognised directly in equity until such time as the investment is sold. At that stage they should be recognised in the statement of profit or loss alongside any gain or loss on disposal of the investment.

Example

USCO holds:

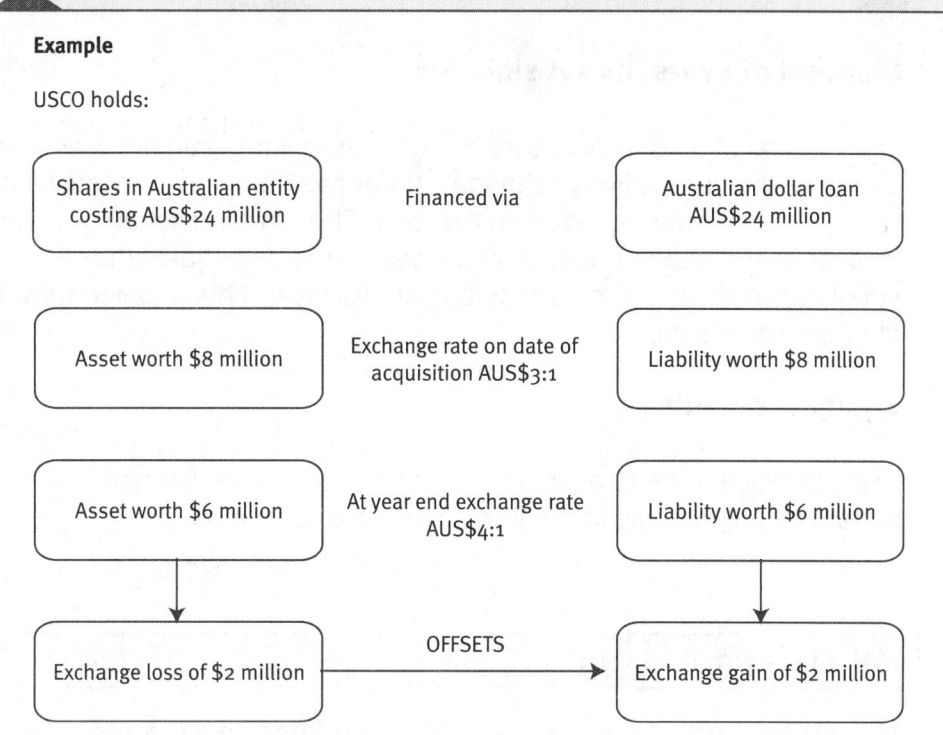

Foreign subsidiaries

If a company has foreign subsidiaries whose functional currency is their local currency, their financial statements must be translated into the parent's presentation currency.

- All assets and liabilities are translated into the parent's presentation currency at the closing rate at the statement of financial position date.

- Goodwill is calculated in the functional currency of the subsidiary, and translated at each reporting date at the closing rate into the presentation currency of the parent.

- Income and expenses in the statement of profit or loss must be translated at the average rate for the period.

- Exchange differences arising on consolidation are recognised in equity until disposal of the subsidiary when they are part of the gain or loss on disposal reported in profit or loss for the year.

- Exchange differences arise from:
    - the retranslation of the opening net assets using the closing rate
    - retranslation of the profit for the year from the average rate (used in the statement of profit or loss) to the closing rate (for inclusion in the statement of financial position).

Disposal of overseas subsidiaries

On disposal of a subsidiary that has been translated into presentational currency, the cumulative exchange differences that have previously been recognised in reserves become realised. The foreign exchange reserve is taken to the statement of profit or loss on the disposal of the subsidiary as part of the gain or loss on disposal. This is called recycling of gains and losses.

Equity accounting

The principles to be used in translating a subsidiary's financial statements also apply to the translation of an associate's.

IAS 23 Borrowing costs

IAS 23 Borrowing costs (revised 2007) requires finance costs to be capitalised providing they are directly attributable to the asset being constructed. Capitalisation commences when construction expenditure is being incurred and ceases when the asset is ready for.

The examiner might expect you to offer opinions or justifications for the accounting treatment required by particular IASs or IFRSs.

It might make sense to capitalise interest associated with the construction of a building (or any other asset that takes a long time to get ready). Arguably, the borrowing costs could be seen as part of the cost in exactly the same way as the cost of the materials or labour applied.

On the other hand, it might be difficult to identify the actual costs of borrowing associated with this asset (unless the company took out a loan that was specifically for this purpose). It can also lead to inconsistencies (such as two identical buildings having different carrying values because one was financed with debt and the other with equity).

If you do have to justify the treatment adopted by a standard then think about its impact on the financial statements.

- Will it increase reported profit?
- What will it do to the statement of financial position?
- Is it more relevant and reliable to users?

Borrowing costs incurred after the asset has been completed or while work is suspended must be written off as revenue expenditure.

Capitalised borrowing costs are those actually incurred, although this may be estimated if the entity is financing the cost out of general borrowings.

The disclosures required by IAS 23 are:

- the accounting policy adopted for borrowing costs
- the amount of borrowing costs
- capitalised during the period
- the capitalisation rate used

IAS 24 Related party disclosures

A party is related to an entity if:

(a) directly or indirectly through one or more intermediaries, the party
  (i) controls, is controlled by, or is under common control with the entity
  (ii) has an interest in the entity that gives it significant influence over the entity
  (iii) has joint control over the entity.

(b) the party is an associate of the entity (as defined in IAS 28 Associates)

(c) the party is a joint venture in which the entity is a venturer

(d) the party is a member of the key management personnel of the entity or its parent

(e) the party is a close member of the family of any individual referred to in (a) or (d)

(f) the party is an entity that is controlled, jointly controlled or significantly influenced by, or for which significant voting power in such an entity resides with, directly or indirectly, any individual referred to in (d) or (e)

(g) the party is a post-employment benefit plan for the benefit of employees of the entity, or of any entity that is a related party of the entity.

Financial reporting revision

A related party transaction is the transfer of resources, services or obligations between related parties regardless of whether a price is charged.

Disclosures

- Relationships between parents and subsidiaries irrespective of whether there have been transactions between the parties.
- The name of the parent and the ultimate controlling party (if different).
- Key management personnel compensation in total and for each short term employee benefits, post employment benefits, other long term benefits, termination benefits and share based payment.
- For related party transactions that have occurred, the nature of the relationship and detail of the transactions and outstanding balances.
- The disclosure should be made for each category of related parties (a) to (g)
- above) and include:
  (a) the amount of the transactions
  (b) the amount of outstanding balances and their terms
  (c) allowances for doubtful debts relating to the outstanding balances
  (d) the expense recognised in the period in respect of irrecoverable or doubtful debts due from related parties.

IAS 27 Separate financial statements (revised)

IAS 27 (revised) applies when an entity has interests in subsidiaries, joint ventures or associates and either elects to, or is required to, prepare separate **non-consolidated financial statements**.

If the financial statements are not consolidated, they must therefore present interests in other entities at cost or in accordance with IFRS 9 Financial Instruments.

IAS 28 Investments in associates and joint ventures (revised)

A **joint venture** is a joint arrangement whereby the parties have joint control of the arrangement and have rights to the net assets of the arrangement. This will normally be established in the form of a separate entity to conduct the joint venture activities (IFRS 11).

An **associate** is an entity over which the investor has significant influence and that is neither a subsidiary nor an interest in a joint venture.

Significant influence is the power to participate in the financial and operating policy decisions of the investee but is not control or joint control over those policies.

The definition of significant influence is very broad. You may have to read the question very carefully in order to decide whether an investment creates should be recognised as either an associate or as a joint venture.

It is normally assumed that significant influence exists if the holding company has a shareholding of 20% to 50%. That does not, however, guarantee that the investing entity has any real influence. For example, a 40% shareholding might actually offer very little real influence if the remaining 60% is in the hands of a controlling investor.

Equity accounting

In the consolidated financial statements of a group:

- Acquisition accounting is used to account for subsidiaries.
- Equity accounting is used to account for associates and joint ventures.

Unlike acquisition accounting, which combined the holding company's figures with those of the subsidiary or subsidiaries, equity accounting involves single figure adjustments to the consolidated statement of profit or loss and the consolidated statement of financial position.

An interest in an associate or joint venture should be accounted for in the separate financial statements of an entity in accordance with accordance with IAS 27 (Revised).

Statement of financial position

The consolidated statement of profit or loss and other comprehensive income includes the **investor's share** of the associate or joint venture's results.

The consolidated statement of financial position includes the **investor's share** of the associate or joint venture's net assets.

The investing entity is not required to produce consolidated statements unless it has at least one subsidiary. Associates and joint ventures are accounted for using equity accounting within the consolidated financial statements, but the existence of an associate or joint venture does not, in itself, require the preparation of group accounts.

Consolidated

The initial investment in the associate or joint venture is shown at cost.

The carrying amount is then adjusted to include the group share of any profits arising post-acquisition, less any impairment of the investment.

Sundry points

The accounting treatment of associates and joint ventures has some similarities to accounting for subsidiaries, but there are also some significant differences.

Associates and joint ventures are not members of the group in the same way that subsidiaries are; they are not under common control.

Always remember that subsidiaries are controlled by the holding company, whereas associates are subject to no more than significant interest, and joint ventures subject to joint control.

Fair values

If the fair value of the associate or joint venture's net assets at acquisition are materially different from their book value the net assets should be adjusted in the same way as for a subsidiary.

Balances with the associate

Generally the associate or joint venture is considered to be outside the group. Therefore balances between group companies and the associate or joint venture will remain in the consolidated statement of financial position.

If a group company trades with the associate or joint venture, the resulting payables and receivables will remain in the consolidated statement of financial position.

Sales to and from associates

Sales between group members and associates or joint ventures are left in the consolidated statement of profit or loss. The only adjustments are in respect of any closing inventory that remains from such transactions.

Unrealised profit in inventory

The group share of unrealised profit in closing inventory arising from sales between group members and associates or joint ventures should still be cancelled.

If the sale was made to the associate then the amount of the unrealised profit should be added back to group cost of sales.

If the sale was made by the associate or joint venture then it would be more appropriate to deduct the unrealised profit from the group's share of the associate's profit. However, it would be acceptable to make the adjustment to the group cost of sales for the sake of simplicity.

Dividends from associates

Dividends from associates and joint ventures are not included in the consolidated statement of profit or loss. This is because the dividend is effectively being paid out of the group's share of the associate or joint venture's profit, which has already been recognised in the group accounts.

IAS 32 Financial instruments: Disclosure and presentation

IAS 32 Financial Instruments: Presentation classifies financial instruments as debt or equity according to the substance of the contractual arrangement.

It does not matter whether a financial instrument is called a 'share' or 'equity'. IAS 32 might still classify it as a liability if it has the characteristics of debt.

A financial instrument is classified as **debt** if the issuer has a contractual obligation either to deliver cash or another financial asset to the holder or to exchange another financial asset/liability with the holder under conditions that are potentially unfavourable to the issuer.

A financial instrument is classified as **equity** if it does not give rise to such a contractual obligation.

For example, preference shares:

- are classified as equity if they are irredeemable
- are classified as debt if they are redeemable.

Compound instruments

A compound instrument is one which has both a liability and an equity component.

For example, a convertible bond pays interest for the first part of its life, until it is redeemed or converted into ordinary share capital. The interest paid during the debt phase is usually lower than the rate offered on equivalent debt capital that does not carry conversion rights.

Compound instruments must be broken down between their liability element and equity element and each is shown in the appropriate part of the statement of financial position. This is usually accomplished by subtracting the net present value of the cash payments associated with the debt element from the fair value of the proceeds of issuing the instrument. That remainder is the equity element.

IAS 33 Earnings per share

- Earnings per share is an important ratio that is used as a comparison for company performance and forms part of the Price / Earnings ratio.
- IAS 33 applies to all listed companies. Private companies must follow the standard if they disclose an EPS figure.

Basic earnings per share is:

$$\frac{\text{Profit or loss for the period attributable to the equity shareholders}}{\text{Weighted average number of equity shares outstanding in the period}}$$

- Basic earnings are profit after tax less non-controlling investment and preference dividends.
- Weighted average number of equity shares must take into account when the shares were issued in the year.
- Partly paid shares are treated as a fraction of an equity share to the extent that they were entitled to participate in dividends relative to a fully paid share.

Changes in share capital

- Issue at full market price – as this share issue will bring cash into the business and increase earnings from the date the shares were issued, the weighted average number of shares must be calculated to ensure that the increase in earnings is matched with the increase in shares.

- Bonus issue – as there is no cash received; there is no effect on earnings.

- Therefore a bonus issue reduces EPS as share capital increases but earnings do not. The bonus issue is treated as if it has always been in issue, so share capital is adjusted at the beginning of the year and the comparative figures are adjusted for the effect of the bonus issue for comparability.

- Rights issue – the rights issue will bring cash into the business but not full price per share as the shares are issued below full market price. This share issue is treated as a combination of a bonus issue and a rights issue. Firstly, the bonus element must be dealt with by adjusting the opening capital by the rights issue bonus fraction:

$$\frac{\text{Fair value of share before exercise of rights}}{\text{Theoretical ex rights price}}$$

The theoretical ex rights price is the average price of the shares after the rights issue has taken place.

Secondly, the weighted average no of shares is calculated by time apportioning the shares according to the date of issue to match the increase in earnings with the increase in shares.

As there is a bonus element with a rights issue, the comparative must be adjusted.

Diluted earnings per share

- IAS 33 requires diluted earnings per share to be disclosed as well as basic EPS

- Diluted EPS shows the effect on the current EPS if all the potential equity shares had been issued under the greatest possible dilution.

- Potential equity shares consist of:
  - convertible loan stock
  - convertible preference shares
  - share warrants and options
  - partly paid shares
  - rights granted under employee share schemes
  - rights to equity shares that are conditional.
- The profit used in the basic EPS calculation is adjusted for any expenses that would no longer be paid if the convertible instrument was converted into shares, e.g. preference dividends, loan interest.
- The weighted average number of shares used in the basic EPS calculation is adjusted for the conversion of the potential equity shares. This deemed to occur at the beginning of the period or the date of issue if they were not in existence at the beginning of the period.

Other DEPS considerations

- Options and warrants are included in the DEPS calculation by calculating the number of shares that were issued for no consideration, i.e. the bonus element. Calculate the number of shares that would be issued if the cash has been used to buy shares at the fair value in the period. The remainder of the shares are treated like a bonus issue (i.e. for no consideration) and are included in the DEPS calculation.
- If there is more than one source of potential equity shares, then the DEPS calculation must be done in two stages as only potential equity shares that are dilutive can be included in the DEPS calculation. Firstly, calculate earnings per incremental share and then rank each potential share with the most dilutive being first. Secondly, starting with basic EPS, add in each potential share, with the most dilutive being added in first, giving a DEPS figure calculated in stages. DEPS is the most diluted figure – any potential share that increases EPS must be ignored as it is anti-dilutive.

Disclosure of EPS

- Basic and diluted earnings per share for continuing operations should be presented on the face of the statement of profit or loss for each class of equity share.
- Basic and diluted earnings per share for discontinued operations should be presented on the face of the statement of profit or loss or in the notes to the accounts for each class of equity share.

- If a company discloses an EPS using a different earnings figure, the alternative calculation must show basic and diluted EPS with equal prominence.

These alternative calculations must be presented in the notes to the financial statements, not on the face of the statement of profit or loss.

IAS 36 Impairment of assets

An impairment loss is the amount by which the carrying amount of an asset or cash generating unit exceeds its recoverable amount.

- Impairment is measured by comparing the carrying value of an asset with its recoverable amount.
- If the carrying value exceeds the recoverable amount, the asset is impaired and must be written down.

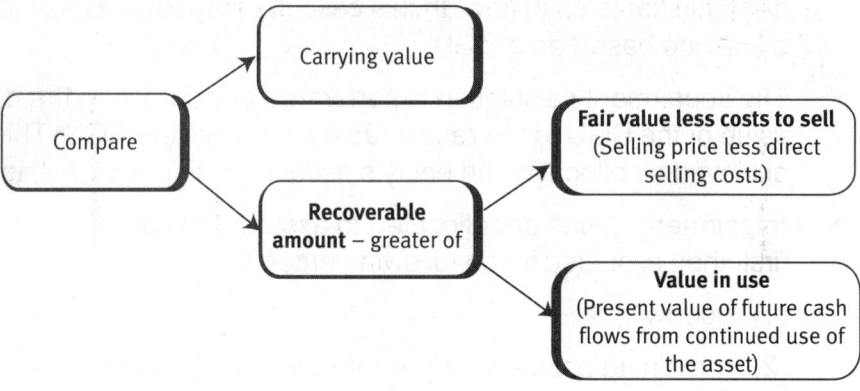

Indicators of impairment

Unless an impairment review is required by another standard (e.g. IAS 38 for intangible assets not amortised or IFRS 3 for purchased goodwill), then impairment reviews are required where there is an indicator for impairment.

Examples

Internal

- Physical damage to the asset.
- Management committed to reorganisation of the business.
- Obsolete assets.
- Idle assets.
- Major loss of key employees.

- Operating losses in the business where the assets are used.

External

- Competitor actions.
- Increasing interest rates (affect value in use).
- Market values of assets falling.
- Change in the business or market where assets are used (e.g. govt action).

Cash-generating units (CGU)

A **cash-generating unit** is the smallest identifiable group of assets that generates external cash inflows from use of those assets.

- It will not always be possible to base the impairment review on individual assets as an individual asset may not generate a distinguishable cash flow. In this case the impairment calculations should be based on a CGU.
- The impairment calculation is performed by comparing the carrying value of the CGU to the recoverable amount of the CGU. This is achieved by allocating an entity's asset including goodwill, to CGUs.
- Impairment losses are allocated to assets with specific impairments first, then allocated in the following order:
    (1) goodwill
    (2) remaining assets on a pro rata basis. No asset can be written down below the higher of fair value less costs to sell, value in use and zero.

Recognition of impairment losses

Assets held at cost: The amount of the impairment is charged to the statement of profit or loss for the period in which the impairment occurs.

Revalued assets: The impairment is charged first to the revaluation reserve to reverse any previous surplus on that asset in the same way as a downward revaluation. Any further impairment is charged to the statement of profit or loss and other comprehensive income.

chapter 20

IAS 37 Provisions, contingent liabilities and contingent assets

- A provision is a liability of uncertain timing or amount.
- A contingent liability is a possible obligation arising from past events whose existence will only be confirmed on the occurrence of uncertain future event outside of the entity's control.
- A contingent asset is a possible asset that arises from past events and whose existence will only be confirmed on the occurrence of uncertain future events outside of the entity's control.

Provisions

Recognition
Recognise when:
- an entity has a present obligation (legal or constructive) as a result of a past event,
- It is probable that an outflow of resources embodying economic benefits will be required to settle the obligation, and
- a reliable estimate can be made of the amount of the obligation.

Measurement
- The amount recognised as a provision should be the best estimate of the expenditure required to settle the present obligation at the balance sheet date.
- Where the time value of money is material, the provision should be discounted to present value.

Contingent liabilities should not be recognised. They should be disclosed unless the possibility of a transfer of economic benefits is remote.

Contingent assets should not be recognised. If the possibility of an inflow of economic benefits is probable they should be disclosed.

Financial reporting revision

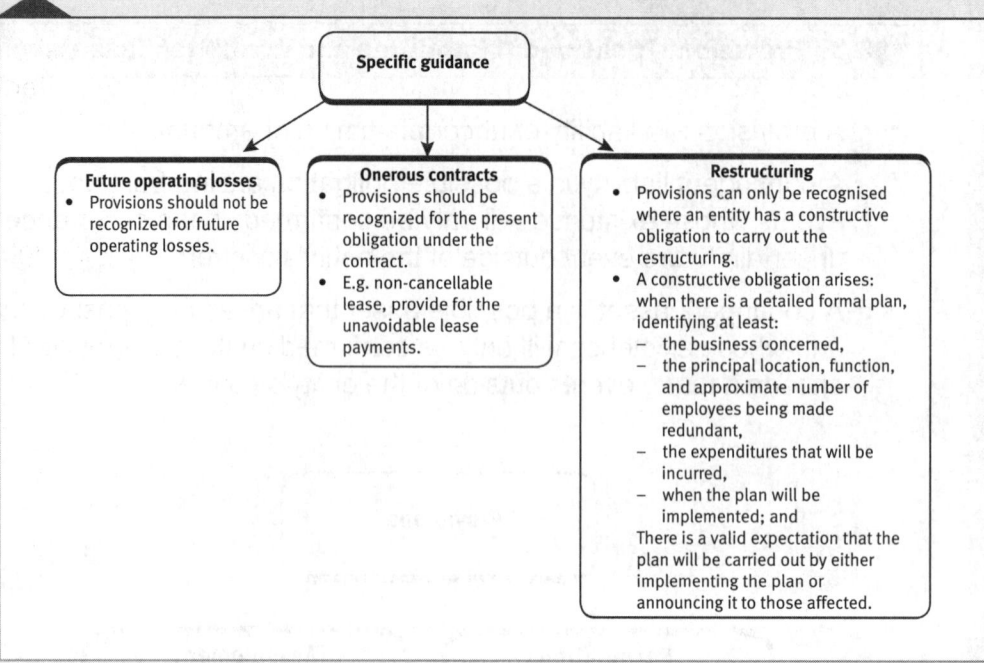

IAS 38 Intangible assets

An **intangible asset** is an identifiable non-monetary asset without physical substance.

Accounting treatment

- An intangible asset is initially recognised at cost if all of the following criteria are met.
  (1) It is identifiable – it could be disposed of without disposing of the business at the same time.
  (2) It is controlled by the entity
      – the entity has the power to obtain economic benefits from it, for example patents and copyrights give legal rights to future economic benefits.
  (3) It will generate probable future economic benefits for the entity
      – this could be by a reduction in costs or increasing revenues.
  (4) The cost can be measured reliably
      – this is straightforward if the asset was purchased outright. If the asset was acquired in a business combination then the initial cost will be the fair value.

- If an intangible does not meet the recognition criteria, then it should be charged to the statement of profit or loss as it is incurred. Items that do not meet the criteria are internally generated goodwill, brands, mastheads, publishing titles, customer lists, research, advertising, start-up costs and training.

- Intangible assets should be amortised, normally using the straight line method, over the term of their useful lives.

- If it can be demonstrated that the useful life is indefinite; no amortisation should be charged but an annual impairment review must be carried out.

- Intangible assets can be revalued but fair values must be determined with reference to an active market. This will have homogenous products, willing buyers and seller at all times and published prices. In practical terms, most intangible assets are likely to be valued using the cost model.

- The recognition of internally generated intangible assets is split into a research phase and a development phase. Costs incurred in the research phase must be charged to the statement of profit or loss as they are incurred. Costs incurred in the development phase should be recognised if they meet the following criteria:

    (a) the project is technically feasible

    (b) the asset will be completed then used or sold

    (c) the entity is able to use or sell the asset

    (d) the asset will generate future economic benefits (either by internal use or there is a market for it)

    (e) the entity has adequate technical, financial and other resources to complete the project

    (f) the expenditure on the project can be reliably measured.

- Amortisation of development costs will occur over the period that commercial benefits are expected to be received.

IAS 39 Financial instruments

IAS 39 is being replaced, in stages, by IFRS 9. Measurement and recognition of financial assets and financial liabilities are now dealt with by IFRS 9. The remaining requirements of IAS 39 relating to derivatives and hedging arrangements continue to apply until superseded by future instalments of IFRS 9.

Financial instruments

This standard requires the recognition of financial instruments in the financial statements.

Derivatives

A derivative is a financial instrument with all three of the following characteristics:

(1) its value changes in response to the change in a specified interest rate, security price, commodity price, foreign exchange rate or similar variable
(2) it requires little or no initial investment
(3) it is settled at a future date.

Derivatives include:

- options
- forward contracts
- futures
- swaps.

Derivatives which are not part of a hedging arrangement are classified to be measure as fair value through profit or loss.

Hedge accounting

Hedge accounting is the accounting treatment where the gains or losses on the **hedging instruments** are recognised in the same performance statement and in the same period as the offsetting gains or losses on the **hedged items**.

A hedging relationship exists when a company can define three elements.

(1) A hedged item – the asset/liability or transaction on which risks need to be reduced;
(2) A hedging instrument – the instrument (usually a derivative) used to offset the risks on the hedged item; and
(3) The hedged risks – the specific risk (currency, interest rate etc) that is being hedged.

In order to follow the hedge accounting rules in IAS 39, the following criteria need to be met.

(1) The hedge must be documented at inception and the elements of the hedging relationship defined (hedged item and instrument).
(2) The hedge is expected to be highly effective
(3) The effectiveness of the hedge can be measured reliably.
(4) Forecast transactions must be highly probable in order to be hedged'.
(5) The effectiveness of the hedge must be able to be assessed and measured on an on-going basis.

Types of hedge

There are three types of hedge:

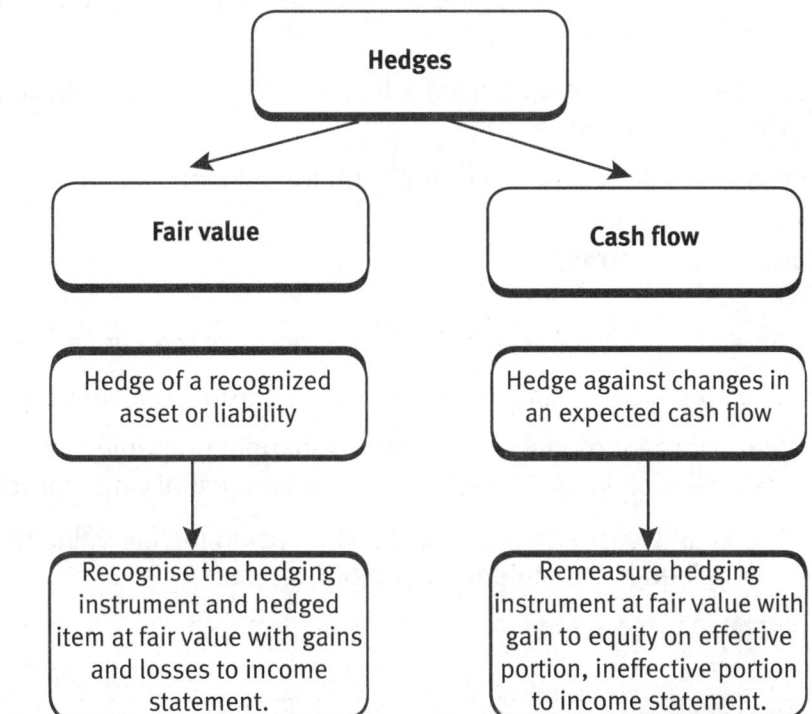

Financial reporting revision

IAS 40 Investment property

Investment property is property (land or a building - or part of a building) held to earn rentals or for capital appreciation or both, rather than for:

- use in the production or supply of goods or services or for administration purposes or
- sale in the ordinary course of business.

Investment property is not:

- property held for use in the production or supply of goods or services or for administrative purposes
- owner occupied property (deal with under IAS 16)
- property held for sale in the normal course of business (deal with under IAS 2 inventories)
- property being constructed for third parties (deal with under IAS 11 Construction contracts)
- property leased to another entity under a finance lease.

Accounting treatment

- An entity can choose either the cost model or the fair value model.
- The cost model is the normal accounting treatment set out in IAS 16.
- The fair value model recognises investment properties in the statement of financial position at fair value (usually market value).
- Gains and losses on revaluation when using the fair value model are recognised in the statement of profit or loss.

IFRS 2 Share based payments

A **share based payment** transaction is one where an entity obtains goods or services from other parties with payment taking the form of shares or share options issued by the entity.

There are two types of share based payment transactions:

(1) equity-settled share based payment transactions where an entity receives goods or services in exchange for equity instruments (e.g. shares or share options).

526   KAPLAN PUBLISHING

(2) cash-settled share based payment transactions, where an entity receives goods and services in exchange for a cash amount paid based on its share price.

Accounting

- IFRS 2 requires that all share-based payments are recognised in the financial statements.
- When a share based transaction is entered into, the goods or services received and corresponding increase in equity should be measured at fair value.
- If an entity issues share options (e.g. to employees), the fair value of the option at the grant date should be used as the cost of the services received.
- For cash settled share based payments, the fair value of goods and services is measured and a liability recognised. The, liability is re-measured at each statement of financial position until it is settled with changes in value being taken to the statement of profit or loss.
- The expense in relation to the share based transaction must be recognised over the period in which the services are rendered or goods are received.

Grant date: the date a share based-payment transaction is entered into.

Vesting date: the date on which the cash or equity instruments can be received by the other party to the agreement.

IFRS 3 (revised) business combinations

IFRS 3 requires that on acquisition both the cost of investment and the net assets acquired are recorded at their fair value. Assets and liabilities must be recognised if they are separately identifiable and can be reliably measured. The future intentions of the acquirer must not be taken into account when calculating fair values.

Fair value is the amount for which an asset could be exchanged, or a liability settled, between knowledgeable, willing parties in an arm's length transaction.

Type of asset/ liability	Fair value
Tangible non-current/assets	(a) land and buildings – market value (b) plant and equipment – market value or if not available, depreciated replacement cost.

Financial reporting revision

Intangible assets	Recognise at market value if there is an active market or estimated value if not (see IAS 38).
Inventory and work-in-progress	Finished goods – the selling price less the cost of disposal and a reasonable profit allowance Work in progress – the selling price of finished goods less costs to complete, the cost of disposal and a reasonable profit allowance Raw materials – current replacement cost
Quoted investments	Quoted investments should be valued at market price.
Contingencies	Contingent assets and liabilities should be measured at fair values where these can be determined (reasonable estimates of the expected outcome may be used).
Pensions and other post retirement benefits	The fair value of a deficit or surplus in a pension or other post retirement benefits scheme should be recognised as a liability or an asset of the acquiring group.
Deferred tax	Deferred tax on adjustments to record assets and liabilities at their fair values should be recognised in accordance with the requirements of IAS 12 Income taxes.

Fair value of the cost of acquisition

The cost of acquisition is:

(a) the amount of cash paid; plus

(b) the fair value of other purchase consideration given by the acquirer; plus

Note:

- If payment of cash is deferred it should be discounted to present value using a rate at which the acquirer could obtain similar borrowing.

- If the acquirer issues shares, fair value is normally the market price at the date of acquisition.

- The revised IFRS 3 requires the acquirer to recognise the acquisition-date fair value of contingent consideration as part of the consideration.

Goodwill and the non-controlling interest

The standard now allows the acquirer (parent) to measure any non-controlling interest (NCI) in one of two ways:

- either at the full goodwill method - this measures goodwill for the entity as a whole (the 'new' method); or
- at the NCI's proportionate share of the acquiree's (subsidiary's) identifiable net assets (this is the 'old' method).

Negative goodwill

If the net assets acquired exceed the fair value of consideration, then negative goodwill arises.

After checking that the calculations have been done correctly, negative goodwill is credited to the statement of profit or loss and other comprehensive income immediately.

Other adjustments

Don't forget that there are other adjustments that you may be required to make. These have been seen in previous studies and include:

- dividends declared by the subsidiary or associate and not accounted for by the parent
- interest on intercompany loans that has not been accounted for by the receiving party
- intercompany management charges that have not been accounted for by the receiving party
- intercompany sales, purchases and unrealised profit in inventory
- intercompany transfer of non-current assets and unrealised profit on transfer
- intercompany receivables, payables and loans that need eliminating.

IFRS 5 Non-current assets held for sale & discontinued activities

A **discontinued operation** is a component of an entity that either has been disposed of, or is classified as held for sale; and

- represents a separate major line of business or geographical area of operations
- is part of a single coordinated plan to dispose of a separate major line of business or geographical area of operations
- is a subsidiary acquired exclusively with a view to resale.

An entity should classify a non-current asset or a disposal group as held for sale if its carrying value will be recovered principally through a sale transaction rather than continued use in the business.

A **disposal group** is a group of assets to be disposed of, by sale or otherwise, together as a group in a single transaction, and liabilities directly associated with those assets that will be transferred in the transaction.

Assets can only be classified as held for sale (and therefore a discontinued operation) if they meet all of the criteria below:

- management commits itself to a plan to sell
- the asset (or disposal group) is available for immediate sale in its present condition
- sale is highly probable and is expected to be completed within a year from date of classification
- the asset (or disposal group) is being actively marketed for sale at a reasonable price compared to its fair value
- it is unlikely that significant changes will be made to the plan or it will be withdrawn.

If there are events outside the entity's control that mean that the sale cannot be completed within one year and there is evidence that the entity remains committed to the plan to sell, then the asset or disposal group can still be classified as held for sale.

If the criteria are met after the statement of financial position date but before the accounts are authorised for issue, the assets should not be classed as held for sale but the information should be disclosed.

Measurement

- A non-current asset (or disposal group) classified as held for sale should be measured at the lower of its carrying value and fair value less costs to sell.
- Assets classified as held for sale should not be depreciated, regardless of whether they are still in use by the reporting entity.

Presentation

Information about discontinued operations should be presented in the financial statements.

- On the face of the statement of profit or loss, a single amount comprising:
  - the total of the post tax profit or loss of discontinued operations
  - the post tax gain or loss on the measurement to fair values less costs to sell or the disposal of the discontinued operation.
- Either on the face of or in the notes to the statement of profit or loss, an analysis of the single amount broken down into:
- the revenue, expenses and pre tax profit or loss of discontinued operations
- the related tax expense
- the gain or loss recognised on the measurement to fair value less costs to sell or on the disposal of the discontinued operations
- the related tax expense.

IFRS 7 Financial instruments: Disclosures

As part of the response to the global financial crisis, the nature and extent of disclosures required by IFRS 7 has been updated to require improved and extended discloses. This will enable users to understand the nature and extent of transactions, balances and associated risks of financial assets and liabilities included in the statement of financial position of an entity.

IFRS 7 requires the following disclosures:
The two main categories of disclosures required are:

(1) information about the significance of financial instruments
(2) information about the nature and extent of risks arising from financial instruments.

The qualitative disclosures describe:

- risk exposures for each type of financial instrument
- management's objectives, policies, and processes for managing those risks
- changes from the prior period.

The quantitative disclosures provide information about the extent to which the entity is exposed to risk, based on information provided internally to the entity's key management personnel. These disclosures include:

- summary quantitative data about exposure to each risk at the reporting date
- disclosures about credit risk, liquidity risk, and market risk as further described below
- concentrations of risk.

IFRS 8 Operating segments

IFRS 8 Operating segments requires an entity to disclose information about each of its operating segments.

An **operating segment** is a component of an entity:

- that engages in business activities from which it may earn revenues and incur expenses;
- whose operating results are regularly reviewed by the entity's chief operating decision maker to make decisions about resources to be allocated to the segment and assess its performance; and
- for which discrete financial information is available.

A **reportable segment** is an operating segment that is used in an entity's internal management reports. Therefore management identifies the operating segments

Reporting thresholds

An entity must separately report information about an operating segment that meets any of the following quantitative thresholds:

- sales, are 10 per cent or more of the combined revenues of all operating segments, both international and external sales revenues.

- its reported profit or loss is 10 per cent or more of the greater, in absolute amount, of:
  - the combined reported profit of all operating segments that did not report a loss and
  - the combined reported loss of all operating segments that reported a loss.
- Its assets are 10 per cent or more of the combined assets of all operating segments.

At least 75% of the entity's **external revenue** should be included in reportable segments. If the quantitative test results segmental disclosure of less than this, other reportable segments should be identified until this 75% is reached.

Disclosures

IFRS 8 requires detailed disclosures, including:

- factors used to identify the entity's reportable segments, including the basis of organisation (for example, whether segments are based on products and services, geographical areas or a combination of these).
- the types of products and services from which each reportable segment derives its revenues.

For each reportable segment an entity should report:

- a measure of profit or loss
- a measure of total assets
- a measure of total liabilities (if such an amount is regularly used in decision making).

IFRS 9 Financial instruments

IFRS 9 was introduced in November 2010 as part of the response of the IASB to the global financial crisis and will result in IAS 39 being superseded and withdrawn in stages. Initially, IFRS 9 dealt only with financial assets, but was revised in October 2010 to also include recognition and measurement of financial liabilities.

> Initially, IFRS 9 was to be effective for accounting periods commencing on or after 1 January 2013, with early adoption permitted. The effective date has now been revised to 1 January 2015.

Financial reporting revision

IFRS 9 classifies financial assets under three headings as follows:

(1) **Financial assets at fair value through profit or loss (FVTPL)**: This is the **default classification for financial assets** and will include any financial assets held for trading or speculative transactions. They will also include derivatives, unless they are part of a designated hedging arrangement. They will also include debt instruments unless they have been correctly designated to be measured at amortised cost. Initial recognition at fair value is normally cost incurred and this will exclude transactions costs which are charged to profit or loss as incurred. This accounting treatment automatically incorporates an annual impairment review.

(2) **Financial assets at fair value through other comprehensive income (FVTOCI)**: This classification applies to equity instruments only and requires an election for classification upon initial recognition. It will typically be applicable for equity interests which an entity wishes to retain ownership of on a continuing basis. Initial recognition at fair value would normally include the associated transaction costs of purchase. The accounting treatment automatically incorporates an impairment review, with any change in fair value taken to other comprehensive income in the year. Upon derecognition, any gain or loss is based upon the carrying value at the date of disposal; there is no recycling of any amounts previously taken to equity in earlier years.

(3) **Financial assets measured at amortised cost**: This classification applies only to debt instruments and requires an election for classification upon initial recognition. For the election to be effective, the financial instrument must pass two tests as follows:

(i) **The business model test** – to pass this test, the entity must be holding the financial asset to collect in the contractual cash flows associated with the financial asset. If this is not the case, such as the financial asset being held to take advantage of changes in *fair* value, then the test is failed and the financial asset must be measured at FVTPL.

(ii) **The cash flow characteristics test** – to pass this test, the contractual cash flows collect must solely consist of payment of interest and capital. If this is not the case (e.g. with convertible bonds) the test is failed and the financial asset must be measured at FVTPL.

This classification of financial asset requires annual review for evidence of possible impairment and, if there is evidence, there must be an impairment review.

Normally, financial liabilities will be measured at FVTPL, with all other financial liabilities measured at amortised cost.

IFRS 9 also retains the option for some liabilities to be measured at fair value if, in doing so, it eliminates or reduces an accounting mismatch. Where this is the case, to the extent that part of the change in fair value of the financial liability is due to a change on own credit risk, this must be taken to other comprehensive income in the year, with the balance of any change in fair value taken to profit or loss.

IFRS 10 Consolidated financial statements

IFRS 10 requires consideration of whether or not an entity is controlled by another entity, to determine if it is a subsidiary that should be consolidated.

There is a **single basis of control** to determine whether consolidation of entities is required.

Control consists of three components:

(1) **Power** over the investee; this is normally exercised through the **majority of voting rights**, but could also arise through other contractual arrangements. Power relates only to substantive, rather than protective rights. The former arises where there is practical ability to exercise rights of control at the time when relevant decisions are made. The latter may arise where control can be exercised only upon pre-determined circumstances arising at some later date.

(2) **Exposure** or rights to variable returns (positive and/or negative) from involvement; and

(3) The **ability to use power** over the investee to affect the amount of investor returns. The ability to use power over an investee to affect returns is regarded as a crucial determinant in deciding whether or not control is exercised.

This definition should be subject to **continuous assessment**, and should be considered at least at each reporting date to determine that control continues to apply.

IFRS 10 also considers whether a portion of an entity (referred to as a "silo") can be considered as a separate entity for the purposes of consolidation.

This may lead to the situation of consolidation of only that part of a separate entity over which control is exercised. For this to be the case, the definition of control as previously outlined must apply to distinguishable or ring-fenced assets and liabilities.

> Note that IFRS 10 recognises that it may be possible for one entity to have a controlling interest in an investee (say 70%) whilst another entity has a shareholding (say 30%) which enables it to exercise significant influence over the same investee. In many cases, such a situation would result in the 30% investor having no influence. However, IFRS 10 requires that an assessment of the true position at each reporting date is evaluated so that it can be properly reported.

IFRS 11 Joint arrangements

A joint arrangement is a contractual arrangement whereby two or more parties undertake an economic activity that is subject to joint control.

IFRS 11 includes the following definitions:

- **Joint arrangements**: where two or more parties have joint control. This will only apply if the relevant activities require unanimous consent of those who collectively control the arrangement. They may take the form of either joint operations or joint ventures. The key distinction between the two forms is based upon the parties' rights and obligations under the joint arrangement.
    - **Joint operations**: the parties that have joint control have rights to the assets and obligations for the liabilities. Normally, there will not be a separate entity established to conduct joint operations.
    - **Joint ventures**: the parties have joint control of the arrangement and have rights to the net assets of the arrangement. This will normally be established in the form of a separate entity to conduct the joint venture activities.

IFRS 11 requires that:

Joint operators each recognise their share of assets, liabilities, revenues and expenses of the joint operation. This may consist of maintaining a joint operation account to record transactions undertaken on behalf of the joint operation, together with balances due to or from other parties to the joint operation.

Joint ventures are accounted for using the equity method.

Proportionate consolidation is not permitted.

chapter 20

IFRS 12 Disclosure of interests in other entities

IFRS 12 applies to entities that have an interest in subsidiaries, joint arrangements and associates, i.e where there is control, joint control or significant influence.

IFRS 9 details accounting requirements where control, joint control or significant influence does not apply.

IFRS 12 is designed to provide relevant information to users of financial statements. It requires disclosure of:

- details relating to the composition of the group;
- details of non-controlling interests within the group; and
- identification and evaluation of risks associated with any interests held in other entities which give rise to control, joint control or significant influence.

IFRS 13 Fair value measurement

The objective of IFRS 13 is to provide a single source of guidance for fair value measurement.

Note that IFRS 13 does not apply to IFRS 2 Share-based Payment and IAS 17 Leases. IFRS 13 also does not apply to situations where different measurements are required, such as net realisable value or value in use which may be required by some reporting standards.

Key definitions are as follows:

- Fair value is defined as the price that would be received to sell an asset or paid to transfer a liability in an orderly transaction between market participants at the measurement date. Fair value may be required to be measured on a recurring basis or a non-recurring basis.
- Fair value on a recurring basis arises when a reporting standard requires fair value to be measured on an ongoing basis. Examples of this include IAS 40 Investment Property, or IFRS 9 Financial Instruments which require some financial assets and liabilities to be measured at fair value at each reporting date.
- Fair value on a non-recurring basis arises when a reporting standard requires fair value to be measured at fair value only in certain specified circumstances. This would apply, for example with the application of IFRS 3 Business Combinations (Revised) where items are measured at fair value at the date of acquisition.

KAPLAN PUBLISHING

chapter 21

Additional practice questions

Additional practice questions

Test your understanding 1

Hydrasports, a limited liability company and national leisure group, has sixteen centres around the country and a head office. Facilities at each centre are of a standard design which incorporates a heated swimming pool, sauna, air-conditioned gym and fitness studio with supervised childcare. Each centre is managed on a day-to-day basis, by a centre manager, in accordance with company policies. The centre manager is also responsible for preparing and submitting monthly accounting returns to head office.

Each centre is required to have a licence from the local authority to operate. Licences are granted for periods between two and five years and are renewable subject to satisfactory reports from local authority inspectors. The average annual cost of a licence is $900.

Members pay a $100 joining fee, plus either $50 per month for 'peak' membership or $30 per month for 'off-peak', payable quarterly in advance. All fees are stated to be non-refundable.

The centre at Verne was closed from July to September 2003 after a chemical spill in the sauna caused a serious accident. Although the centre was re-opened, Hydrasports has recommended to all centre managers that sauna facilities be suspended until further notice.

In response to complaints to the local authorities about its childcare facilities, Hydrasports has issued centre managers with revised guidelines for minimum levels of supervision. Centre managers are finding it difficult to meet the new guidelines and have suggested that childcare facilities should be withdrawn.

Staff lateness is a recurring problem and a major cause of 'early bird' customer dissatisfaction with sessions which are scheduled to start at 07.00. New employees are generally attracted to the industry in the short-term for its non-cash benefits, including free use of the facilities – but leave when they require increased financial rewards. Training staff to be qualified life-guards is costly and time-consuming and retention rates are poor. Turnover of centre managers is also high, due to the constraints imposed on them by company policy.

Three of the centres are expected to have run at a loss for the year to 31 December 2003 due to falling membership. Hydrasports has invested heavily in a hydrotherapy pool at one of these centres, with the aim of attracting retired members with more leisure time. The building contractor has already billed twice as much and taken three times as long as budgeted for the work. The pool is now expected to open in February 2004.

Cash flow difficulties in the current year have put back the planned replacement of gym equipment for most of the centres.

Insurance premiums for liability to employees and the public have increased by nearly 45%. Hydrasports has met the additional expense by reducing its insurance cover on its plant and equipment from a replacement cost basis to a net realisable value basis.

Required:

(a) (i) Identify and explain the business risks which should be assessed by the management of Hydrasports. **(8 marks)**

(ii) Explain how each of the business risks identified in (i) may be linked to financial statement risk. **(8 marks)**

(b) Describe the principal audit work to be performed in respect of the carrying amount of the following items in the statement of financial position of Hydrasports as at 31 December 2003:

(i) deferred income; and **(3 marks)**

(ii) hydrotherapy pool. **(3 marks)**

(c) Suggest performance indicators that could be set to increase the centre managers' awareness of Hydrasports' social and environmental responsibilities and the evidence which should be available to provide assurance on their accuracy. **(8 marks)**

(Total: 30 marks)

Test your understanding 2

Cerise, a limited liability company, manufactures computer-controlled equipment for production-line industries such as cars, washing machines, cookers, etc. On 1 September 2004 the shareholder-managers decided, unanimously, to accept a lucrative offer from a multi-national corporation to buy the company's patented technology and manufacturing equipment.

By 10 September 2004 management had notified all the employees, suppliers and customers that Cerise would cease all manufacturing activities on 31 October 2004. The 200-strong factory workforce and the majority of the accounts department and support staff were made redundant with effect from that date, when the sale was duly completed.

The marketing, human resources and production managers will cease to be employed by the company at 31 December 2004. However, the chief executive, sales manager, finance manager, accountant and a small number of accounting and other support staff expect to be employed until the company is wound down completely.

Additional practice questions

Cerise's operations extend to fourteen premises, nine of which were put on the market on 1 November 2004. Cerise accounts for all tangible, non-current assets under the cost model (i.e. at depreciated cost). Four premises are held on leases that expire in the next two to seven years and cannot be sold or sub-let under the lease terms. The small head office premises will continue to be occupied until the lease expires in 2007. No new lease agreements were entered into during 2004.

All Cerise's computer-controlled products carry a one-year warranty. Extended warranties of three and five years, previously available at the time of purchase, have not been offered on sales of remaining inventory from 1 November onwards.

Cerise has three-year agreements with its national and international distributors for the sale of equipment. It also has annual contracts with its major suppliers for the purchase of components. So far, none of these parties have lodged any legal claim against Cerise. However, the distributors are withholding payment of their account balances pending settlement of the significant penalties which are now due to them.

Required:

You are required to answer the following in the context of the final audit of the financial statements of Cerise for the year ending 31 December 2004:

(a) Using the information provided, identify and explain the financial statement risks to be taken into account in planning the audit. **(12 marks)**

(b) Explain how the extent of the reliance to be placed on:
   (i) analytical procedures; and **(4 marks)**
   (ii) management representations, **(4 marks)**

   should compare with that for the prior year audit.

(c) Describe the principal audit work to be performed in respect of the carrying amount of the following items in the statement of financial position:
   (i) amounts due from distributors; and **(3 marks)**
   (ii) lease liabilities. **(3 marks)**

(Total: 26 marks)

chapter 21

Test your understanding 3

Geno Vesa Farm (GVF), a limited liability company, is a cheese manufacturer. Its principal activity is the production of a traditional 'Farmhouse' cheese that is retailed around the world to exclusive shops, through mail order and web sales. Other activities include the sale of locally produced foods through a farm shop and cheese-making demonstrations and tours.

The farm's herd of 700 goats is used primarily for the production of milk. Kids (i.e. goat offspring), which are a secondary product, are selected for herd replacement or otherwise sold. Animals held for sale are not usually retained beyond the time they reach optimal size or weight because their value usually does not increase thereafter.

There are two main variations of the traditional farmhouse cheese; 'Rabida Red' and 'Bachas Blue'. The red cheese is coloured using Innittu, which is extracted from berries found only in South American rain forests. The cost of Innittu has risen sharply over the last year as the collection of berries by local village workers has come under the scrutiny of an international action group. The group is lobbying the South American government to ban the export of Innittu, claiming that the workers are being exploited and that sustaining the forest is seriously under threat.

Demand for Bachas Blue, which is made from unpasteurized milk, fell considerably in 2003 following the publication of a research report that suggested a link between unpasteurized milk products and a skin disorder. The financial statements for the year ended 30 September 2004 recognized a material impairment loss attributable to the equipment used exclusively for the manufacture of Bachas Blue. However, as the adverse publicity is gradually being forgotten, sales of Bachas Blue are now showing a steady increase and are currently expected to return to their former level by the end of September 2005.

Cheese is matured to three strengths – mild, medium and strong – depending on the period of time it is left to ripen, which is six, 12 and 18 months respectively. When produced, the cheese is sold to a financial institution, Abingdon Bank, at cost. Under the terms of sale, GVF has the option to buy the cheese on its maturity at cost plus 7% for every six months which has elapsed.

All cheese is stored to maturity on wooden boards in GVF's cool and airy sheds. However, recently enacted health and safety legislation requires that the wooden boards be replaced with stainless steel shelves with effect from 1 July 2005. The management of GVF has petitioned the government health department that to comply with the legislation would interfere with the maturing process and the production of medium and strong cheeses would have to cease.

Additional practice questions

In 2003, GVF applied for and received a substantial regional development grant for the promotion of tourism in the area. GVF's management has deferred its plan to convert a disused barn into holiday accommodation from 2004 until at least 2006.

Required:

(a) Identify and explain the principal audit risks to be considered when planning the final audit of GVF for the year ending 30 September 2005. **(14 marks)**

(b) Describe the audit work to be performed in respect of the carrying amount of the following items in the statement of financial position of GVF as at 30 September 2005:

   (i) goat herd; **(4 marks)**

   (ii) equipment used in the manufacture of Bachas Blue; and **(4 marks)**

   (iii) cheese. **(4 marks)**

(Total: 26 marks)

Test your understanding 4

Shire Oil Co ('Shire'), a listed company, is primarily an oil producer with interests in the North Sea, West Africa and South Asia. Shire's latest interim report shows:

	30 June 2005	30 June 2004	31 December 2004
	Unaudited $000	Audited $000	Unaudited $000
Revenue	22,000	18,300	37,500
Profit before tax	5,500	4,200	7,500
Total assets	95,900	92,300	88,400
Earnings per share (basic)	$1.82	$2.07	$3.53

In April 2005, the company was awarded a new five-year licence, by the central government, to explore for oil in a remote region. The licence was granted at no cost to Shire. However, Shire's management has decided to recognize the licence at an estimated fair value of $3 million.

The most significant of Shire's tangible non-current assets are its 17 oil rigs (2004 – 15). Each rig is composed of numerous items including a platform, buildings thereon and drilling equipment. The useful life of each platform is assessed annually on factors such as weather conditions and the period over which it is estimated that oil will be extracted. Platforms are depreciated on a straight line basis over 15 to 40 years.

A provision for the present value of the expected cost of decommissioning an oil rig is recognized in full at the commencement of oil production. One of the rigs in South Asia sustained severe cyclone damage in October 2005. Shire's management believes the rig is beyond economic recovery and that there will be no alternative but to abandon it where it is. This suggestion has brought angry protests from conservationists.

In July 2005, Shire entered into an agreement to share in the future economic benefits of an extensive oil pipeline.

You are the manager responsible for the audit of Shire. Last year your firm modified its auditor's report due to a lack of evidence to support management's schedule of proven and probable oil reserves to be recoverable from known reserves.

Required:

(a) Using the information provided, identify and explain the audit risks to be addressed when planning the final audit of Shire Oil Co for the year ending 31 December 2005. **(12 marks)**

(b) Describe the principal audit work to be performed in respect of the useful lives of Shire Oil Co's rig platforms. **(6 marks)**

You have just been advised of management's intention to publish its yearly marketing report in the annual report that will contain the financial statements for the year ending 31 December 2005. Extracts from the marketing report include the following:

'Shire Oil Co sponsors national school sports championships and the 'Shire Ward' at the national teaching hospital. The company's vision is to continue its investment in health and safety and the environment.

'Our health and safety, security and environmental policies are of the highest standard in the energy sector. We aim to operate under principles of no-harm to people and the environment.

'Shire Oil Co's main contribution to sustainable development comes from providing extra energy in a cleaner and more socially responsible way. This means improving the environmental and social performance of our operations. Regrettably, five employees lost their lives at work during the year.'

Additional practice questions

Required:

(c) Suggest performance indicators that could reflect the extent to which Shire Oil Co's social and environmental responsibilities are being met, and the evidence that should be available to provide assurance on their accuracy. **(6 marks)**

(d) Explain the nature and value of a social report, and draft out the typical contents of a social report attestation. **(10 marks)**

(Total: 34 marks)

Test your understanding 5

You are the manager responsible for the audit of Volcan, a long-established limited liability company. Volcan operates a national supermarket chain of 23 stores, five of which are in the capital city, Urvina. All the stores are managed in the same way with purchases being made through Volcan's central buying department and product pricing, marketing, advertising and human resources policies being decided centrally. The draft financial statements for the year ended 31 March 2005 show revenue of $303 million (2004 – $282 million), profit before taxation of $9.5 million (2004 – $7.3 million) and total assets of $178 million (2004 – $173 million).

The following issues arising during the final audit have been noted on a schedule of points for your attention:

(a) On 1 May 2005, Volcan announced its intention to downsize one of the stores in Urvina from a supermarket to a 'City Metro' in response to a significant decline in the demand for supermarket-style shopping in the capital.

The store will be closed throughout June, re-opening on 1 July 2005. Goodwill of $5.5 million was recognized three years ago when this store, together with two others, was bought from a national competitor. 60% of the goodwill has been written off due to impairment. **(7 marks)**

(b) On 1 April 2004 Volcan introduced a 'reward scheme' for its customers. The main elements of the reward scheme include the awarding of a 'store point' to customers' loyalty cards for every $1 spent, with extra points being given for the purchase of each week's special offers. Customers who hold a loyalty card can convert their points into cash discounts against future purchases on the basis of $1 per 100 points. **(6 marks)**

(c) In October 2004, Volcan commenced the development of a site in a valley of 'outstanding natural beauty' on which to build a retail 'megastore' and warehouse in late 2005. Local government planning permission for the development, which was received in April 2005, requires that three 100-year-old trees within the valley be preserved and the surrounding valley be restored in 2006. Additions to property, plant and equipment during the year include $4.4 million for the estimated cost of site restoration. This estimate includes a provision of $0.4 million for the relocation of the 100-year-old trees.

In March 2005 the trees were chopped down to make way for a car park. A fine of $20,000 per tree was paid to the local government in May 2005. **(7 marks)**

Required:

For each of the above issues:

(i) comment on the matters that you should consider; and

(ii) state the audit evidence that you should expect to find,

in undertaking your review of the audit working papers and financial statements of Volcan for the year ended 31 March 2005. **Note:** The mark allocation is shown against each of the three issues.

(Total: 20 marks)

Test your understanding 6

You are the manager responsible for the audit of Albreda Co, a limited liability company, and its subsidiaries. The group mainly operates a chain of national restaurants and provides vending and other catering services to corporate clients. All restaurants offer 'eat-in', 'take-away' and 'home delivery' services. The draft consolidated financial statements for the year ended 30 September 2005 show revenue of $42.2 million (2004 – $41.8 million), profit before taxation of $1.8 million (2004 – $2.2 million) and total assets of $30.7 million (2004 – $23.4 million).

The following issues arising during the final audit have been noted on a schedule of points for your attention:

Additional practice questions

(a) In September 2005 the management board announced plans to cease offering 'home delivery' services from the end of the month. These sales amounted to $0.6 million for the year to 30 September 2005 (2004 – $0.8 million). A provision of $0.2 million has been made as at 30 September 2005 for the compensation of redundant employees (mainly drivers). Delivery vehicles have been classified as non-current assets held for sale as at 30 September 2005 and measured at fair value less costs to sell, $0.8 million (carrying amount, $0.5 million). **(8 marks)**

(b) Historically, all owned premises have been measured at cost depreciated over 10 to 50 years. The management board has decided to revalue these premises for the year ended 30 September 2005. At the statement of financial position date two properties had been revalued by a total of $1.7 million. Another 15 properties have since been revalued by $5.4 million and there remain a further three properties which are expected to be revalued during 2006. A revaluation surplus of $7.1 million has been credited to equity. **(7 marks)**

(c) During the year Albreda paid $0.1 million (2004 – $0.3 million) in fines and penalties relating to breaches of health and safety regulations. These amounts have not been separately disclosed but included in cost of sales. **(5 marks)**

Required:

For each of the above issues:

(i) comment on the matters that you should consider; and

(ii) state the audit evidence that you should expect to find,

in undertaking your review of the audit working papers and financial statements of Albreda Co for the year ended 30 September 2005.

Note: The mark allocation is shown against each of the three issues.

(Total: 20 marks)

chapter 21

Test your understanding 7

(a) Explain the importance of the role of objectivity to the auditor-client relationship. **(5 marks)**

(b) You are the audit partner in a firm which provides a variety of accountancy-related services to a large portfolio of clients. The firm's gross practice income is $1 million. The firm has a particularly successful tax department, which carries out a great deal of recurring and special tax work for both audit and non-audit clients. The tax manager has recently involved you in discussions with a major tax client who is considering changing its auditors. The client, Rainbow, would expect audit fees of around $100,000 (which is a reasonable fee for the audit). Your adult daughter has been working as an administrative assistant in the sales department of Rainbow for a year, after being introduced by the tax manager. She has just joined an employee share benefit scheme.

The client is keen to use the firm to provide audit services as he is pleased with the taxation services they provide. The managing director and major shareholder, Mr Parkes, has therefore offered an incentive to the audit fee of an additional 1% of profits in excess of $20 million, annually where relevant. The current recurring taxation fees from Rainbow are $35,000, and last year special tax work amounted to $25,000. Last year's fees remain outstanding.

The managing director has suggested that you give consideration to the matter while staying for the weekend at his villa in Tenerife. He has arranged flights for both you and your spouse.

Required:

Comment on the matters that you should consider in deciding whether or not your audit firm can accept appointment as auditors of Rainbow. **(10 marks)**

(Total: 15 marks)

Test your understanding 8

You are an audit manager in Sepia, a firm of Chartered Certified Accountants. Your specific responsibilities include advising the senior audit partner on the acceptance of new assignments. The following matters have arisen in connection with three prospective client companies:

Additional practice questions

(a) Your firm has been nominated to act as auditor to Squid, a private limited company. You have been waiting for a response to your letter of 'professional enquiry' to Squid's auditor, Krill & Co, for several weeks. Your recent attempts to call the current engagement partner, Anton Fargues, in Krill & Co have been met with the response from Anton's personal assistant that 'Mr Fargues is not available'.
(5 marks)

(b) Sepia has been approached by the management of Hatchet, a company listed on a recognized stock exchange, to advise on a take-over bid which they propose to make. The target company, Vitronella, is an audit client of your firm. However, Hatchet is not.
(5 marks)

(c) A former colleague in Sepia, Edwin Stenuit, is now employed by another audit firm, Keratin. Sepia and Keratin and three other firms have recently tendered for the audit of Benthos, a limited liability company. Benthos is expected to announce the successful firm next week. Yesterday, at a social gathering, Edwin confided to you that Keratin 'lowballed' on their tender for the audit as they expect to be able to provide Benthos with lucrative other services. **(5 marks)**

Required:

Comment on the professional issues raised by each of the above matters and the steps, if any, that Sepia should now take.
Note: The mark allocation is shown against each of the three issues.

(Total: 15 marks)

Test your understanding 9

(a) Explain why quality control may be difficult to implement in a smaller audit firm and illustrate how such difficulties may be overcome.
(5 marks)

(b) Kite Associates is an association of small accounting practices. One of the benefits of membership is improved quality control through a peer review system. Whilst reviewing a sample of auditor's reports issued by Rook & Co, a firm only recently admitted to Kite Associates, you come across the following modified opinion on the financial statements of Lammergeier Group:

Qualified opinion arising from material misstatement accounting treatment relating to the non-adoption of IAS 7

The management has not prepared a group statement of cashflows and its associated notes. In the opinion of the management it is not practical to prepare a group statement of cashflows due to the complexity involved. In our opinion the reasons for the departure from IAS 7 are sound and acceptable and adequate disclosure has been made concerning the departure from IAS 7. The departure in our opinion does not impact on the truth and fairness of the financial statements.

'In our opinion, except for the non-preparation of the group statement of cashflows and associated notes, the financial statements give a true and fair view of the financial position of the Company as at 31 December 2003 and of the profit of the group for the year then ended, and have been properly prepared in accordance with …'

Your review of the prior year auditor's report has revealed that the 2002 year-end audit opinion was identical.

Required:

Critically appraise the appropriateness of the audit opinion given by Rook & Co on the financial statements of Lammergeier Group for the years ended 31 December 2003 and 2002. **(10 marks)**

(Total: 15 marks)

Test your understanding 10

(a) Explain the auditor's responsibilities for other information in documents containing audited financial statements. **(5 marks)**

(b) You are an audit manager with specific responsibility for reviewing other information in documents containing audited financial statements before your firm's auditor's report is signed. The financial statements of Hegas, a privately-owned civil engineering company, show total assets of $120 million, revenue of $261 million, and profit before tax of $9.2 million for the year ended 31 March 2005. Your review of the Annual Report has revealed the following:

(i) The statement of changes in equity includes $4.5 million under a separate heading of 'miscellaneous item' which is described as 'other difference not recognized in income'. There is no further reference to this amount or 'other difference' elsewhere in the financial statements. However, the Management Report, which is required by statute, is not audited. It discloses that 'changes in shareholders' equity not recognized in income includes $4.5 million arising on the revaluation of investment properties'.

The notes to the financial statements state that the company has implemented IAS 40 Investment Property for the first time in the year to 31 March 2005 and also that 'the adoption of this standard did not have a significant impact on Hegas's financial position or its results of operations during 2005'.

(ii) The chairman's statement asserts 'Hegas has now achieved a position as one of the world's largest generators of hydro-electricity, with a dedicated commitment to accountable ethical professionalism'. Audit working papers show that 14% of revenue was derived from hydro-electricity (2004: 12%). Publicly available information shows that there are seven international suppliers of hydro-electricity in Africa alone, which are all at least three times the size of Hegas in terms of both annual turnover and population supplied.

Required:

Identify and comment on the implications of the above matters for the auditor's report on the financial statements of Hegas for the year ended 31 March 2005. **(10 marks)**

(Total: 15 marks)

chapter 21

Test your understanding answers

Test your understanding 1

(a) **Business/financial statements risk**

The standard design of facilities increases operational risk as any difficulties encountered in one facility will be compounded by the number of other facilities (potentially all) which are similarly affected. This is illustrated by the closure of the saunas. The carrying amount of the associated non-current assets (i.e. equipment, fixtures and fittings) is likely to be overstated as they are likely to be impaired if they are not in use.

Centralized control through company policy is resulting in inefficient and ineffective operations as managers cannot respond on a timely basis to local needs. Management circumvention or override of control procedures laid down by head office may result in system weaknesses. If errors arising are not detected and corrected the risk of misstatement in the financial statements is increased.

Business reporting risk is likely to be increased by centre managers preparing monthly accounting returns. Operational risk may be increased if centre managers cannot fulfil their day-to-day responsibilities (e.g. relating to customer satisfaction, human resources, health and safety). Information processing risk is increased as accounting information flowing into the financial statements may not be properly captured, input, processed or output by the centre managers. Inherent risk, of errors arising, in monthly 'branch' returns is high.

Advanced payments contribute to business reporting and financial (cash flow) risk. Cash received must be available to meet the costs of providing future services. Revenue may be overstated if an accurate cut-off is not achieved. In particular, there is an estimate risk in determining the amount of deferred income at the statement of financial position date. An error of principle may also arise if Hydrasports' revenue recognition policy does not comply with IAS 18 Revenue.

Hydrasports cannot operate a centre if a licence is suspended, withdrawn or not renewed (e.g. through failing a local authority inspection or failing to apply for renewal). An error of principle arises if licences are not capitalized as intangible assets (but instead written off as expenses when incurred). Intangible assets (licences) should be reviewed for impairment at each statement of financial position date (e.g. for centres which are closed).

Closure may result in customers finding alternative facilities with permanent loss of fee revenue. Failure risk (i.e. that Hydrasports will not continue to operate as a going concern) is increased.

'Early bird' customer dissatisfaction similarly increases operational risk. This creates disclosure risk if the disclosures relating to going concern as the basis of accounting do not meet the requirements of IAS 1 Presentation of Financial Statements.

Serious accidents may prompt investigation by local authority – resulting in penalties, fines and/or withdrawal of licence to operate. If licences are withdrawn, the intangible asset (amounts prepaid) should be written off to the extent that monies are not refundable. The likelihood of contingent (if not actual) liabilities increases disclosure risk.

Although fees are non-refundable, suspension of a facility (e.g. sauna) may result in customers asking for partial refund. In particular Hydrasports may have an obligation to refund fees paid in advance when centres are closed (e.g. the Verne centre from July–September 2003). Provisions may be understated at 31 December 2003 if Hydrasports has a legal obligation to refund fees where it has failed to provide services.

Permanent loss of customers requiring childcare facilities increases operating risk. Compliance risk is increased if the new guidelines are not met. Disclosure risk is (again) increased if fines/penalties arising are material and not disclosed.
Similarly, inability to retain lifeguards increases operational risk that pools cannot open (due to health and safety regulations). Compliance risk is increased by the possibility that pools may be operated without a lifeguard being on duty.

High staff turnover indicates increased operational risk (poor human resource management, inefficiency in working practices, reduced capacity, etc). Staff costs may be overstated as the risk that payments may be made to leavers is increased.

Limitations on centre managers' levels of authority may not be commensurate with their responsibilities. Empowerment risk arises if managers are not properly led (and if they, in turn, do not properly lead their centre staff). Any lack of integrity may increase the risk of management and/or employee fraud, illegal acts and unauthorized use of company assets. In particular the assertion of existence of assets may be at risk (resulting in overstatement).

More centres may become loss-making if the reasons for falling membership are not addressed. Loss-making centres should be tested for impairment as cash-generating units.

The hydrotherapy pool cannot operate until construction is complete, which may be threatened by cash flow problems. The value of the asset in construction should be written down if it is impaired (even if it has not yet been brought into use)

Cash flow difficulties increase liquidity/financial risk. See above reference to going concern and disclosure risk.

Obsolete gym equipment increases operational risk as customer satisfaction decreases and health and safety risks are increased. Depreciation may be overstated if Hydrasports continues to calculate depreciation on fully-depreciated assets. Disclosures for capital commitments (e.g. to replace equipment) in the financial statements may be inappropriate if Hydrasports does not have funds to finance such commitments.

The reduction in insurance cover reduces the recoverable amount of assets in the event of loss through fire (for example). Inability to replace lost/damaged assets increases operational risk (see obsolete gym equipment above).   See above reference to going concern and disclosure risk.

Operational risk is increased if the substantial increase in liability insurance premiums is a reflection of an increase in the level of claims being made. Disclosure risk is increased in relation to contingent assets (for reimbursement under insurance policies).

(b) **Principal audit work**

(i) Deferred income

– Agreeing Hydrasports' analysis of joining fee and peak/off-peak membership fees on a sample basis.

– Reconciling membership income to fees paid. If customers can renew their membership without payment there should be no deferral of income (unless the debt for unpaid fees is also recognized).

– Assessing the collectability of unpaid fees (if any) by reviewing after date receipts and correspondence with members.

– Recomputing the deferred income element of fees received in the three months before the statement of financial position date.

– Comparison of year-end balance with prior year and investigation of variance.

(ii) Hydrotherapy pool
- Verifying the initial cost of this constructed asset will include an examination of:
    - the contract with the builder
    - contractors billings; and
    - stage payments.
- Hydrasports is likely to be advised by its own expert (a quantity surveyor) on how the contract is progressing. Audit work will include a review of the expert's assessment of stage of completion as at the statement of financial position date, estimated costs to completion, etc.
- Physical inspection of the construction at the year end to confirm work to date and assess the reasonableness of stage of completion.
- Borrowing costs associated with this substantial ('heavy') investment should be agreed to finance terms and payments. The calculation of any amount capitalized should be recomputed to confirm accuracy.
- The basis of capitalization, if any, should be agreed to comply with IAS 23 Borrowing Costs (e.g. interest accruing during any suspension of building work should not be capitalized).
- As the construction has already cost twice as much as budgeted, its value in use (when brought into use) may be less than cost. Management's assessment of possible impairment (of the hydrotherapy pool and the centre) should be critically appraised.

(c) **Performance indicators – social/environmental responsibility**

Member satisfaction

- Number of people on membership waiting lists (if any).
- Number of referrals/recommendations to club membership by existing members.
- Proportion of renewed memberships.
- Actual members: 100% capacity membership (sub-analysed between 'peak' and 'off-peak').

Membership dissatisfaction

- Proportion of members requesting refunds per month/quarter.
- Proportion of memberships 'lapsing' (i.e. not renewed).

Staff

- Average number of staff employed per month.
- Number of starters/leavers per month.
- Staff turnover/average duration of employment.
- Number of training courses for lifeguards per annum.

Predictability

- Number of late openings (say more than 5, 15 and 30 minutes after advertised opening times).
- Number of days closure per month/year of each facility (i.e. pool, crèche, sauna, gym) and centre.

Safety

- Incidents reports documenting the date, time and nature of each incident, the extent of damage and/or personal injury, and action taken.
- Number of accident free days.

Other society

- Local community involvement (e.g. facilities offered to schools and clubs at discount rates during 'off-peak' times).
- Range of facilities offered specifically to pensioners, mothers and babies, disabled patrons, etc.
- Participation in the wider community (e.g. providing facilities to support sponsored charity events).

Environment

- Number of instances of non-compliance with legislation/regulations (e.g. on chemical spills).
- Energy efficiency (e.g. in maintaining pool at a given temperature throughout the year).
- Incentives for environmental friendliness such as discouraging use of cars/promoting use of bicycles (e.g. by providing secure lock-ups for cycles and restricted car parking facilities).

Additional practice questions

Evidence

- Membership registers clearly distinguishing between new and renewed members, also showing lapsed memberships.
- Pool/gym timetables – showing sessions set aside for 'over 60s', 'ladies only', schools, clubs, special events, etc.
- Staff training courses and costs.
- Staff timesheets – showing arrival/departure times and adherence to staff rotas.
- Documents supporting additions to/deletions from payroll standing data (e.g. new joiner/leaver notifications).
- Engineer's inspection reports – confirming gym equipment, etc is in satisfactory working order. Also, engineer and safety check manuals and the maintenance program.
- Levels of expenditure on repairs and maintenance.
- Energy saving equipment/measures (e.g. insulated pool covering).
- Safety drill reports (e.g. alarm tests, pool evacuations).
- Accident report register – showing date, nature of incident, personal injury sustained (if any), action taken (e.g. emergency services called in).
- Any penalties/fines imposed by the local authorities and the reasons for them.
- Copies of reports of local authority investigations.
- The frequency and nature of insurance claims (e.g. to settle claims of injury to members and/or staff).

Test your understanding 2

(a) **Financial statement risks – planning the final audit 31 December 2004**

Computer-controlled equipment for production-line industries

- Cerise is manufacturing a relatively high-tech range of products. Inventory will be overstated if sufficient allowance is not made for technical obsolescence and slow-moving items (i.e. writing inventory down to lower of cost and net realisable value).

- As Cerise is ceasing manufacture two months prior to the year end the items remaining in inventory at the year end are likely to require being written down in value. The amount of write down is required to be disclosed in accordance with IAS 2 Inventories.

Cessation of trade

- Cerise ceased to trade during the year. The financial statements should not therefore be prepared on a going concern basis, but on a 'break-up' or other 'realisable' basis.

  This has implications for:

  - the reclassification of assets and liabilities (from non-current to current);
  - the carrying amount of assets (at recoverable amount); and
  - the completeness of recorded liabilities.

Redundant workforce

- Liabilities may not be disclosed (if contingent) or provided for, if there are claims arising from the redundant workers (e.g. if their statutory or contractual rights have been breached).
- Although statutory redundancy pay, holiday pay, accrued overtime etc may well have all been settled before the year end there may be additional liabilities in respect of former employees (e.g. pension obligations).

Sale of patented technology and manufacturing equipment

- All assets sold should be derecognized and the profit on disposal disclosed as an exceptional item arising from the discontinuance of operations.
- Plant and equipment will be overstated if:
  - manufacturing equipment that has been sold is left 'on the books';
  - assets that were not part of the sale are not:
  - tested for impairment (in accordance with IAS 36 Impairment of Assets);
  - written down to the higher of net selling price and value in use.

Accounts department

- Fewer ('skeleton') staff being employed in the accounts department may increase the risk of errors arising as staff assume wider areas of responsibility as the volume of transactions is reduced.

- The risk of errors arising not being detected (i.e. control risk) is also likely to increase. For example, levels of supervision and degrees of segregation of duties may be reduced and adherence to control procedures may slacken.

Premises

- If the unsold properties meet all the criteria of IFRS 5 Non-current Assets Held for Sale and Discontinued Operations at the statement of financial position date they should be:
    - separately classified as held for sale.
    - carried at the lower of carrying amount (i.e. depreciated cost) and fair value less estimated costs to sell.

- Any after-date losses on disposal would provide evidence of impairment. (However, as it is Cerise's policy to carry non-current assets at depreciated cost, impairment is less likely than if they were carried at revalued amounts.)

- Unoccupied premises may fall into disrepair with time. The financial statements would be misstated if the management of Cerise sought to provide for:
    - dilapidations on the properties arising after the statement of financial position date; and/or
    - future expectation of repairs on unsold properties.

Such provisions are contrary to IAS 37 Provisions, Contingent Liabilities and Contingent Assets.

Onerous contracts

- Full provision should be made for the lease obligations under onerous contracts on four premises in accordance with IAS 37. This should not be extended to the head office premises.

Product warranties

- Adequate provision must be made for warranties of:
    - one year (sales in the year to 31 December 2004);
    - up to three years (sales between 1 January 2002 and 31 October 2004); and
    - up to five years (sales between 1 January 2000 and 31 October 2004).
- The provision may be understated if the basis of its calculation is no longer appropriate. For example, if Cerise must now outsource warranty work as it no longer has an in-house capability.

Breach of agreements/contracts

- Since Cerise no longer has the means of fulfilling contracts with distributors, provision should be made for any compensation or penalties arising. Where the penalties due to distributors for breach of supply agreements exceed the amounts due from them, the receivables should be written down and provision made for any excess.
- Adequate provision should be made for breaches of contracts with suppliers (non-purchase). If suppliers do not exercise their rights to invoke penalty clauses disclosure of the contingent liability may be more appropriate than a provision.

(b) **Reliance on audit work**

   (i) Analytical procedures

   Note: Reliance on analytical procedures is only obtained through those that provide substantive audit evidence. This question therefore concerns substantive analytical procedures as evidence – which are optional – not those at the planning and review stages (which are mandatory).

   - Overall the extent of reliance on analytical procedures is likely to be less than that for the prior year audit as the scale and nature of Cerise's activities will differ from the prior year.
   - There are a number of individually material transactions in the current year which will require detailed substantive testing (e.g. sale of patented technology and manufacturing equipment and sale of premises).

- Budgetary information used for analytical procedures in prior periods (e.g. budgeted production/sales) will have less relevance in the current year as the cessation of trade is unlikely to have been forecast.

- Information will be comparable with the prior year for at most 10 months (i.e. January to October). Costs incurred in November/December will relate to winding down operations – rather than operational activities.

- The impact of the 'one-off' circumstance on carrying amounts is more likely to be assessed through detailed substantive testing (e.g. after-date realization) than reliance on ratios and past history.

- For example, analytical procedures on an aged-trade receivables analysis and calculation of average collection period used in prior years will not be relevant to assessing the adequacy of the write-down now needed. Similarly, inventory turnover ratios will no longer be comparable when inventory is no longer being replenished.

- However, some reliance will still be placed on certain analytical procedures. For example, in substantiating charges to the statement of comprehensive income for the 10 months of operations.

(ii) Management representations

- Overall the extent of reliance on management representations is likely to be increased as compared with the prior year audit.

- The magnitude of matters of judgement and opinion is greater than in prior years. For example, inventory/trade receivable write-downs, impairment losses and numerous provisions. The auditor will seek to obtain as much corroborative evidence as is available. However, where amounts of assets have still to be recovered and liabilities settled, management will be asked to make representations on the adequacy of write-downs, provisions, etc and the completeness of disclosures (e.g. for claims and other contingent liabilities).

- Where negotiations are under discussion but not yet formalized (e.g. with a prospective buyer for premises), management may be the only source of evidence (e.g. for the best estimate of sale proceeds).

- However, the extent to which reliance can be placed on representations depends on the extent to which those making the representation can be expected to be well-informed on the particular matters. Therefore, as the human resources and production directors will not be available after the statement of financial position date particular thought should be given to obtaining representations on matters pertaining to employee obligations and product warranties (say).

(c) **Principal audit work – carrying amount**

   (i) Amounts due from distributors

   - Agreeing gross amounts due to accounts receivable balances (for sales made in the normal course of business up to 31 October 2004 and in the 'running down' of inventory to 31 December 2004).

   - As a significant portion of account balances outstanding will already be two months old at 31 December 2004, all receipts of after-date cash (if any) should be monitored for evidence of recoverability.

   - Review of agreements with distributors to confirm the unexpired period (up to three years) and the penalties stipulated.

   - Recalculation of amounts due to distributors for the early termination of the agreements with them.

   - Review of Cerise's correspondence to the distributors (e.g. offering financial settlement) and responses received.

   (ii) Lease liabilities

   - Confirm the leases as operating leases to prior period working papers/disclosures in the previous year's financial statements.

   - To confirm contracts as onerous and justify full provision: review Cerise's correspondence with the lessors requesting terms for an early exit from the lease period; and visit premises to confirm that Cerise is not receiving any economic benefit from them (i.e. they are not still occupied or sub-let).

   - Agree/reconcile the amounts provided for liabilities under onerous contracts to the present value of the future minimum lease payments under non-cancellable operating leases.

Additional practice questions

– Agree/reconcile the future minimum lease payments used in the calculation of the provision to those disclosed (under IAS 17 Leases) in the financial statements to 31 December 2003 as:

– later than one year and not later than five years; plus

– later than five years.

Test your understanding 3

(a) **Principal audit risks**

Industry

'Farming' is an inherently risky business activity – being subject to conditions (e.g. disease, weather) outside management's control. In some jurisdictions, where the industry is highly regulated, compliance risk may be high.

The risks of mail order retailing 'exclusive' products are higher (than for 'essential' products, say) as demand fluctuations are more dramatic (e.g. in times of recession). However, the Internet has provided GVF with a global customer base.

The planned audit approach should be risk-based combined with a systems approach to (say) controls in the revenue cycle.

Goat herd

The goat herd will consist of:

– mature goats held for use in the production of milk (i.e. accounted for as depreciable non-current tangible assets – IAS 16 Property, Plant and Equipment);

– kids which are held for replacement purposes (accounted for as biological assets under IAS 41 Agriculture); and

– kids which are to be sold (held as inventory under IAS 2).

Therefore, the number of animals in each category must be accurately ascertained to determine:

– the statement of financial position carrying amounts analysed between current and non-current assets; and

– the charge to the statement of comprehensive income (e.g. for depreciation and fair value adjustments).

There is a risk that the carrying amount of the production animals will be misstated if, for example:

- useful lives/depreciation rates are unreasonable;
- estimates of residual values are not kept under review.

Animals raised during the year should be recognized initially and at each statement of financial position date at fair value less estimated point-of-sale costs. Such biological assets will be understated in the statement of financial position if they are not recorded on birth.

The net realisable value of animals held for sale may fall below cost if they are not sold soon after reaching optimal size and weight.

Unrecorded revenue

Raised (bred) animals are not purchased and, in the absence of documentation supporting their origination, could be sold for cash (and the revenue unrecorded).

Although the controls over retailing around the world are likely to be strong, there are other sources of income – the shop and other activities at the farm. Although revenue from these sundry sources may not be material, there is a risk that it could go unrecorded due to lack of effective controls.

'Rabida Red'

The cost of an ingredient which is essential to the manufacturing process has increased significantly. If the cost is passed on to the customers, demand may fall (increasing going concern risk).

Supplies of the ingredient, Innittu, may be restricted – further increasing going concern risk.

Any disclosure of GVF's socio-environmental policies (e.g. in other information presented with the audited financial statements), if any, should be scrutinized to ensure that it does not mislead the reader and/or undermine the credibility of the financial statements.

'Bachas Blue'

If 'Bachas Blue' has been specifically cited as a cause of a skin disorder then GVF could face contingent liabilities for pending litigation. However, it is more likely that the fall in demand has threatened GVF's going concern. As the fall in demand has not been permanent, this threat has been removed for the time being.

The impairment loss previously recognized in respect of the equipment used exclusively in the manufacture of Bachas Blue should be reversed if there has been a change in the estimates used to determine their recoverable amount (IAS 36 Impairment of Assets).

The recoverable amount would have been based on value in use (since net selling price would not have been applicable). GVF's management will have to provide evidence to support their best estimates of future cash flows for the recalculation of value in use at 30 September 2005.

Maturing cheese

The substance of the sale and repurchase of cheese is that of a loan secured on the inventory. Therefore revenue should not be recognized on 'sale' to Abingdon Bank. The principal terms of the secured borrowings should be disclosed, including the carrying amount of the inventory to which it applies.

Borrowing costs should all be recognized as an expense in the period unless it is GVF's policy to capitalize them (the allowed alternative treatment under IAS 23 Borrowing Costs). Since the cost of inventories should include all costs incurred in bringing them to their present location and condition (of maturity), the cost of maturing cheese should include interest at 7% per six months (as clearly the borrowings are specific). There is a risk that, if the age of maturing cheeses is not accurately determined, the cost of cheese will be misstated.

Health and safety legislation

At 30 September 2005 the legislation will have been in effect for three months. If GVF's management has not replaced the shelves, a provision should be made for the penalties/fines accruing from non-compliance.

If the legislation is complied with:

- plant and equipment may be overstated e.g.:
    - if the replaced shelves are not written off;
    - if the value of equipment, etc is impaired because the maturing cheese business is to be downsized;
- inventory may be overstated (e.g. if insufficient allowance is made for the deterioration in maturing cheese resulting from handling it to replace the shelves);
- GVF may no longer be a going concern if it does not have the produce to sell to its exclusive customers.

Grant

There is a risk that the grant received has become repayable. For example, if the terms of the grant specified a timeframe for the development which is now to be exceeded. In this case the grant should be presented as a payable in the statement of financial position.

If the reason for deferring the implementation is related to cash flow problems, this could have implications for the going concern of GVF.

(b) **Audit work on carrying amounts**

   (i) Goat herd

   – Physical inspection of the number and condition of animals in the herd and confirming, on a test basis, that they are tagged (or otherwise 'branded' as being owned by GVF).

   – Tests of controls on management's system of identifying and distinguishing held-for-sale animals (inventory) from the production herd (depreciable non-current assets).

   – Comparison of GVF's depreciation policies (including useful lives, depreciation methods and residual values) with those used by other farming entities.

   – 'Proof in total', or other reasonableness check, of the depreciation charge for the herd for the year.

   – Observing test counts or total counts of animals held for sale.

   – Market values of kids, according to their weight and age, as at 30 September 2005 – for both held-for-sale and held-for-replacement animals.

   – For held-for-sale animals only, vouching (on a sample basis) management's schedule of point-of-sale costs (e.g. market dealers' commissions).

   (ii) Equipment used in the manufacture of Bachas Blue

   – Agree cost less accumulated depreciation and impairment losses at the beginning of the year to prior year working papers (and/or last year's published financial statements).

   – Recalculate the current year depreciation charge based on the carrying amount (as reduced by the impairment loss).

   – Calculate the carrying amount of the equipment as at 30 September 2005 without deduction of the impairment loss.

- Agree management's schedule of future cash flows estimated to be attributable to the equipment for a period of up to five years (unless a longer period can be justified) to approved budgets and forecasts.

- Recalculate: on a sample basis, the make up of the cash flows included in the forecast; and GVF's weighted average cost of capital.

- Review production records and sales orders for the year, as compared with the prior period, to confirm a 'steady increase'.

- Compare sales volume at 30 September 2005 with the pre-'scare' level to assess how much of the previously recognized impairment loss it would be prudent to write back (if any).

- Scrutinize sales orders in the post statement of financial position event period. Sales of such produce can be very volatile and another 'incident' could have sales plummeting again – in which case the impairment loss should not be reversed.

(iii) Cheese

- Examine the terms of sales to Abingdon Bank – confirm the bank's legal title (e.g. if GVF were to cease to trade and so could not exercise buy-back option).

- Obtain a direct confirmation from the bank of the cost of inventory sold by GVF to Abingdon Bank and the amount re-purchased as at 30 September 2005 (the net amount being the outstanding loan).

- Inspect the cheese as at 30 September 2005 (e.g. during the physical inventory count) paying particular attention to the factors which indicate the age (and strength) of the cheese (e.g. its location or physical appearance).

- Observe how the cheese is stored – if on steel shelves discuss with GVF's management whether its net realisable value has been reduced below cost.

- Test check, on a sample basis, the costing records supporting the cost of batches of cheese.

- Confirm that the cost of inventory sold to the bank is included in inventory as at 30 September 2005 and the nature of the bank security adequately disclosed.

- Agree the repurchase of cheese which has reached maturity at cost plus 7% per six months to purchase invoices (or equivalent contracts) and cash book payments.

- Test check GVF's inventory-ageing records to production records. Confirm the carrying amount of inventory as at 30 September 2005 that will not be sold until after 30 September 2006, and agree to the amount disclosed in the notes to inventory as a 'non-current' portion.

Test your understanding 4

(a) **Audit risks**

Inherent – financial statements level

- As Shire is a listed company there will be pressures on its management to meet the expectations of users, in particular shareholders and analysts, thereby increasing inherent risk.

- The oil industry is exposed to a volatile market (e.g. in futures trading). This increases going concern (failure) risk.

- Shire operates in different regions with exposure to economic instability, currency devaluation and high inflation. Increased disclosure risk arises as IAS 1 Presentation of Financial Statements requires that key assumptions concerning the future of such sources of estimation uncertainty be disclosed.

- Disclosure risk is increased as Shire is required to comply with the extensive disclosure requirements of IAS 14 Segment Reporting.

- The fall in basic EPS (as compared with the first six months of the previous half year) may increase management bias to overstate performance in the second half year (to 31 December 2005).

Inherent – assertion level

- The grant of a licence may be valued at either cost or fair value (IAS 20 Accounting for Government Grants and Disclosure of Government Assistance). However, valuation other than at cost ($nil) is inherently risky as fair value has been estimated by management. The licence may be unique (being for five years in a remote region) and in the absence of an active market in them – or recent transactions for which prices can be observed – it seems unlikely that any estimate of fair value made by management can be substantiated.

- The licence is an intangible asset. If recognized other than at cost it should be amortized on a straight-line basis over five years (IAS 38 Intangible Assets).

- Item replacements (e.g. of drilling equipment) should be recognized as items of property, plant and equipment (and the replaced items as disposals) in accordance with (IAS 16 Property, Plant and Equipment). Constituent items of each rig should be depreciated over their useful lives.

- If management is properly re-assessing the useful life of each rig annually then this should be reflected in the change, from time to time, of the number of years over which each rig is depreciated.

- Although the treatment of decommissioning provisions (Debit Asset/Credit Provision) appears to be correct (IAS 16 and IAS 37 Provisions, Contingent Liabilities and Contingent Assets) abandoning the cyclone-damaged rig calls into question Shire's recognition of such provisions. In the absence of a legal or constructive obligation there is no liability to be provided for.

- The abandoned rig may be overstated. Depreciation should cease and the rig tested for impairment. In particular, the decommissioning provision should be reversed against the undepreciated balance included in cost (and any difference included in profit or loss).

- Actual and/or contingent liabilities may arise if Shire is exposed to fines/penalties as a result of abandoning the rig (IAS 37). As the rig was damaged before the year end, provisions should be made as at 31 December 2005 unless they cannot be reliably measured (unlikely). (This could include provision for redundancy of rig workers)

- The oil pipeline is a jointly controlled asset that should be accounted for to reflect its economic substance (IAS 31 Interests in Joint Ventures). Shire must recognize its share of the asset, liabilities and expenditure incurred and any income from the sale of its share of the oil output (as well as its own liabilities and expenses separately incurred).

- The prior year modification would have been 'qualified – except for'. If there is a similar lack of evidence in the current year the auditor's report should be similarly qualified. Even if the correct position at 31 December 2005 is determinable, the audit opinion at that date should be modified in respect of the impact, if any, on the opening position and comparative information (unless the opening oil reserves position has since been ascertained and can be corrected with a prior period adjustment).

Credit will be given for additional answer points relevant to the scenario and the industry. For example:

- Going concern (failure) risk is increased if significant operating licences (withdrawal of the new licence would not create a going concern issue) are withdrawn from oil-producing areas (e.g. as a result of non-compliance with environmental legislation).

- Research and development (may also be described as 'exploration and evaluation' costs or 'discovery and assessment') costs must be expensed unless/until Shire has a legal right to explore the area in which they are incurred. So, in the remote region, Shire can only capitalize costs incurred from April. (Risk is asset overstatement)

- Exploration and evaluation assets should be classified as tangible (e.g. rigs) or intangible (e.g. drilling rights) according to their nature (IFRS 6 Exploration for and Evaluation of Mineral Resources).

- When a technical feasibility and commercial viability of extracting oil from an area of interest can be demonstrated, exploration and evaluation assets must be tested for impairment before reclassification (as tangible/intangible assets).

(b) **Principal audit work – useful life of rig platforms**

- Review of management's annual assessment of the useful life of each rig at 31 December 2005 and corroboration of any information that has led to a change in previous estimates. For example, for the abandoned rig, where useful life has been assessed to be at an end, obtain:
    - weather reports;
    - incident report supported by photographs;
    - insurance claim, etc.

- Consider management's past experience and expertise in estimating useful lives. For example, if all lives initially assessed as short (c. 15 years) are subsequently lengthened (or long lives consistently shortened) this would suggest that management is being over (under) prudent in its initial estimates.

- Review of industry comparatives as published in the annual reports of other oil producers.

- Comparison of actual maintenance costs against budgeted to confirm that the investment needed in maintenance, to achieve expected life expectancy, is being made.

- Comparison of actual output (oil extracted) against budgeted. If actual output is less than budgeted the economic life of the platform may be:
  - shorter (e.g. because there is less oil to be extracted than originally surveyed); or
  - longer (e.g. because the rate of extraction is less than budgeted).
- A review of the results of management's impairment testing of each rig (i.e. the cash-generating unit of which each platform is a part).
- Recalculations of cash flow projections (based on reasonable and supportable assumptions) discounted at a suitable pre-tax rate.
- Review of working papers of geologist/quantity surveyor(s) employed by Shire supporting estimations of reserves used in the determination of useful lives of rigs.

(c) **Social and environmental responsibilities**

Performance indicators

- Absolute ($) and relative (%) level of investment in sports sponsorship, and funding to the Shire Ward.
- Increasing number of championship events and participating schools/students as compared with prior year.
- Number of medals/trophies sponsored at events and/or number awarded to Shire sponsored schools/students.
- Number of patients treated (successfully) a week/month. Average bed occupancy (daily/weekly/monthly and cumulative to date).
- Staffing levels (e.g. of volunteers for sports events, Shire Ward staff and the company):
  - ratio of starters to leavers/staff turnover;
  - absenteeism (average number of days per person per annum).
- Number of:
  - breaches of health and safety regulations and environmental regulations;
  - oil spills;
  - accidents and employee fatalities;
  - insurance claims.

Evidence

- Actual level of investment ($) compared with budget and budget compared with prior period.
- Physical evidence of favourable increases on prior year, for example:
  - medals/cups sponsored;
  - number of beds available.
- Increase in favourable press coverage/reports of sponsored events. (Decrease in adverse press about accidents/fatalities.)
- Independent surveys (e.g. by marine conservation organizations, welfare groups, etc) comparing Shire favourably with other oil producers.
- A reduction in fines paid compared with budget (and prior year).
- Reduction in legal fees and claims being settled as evidenced by fee notes and correspondence files.
- Amounts settled on insurance claims and level of insurance cover as compared with prior period.

(d) Many companies now publish social and environmental reports, but few attach audit reports to these. However it is possible to:

- conduct an audit on social, environmental or health and safety issues, and/or
- attest to the report to add assurance to its authenticity.

Whether an audit firm is the right agent to perform a 'social audit' is debatable. There are specialized firms which carry out such audits.

The benefit of such a report to the company is to enable it to demonstrate its responsible social attitude and be compared (hopefully favourably) to other companies.

The benefit of the attestation report issued by reporting accountants is to add credibility to the statements made by the company, thereby enhancing its standing from a social and ethical point of view.

Audit firms may provide an attestation on a social report issued by the company; the report might be framed as follows:

SOCIAL REPORT ATTESTATION

To: The Board of Directors, Shire Oil

We have examined the information which has been included in the Social Report on pages XX to XX in accordance with the instructions set out in your letter of (date).

In accordance with our terms of reference, the purpose of the attestation is to test the assertions and statements made in the Social Report in order to give assurance to the reader from an independent third party regarding the information in the report. The report has been prepared by the directors, who are responsible for the collection and presentation of information within it. The attestation statement in itself should not be taken as a basis for interpreting Shire Oil's performance in relation to its non-financial policies.

There are currently no statutory requirements or generally accepted standards in (country) relating to the preparation, public reporting and attestation of corporate social reports.

We have therefore developed an attestation approach which addresses the requirements of our terms of reference and which involves challenging the Social Report's contents in detail. The approach has three main components. These are summarized below:

- Challenging and substantiating the assertions and claims made in the Social Report to ensure that the information as reported is consistent with the evidence obtained. We carry out a number of specific procedures to gain this assurance.

- Reviewing the consistency of social performance data collection and reporting processes in order to gain assurance of the reliability of data reported.

- Reviewing implementation of the non-financial policies through a sample of site visits and discussions with executives and senior managers to gather supporting evidence relating to the data, statements and assertions made in the report.

In our opinion the information is fairly stated.

Signed

Reporting accountants

Address

Date

If an attesting accountant found that the work done revealed an inconsistency or misstatement in the social report then clearly the matter would need to be discussed with management and the report amended. An attest report would not be issued if the matter could not be resolved. A qualified report is probably not an option.

Test your understanding 5

(a) **Store impairment**

   (i) Matters

   The cost of goodwill represents 3.1% of total assets and is therefore material.

   However, after three years the carrying amount of goodwill ($2.2m) represents only 1.2% of total assets –and is therefore immaterial in the context of the statement of financial position.

   The impact of writing off the whole of the carrying amount would be material to PBT (23%).

   The announcement is after the statement of financial position date and is therefore a non-adjusting event (IAS 10 Events After the Statement of financial position Date) insofar as no provision for restructuring (for example) can be made.

   However, the event provides evidence of a possible impairment of the cash-generating unit which is this store and, in particular, the value of goodwill assigned to it.

   If the carrying amount of goodwill ($2.2m) can be allocated on a reasonable and consistent basis to this and the other two stores (purchased at the same time) Volcan's management should have applied a 'bottom-up' test to determine whether or not there is an impairment loss.

   If more than 22% of goodwill is attributable to the City Metro store – then its write-off would be material to PBT (22% × $2.2m ÷ $9.5m = 5%).

   If the carrying amount of goodwill cannot be so allocated; a 'top-down' test should have been applied also.

Management should have considered whether the other four stores in Urvina (and elsewhere) are similarly impaired.

Going concern is unlikely to be an issue unless all the supermarkets are located in cities facing a downward trend in demand.

(ii) **Audit evidence**

Board minutes approving the store's 'facelift' and documenting the need to address the fall in demand for it as a supermarket.

Recomputation of the carrying amount of goodwill (2/5 × $5.5m = $2.2m).

A schedule identifying all the assets that relate to the store under review and the carrying amounts thereof agreed to the underlying accounting records (e.g. non-current asset register).

Recalculation of value in use and/or net selling price of the cash-generating unit (that is to become the City Metro) as at 31 March 2005.

Agreement of cash flow projections (e.g. to approved budgets/forecast revenues and costs for a maximum of five years, unless a longer period can be justified).

Written management representation relating to the assumptions used in the preparation of financial budgets.

Agreement that the pre-tax discount rate used reflects current market assessments of the time value of money (and the risks specific to the store) and is reasonable. For example, by comparison with Volcan's weighted average cost of capital.

Inspection of the store (if this month it should be closed for refurbishment).

Revenue budgets and cash flow projections for:

- the two stores purchased at the same time;
- the other stores in Urvina; and
- the stores elsewhere.
- Also actual after-date sales by store compared with budget.

chapter 21

(b) **Reward scheme**

  (i) Matters

   If the entire year's revenue ($303m) attracted store points then the cost of the reward scheme in the year is at most $3.03m. This represents 1% of revenue, which is material to the statement of comprehensive income and very material (31.9%) to profit before tax (PBT).

   The proportion of customers who register for loyalty cards and the percentage of revenue (and profit) which they represent (which may vary from store to store depending on customer profile).

   In accordance with the assumption of accruals, which underlies the preparation and presentation of financial statements (The Framework/IAS 1 Presentation of Financial Statements), the expense and liability should be recognized as revenue is earned. (It is of the nature of a discount.)

   Any restrictions on the terms for converting points (e.g. whether they expire if not used within a specified time).

   To the extent that points have been awarded but not redeemed at 31 March 2005, Volcan will have a liability at the statement of financial position date.

   Agree the total balance due to customers at the year end under the reward scheme to the sum of the points on individual customer reward cards.

   The proportion of reward points awarded which are not expected to be claimed (e.g. the 'take up' of points awarded may be only 80%, say).

   Whether reward points are valued at selling price or cost. For example, if the average gross profit margin is 20%, one point is equivalent to 0.8 cents of goods at cost.

  (ii) Audit evidence

   New/updated systems documentation explaining how:

   – loyalty cards (and numbers) are issued to customers;
   – points earned are recorded at the point of sale; and
   – points are later redeemed on subsequent purchases.

Walk-through tests (e.g. on registering customer applications and issuing loyalty cards, awarding of points on special offer items).

Tests of controls supporting the extent to which audit reliance is placed on the accounting and internal control system. In particular, how points are extracted from the electronic tills (cash registers) and summarized into the weekly/monthly financial data for each store which underlies the financial statements.

Analytical procedures on the value of points awarded by store per month with explanations of variations ('variation analysis'). For example, similar proportions (not exceeding 1% of revenue) of points in each month might be expected by store – possibly increasing following any promotion of the 'loyalty' scheme.

Tests of detail on a sample of transactions with customers undertaken at store visits. For example, for a sample of copy till receipts:

- check the arithmetic accuracy of points awarded (1 per $1 spent + special offers);
- agree points awarded for special offers to that week's special offers;
- for cash discounts taken confirm the conversion of points is against the opening balance of points awarded (not against purchases just made)

(c) **Site restoration**

(i) Matters

The provision for site restoration represents nearly 2.5% of total assets and is therefore material if it is not warranted.

The estimated cost of restoring the site is a cost directly attributable to the initial measurement of the tangible fixed asset to the extent that it is recognized as a provision under IAS 37 Provisions, Contingent Liabilities and Contingent Assets (IAS 16 Property, Plant and Equipment).

A provision should not be recognized for site restoration unless it meets the definition of a liability, i.e:

- a present obligation;
- arising from past events;

– the settlement of which is expected to result in an outflow of resources embodying economic benefits.

The provision is overstated by nearly $0.34m since Volcan is not obliged to relocate the trees and de facto has only an obligation of $60,000 as at 31 March 2005 (being the penalty for having felled them). When considered in isolation, this overstatement is immaterial (representing only 0.2% of total assets and 3.6% of PBT).

It seems that even if there are local government regulations calling for site restoration there is no obligation unless the penalties for non-compliance are prohibitive (unlike the fines for the trees).

It is unlikely that commencement of site development has given rise to a constructive obligation, since past actions (disregarding the preservation of the trees) must dispel any expectation that Volcan will honour any pledge to restore the valley.

Whether commencing development of the site, and destroying the trees, conflicts with any statement of socio-environmental responsibility in the annual report.

(ii) Audit evidence

A copy of the planning application and permission granted setting out the penalties for non-compliance.

Payment of $60,000 to local government in May 2005 agreed to the bank statement.

The present value calculation of the future cash expenditure making up the $4.0m provision.

Agreement that the pre-tax discount rate used reflects current market assessments of the time value of money (as for (a)).

Asset inspection at the site as at 31 March 2005.

Any contracts entered into which might confirm or dispute management's intentions to restore the site. For example, whether plant hire (bulldozers, etc) covers only the period over which the warehouse will be constructed – or whether it extends to the period in which the valley would be 'made good'.

Additional practice questions

Test your understanding 6

(a) **Cessation of 'home delivery' service**

(i) Matters

$0.6 million represents 1.4% of reported revenue (prior year 1.9%) and is therefore material.

The home delivery service is not a component of Albreda and its cessation does not classify as a discontinued operation (IFRS 5 Non-current Assets Held for Sale and Discontinued Operations).

It is not a cash-generating unit because home delivery revenues are not independent of other revenues generated by the restaurant kitchens.

1.4% of revenue is not a 'major line of business'.

Home delivery does not cover a separate geographical area (but many areas around the numerous restaurants).

The redundancy provision of $0.2 million represents 11.1% of profit before tax (10% before allowing for the provision) and is therefore material. However, it represents only 0.6% of total assets and is therefore immaterial to the statement of financial position.

As the provision is a liability it should have been tested primarily for understatement (completeness).

The delivery vehicles should be classified as held for sale if their carrying amount will be recovered principally through a sale transaction rather than through continuing use. For this to be the case the following IFRS 5 criteria must be met:

– the vehicles must be available for immediate sale in their present condition; and

– their sale must be highly probable.

However, even if the classification as held for sale is appropriate the measurement basis is incorrect.

Non-current assets classified as held for sale should be carried at the lower of carrying amount and fair value less costs to sell.

It is incorrect that the vehicles are being measured at fair value less costs to sell which is $0.3 million in excess of the carrying amount. This amounts to a revaluation. Wherever the credit entry is (equity or statement of comprehensive income) it should be reversed. $0.3 million represents just less than 1% of assets (16.7% of profit if the credit is to the statement of comprehensive income).

Comparison of fair value less costs to sell against carrying amount should have been made on an item by item basis (and not on their totals).

(ii) Audit evidence

Copy of board minute documenting management's decision to cease home deliveries (and any press releases/internal memoranda to staff).

An analysis of revenue (e.g. extracted from management accounts) showing the amount attributed to home delivery sales.

Redundancy terms for drivers as set out in their contracts of employment.

A 'proof in total' for the reasonableness/completeness of the redundancy provision (e.g. number of drivers × sum of years employed × payment per year of service).

A schedule of depreciated cost of delivery vehicles extracted from the non-current asset register.

Checking of fair values on a sample basis to second hand market prices (as published/advertised in used vehicle guides).

After-date net sale proceeds from sale of vehicles and comparison of proceeds against estimated fair values.

Physical inspection of condition of unsold vehicles.

Separate disclosure of the held for sale assets on the face of the statement of financial position or in the notes.

Assets classified as held for sale (and other disposals) shown in the reconciliation of carrying amount at the beginning and end of the period.

Additional descriptions in the notes of:

- the non-current assets; and
- the facts and circumstances leading to the sale/disposal (i.e. cessation of home delivery service).

(b) **Revaluation of owned premises**

(i) Matters

The revaluations are clearly material as $1.7 million, $5.4 million and $7.1 million represent 5.5%, 17.6% and 23.1% of total assets, respectively.

The change in accounting policy, from a cost model to a revaluation model, should be accounted for in accordance with IAS 16 Property, Plant and Equipment (i.e. as a revaluation).

The basis on which the valuations have been carried out, for example, market-based fair value (IAS 16).

Independence, qualifications and expertise of valuer(s).

IAS 16 does not permit the selective revaluation of assets thus the whole class of premises should have been revalued.

The valuations of properties after the year end are adjusting events (i.e. providing additional evidence of conditions existing at the year end) per IAS 10 Events after the Statement of Financial Position Date.

If $5.4 million is a net amount of surpluses and deficits it should be grossed up so that the credit to equity reflects the sum of the surpluses with any deficits being expensed through profit and loss (IAS 36 Impairment of Assets).

The revaluation exercise is incomplete. If the revaluations on the remaining three properties are expected to be material and cannot be reasonably estimated for inclusion in the financial statements for the year ended 30 September 2005 perhaps the change in policy should be deferred for a year.

Depreciation for the year should have been calculated on cost as usual to establish carrying amount before revaluation.

Any premises held under finance leases should be similarly revalued.

(ii) Audit evidence

A schedule of depreciated cost of owned premises extracted from the non-current asset register.

Calculation of difference between valuation and depreciated cost by property. Separate summation of surpluses and deficits.

Copy of valuation certificate for each property.

Physical inspection of properties with largest surpluses (including the two valued before the year end) to confirm condition.

Extracts from local property guides/magazines indicating a range of values of similarly styled/sized properties.

Separate presentation of the revaluation surpluses (gross) in:

– the statement of changes in equity; and
– reconciliation of carrying amount at the beginning and end of the period.

IAS 16 disclosures in the notes to the financial statements including:

– the effective date of revaluation;
– whether an independent valuer was involved;
– the methods and significant assumptions applied in estimating fair values; and
– the carrying amount that would have been recognized under the cost model.

(c) **Fines and penalties**

(i) Matters

$0.1 million represents 5.6% of profit before tax and is therefore material. However, profit has fallen, and compared with prior year profit it is less than 5%. So 'borderline' material in quantitative terms.

Prior year amount was three times as much and represented 13.6% of profit before tax.

Even though the payments may be regarded as material 'by nature' separate disclosure may not be necessary if, for example, there are no external shareholders.

Treatment (inclusion in cost of sales) should be consistent with prior year ('The Framework'/IAS 1 Presentation of Financial Statements).

The reason for the fall in expense. For example, whether due to an improvement in meeting health and safety regulations and/or incomplete recording of liabilities (understatement).

The reason(s) for the breaches. For example, Albreda may have had difficulty implementing new guidelines in response to stricter regulations.

Whether expenditure has been adjusted for in the income tax computation (as disallowed for tax purposes).

Management's attitude to health and safety issues (e.g. if it regards breaches as an acceptable operational practice or cheaper than compliance).

Any references to health and safety issues in other information in documents containing audited financial statements that might conflict with Albreda incurring these costs.

Any cost savings resulting from breaches of health and safety regulations would result in Albreda possessing proceeds of its own crime which may be a money laundering offence.

(ii) Audit evidence

A schedule of amounts paid totalling $0.1 million with larger amounts being agreed to the cash book/bank statements.

Review/comparison of current year schedule against prior year for any apparent omissions.

Review of after-date cash book payments and correspondence with relevant health and safety regulators (e.g. local authorities) for liabilities incurred before 30 September 2005.

Notes in the prior year financial statements confirming consistency, or otherwise, of the lack of separate disclosure.

A 'signed off' review of 'other information' (i.e. directors' report, chairman's statement, etc).

Written management representation that there are no fines/penalties other than those which have been reflected in the financial statements.

Test your understanding 7

(a) Objectivity is one of the fundamental principles for a member of ACCA. It is defined as being 'The state of mind which has regard to all considerations relevant to the task in hand and no other. It presupposes intellectual honesty'.

Objectivity is particularly important to an auditor, whose role it is to provide an independent opinion on financial statements. ACCA's detailed guidance on the question of objectivity of auditors states that:

'A member's objectivity must be beyond question if he is to report as an auditor. That objectivity can only be assured if the member is and is seen to be independent'.

The ACCA then provides detailed guidance on how auditors should maintain their objectivity and independence. The guidance covers issues such as dependence on an audit client (fee-related issues), close relationships with the client, provision of other accountancy or other services to the client, and accepting goods and services.

The auditor must always strive to maintain his objectivity in all his dealings with the client.

(b) **Audit engagement**

There are a number of matters to be considered in relation to accepting the audit of Rainbow.

Undue dependence

Accepting the work of Rainbow may lead to the firm having an undue dependence on the client. The audit fee discussed is substantial and, in connection with the tax work, may affect the objectivity of the firm. ACCA suggest that recurring fees from one client should not exceed 15% of gross practice income.

The recurring work outlined in the scenario amounts to $135,000 plus contingent element; this means that it does not meet the 15% guideline ($150,000).

However, consideration should be given to the regularity of special work undertaken by the firm on behalf of the client. It may be arguable that this work is in some sense 'recurring' and this would mean objectivity was impaired.

Contingency fee

This would be unacceptable. Linking the audit fee to the success of the client's business clearly affects objectivity. The firm should not accept these terms.

Unpaid fees

Overdue fees can be construed as a loan to the client, which would adversely affect objectivity. The auditor should consider whether the unpaid fees are overdue, or whether it is normal practice for the firm to have such outstanding fees.

Relationships

The audit partner is related to a member of the client's staff. This could affect objectivity. However, the staff member appears to be junior in the organization, and is an adult daughter and therefore not dependent on the auditor. This should not therefore adversely affect the auditor's objectivity.

Shareholding

As the daughter is not a dependant of the auditor, her shareholding should not affect his objectivity towards this audit.

Other services

Provision of other services to an audit client can affect objectivity of an audit. It appears that different staff would be involved in tax and audit work so (other than the fee issue above) this should not pose any issues in relation to objectivity.

Hospitality

Auditors should beware accepting excessive gifts which are given on terms other than normal commercial ones. The weekend in Tenerife appears to be excessive and should not be accepted. The auditor should consider whether the offer of the free holiday casts significant doubt on the integrity of the director, and whether this would affect his decision to accept the audit work.

chapter 21

Test your understanding 8

(a) **'Professional enquiry'**

Professional issues raised

Krill has a professional duty of confidentiality to its client, Squid. If Krill's lack of response is due to Squid not having given them permission to respond, Sepia should not accept the appointment. However, in this case, Anton Fargues should have:

– notified Squid's management of the communication received from Sepia; and

– written to Sepia to decline to give information and state his reasons.

Krill should not have simply failed to respond.

Krill may have suspicions of some unlawful act (e.g. defrauding the taxation authority), but no proof, which they do not wish to convey to Sepia in a written communication. However, Krill has had the opportunity of oral discussion with Sepia to convey a matter which may provide grounds for the nomination being declined by Sepia.

Steps by Sepia

Obtain written representation from Squid's management, that Krill & Co has been given Squid's written permission to respond to Sepia's communication.

Send a further letter to Krill by a recorded delivery service (i.e. requiring a signature) which states that if a reply is not received in the next seven days (say) Sepia will assume that there are no matters of which they should be aware and so proceed to accept the appointment. (Advise also that unless a response is received, a written complaint will be made to the relevant professional body.)

Make a written complaint to the disciplinary committee of the professional body of which Anton Fargues is a member – so that his unprofessional conduct can be investigated.

(b) **Take-over bid**

Professional issues raised

Sepia has a professional duty of confidentiality to its existing audit client, Vitronella.

KAPLAN PUBLISHING

Additional practice questions

Vitronella may ask Sepia to give corporate finance advice on Hatchet's take-over bid which would be incidental to the audit relationship. Providing Sepia can maintain and demonstrate integrity and objectivity throughout, there would be no objection to Sepia providing such an additional service, to advance their existing clients' case.

It is often in a company's best interests to have financial advice provided by their auditors, and there is nothing ethically improper in this. So it seems unusual that Hatchet should have approached Sepia, rather than their current auditors.

ACCA's 'Code of Ethics and Conduct' consider that it would not be improper for an audit firm to audit two parties, even if the take-over is contested, and that to cease to act could damage the client's interests. However, the situation is different here in that Sepia is not Hatchet's auditor.

Sepia should take all reasonable steps to avoid conflicts of interest arising from new engagements and the possession of confidential information. Sepia cannot therefore resign from Vitronella in order to undertake the advisory role for Hatchet. (A relationship which has ended only in the last two years is still likely to constitute a conflict.)

Steps by Sepia

As it is clear that a material conflict of interest exists, Sepia should decline to act as adviser to Hatchet.

Advise Vitronella's management that Hatchet's approach has been declined.

(c) **Lowballing**

Professional issues raised

'Lowballing' is a practice in which auditors compete for clients by reducing their fees for statutory audits. Lower audit fees are compensated by the auditor carrying out more lucrative non-audit work (e.g. consultancy and tax advice).

The fact that Keratin has quoted a lower fee than the other tendering firms (if that is the case) is not improper providing that the prospective client, Benthos, is not misled about:

– the precise range of services that the quoted fee is intended to cover; and

– the likely level of fees for any other work undertaken.

Although an admission to lowballing 'Setting the early price in an arrangement at a low amount to secure business with the intent later to raise the price' may sound improper, it does not breach current ethical guidance providing Benthos understands the situation. So, for example, Keratin could offer Benthos a 'free' first-year audit, providing Benthos appreciates what the cost of future audits would be.

The risk is, that if the non-audit work does not materialize, Keratin may be under pressure to cut corners or resort to irregular practices (e.g. the falsification of audit working papers) in order to 'keep within budget'. If a situation of negligence (say) were then to arise, Keratin could be found guilty of incompetence.

As the provision of other services is under scrutiny and becoming increasingly restricted this risk is likely to be high. For example, non-audit services which are prohibited in the US include bookkeeping, financial information systems design and implementation, valuation services, actuarial services, internal audit (outsourced), human resource services for executive positions, investment and legal services.

Keratin may not be just lowballing on the first year audit fee, but in the longer term. Perhaps indicating that future increases might only be in line with inflation. In this case if, rather than comprise the quality of the audit, Keratin were to substantially increase Benthos' audit fees, a fee dispute could arise. In this event Benthos could refuse to pay the higher fee. It might be difficult then for Keratin to take the matter to arbitration if Benthos was misled.

Steps by Sepia

There are no steps which Sepia can take to prevent Benthos from awarding the tender to whichever firm it chooses.

If Keratin is successful in being awarded the tender, Sepia should consider its own policy on pricing in future competitive tendering situations.

Additional practice questions

Test your understanding 9

(a) **Quality control in a smaller audit firm**

Why difficult to implement

Audit quality depends, inter alia, on the quality of the people. Smaller firms may lack resources and specialist (audit) expertise. In particular, small firms may not be able to offer the same reward structures to attract and retain staff as larger firms.

Also, whereas larger firms can afford to recruit staff in sufficient numbers to allow for subsequent leavers and provide for their training needs, smaller firms may not be able to offer the same training opportunities. Prospective trainees may perceive a smaller firm's client base to be less attractive than that of a larger firm (e.g. in terms of the on-the-job training which it offers).

Smaller practices may have less scope to provide staff with internal and on-the-job training and costs of external training may be costly in comparison and also fail to provide the 'hands-on' experience necessary for professional development.

The cost of access to external specialists may be prohibitive for smaller firms.

Audit committees play an oversight role which contributes to quality control in larger firms (e.g. on matters of client acceptance/retention, independence issues, etc). When the client base is largely of owner-managed businesses, as for many smaller audit firms, there are no non-executive directors to support the auditor when difficult issues arise.

Quality control requires leadership within the firm. In a larger firm one senior partner may have responsibility for establishing quality control policies and procedures and another, responsibility for monitoring work performed. Splitting these roles may not be practical for a smaller firm (and impossible for sole practitioners).

Small firms operate in a highly competitive environment for audit work and are often busy with non-audit work and under-resourced. Technical updating on audit matters may not be as regular as desirable and audit practice may become inefficient.

How overcome

Where in a larger firm quality control procedures might be the responsibility of a central technical team, in a smaller firm those same responsibilities might be distributed between the reporting partners.

Smaller firms may draw, judiciously, on the expertise of suitably qualified external consultants (e.g. on technical matters). Small firms and sole practitioners have the same access to a wide range of technical and ethical advisory services provided by ACCA (and other professional bodies) and should take advantage of these.

Small firms may work together as a consortium to share training opportunities and sometimes staff. For example, an association of small firms may adopt the same methodology and meet annually (say) for technical updates.

(b) **Lammergeier Group - auditor's report**

The report is confused. It is clearly headed 'Qualified opinion arising from material misstatement ...' yet the reasons for departure (from IAS 7) are 'sound and acceptable'. The heading is a statement of disagreement with the application of a standard, the latter a statement of concurrence. If the auditor concurs with a departure the opinion should not be modified.

What is 'IAS 7'? This should be stated in full, i.e. 'International Accounting Standard 7 Cash Flow Statements'. It might be simpler/clearer to head the opinion paragraph 'Qualified opinion arising from omission of statement of cashflows'.

The auditors should not be expressing an opinion of Lammergeier's management in their report. Management's 'justification' should be set out in a note to the financial statements (e.g. in the accounting policies section). The auditor's report should clearly state that there is noncompliance with IAS 7. For example, 'As explained in note ... the financial statements do not contain

It cannot be true that the departure 'does not impact on the truth and fairness ...'. The requirement to prepare a statement of cashflows (and its associated notes) stems from the need to provide users of financial statements with information about changes in financial resources. If this information is omitted the financial statements cannot show a true and fair view.

'Except for [the non-preparation of the group statements of cashflows and associated notes] ....' is a modified audit opinion. This contradicts Rook & Co's assertion that the matter 'does not impact on the truth and fairness ...'.

If the departure from IAS 7 were justified it would assist the user of the financial statements to know precisely where the 'adequate disclosure has been made'. If the auditor wished to draw attention to the matter, without modifying the audit opinion, an Other Matter paragraph should refer to the specific note where the departure is explained.

The grounds for non-compliance is 'the complexity involved'. This does not seem likely. IAS 7 offers no exemption on these (or any other) grounds.

The fact that the audit opinion was similarly modified in the prior year shows that the matter has not been resolved even after a year.

It is possible that, having modified on the prior year, it was an 'easy option' to do so again in the same terms rather than draft a more appropriate opinion for the consecutive year.

The 2003 opinion makes no reference to the fact that the matter is 'not new' and that the opinion was similarly modified in the prior year.

Test your understanding 10

(a) **Auditor's responsibilities for 'other information'**

The auditor has a professional responsibility to read other information to identify material inconsistencies with the audited financial statements (ISA 720 The Auditor's Responsibilities Relating to Other Information in Documents Containing Audited Financial Statements).

A 'material inconsistency' arises when other information contradicts that which is contained in the audited financial statements. It may give rise to doubts about:

– the auditor's conclusions drawn from audit evidence; and
– the basis for the auditor's opinion on the financial statements.

In certain circumstances, the auditor may have a statutory obligation (under national legislation) to report on other information (e.g. Management Report).

Even where there is no such obligation (e.g. chairman's statement), the auditor should consider it, as the credibility of the financial statements may be undermined by any inconsistency.

The auditor must arrange to have access to the other information on a timely basis prior to dating the auditor's report.

Material inconsistency

If a material inconsistency is identified, the auditor should determine whether it is the audited financial statements or the other information which needs amending.

If an amendment to the audited financial statements is required but not made, there will be misstatement, which may result in the expression of a qualified or adverse opinion. (Such a situation would be extremely rare.)

Where an amendment to other information is necessary, but refused, the auditor's report may include an Other Matter paragraph (since the audit opinion cannot be other than unmodified with respect to this matter)

Material misstatement of fact

A material misstatement of fact in other information exists when information which is not related to matters appearing in the audited financial statements is incorrectly stated or presented in a misleading manner.

If management do not act on advice to correct a material misstatement the auditors should document their concerns to those charged with corporate governance and obtain legal advice.

(b) **Implications for the auditor's report**
  (i) Management Report

   $4.5 million represents 3.75% of total assets, 1.7% of revenue and 48.9% profit before tax. As this is material by any criteria (exceeding all of 2% of total assets, 1/2% revenue and 5% PBT), the specific disclosure requirements of IASs need to be met (IAS 1 Presentation of Financial Statements).

Additional practice questions

The Management Report discloses the amount and the reason for a material change in equity whereas the financial statements do not show the reason for the change and suggest that it is immaterial. As the increase in equity attributable to this adjustment is nearly half as much as that attributable to PBT there is a material inconsistency between the Management Report and the audited financial statements.

Amendment to the Management Report is not required.

Amendment to the financial statements is required because the disclosure is:

- incorrect – as, on first adoption of IAS 40, the fair value adjustment should be against the opening balance of retained earnings; and
- inadequate – because it is being 'supplemented' by additional disclosure in a document which is not within the scope of the audit of financial statements.

Whilst it is true that the adoption of IAS 40 did not have a significant impact on results of operations, Hegas's financial position has increased by nearly 4% in respect of the revaluation (to fair value) of just one asset category (investment properties). As this is significant, the statement in the notes should be redrafted.

If the financial statements are not amended, the auditor's report should be modified 'except for' on grounds of misstatement (non-compliance with IAS 40) as the matter is material but not pervasive. Additional disclosure should also be given (e.g. that the 'other difference' is a fair value adjustment).

However, it is likely that when faced with the prospect of a modified auditor's report Hegas' management will rectify the financial statements so that an unmodified auditor's report can be issued.

(ii) Chairman's statement

The assertion in the chairman's statement, which does not fall within the scope of the audit of the financial statements, claims two things, namely that the company:

- is 'one of the world's largest generators of hydro-electricity'; and
- has 'a dedicated commitment to accountable ethical professionalism'.

To the extent that this information does not relate to matters disclosed in the financial statements it may give rise to a material misstatement of fact. In particular, the first statement presents a misleading impression of the company's size. In misleading a user of the financial statements with this statement, the second statement is not true (as it is not ethical or professional to mislead the reader and potentially undermine the credibility of the financial statements).

The first statement is a material misstatement of fact because, for example:

- the company is privately-owned, and publicly-owned international/multi-nationals are larger;
- the company's main activity is civil engineering not electricity generation (only 14% of revenue is derived from HEP);
- as the company ranks at best eighth against African companies alone it ranks much lower globally.

Hegas should be asked to reconsider the wording of the chairman's statement (i.e. removing these assertions) and consult, as necessary, the company's legal advisor.

If the statement is not changed there will be no grounds for modification of the opinion on the audited financial statements. The audit firm should therefore take legal advice on how the matter should be reported.

However, an Other Matter paragraph may be used to report on matters other than those affecting the audited financial statements. For example, to explain the misstatement of fact if management refuses to make the amendment.

Additional practice questions

Index

A

Accepting a new client or engagement.....68, 132
Administration..... 477, 478
Adverse opinion.....350, 351, 353
Advocacy threat.....31, 32, 37, 38, 446
Analytical procedures.....149, 187, 189, 233, 267, 268, 269, 305, 306, 395, 403, 431
Appointment as auditor.....18, 68-73
Assurance services.....385-437
Attestation.....390-391, 393, 411, 462
Audit committees.....12, 14-16, 123, 243, 377
Audit risk.....89, 185, 186, 190, 191, 234
Audit strategy.....184, 204, 230

B

Business combinations.....227-240
Business risks.....188, 190, 191-193, 375, 377, 414

C

Changing auditors.....118-120, 123
Client acceptance.....68, 69, 79, 80
Client identification procedures..... 132-134
Code of ethics and conduct.....27-48, 80, 136, 234, 275
Cold reviews.....88-89, 302, 303
Confidentiality.....29, 30, 40-41, 42, 133, 134, 136, 137, 145, 274, 447
Conflicts of interest.....30, 41-42
Contingent fees....37, 46, 107, 108
Continuous auditing.....285,286
Corporate governance.....10-20, 33, 123, 241, 242, 344, 377, 414, 464
Criminal liability..... 131, 156, 480
Customer due diligence (CDD).....129, 132-133, 134, 136, 401

D

Direct reporting.....390-391, 393, 400
Disclaimer of opinion.....68, 229, 239, 315, 350, 351, 353, 354
Due diligence..... 129, 132-134, 136, 388, 399, 400-404, 445, 457
Duty of care.....157-161, 346

E

Emphasis of matter..... 315, 349, 355-356
Engagement acceptance..... 68, 69, 79, 80
Engagements to review financial statements.....386-388, 393-398

Environmental and social auditing.....399, 405, 408-414
Expectation gap.....164-165, 343-344, 347

F

Familiarity threat.....31, 32, 34-36, 39
Fees.....37, 42, 46, 72, 106-109
Forensic audits.....148, 150, 388, 443-449
Fraud and error..... 41, 147-148, 150-154, 165, 190, 193-195, 269-270, 279-280, 304-305, 343-344, 444-445
Fraudulent trading...480

G

Group and transnational audits.....6, 73, 120, 227-245, 278, 310

H

Hot reviews.....85, 88-89
Human resources.....82-83

I

IFAC – the International Federation of Accountants..... 4-7, 9, 29, 80, 142
Independent verification statements.....312-314
Insolvency.....156, 473-481
Integrity.....29, 30, 42-45, 154, 197, 272, 446
Internal audit.....15, 39. 47, 72, 141, 186-188, 231, 238, 275-277, 456, 463-466
Intimidation threat.....31, 32, 34, 35, 39

K

Key performance indicators.....404-407

L

Leadership.....19, 78, 80-81
Legal liability.....155-164, 170
Letters of support.....239-240
Levels of assurance.....185, 387, 389, 390, 392, 430
Limited assurance.....387, 390, 392-393, 395-398, 434
Liquidation.....474-478
Low-balling.....108-109, 121

Index

M
Management and those charged with governance.....37, 48, 71, 89, 140, 143, 148, 152, 153, 154, 237, 269, 278, 305, 308, 359, 374-378

Materiality.....89, 198-200, 232, 237, 239, 279, 304, 305

Modified audit reports.....239, 298-300, 315, 349-357

Money laundering.....40, 127-138, 145, 401

Money laundering reporting officer.....131, 132, 134, 135

N
Negative assurance.....387, 390, 392-393, 395-398, 434

Negligence.....78, 155-164, 170, 186, 445

O
Objectivity.....29-39, 41-42, 44-48, 195, 274-277, 446

Outsourcing.....414, 455-455

P
Positive assurance.....387, 390, 392

Proceeds of Crime Act 2002 (POCA).....130, 133

Professional competence and due care.....29, 30, 108, 157, 230, 234, 447

Professional negligence..... 78, 155-164, 170, 186, 445

Prospective financial information (PFI).....427-434

Q
Quality control.....33, 77-91, 195, 205, 275-277, 302

R
Reasonable assurance....141, 185, 387, 390, 392, 462

Related parties.....193, 204, 237, 278-281, 511-512

Restricting auditors' liability.....161-165

Risk assessment engagements.....414-415

Risk assessment procedures.....24, 149, 184, 187-190

Risk.... 89, 149, 184-193, 234 375, 377, 414-415

S
Sarbanes Oxley act.....9, 13, 109

Substantive analytical procedures.....187, 194, 201, 233, 251, 267, 268

T
Tipping off..... 131, 133

Transnational audit committee (TAC).....5-6, 243

U
UK Corporate Governance Code.....18-20, 123, 377

W
Wrongful trading....480-481